FAUST.

FAUST

A TRAGEDY

BY

JOHANN WOLFGANG VON GOETHE

TRANSLATED, IN THE ORIGINAL METRES

BY

BAYARD TAYLOR

WITH EXPLANATORY NOTES

LONDON
FREDERICK WARNE & CO.
BEDFORD STREET, STRAND

PUBLISHER'S PREFACE.

———◆———

THIS translation has had the advantage of being the work of a Poet of some repute, who was a master of both English and German, and who had long studied Goethe's masterpiece. His edition has been simply reproduced. But it has been found necessary to compress the notes, which were very voluminous. For this purpose, those relating to the conflicting views of the numerous German commentators have been omitted, and certain passages from Goethe's letters to and conversation with his friends about the period of production, &c., &c. But all the notes illustrating the text and explaining the allegory have been carefully retained.

THE TRANSLATOR'S PREFACE.

It is twenty years since I first determined to attempt the translation of *Faust*, in the original metres. At that time, although more than a score of English translations of the First Part, and three or four of the Second Part, were in existence, the experiment had not yet been made. The prose version of Hayward seemed to have been accepted as the standard, in default of anything more satisfactory: the English critics, generally sustaining the translator in his views concerning the secondary importance of form in Poetry, practically discouraged any further attempt; and no one, familiar with rhythmical expression through the needs of his own nature, had devoted the necessary love and patience to an adequate reproduction of the great work of Goethe's life. Mr. Brooks was the first to undertake the task, and the publication of his translation of the First Part (in 1856) induced me, for a time, to give up my own design. No previous English version exhibited such abnegation of the translator's own tastes and habits of thought, such reverent desire to present the original in its purest form. The care and conscience with which the work had been performed were so apparent, that I now state with reluctance what then seemed to me to be its only deficiencies,—a lack of the lyrical fire and fluency of the original in some passages, and an occasional lowering of the tone through the use of words which are literal, but not equivalent. The plan of translation adopted by Mr. Brooks was so entirely my own, that when further residence in Germany and a more careful study of both parts of *Faust* had satisfied me that the field was still open,—that the means furnished by the poetical affinity of the two languages had not yet been exhausted,—nothing remained for me but to follow him in all essential particulars. His example confirmed me in the belief that there were few difficulties in the way of a nearly literal yet thoroughly rhythmical version of *Faust*, which might not be overcome by loving labour. A comparison of seventeen English translations, in the arbitrary metres adopted by the translators, sufficiently showed the danger of allowing licence in this respect: the white light of Goethe's thought was thereby passed through the tinted glass of other minds, and assumed the colouring of each. Moreover, the plea of selecting different metres in the hope of producing a similar effect is unreasonable, where the identical metres are possible.

The value of form, in a poetical work, is the first question to be considered. No poet ever understood this question more thoroughly than Goethe himself, or expressed a more positive opinion in regard to it. The alternative modes of translation which he presents (reported by Riemer, quoted by Mrs. Austin, in her "Characteristics of Goethe," and accepted by Mr. Hayward), are quite independent of his views concerning the value of form, which we find given elsewhere, in the clearest and most emphatic manner.[1] Poetry is not simply a fashion of expression : it is the form of expres-

---

[1] "You are right," said Goethe; "there are great and mysterious agencies included in the various forms of Poetry. If the substance of my 'Roman Elegies' were to be expressed in the tone and measure of Byron's 'Don Juan,' it would really have an atrocious effect."—*Eckermann*

sion absolutely required by a certain class of ideas.
Poetry, indeed, may be distinguished from Prose by the
single circumstance, that it is the utterance of whatever
in man cannot be perfectly uttered in any other than a
rhythmical form : it is useless to say that the naked
meaning is independent of the form : on the contrary,
the form contributes essentially to the fulness of the
meaning. In Poetry which endures through its own
inherent vitality, there is no forced union of these two
elements. They are as intimately blended, and with the
same mysterious beauty, as the sexes in the ancient
Hermaphroditus. To attempt to represent Poetry in
Prose, is very much like attempting to translate music
into speech.[1]

The various theories of translation from the Greek and
Latin poets have been admirably stated by Dryden in his
Preface to the "Translations from Ovid's Epistles," and
I do not wish to continue the endless discussion,—
especially as our literature needs examples, not opinions.
A recent expression, however, carries with it so much
authority, that I feel bound to present some considera-
tions which the accomplished scholar seems to have
overlooked. Mr. Lewes[2] justly says : "The effect of
poetry is a compound of music and suggestion ; this
music and this suggestion are intermingled in words,
which to alter is to alter the effect. For words in poetry
are not, as in prose, simple representatives of objects and
ideas : they are parts of an organic whole,—they are
tones in the harmony." He thereupon illustrates the
effect of translation by changing certain well-known
English stanzas into others, equivalent in meaning, but

---

[1] "Goethe's poems exercise a great sway over me, not only by
their meaning, but also by their rhythm. It is a language which
stimulates me to composition."—*Beethoven.*

[2] Life of Goethe (Book VI.).

lacking their felicity of words, their grace and melody. I cannot accept this illustration as valid, because Mr. Lewes purposely omits the very quality which an honest translator should exhaust his skill in endeavouring to reproduce. He turns away from the *one best* word or phrase in the English lines he quotes, whereas the translator seeks precisely that one best word or phrase (having *all* the resources of his language at command), to represent what is said in *another* language. More than this, his task is not simply mechanical: he must feel, and be guided by, a secondary inspiration. Surrendering himself to the full possession of the spirit which shall speak through him, he receives, also, a portion of the same creative power. Mr. Lewes reaches this conclusion: "If, therefore, we reflect what a poem *Faust* is, and that it contains almost every variety of style and metre, it will be tolerably evident that no one unacquainted with the original can form an adequate idea of it from translation,"[1] which is certainly correct of any translation wherein something of the rhythmical variety and beauty of the original is not retained. That very much of the rhythmical character may be retained in English, was long ago shown by Mr. Carlyle,[2] in the passages which he translated, both literally and rhythmically, from the *Helena* (Part Second). In fact, we have so many instances of the possibility of reciprocally transferring the finest qualities of English and German poetry, that there is no sufficient excuse for an unmetrical trans-

---

[1] Mr. Lewes gives the following advice: "The English reader would perhaps best succeed who should first read Dr. Anster's brilliant paraphrase, and then carefully go through Hayward's prose translation." This is singularly at variance with the view he has just expressed. Dr. Anster's version is an almost incredible dilution of the original, written in *other* metres; while Hayward's entirely omits the element of poetry.

[2] *Foreign Review*, 1828.

lation of *Faust*. I refer especially to such subtile and melodious lyrics as "The Castle by the Sea," of Uhland, and the "Silent Land" of Salis, translated by Mr. Longfellow; Goethe's "Minstrel" and "Coptic Song," by Dr. Hedge; Heine's "Two Grenadiers," by Dr. Furness, and many of Heine's songs by Mr. Leland; and also to the German translations of English lyrics, by Freiligrath and Strodtmann.

I have a more serious objection, however, to urge against Mr. Hayward's prose translation. Where all the restraints of verse are flung aside, we should expect, at least, as accurate a reproduction of the sense, spirit, and tone of the original, as the genius of our language will permit. So far from having given us such a reproduction, Mr. Hayward not only occasionally mistakes the exact meaning of the German text,[1] but, wherever two phrases may be used to express the meaning with equal fidelity, he very frequently selects that which has the less grace, strength, or beauty.[2] For there are few things which

---

[1] On his second page, the line *Mein Lied ertönt der unbekannten Menge,* "My song sounds to the unknown multitude," is translated: "My *sorrow* voices itself to the strange throng." Other English translators, I notice, have followed Mr. Hayward in mistaking *Lied* for *Leid*.

[2] I take but one out of numerous instances, for the sake of illustration. The close of the Soldier's Song (Part I., Scene II.) is:—

> " Kühn is das Mühen,
> Herrlich der Lohn !
> Und die Soldaten
> Ziehen davon."

Literally :—

> Bold is the endeavour,
> Splendid the pay !
> And the soldiers
> March away.

This Mr. Hayward translates :—

> Bold the adventure,
> Noble the reward—
> And the soldiers
> Are off.

may not be said, in English, in a twofold manner,—one poetic, and the other prosaic. In German, equally, a word which in ordinary use has a bare prosaic character may receive a fairer and finer quality from its place in verse. The prose translator should certainly be able to feel the manifestation of this law in both languages, and should so choose his words as to meet their reciprocal requirements.

While, therefore, I heartily recognise Mr. Hayward's lofty appreciation of *Faust*,—while I honour him for the patient and conscientious labour he has bestowed upon his translation,—I cannot but feel that he has himself illustrated the unsoundness of his argument. Nevertheless, the circumstance that his prose translation of *Faust* has received so much acceptance proves those qualities of the original work which cannot be destroyed by a test so violent. From the cold bare outline thus produced, the reader unacquainted with the German language would scarcely guess what glow of colour, what richness of changeful life, what fluent grace and energy of movement have been lost in the process. We must, of course, gratefully receive such an outline, where a nearer approach to the form of the original is impossible, but, until the latter has been demonstrated, we are wrong to remain content with the cheaper substitute.

It seems to me that in all discussions upon this subject the capacities of the English language have received but scanty justice. The intellectual tendencies of our race have always been somewhat conservative, and its standards of literary taste or belief, once set up, are not varied without a struggle. The English ear is suspicious of new metres and unaccustomed forms of expression: there are critical detectives on the track of every author, and a violation of the accepted canons is followed by a summons to judgment. Thus the tendency is to con

tract rather than to expand the acknowledged excellences
of the language. The difficulties in the way of a nearly
literal translation of *Faust* in the original metres have
been exaggerated, because certain affinities between the
two languages have not been properly considered. With
all the splendour of versification in the work, it contains
but few metres of which the English tongue is not
equally capable. Hood has familiarised us with dactylic
(triple) rhymes, and they are remarkably abundant and
skilful in Mr. Lowell's "Fable for the Critics:" even the
unrhymed iambic hexameter of the *Helena* occurs now
and then in Milton's *Samson Agonistes*. It is true that
the metrical foot into which the German language most
naturally falls is the *trochaic*, while in English it is the
iambic : it is true that German is rich, involved, and
tolerant of new combinations, while English is simple,
direct, and rather shy of compounds; but precisely these
differences are so modified in the German of *Faust* that
there is a mutual approach of the two languages. In
Faust, the iambic measure predominates; the style is
compact; the many licences which the author allows
himself are all directed towards a shorter mode of construction. On the other hand, English metre compels
the use of inversions, admits many verbal liberties prohibited to prose, and so inclines towards various flexible
features of its sister-tongue that many lines of *Faust*
may be repeated in English without the slightest change
of meaning, measure, or rhyme. There are words, it is
true, with so delicate a bloom upon them that it can in
no wise be preserved; but even such words will always
lose less when they carry with them their rhythmical
atmosphere. The flow of Goethe's verse is sometimes so
similar to that of the corresponding English metre, that
not only its harmonies and cæsural pauses, but even its
punctuation, may be easily retained.

I am satisfied that the difference between a translation of *Faust* in prose or metre is chiefly one of labour,—and of that labour which is successful in proportion as it is joyously performed. My own task has been cheered by the discovery, that the more closely I reproduced the language of the original, the more of its rhythmical character was transferred at the same time. If, now and then, there was an inevitable alternative of meaning or music, I gave the preference to the former. By the term "original metres" I do not mean a rigid, unyielding adherence to every foot, line, and rhyme of the German original, although this has very nearly been accomplished. Since the greater part of the work is written in an irregular measure, the lines varying from three to six feet, and the rhymes arranged according to the author's will, I do not consider that an occasional change in the number of feet, or order of rhyme, is any violation of the metrical plan. The single slight liberty I have taken with the lyrical passages is in Margaret's song,—"The King of Thule,"—in which, by omitting the alternate feminine rhymes, yet retaining the metre, I was enabled to make the translation strictly literal. If, in two or three instances, I have left a line unrhymed, I have balanced the omission by giving rhymes to other lines which stand unrhymed in the original text. For the same reason, I make no apology for the imperfect rhymes, which are frequently a translation as well as a necessity. With all its supreme qualities, *Faust* is far from being a technically perfect work.

The feminine and dactylic rhymes, which have been for the most part omitted by all metrical translators except Mr. Brooks, are indispensable. The characteristic tone of many passages would be nearly lost, without them. They give spirit and grace to the dialogue, point to the aphoristic portions (especially in the Second Part), and an ever-changing music to the lyrical passages. The English language, though not so rich as the German in such rhymes, is less deficient than is generally supposed. The difficulty to be overcome is one of construction rather than of the vocabulary. The present participle can only be used to a limited extent, on account of its weak termination, and the want of an accusative form to the noun also restricts the arrangement of words in English verse. I cannot hope to have been always successful; but I have at least laboured long and patiently, bearing constantly in mind not only the meaning of the original and the mechanical structure of the lines, but also that subtile and haunting music which seems to govern rhythm instead of being governed by it.

The Second Part of *Faust* has been translated five times into English (by Birch, Bernays, Macdonald, Archer Gurney, and Anster). Inasmuch as this part was included in Goethe's original design, the First Part, although apparently complete as a tragic episode, is in reality but a fragment, wherein the deeper problems upon which the work is based are left unsolved. I consider, therefore, that the Second Part is necessary (as necessary, indeed, as the *Paradiso* to the *Divina Commedia* of Dante); and my aim will be to make that necessity clear, alike to the English reader and to those who follow various German and English critics in disparaging the original.

THE FAUST-LEGEND.

THE slow revival of science in Germany, France, and Italy, furnished the ignorant multitude with many new names which passed with them for those of sorcerers, and gradually displaced the traditions of Virgilius, Merlin, and others who had figured in their lore for many centuries. Raymond Lully, Roger Bacon, Paracelsus, Cornelius Agrippa, the Abbot Tritheim (Trithemius), and many other sincere though confused workers, were believed by the people to be in league with evil spirits, and their names became nuclei, around which gathered all manner of floating traditions. The fifteenth and sixteenth centuries, from the movements in human thought which they brought forth, were naturally rich in such stories, for even the most advanced minds still retained a half-belief in occult spiritual forces. Melancthon, himself, is our chief evidence in relation to the person and character of the Faust of the legend.

It is possible that there was another person of this name, and of some local reputation, in the fifteenth century. George Sabellicus, a noted charlatan, of whom the Abbot Tritheim writes in 1509, called himself *Faustus minor*. The name (signifying fortunate, of good omen) was not unusual ; it was the baptismal name of the younger Socinus, who taught his Unitarian doctrines in Poland and Transylvania, and whom some have very absurdly attempted to connect with the legend ; for he was not born until 1539. The Johann Faust of the popular stories was undoubtedly an individual of that name, born towards the close of the fifteenth century, in the little town of Knittlingen, near Maulbronn, in Würtemberg. His parents were poor, but he was enabled by the bequest of a rich uncle to study medicine. He attended the University of Cracow (where he probably received his Doctor s degree), studied magic, which was there taught as an accepted branch of knowledge, and appears to have afterwards travelled for many years through Europe. Manlius, the disciple of Melancthon, quotes the latter as having said :—"This fellow Faust escaped from our town of Wittenberg, after our Duke John had given the order to have him imprisoned. He also escaped from Nuremberg, under the like circumstances. This sorcerer Faust, an abominable beast, a common

FAUST.

sewer (*cloaca*) of many devils, boasted that he, by his magic arts, had enabled the Imperial armies to win their victories in Italy." It was probably the famous battle of Pavia (1525) of which Faust spoke, as the time of his visit to Wittenberg appears to have been about the year 1530.

Another evidence of Faust is found in the *Index Sanitatis* of the physician, Philip Begardi, which was published at Worms in 1539. He therein says : "Since several years he has gone through all regions, provinces and kingdoms, made his name known to everybody, and is highly renowned for his great skill, not alone in medicine, but also in chiromancy, necromancy, physiognomy, visions in crystal, and the like other arts. And also not only renowned, but written down and known as an experienced master. Himself admitted, nor denied that it was so, and that his name was Faustus, and called himself *philosophum philosophorum*. But how many have complained to me that they were deceived by him—verily a great number ! "

The third witness is the theologian, Johann Gast, who in his *Sermones Conviviales* describes a dinner given by Faust at Basle, at which he was present. After mentioning the two devils who attended Faust in the form of a dog and a horse, he says : "The wretch came to an end in a terrible manner ; for the Devil strangled him. His dead body lay constantly on its face on the bier, although it had been five times turned upwards." Gast probably makes this last statement on the strength of some popular rumour. Faust seems to have gradually passed out of notice, and we have no particulars of his death which possess the least authenticity. Melancthon, in his discourses as Professor at Wittenberg, Luther in his "table-talk," and the other Protestant theologians of that period, almost without exception, expressed their belief in a personal, visible Devil, then specially active in their part of the world. Luther even describes the annoyances to which the Devil subjects him, with a candour which cannot now be imitated ; and the same belief naturally took grosser and more positive forms among the common people. The wandering life of Johann Faust, as physician and necromancer, must have made his name well known throughout Germany ; his visit to Wittenberg and the reference to him in the three works already quoted, would distinguish him above others of his class, and every floating rumour of diabolical compact, power, and final punishment would thenceforth gather around his name as iron filings around a magnet.

The various books of magic entitled *Faust's Höllenzwang* (Infernal Influences) were all published with false early dates, after Faust's name became generally known, and are therefore of no value as evidence. The attempt, also, to connect him with Fust, Guttenberg's associate in printing, has no foundation whatever.

The original form of the legend is the book published by Spiess, in Frankfurt, in 1587. Its title runs thus : "History of Dr. Joh. Faust, the notorious sorcerer and black-artist : How he bound himself to the Devil for a certain time : What singular adventures befell him therein, what he did and carried on until finally he received his well-deserved pay. Mostly from his own posthumous writings ; for all presumptuous, rash and godless men, as a terrible example, abominable instance and well-meant warning, collected and put in print. James, IIII., Submit yourselves therefore to God : resist the Devil, and he will flee from you." The book must have been instantly and widely popular, for a second edition was published in 1588 ; a Low-German version in Lübeck and an English ballad on the subject, the same year ; an English translation in 1590, two Dutch translations in 1592, and one French in 1598. From the first of these Marlowe obtained the material for his tragedy of "Dr. Faustus," which appears to have been first acted in London in 1593, the year of his death. It was published in 1604, and no doubt formed part of the repertory of the companies of English strolling-players who were accustomed to visit Germany.

In the Dutch translation dates are given, apparently for the purpose of making the story more credible. The year 1491 is mentioned as that of Faust's birth ; his first compact with the Devil, for seventeen years, was made on the 23rd of October, 1514 ; his second, for seven years, on the 3rd of August, 1531 ; and he was finally carried off by the Devil at midnight, on the 23rd of October, 1538. The term of twenty-four years, which is not a mystical number, is thus obtained by adding the two mystical terms, 17 and 7. In the English translation the village of Kindling, in Silesia, is given as Faust's birthplace; another tradition, adopted in the original Frankfurt work, says Roda, near Weimar.

This oldest book repeats Melancthon's statement of Faust's studies at Cracow, and his fame as a physician and sorcerer. It then describes the manner of his summoning the Devil at night, in a forest near Wittenberg. Afterwards the evil spirit visits him in his dwelling, and three several "disputations" take place, at the third of which the spirit gives his name as *Mephostophiles.* The compact for the term of twenty-four years is thereupon concluded. When Faust pierces his hand with the point of a knife in order to sign the compact, the blood flows into the form of the words *O Homo Fuge !* signifying : "O man, fly from him !" Mephostophiles first serves him in the form of a monk, supplying him with food and wine from the cellars of the Bishop of Salzburg and other prelates, and with rich garments from Augsberg and Frankfurt, so that Faust and his Famulus, Christopher Wagner, are enabled to live in the utmost luxury. It was not long, however, before Faust desired to marry, but this was in no wise permitted, Mephostophiles saying that marriage was pleasing to God, and therefore a violation of the compact. This feature of the legend grew directly from the questions of the Reformation ; and there was a special meaning in giving the evil spirit the form of a monk. Wagner, moreover, is said to have been the son of a Catholic priest, picked up by Faust as a boy of fifteen, and by him educated.

b

Then follow many chapters wherein Faust questions Mephosto-philes in regard to the creation of the world, the seasons, the planets, Hell and the infernal hierarchy, and is himself taken to the latter place in a chariot drawn by dragons. Afterwards, he wishes to visit the different parts of the earth : Mephostophiles changes himself into a horse, "but with wings like a dromedary," and flies with him through the air. They travel to all parts of Europe and finally come to Rome, where Faust lives three days in the Vatican, invisible. As often as the Pope makes the sign of the cross, he blows in his face : he also eats off the Pope's table and drinks the wine from his goblets, until His Holiness commands all the bells of Rome to be rung, to dispel the evil magic. Faust then goes to Constantinople, where he appears in the Sultan's palace in the form of Mahomet, and lives in state. He next traverses Egypt, then Morocco, the Orkney Islands, Scythia, Arabia, and Persia, and finally, "from the highest peak of the Island of Caucasus" has a distant view of the Garden of Eden. After his return to Germany he visits the Court of the Emperor Charles V. at Innsbruck, and at the desire of the latter calls up before him the shades of Alexander the Great and his wife. Many pranks are also related, which he plays upon the knights attending the Emperor.

The remaining part of the book is principally taken up with an account of the tricks and magical illusions with which Faust diverted himself in Leipzig, Erfurt, Gotha, and other parts of Northern Germany. He here resembles Till Eulenspiegel much more than the ambitious student of Cracow, who "took to himself the wings of an eagle, and would explore all the secrets of heaven and earth." He swallows a pair of horses and a load of hay ; he cuts off heads and replaces them ; makes flowers bloom at Christmas, draws wine from a table, calls Helen of Troy from the shades at the request of a company of students ; and shows himself everywhere as a gay, jovial companion, full of pranks, but exercising his super-natural power quite as often for good as for evil purposes. Finally in the twenty-third year of his compact, Mephostophiles brings the Grecian Helena to him ; he becomes infatuated with her beauty, lives with her, and by her has a son whom he names Justus Faustus. On the night when his term of years expires, we find him in com-pany with some students in a tavern of the village of Rimlich, near Wittenberg. He is overcome with melancholy, and makes the students an address wherein he expresses his great penitence, and his willingness that the Devil should have his body, provided his soul may receive pardon. At midnight a fearful storm arose : the next morning the walls and floor of the room were sprinkled with the bloody fragments of Faust, who had been so torn to pieces that no member was left whole. Helena and her child had disappeared. Wagner, by Faust's will, became heir to his property, part of which was a dwelling in the town of Wittenberg.

The great popularity of the legend in this form led to the pre-paration of Widmann's larger and more ambitious work, which was published at Hamburg, in 1599. Its title is: "The Veritable History of the hideous and abominable sins and vices, also of many wonderful and strange adventures, which D. Johannes Faustus, a notorious black-artist and arch-sorcerer, by means of his black art, committed even until his terrible ending. Fitted out and expounded with necessary reminders and admirable instances, for manifold instruction and warning." The story is substantially the same as in Spiess's book, but many additional anecdotes are inserted, and all the details are amplified. Instead of three "disputations" between Faust and Mephostophiles, there are *ten*, and each is followed—as, in fact, every chapter in the work—by a long-winded theological discourse, called a Reminder (*Erinnerung*). These Reminders are pedantic and fiercely Protestant in character: no opportunity is let slip to illustrate the vices of Faust by references to the Roman Church and its Popes. The name of the Famulus is changed to Johann Wayger, and two or three stories, taken from Luther's table-talk, are arbitrarily applied to Faust; whence the work is not considered by scholars to be so fair a representation of the popular traditions as that of Spiess.

A new edition of Widmann's book, revised but not improved by Dr. Pfitzer, was published in Nuremberg in 1674, and revived the somewhat faded popularity of the legend. The references to Faust in the *Centuriæ* of Camerarius (1602) and in Neumann's *Disquisitio Historica*, were known only to the scholars, and Pfitzer's reprint of Widmann was therefore welcomed by the people, several editions having been called for in a few years. By this time it was also represented as a puppet-play, and the knowledge of Faust and his history thus became universal in Germany.

The only other work which requires notice is an abbreviation of the legend, with some variations, written in a lively narrative style, and published at Frankfurt and Leipzig in the year 1728. The title is as follows: "The Compact concluded by the Devil with Dr. Johann Faust, notorious through the whole world as a sorcerer and arch-professor of the Black Art, together with his adventurous course of life and its terrifying end, all most minutely described. Now again newly revised, compressed into an agreeable brevity, and furnished in print as a hearty admonition and warning to all wilful sinners, by One with Christian Intentions." This quaint and curious narrative was certainly known to Goethe, as well as Widmann's work. It is the last appearance of the legend in a popular form: thenceforth, through many channels, the latter found its way into literature.

The original book of Spiess was followed in 1594 by an account of the life of Christopher Wagner, whom the Devil accompanied in the form of an ape, under the name of *Auerhahn* (moor-cock). It is an evident imitation of the story of Faust; there is a similar compact, there are magical tricks, adventures, and airy travels, with a like tragical conclusion. This book was translated into English the same year, and immediately afterwards into Dutch; but there appears to have been no further German edition until 1712, when the original, with some additions, was reprinted in Berlin. In 1742, a play entitled "The Vicious Life and Terrible End of Joh. Christoph Wagner" was acted in the Frankfurt theatre.

The stamp of the sixteenth century—of its beliefs, its super-stitions, its struggles and its antagonisms—is unmistakably im-pressed on the legend. The singular individual, half genius, half impostor, who bore the name of Faust, must have typified then, as now, the activity of blind, formless, unresting forces in the nature of the people ; and through all the coarseness and absurdity of the stories which they have gathered around him, there are constant suggestions of the general craving for some withheld knowledge or right. In spite of Widmann's "Reminders" and the "One with Christian Intentions," it is very doubtful whether the moral of Faust's ending overcame the sympathy of the people with his courage or their admiration of his power. There are elements in the legend, the value of which even a purblind poet could not help seeing, yet which the loftiest genius may admit to be almost beyond his grasp. It is not the least of Goethe's deserts, that, although in his youth "a new *Faust* was announced in every quarter of Ger-many," he took up the theme already hackneyed by small talents, and made it his own solely and for ever.

CONTENTS.

		PAGE
An Goethe	. . . .	xxiii
Dedication	. . . .	xxiv
Prelude on the Stage	. . . . . .	1
Prologue in Heaven	. . . . . .	7
Scene I.	Night (*Faust's Monologue*)	13
II.	Before the City-Gate	25
III.	The Study (*The Exorcism*) . . .	35
IV.	The Study (*The Compact*) . . .	45
V.	Auerbach's Cellar	59
VI.	Witches' Kitchen	68
VII.	A Street	76
VIII.	Evening	79
IX.	Promenade	83
X.	The Neighbour's House	85
XI.	Street	89
XII.	Garden	91
XIII.	A Garden-Arbour	95
XIV.	Forest and Cavern	96
XV.	Margaret's Room	101
XVI.	Martha's Garden	102
XVII.	At the Fountain	106
XVIII.	Donjon (*Margaret's Prayer*) . . .	108
XIX.	Night (*Valentine's Death*) . . .	109
XX.	Cathedral	114
XXI.	Walpurgis-Night	116
XXII.	Oberon and Titania's Golden Wedding .	127
XXIII.	Dreary Day	132
XXIV.	Night	134
XXV.	Dungeon	134

SECOND PART OF THE TRAGEDY.

PAGE

INTRODUCTION 143

ACT I.

SCENE
I. A PLEASANT LANDSCAPE 119
II. THE EMPEROR'S CASTLE 153
III. SPACIOUS HALL (*Carnival Masquerade*) . . . 162
IV. PLEASURE-GARDEN (*Paper-Money Scheme*) . . 188
V. A GLOOMY GALLERY (*The Mothers*) . . . 193
VI. BRILLIANTLY LIGHTED HALLS 197
VII. HALL OF THE KNIGHTS (*Paris and Helena*) . . 200

ACT II.

I. A GOTHIC CHAMBER, FORMERLY FAUST'S . . 206
II. LABORATORY (*Homunculus*) 213
III. CLASSICAL WALPURGIS-NIGHT 219
     I. THE PHARSALIAN FIELDS 219
     II. PENEUS 226
     III. ON THE UPPER PENEUS, AS BEFORE . . 233
     IV. ROCKY COVES ON THE ÆGEAN SEA . . 243
     V. TELCHINES OF RHODES 255

ACT III.

THE HELENA 261

ACT IV.

I. HIGH MOUNTAINS 309
II. ON THE HEADLAND (*The Battle*) 318
III. THE RIVAL EMPEROR'S TENT 330

ACT V.

I. OPEN COUNTRY 339
II. IN THE LITTLE GARDEN 341
III. PALACE 342
IV. DEAD OF NIGHT 346
V. MIDNIGHT (*Faust's Blindness*) 349
VI. GREAT OUTER COURT OF THE PALACE (*Faust's Death*) 353
VII. MOUNTAIN-GORGES, FOREST, ROCK, DESERT . . 362

NOTES 371
THE CHRONOLOGY OF FAUST 418

AN GOETHE.

—◆—

I.

Erhabener Geist, im Geisterreich verloren!
Wo immer Deine lichte Wohnung sey,
Zum höh'ren Schaffen bist Du neugeboren,
Und singest dort die voll're Litanei.
Von jenem Streben das Du auserkoren,
Vom reinsten Æther, drin Du athmest frei,
O neige Dich zu gnädigem Erwiedern
Des letzten Wiederhalls von Deinen Liedern!

II.

Den alten Musen die bestäubten Kronen
Nahmst Du, zu neuem Glanz, mit kühner Hand.
Du löst die Räthsel ältester Æonen
Durch jüngeren Glauben, helleren Verstand,
Und machst, wo rege Menschengeister wohnen,
Die ganze Erde Dir zum Vaterland;
Und Deine Jünger, sehn in Dir, verwundert,
Verkörpert schon das werdende Jahrhundert.

III.

Was Du gesungen, Aller Lust und Klagen,
Des Lebens Wiedersprüche, neu vermählt,—
Die Harfe tausendstimmig frisch geschlagen,
Die Shakspeare einst, die einst Homer gewählt,—
Darf ich in fremde Klänge übertragen
Das Alles, wo so Mancher schon gefehlt?
Lass Deinen Geist in meiner Stimme klingen,
Und was Du sangst, lass mich es Dir nachsingen!

B. T.

DEDICATION.

Again ye come, ye hovering Forms! I find ye,
As early to my clouded sight ye shone!
Shall I attempt, this once, to seize and bind ye?
Still o'er my heart is that illusion thrown?
Ye crowd more near! Then, be the reign assigned ye,
And sway me from your misty, shadowy zone!
My bosom thrills, with youthful passion shaken,
From magic airs that round your march awaken.

Of joyous days ye bring the blissful vision;
The dear, familiar phantoms rise again,
And, like an old and half-extinct tradition,
First Love returns, with Friendship in his train.
Renewed is Pain: with mournful repetition
Life tracks his devious, labyrinthine chain,
And names the Good, whose cheating fortune tore them
From happy hours, and left me to deplore them.

They hear no longer these succeeding measures,
The souls, to whom my earliest songs I sang;
Dispersed the friendly troop, with all its pleasures,
And still, alas; the echoes first that rang!
I bring the unknown multitude my treasures!
Their very plaudits give my heart a pang,
And those beside, whose joy my Song so flattered,
If still they live, wide through the world are scattered.

And grasps me now a long-unwonted yearning
For that serene and solemn Spirit-Land:
My song, to faint Æolian murmurs turning,
Sways like a harp-string by the breezes fanned.
I thrill and tremble; tear on tear is burning,
And the stern heart is tenderly unmanned.
What I possess, I see far distant lying,
And what I lost, grows real and undying.

FAUST.

PRELUDE ON THE STAGE.

MANAGER. DRAMATIC POET. MERRY-ANDREW

MANAGER. You two, who oft a helping hand
Have lent, in need and tribulation,
Come, let me know your expectation
Of this, our enterprise, in German land !
I wish the crowd to feel itself well treated,
Especially since it lives and lets me live ;
The posts are set, the booth of boards completed,[1]
And each awaits the banquet I shall give.
Already there, with curious eyebrows raised,
They sit sedate, and hope to be amazed.
I know how one the People's taste may flatter,
Yet here a huge embarrassment I feel :
What they're accustomed to, is no great matter,
But then, alas ! they've read an awful deal.
How shall we plan, that all be fresh and new,—
Important matter, yet attractive too ?
For 'tis my pleasure to behold them surging,
When to our booth the current sets apace,
And with tremendous, oft-repeated urging,
Squeeze onward through the narrow gate of grace :
By daylight even, they push and cram in
To reach the seller's box, a fighting host,
And as for bread, around a baker's door, in famine,
To get a ticket break their necks almost.

B

This miracle alone can work the Poet
On men so various : now, my friend, pray show it.
    POET. Speak not to me of yonder motley masses,
Whom but to see, puts out the fire of Song !
Hide from my view the surging crowd that passes,
And in its whirlpool forces us along !
No, lead me where some heavenly silence glasses
The purer joys that round the Poet throng,—
Where Love and Friendship still divinely fashion
The bonds that bless, the wreaths that crown his passion !

Ah, every utterance from the depths of feeling
The timid lips have stammeringly expressed,—
Now failing, now, perchance, success revealing,—
Gulps the wild Moment in its greedy breast ;
Or oft, reluctant years its warrant sealing,
Its perfect stature stands at last confessed !
What dazzles, for the Moment spends its spirit :
What's genuine, shall Posterity inherit.
    MERRY-ANDREW. Posterity ! Don't name the word to me !
If *I* should choose to preach Posterity,
Where would you get cotemporary fun ?
That men *will* have it, there's no blinking :
A fine young fellow's presence, to my thinking,
Is something worth, to every one.
Who genially his nature can outpour,
Takes from the People's moods no irritation ;
The wider circle he acquires, the more
Securely works his inspiration.
Then pluck up heart, and give us sterling coin !
Let Fancy be with her attendants fitted,—
Sense, Reason, Sentiment, and Passion join,—
But have a care, lest Folly be omitted !
    MANAGER. Chiefly, enough of incident prepare !
They come to look, and they prefer to stare.
Reel off a host of threads before their faces,
So that they gape in stupid wonder : then
By sheer diffuseness you have won their graces,
And are, at once, most popular of men.
Only by mass you touch the mass ; for any

Will finally, himself, his bit select :
Who offers much, brings something unto many,
And each goes home content with the effect.
If you've a piece, why, just in pieces give it :
A hash, a stew, will bring success, believe it !
'Tis easily displayed, and easy to invent.
What use, a Whole compactly to present ?
Your hearers pick and pluck, as soon as they receive it !

    POET. You do not feel, how such a trade debases ;
How ill it suits the Artist, proud and true !
The botching work each fine pretender traces
Is, I perceive, a principle with you.

    MANAGER. Such a reproach not in the least offends ;
A man who some result intends
Must use the tools that best are fitting.
Reflect, soft wood is given to you for splitting,
And then, observe for whom you write !
If one comes bored, exhausted quite,
Another, satiate, leaves the banquet's tapers,
And, worst of all, full many a wight
Is fresh from reading of the daily papers.
Idly to us they come, as to a masquerade,
Mere curiosity their spirits warming :
The ladies with themselves, and with their finery, aid,
Without a salary their parts performing.
What dreams are yours in high poetic places ?
You're pleased, forsooth, full houses to behold ?
Draw near, and view your patrons' faces !
The half are coarse, the half are cold.
One, when the play is out, goes home to cards ;
A wild night on a wench's breast another chooses :
Why should you rack, poor, foolish bards,
For ends like these, the gracious Muses ?
I tell you, give but more—more, ever more, they ask :
Thus shall you hit the mark of gain and glory.
Seek to confound your auditory !
To satisfy them is a task.—
What ails you now ? Is't suffering, or pleasure ?

    POET. Go, find yourself a more obedient slave !
What ! shall the Poet that which Nature gave,

The highest right, supreme Humanity,
Forfeit so wantonly, to swell your treasure?
Whence o'er the heart his empire free?
The elements of Life how conquers he?
Is't not his heart's accord, urged outward far and dim,
To wind the world in unison with him?
When on the spindle, spun to endless distance,
By Nature's listless hand the thread is twirled,
And the discordant tones of all existence
In sullen jangle are together hurled,
Who, then, the changeless orders of creation
Divides, and kindles into rhythmic dance?
Who brings the One to join the general ordination,
Where it may throb in grandest consonance?
Who bids the storm to passion stir the bosom?
In brooding souls the sunset burn above?
Who scatters every fairest April blossom
Along the shining path of Love?
Who braids the noteless leaves to crowns, requiting
Desert with fame, in Action's every field?
Who makes Olympus sure, the Gods uniting?
The might of Man, as in the Bard revealed.

   MERRY-ANDREW. So, these fine forces, in conjunction,
Propel the high poetic function,
As in a love-adventure they might play!
You meet by accident; you feel, you stay,
And by degrees your heart is tangled;
Bliss grows apace, and then its course is jangled;
You're ravished quite, then comes a touch of woe,
And there's a neat romance, completed ere you know!
Let us, then, such a drama give!
Grasp the exhaustless life that all men live!
Each shares therein, though few may comprehend:
Where'er you touch, there's interest without end.
In motley pictures little light,
Much error, and of truth a glimmering mite,
Thus the best beverage is supplied,
Whence all the world is cheered and edified.
Then, at your play, behold the fairest flower
Of youth collect, to hear the revelation!

Each tender soul, with sentimental power,
Sucks melancholy food from your creation ;
And now in this, now that, the leaven works,
For each beholds what in his bosom lurks.
They still are moved at once to weeping or to laughter,
Still wonder at your flights, enjoy the show they see :
A mind, once formed, is never suited after ;
One yet in growth will ever grateful be.

    POET. Then give me back that time of pleasures,
While yet in joyous growth I sang,—
When, like a fount, the crowding measures
Uninterrupted gushed and sprang !
Then bright mist veiled the world before me,
In opening buds a marvel woke,
As I the thousand blossoms broke,
Which every valley richly bore me !
I nothing had, and yet enough for youth—
Joy in Illusion, ardent thirst for Truth.
Give, unrestrained, the old emotion,
The bliss that touched the verge of pain,
The strength of Hate, Love's deep devotion,—
O, give me back my youth again !

    MERRY-ANDREW. Youth, good my friend, you certainly
        require
When foes in combat sorely press you ;
When lovely maids, in fond desire,
Hang on your bosom and caress you ;
When from the hard-won goal the wreath
Beckons afar, the race awaiting ;
When, after dancing out your breath,
You pass the night in dissipating :—
But that familiar harp with soul
To play,—with grace and bold expression,
And towards a self-erected goal
To walk with many a sweet digression,—
This, aged Sirs, belongs to you,[2]
And we no less revere you for that reason :
Age childish makes, they say, but 'tis not true ;
We're only genuine children still, in Age's season !

    MANAGER. The words you've bandied are sufficient ;

'Tis deeds that I prefer to see ;
In compliments you're both proficient,
But might, the while, more useful be.
What need to talk of Inspiration ?
'Tis no companion of Delay.
If Poetry be your vocation,
Let Poetry your will obey !
Full well you know what here is wanting :
The crowd for strongest drink is panting,
And such, forthwith, I'd have you brew.
What's left undone to-day, To-morrow will not do.
Waste not a day in vain digression :
With resolute, courageous trust
Seize every possible impression,
And make it firmly your possession ;
You'll then work on, because you must.
Upon our German stage, you know it,
Each tries his hand at what he will ;
So, take of traps and scenes your fill,
And all you find, be sure to show it !
Use both the great and lesser heavenly light,—
Squander the stars in any number,
Beasts, birds, trees, rocks, and all such lumber,
Fire, water, darkness, Day and Night !
Thus, in our booth's contracted sphere,
The circle of Creation will appear,
And move, as we deliberately impel,
From Heaven, across the World, to Hell !

PROLOGUE IN HEAVEN.

——◆——

THE LORD. THE HEAVENLY HOSTS. *Afterwards*
MEPHISTOPHELES.

The THREE ARCHANGELS *come forward.*[3]

RAPHAEL. The sun-orb sings, in emulation,
'Mid brother-spheres, his ancient round :
His path predestined through Creation.
He ends with step of thunder-sound.
The angels from his visage splendid
Draw power, whose measure none can say ;
The lofty works, uncomprehended,
Are bright as on the earliest day.

  GABRIEL. And swift, and swift beyond conceiving,
The splendour of the world goes round,
Day's Eden-brightness still relieving
The awful Night's intense profound :
The ocean-tides in foam are breaking,
Against the rocks' deep bases hurled,
And both, the spheric race partaking,
Eternal, swift, are onward whirled !

  MICHAEL. And rival storms abroad are surging
From sea to land, from land to sea.
A chain of deepest action forging
Round all, in wrathful energy.
There flames a desolation, blazing
Before the Thunder's crashing way :
Yet, Lord, Thy messengers are praising
The gentle movement of Thy Day.

  THE THREE. Though still by them uncomprehended,
From these the angels draw their power,

And all Thy works, sublime and splendid,
Are bright as in Creation's hour.

MEPHIS. Since Thou, O Lord, deign'st to approach again
And ask us how we do, in manner kindest,
And heretofore to meet myself wert fain,
Among Thy menials, now, my face Thou findest.
Pardon, this troop I cannot follow after [4]
With lofty speech, though by them scorned and spurned :
My pathos certainly would move Thy laughter,
If Thou hadst not all merriment unlearned.
Of suns and worlds I've nothing to be quoted ;
How men torment themselves, is all I've noted.
The little god o' the world sticks to the same old way,
And is as whimsical as on Creation's day.
Life somewhat better might content him,
But for the gleam of heavenly light which Thou hast lent
    him :
He calls it Reason—thence his power's increased,
To be far beastlier than any beast.
Saving Thy Gracious Presence, he to me
A long-legged grasshopper appears to be,
That springing flies, and flying springs,
And in the grass the same old ditty sings.
Would he still lay among the grass he grows in !
Each bit of dung he seeks, to stick his nose in.

THE LORD. Hast thou, then, nothing more to mention ?
Com'st ever, thus, with ill intention ?
Find'st nothing right on earth, eternally ?

MEPHIS. No, Lord ! I find things, there, still bad as they
    can be.
Man's misery even to pity moves my nature ;
I've scarce the heart to plague the wretched creature.

THE LORD. Know'st Faust ?

MEPHIS. The Doctor Faust ?

THE LORD. My servant, he !

MEPHIS. Forsooth ! He serves you after strange devices :
No earthly meat or drink the fool suffices :
His spirit's ferment far aspireth ;
Half conscious of his frenzied, crazed unrest,
The fairest stars from Heaven he requireth,

From Earth the highest raptures and the best,
And all the Near and Far that he desireth
Fails to subdue the tumult of his breast.

THE LORD. Though still confused his service unto Me,
I soon shall lead him to a clearer morning.
Sees not the gardener, even while buds his tree,
Both flower and fruit the future years adorning?

MEPHIS. What will you bet? There's still a chance to
       gain him,
If unto me full leave you give,
Gently upon *my* road to train him!

THE LORD. As long as he on earth shall live,
So long I make no prohibition.
While Man's desires and aspirations stir,
He cannot choose but err.[5]

MEPHIS. My thanks! I find the dead no acquisition,
And never cared to have them in my keeping.
I much prefer the cheeks where ruddy blood is leaping,
And when a corpse approaches, close my house:
It goes with me, as with the cat the mouse.

THE LORD. Enough! What thou hast asked is granted.
Turn off this spirit from his fountain-head;
To trap him, let thy snares be planted,
And him, with thee, be downward led;
Then stand abashed, when thou art forced to say:
A good man, through obscurest aspiration,
Has still an instinct of the one true way.[6]

MEPHIS. Agreed! But 'tis a short probation.
About my bet I feel no trepidation.
If I fulfil my expectation,
You'll let me triumph with a swelling breast:
Dust shall he eat, and with a zest,
As did a certain snake, my near relation.

THE LORD. Therein thou'rt free, according to thy merits;
The like of thee have never moved My hate.
Of all the bold, denying Spirits,
The waggish knave least trouble doth create.
Man's active nature, flagging, seeks too soon the level;
Unqualified repose he learns to crave;
Whence, willingly, the comrade him I gave,

Who works, excites, and must create, as Devil.
But ye, God's sons in love and duty,[7]
Enjoy the rich, the ever-living Beauty !
Creative Power, that works eternal schemes,
Clasp you in bonds of love, relaxing never,
And what in wavering apparition gleams
Fix in its place with thoughts that stand for ever !

                      [Heaven closes: the ARCHANGELS *separate.*

MEPHIS. *(solus).* I like, at times, to hear The Ancient's word,
And have a care to be most civil :
It's really kind of such a noble Lord
So humanly to gossip with the Devil !

FIRST PART OF THE TRAGEDY.

I.

NIGHT.

A lofty-arched, narrow, Gothic chamber. FAUST, *in a chair at his desk, restless.*

FAUST. I've studied now Philosophy
And Jurisprudence, Medicine,—
And even, alas! Theology,—
From end to end, with labour keen;
And here, poor fool! with all my lore
I stand, no wiser than before:
I'm Magister—yea, Doctor—hight,
And straight or cross-wise, wrong or right,
These ten years long, with many woes,
I've led my scholars by the nose,—
And see, that nothing can be known!
That knowledge cuts me to the bone.
I'm cleverer, true, than those fops of teachers,
Doctors and Magisters, Scribes and Preachers;
Neither scruples nor doubts come now to smite me,
Nor Hell nor Devil can longer affright me.
For this, all pleasure am I foregoing;
I do not pretend to aught worth knowing,
I do not pretend I could be a teacher
To help or convert a fellow-creature.
Then, too, I've neither lands nor gold,
Nor the world's least pomp or honour hold—
No dog would endure such a curst existence!
Wherefore, from Magic I seek assistance,
That many a secret perchance I reach
Through spirit-power and spirit-speech,
And thus the bitter task forego

Of saying the things I do not know,—
That I may detect the inmost force
Which binds the world, and guides its course;
Its germs, productive powers explore,
And rummage in empty words no more !

O full and splendid Moon, whom I
Have, from this desk, seen climb the sky
So many a midnight,—would thy glow
For the last time beheld my woe !
Ever thine eye, most mournful friend,
O'er books and papers saw me bend ;
But would that I, on mountains grand,
Amid thy blessed light could stand,
With spirits through mountain-caverns hover,
Float in thy twilight the meadows over,
And, freed from the fumes of lore that swathe me,
To health in thy dewy fountains bathe me !

Ah, me ! this dungeon still I see.
This drear, accursed masonry,
Where even the welcome daylight strains
But duskly through the painted panes.
Hemmed in by many a toppling heap
Of books worm-eaten, gray with dust,
Which to the vaulted ceiling creep,
Against the smoky paper thrust,—
With glasses, boxes, round me stacked,
And instruments together hurled,
Ancestral lumber, stuffed and packed—
Such is my world : and what a world !

And do I ask, wherefore my heart
Falters, oppressed with unknown needs ?
Why some inexplicable smart
All movement of my life impedes ?
Alas ! in living Nature's stead,
Where God His human creature set,
In smoke and mould the fleshless dead
And bones of beasts surround me yet !

Fly ! Up, and seek the broad, free land !
And this one Book of Mystery
From Nostradamus' very hand,[8]
Is't not sufficient company ?
When I the starry courses know,
And Nature's wise instruction seek,
With light of power my soul shall glow,
As when to spirits spirits speak.
'Tis vain, this empty brooding here,
Though guessed the holy symbols be :
Ye, Spirits, come—ye hover near—
Oh, if you hear me, answer me !

> [*He opens the Book, and perceives the sign of*
> *the Macrocosm.*[9]

Ha ! what a sudden rapture leaps from this
I view, through all my senses swiftly flowing !
I feel a youthful, holy, vital bliss
In every vein and fibre newly glowing.
Was it a God, who traced this sign,
With calm across my tumult stealing,
My troubled heart to joy unsealing,
With impulse, mystic and divine,
The powers of Nature here, around my path, revealing !
Am I a God ?—so clear mine eyes !
In these pure features I behold
Creative Nature to my soul unfold.
What says the sage, now first I recognize :
" The spirit-world no closures fasten ;
Thy sense is shut, thy heart is dead :
Disciple, up ! untiring, hasten
To bathe thy breast in morning-red ! "

> [*He contemplates the sign.*

How each the Whole its substance gives,
Each in the other works and lives !
Like heavenly forces rising and descending,
Their golden urns reciprocally lending,
With wings that winnow blessing
From Heaven through Earth I see them pressing,
Filling the All with harmony unceasing !
How grand a show ! but, ah ! a show alone.

Thee, boundless Nature, how make thee my own?
Where you, ye breasts?   Founts of all Being, shining,
Whereon hang Heaven's and Earth's desire,
Whereto our withered hearts aspire,—
Ye flow, ye feed: and am I vainly pining?

> [*He turns the leaves impatiently, and perceives the
> sign of the Earth-Spirit.*

How otherwise upon me works this sign!
Thou, Spirit of the Earth, art nearer:
Even now my powers are loftier, clearer;
I glow, as drunk with new-made wine:
New strength and heart to meet the world incite me,
The woe of earth, the bliss of earth, invite me,
And though the shock of storms may smite me,
No crash of shipwreck shall have power to fright me!
Clouds gather over me—
The moon conceals her light—
The lamp's extinguished!—
Mists rise,—red, angry rays are darting
Around my head!—There falls
A horror from the vaulted roof,
And seizes me!
I feel thy presence, Spirit I invoke!
Reveal thyself!
Ha! in my heart what rending stroke!
With new impulsion
My senses heave in this convulsion!
I feel thee draw my heart, absorb, exhaust me:
Thou must! thou must! and though my life it cost me!

> [*He seizes the book, and mysteriously pronounces the
> sign of the Spirit. A ruddy flame flashes: the
> SPIRIT appears in the flame.*

SPIRIT. Who calls me?

FAUST (*with averted head*). Terrible to see!

SPIRIT. Me hast thou long with might attracted,
Long from my sphere thy food exacted,
And now—

FAUST. Woe! I endure not thee!

SPIRIT. To view me is thine aspiration,
My voice to hear, my countenance to see:

Thy powerful yearning moveth me,
Here am I !—what mean perturbation
Thee, superhuman, shakes ? Thy soul's high calling, where ?
Where is the breast, which from itself a world did bear,
And shaped and cherished—which with joy expanded,
To be our peer, with us, the Spirits, banded ?
Where art thou, Faust, whose voice has pierced to me,
Who towards me pressed with all thine energy ?
He art thou, who, my presence breathing, seeing,
Trembles through all the depths of being,
A writhing worm, a terror-stricken form ?
    FAUST. Thee, form of flame, shall I then fear ?
Yes, I am Faust : I am thy peer !
    SPIRIT.   In the tides of Life, in Action's storm,
              A fluctuant wave,
              A shuttle free,
              Birth and the Grave,
              An eternal sea,
              A weaving, flowing
              Life, all-glowing,
Thus at Time's humming loom 'tis my hand prepares
The garment of Life which the Deity wears !
    FAUST. Thou, who around the wide world wendest,
Thou busy Spirit, how near I feel to thee !
    SPIRIT. Thou'rt like the Spirit which thou compre-
        hendest.
Not me !   [*Disappears.*
    FAUST (*overwhelmed*). Not thee !
Whom then ?
I, image of the Godhead !
Not even like thee !   [*A knock.*
O Death !—I know it—'tis my Famulus ! [10]
My fairest luck finds no fruition :
In all the fulness of my vision
The soulless sneak disturbs me thus !

    Enter WAGNER,[11] *in dressing-gown and night-cap, a lamp in*
      his hand. FAUST *turns impatiently.*

    WAGNER. Pardon, I heard your declamation ;
'Twas sure an old Greek tragedy you read ?

In such an art I crave some preparation,
Since now it stands one in good stead.
I've often heard it said, a preacher
Might learn, with a comedian for a teacher.

FAUST. Yes, when the priest comedian is by nature,
As haply now and then the case may be.

WAGNER. Ah, when one studies thus, a prisoned creature,
That scarce the world on holidays can see,—
Scarce through a glass, by rare occasion,
How shall one lead it by persuasion?

FAUST. You'll never attain it, save you know the feeling,
Save from the soul it rises clear,
Serene in primal strength, compelling
The hearts and minds of all who hear.
You sit for ever, gluing, patching;
You cook the scraps from others' fare;
And from your heap of ashes hatching
A starveling flame, ye blow it bare!
Take children's, monkeys' gaze admiring,
If such your taste, and be content;
But ne'er from heart to heart you'll speak inspiring,
Save your own heart is eloquent!

WAGNER. Yet through delivery orators succeed;
I feel that I am far behind, indeed.

FAUST. Seek thou the honest recompense!
Beware, a tinkling fool to be!
With little art, clear wit and sense
Suggest their own delivery;
And if thou'rt moved to speak in earnest,
What need, that after words thou yearnest?
Yes, your discourses, with their glittering show,
Where ye for men twist shredded thought like paper,[12]
Are unrefreshing as the winds that blow
The rustling leaves through chill autumnal vapour!

WAGNER. Ah, God! but Art is long,
And Life, alas! is fleeting.
And oft, with zeal my critic-duties meeting,
In head and breast there's something wrong.
How hard it is to compass the assistance
Whererby one rises to the source!

And, haply, ere one travels half the course
Must the poor devil quit existence.

FAUST. Is parchment, then, the holy fount before thee,
A draught wherefrom thy thirst for ever slakes?
No true refreshment can restore thee,
Save what from thine own soul spontaneous breaks.

WAGNER. Pardon! a great delight is granted
When, in the spirit of the ages planted,
We mark how, ere our time, a sage has thought,
And then, how far his work, and grandly, we have brought.

FAUST. O yes, up to the stars at last!
Listen, my friend: the ages that are past
Are now a book with seven seals protected:
What you the Spirit of the Ages call
Is nothing but the spirit of you all,
Wherein the Ages are reflected.
So, oftentimes, you miserably mar it!
At the first glance who sees it runs away.
An offal-barrel and a lumber-garret,
Or, at the best, a Punch-and-Judy play,[13]
With maxims most pragmatical and hitting,
As in the mouths of puppets are befitting!

WAGNER. But then, the world—the human heart and brain!
Of these one covets some slight apprehension.

FAUST. Yes, of the kind which men attain!
Who dares the child's true name in public mention?
The few, who thereof something really learned,
Unwisely frank, with hearts that spurned concealing,
And to the mob laid bare each thought and feeling,
Have evermore been crucified and burned.
I pray you, Friend, 'tis now the dead of night;
Our converse here must be suspended.

WAGNER. I would have shared your watches with delight,
That so our learned talk might be extended.
To-morrow, though, I'll ask, in Easter leisure,
This and the other question, at your pleasure.
Most zealously I seek for erudition:
Much do I know—but to know all is my ambition. [Exit.

FAUST (solus). That brain, alone, not loses hope, whose
choice is

c 2

To stick in shallow trash for evermore,—
Which digs with eager hand for buried ore,
And, when it finds an angel-worm, rejoices !

Dare such a human voice disturb the flow,
Around me here, of spirit-presence fullest ?
And yet, this once my thanks I owe
To thee, of all earth's sons the poorest, dullest !
For thou hast torn me from that desperate state
Which threatened soon to overwhelm my senses :
The apparition was so giant-great,
It dwarfed and withered all my soul's pretences !

I, image of the Godhead, who began—
Deeming Eternal Truth secure in nearness—
To sun myself in heavenly light and clearness,
And laid aside the earthly man ;—
I, more than Cherub, whose free force had planned
To flow through Nature's veins in glad pulsation,
To reach beyond, enjoying in creation
The life of Gods, behold my expiation !
A thunder-word hath swept me from my stand.

With thee I dare not venture to compare me.
Though I possessed the power to draw thee near me,
The power to keep thee was denied my hand.
When that ecstatic moment held me,
I felt myself so small, so great ;
But thou hast ruthlessly repelled me
Back upon Man's uncertain fate.
What shall I shun ?   Whose guidance borrow ?
Shall I accept that stress and strife ?
Ah ! every deed of ours, no less than every sorrow,
Impedes the onward march of life.

Some alien substance more and more is cleaving
To all the mind conceives of grand and fair ;
When this world's Good is won by our achieving,
The Better, then, is named a cheat and snare.
The fine emotions, whence our lives we mould,

Lie in the earthly tumult dumb and cold.
If hopeful Fancy once, in daring flight,
Her longings to the Infinite expanded,
Yet now a narrow space contents her quite,
Since Time's wild wave so many a fortune stranded.
Care at the bottom of the heart is lurking:
Her secret pangs in silence working,
She, restless, rocks herself, disturbing joy and rest:
In newer masks her face is ever drest,
By turns as house and land, as wife and child, pre-
    sented,—
As water, fire, as poison, steel:
We dread the blows we never feel,
And what we never lose is yet by us lamented!
I am not like the Gods! That truth is felt too deep:
The worm am I, that in the dust doth creep,—
That, while in dust it lives and seeks its bread,
Is crushed and buried by the wanderer's tread.

Is not this dust, these walls within them hold,
The hundred shelves, which cramp and chain me,
The frippery, the trinkets thousand-fold,
That in this mothy den restrain me?
Here shall I find the help I need?
Shall here a thousand volumes teach me only
That men, self-tortured, everywhere must bleed,—
And here and there one happy man sits lonely?
What mean'st thou by that grin, thou hollow skull,
Save that thy brain, like mine, a cloudy mirror,
Sought once the shining day, and then, in twilight dull,
Thirsting for Truth, went wretchedly to Error?
Ye instruments, forsooth, but jeer at me
With wheel and cog, and shapes uncouth of wonder;
I found the portal, you the keys should be;
Your wards are deftly wrought, but drive no bolts asunder!
Mysterious even in open day,
Nature retains her veil, despite our clamours:
That which she doth not willingly display
Cannot be wrenched from her with levers, screws, and
    hammers.

Ye ancient tools, whose use I never knew,
Here, since my father used ye, still ye moulder:
Thou, ancient scroll, hast worn thy smoky hue
Since at this desk the dim lamp wont to smoulder.
'Twere better far, had I my little idly spent,
Than now to sweat beneath its burden, I confess it!
What from your fathers' heritage is lent,
Earn it anew, to really possess it!
What serves not, is a sore impediment:
The Moment's need creates the thing to serve and bless it!

Yet, wherefore turns my gaze to yonder point so lightly?
Is yonder flask a magnet for mine eyes?
Whence, all around me, glows the air so brightly,
As when in woods at night the mellow moonbeam lies?

I hail thee, wondrous, rarest vial!
I take thee down devoutly, for the trial:
Man's art and wit I venerate in thee.
Thou summary of gentle slumber-juices,
Essence of deadly finest powers and uses,
Unto thy master show thy favour free!
I see thee, and the stings of pain diminish;
I grasp thee, and my struggles slowly finish:
My spirit's flood-tide ebbeth more and more.
Out on the open ocean speeds my dreaming;
The glassy flood before my feet is gleaming,
A new day beckons to a newer shore!

A fiery chariot, borne on buoyant pinions,
Sweeps near me now!   I soon shall ready be
To pierce the ether's high, unknown dominions,
To reach new spheres of pure activity!
This godlike rapture, this supreme existence,
Do I, but now a worm, deserve to track?
Yes, resolute to reach some brighter distance,
On Earth's fair sun I turn my back!
Yes, let me dare those gates to fling asunder,
Which every man would fain go slinking by!
'Tis time, through deeds this word of truth to thunder:

That with the height of Gods Man's dignity may vie !
Nor from that gloomy gulf to shrink affrighted,
Where Fancy doth herself to self-born pangs compel,—
To struggle toward that pass benighted,
Around whose narrow mouth flame all the fires of Hell,—
To take this step with cheerful resolution,
Though Nothingness should be the certain, swift conclusion !

And now come down, thou cup of crystal clearest !
Fresh from thine ancient cover thou appearest,
So many years forgotten to my thought !
Thou shon'st at old ancestral banquets cheery,
The solemn guests thou madest merry,
When one thy wassail to the other brought.
The rich and skilful figures o'er thee wrought,
The drinker's duty, rhyme-wise to explain them,
Or in one breath below the mark to drain them,
From many a night of youth my memory caught.
Now to a neighbour shall I pass thee never,
Nor on thy curious art to test my wit endeavour :
Here is a juice whence sleep is swiftly born.
It fills with browner flood thy crystal hollow ;
I chose, prepared it : thus I follow,—
With all my soul the final drink I swallow,
A solemn festal cup, a greeting to the morn !
> [*He sets the goblet to his mouth.   Chime of bells and
> choral song.*

CHORUS OF ANGELS.[14]   Christ is arisen !
>   Joy to the Mortal One,
>   Whom the unmerited,
>   Clinging, inherited
>   Needs did imprison.

FAUST.   What hollow humming, what a sharp, clear
stroke,
Drives from my lip the goblet's, at their meeting ?
Announce the booming bells already woke
The first glad hour of Easter's festal greeting ?
Ye choirs, have ye begun the sweet, consoling chant,
Which, through the night of Death, the angels ministrant
Sang, God's new Covenant repeating ?

CHORUS OF WOMEN. With spices and precious
>   Balm, we arrayed him ;
>   Faithful and gracious,
>   We tenderly laid him :
>   Linen to bind him
>   Cleanlily wound we :
>   Ah ! when we would find him,
>   Christ no more found we !

CHORUS OF ANGELS. Christ is ascended !
>   Bliss hath invested him,—
>   Woes that molested him,
>   Trials that tested him,
>   Gloriously ended !

FAUST. Why, here in dust, entice me with your spell,
Ye gentle, powerful sounds of Heaven ?
Peal rather there, where tender natures dwell.
Your messages I hear, but faith has not been given ;
The dearest child of Faith is Miracle.
I venture not to soar to yonder regions
Whence the glad tidings hither float ;
And yet, from childhood up familiar with the note,
To Life it now renews the old allegiance.
Once Heavenly Love sent down a burning kiss
Upon my brow, in Sabbath silence holy ;
And, filled with mystic presage, chimed the church-bell
>   slowly,
And prayer dissolved me in a fervent bliss.
A sweet, uncomprehended yearning
Drove forth my feet through woods and meadows free,
And while a thousand tears were burning,
I felt a world arise for me.
These chants, to youth and all its sports appealing,
Proclaimed the Spring's rejoicing holiday ;
And Memory holds me now, with childish feeling,
Back from the last, the solemn way.
Sound on, ye hymns of Heaven, so sweet and mild !
My tears gush forth : the Earth takes back her child !

CHORUS OF DISCIPLES. Has He, victoriously,
>   Burst from the vaulted
>   Grave, and all-gloriously

Now sits exalted ?
Is He, in glow of birth,
Rapture creative near ? [15]
Ah ! to the woe of earth
Still are we native here.
We, his aspiring
Followers, Him we miss ;
Weeping, desiring,
Master, Thy bliss !

CHORUS OF ANGELS. Christ is arisen,
Out of Corruption's womb :
Burst ye the prison,
Break from your gloom !
Praising and pleading him,
Lovingly needing him,
Brotherly feeding him,
Preaching and speeding him,
Blessing, succeeding Him,
Thus is the Master near,—
Thus is He here !

II.

BEFORE THE CITY-GATE.

Pedestrians of all kinds come forth.

SEVERAL APPRENTICES. Why do you go that way ?
OTHERS. We're for the Hunters'-lodge, to-day.
THE FIRST. We'll saunter to the Mill, in yonder hollow.
AN APPRENTICE. Go to the River Tavern, I should say.
SECOND APP. But then, it's not a pleasant way.
THE OTHERS. And what will *you* ?
A THIRD.   As goes the crowd, I follow
A FOURTH. Come up to Burgdorf ? There you'll find
    good cheer,

The finest lasses and the best of beer,
And jolly rows and squabbles, trust me !
    A Fifth. You swaggering fellow, is your hide
A third time itching to be tried?
I won't go there, your jolly rows disgust me !
    Servant-Girl. No,—no ! I'll turn and go to town again.
    Another. We'll surely find him by those poplars yonder.
    The First. That's no great luck for me, 'tis plain.
You'll have him, when and where you wander :
His partner in the dance you'll be,—
But what is all your fun to me ?
    The Other. He's surely not alone to-day :
He'll be with Curly-head, I heard him say.
    A Student. Deuce ! how they step, the buxom wenches !
Come, Brother ! we must see them to the benches.
A strong, old beer, a pipe that stings and bites,
A girl in Sunday clothes,—these three are my delights.
    Citizen's Daughter. Just see those handsome fellows
        there !
It's really shameful, I declare ;—
To follow servant-girls, when they
Might have the most genteel society to-day !
    Second Student (*to the First*). Not quite so fast ! Two
        others come behind,—
Those, dressed so prettily and neatly.
My neighbour's one of them, I find,
A girl that takes my heart, completely.
They go their way with looks demure,
But they'll accept us, after all, I'm sure.
    The First. No, Brother ! not for me their formal ways.
Quick ! lest our game escape us in the press :
The hand that wields the broom on Saturdays
Will best, on Sundays, fondle and caress.
    Citizen. He suits me not at all, our new-made Burgo-
        master !
Since he's installed, his arrogance grows faster.
How has he helped the town, I say ?
Things worsen,—what improvement names he ?
Obedience, more than ever, claims he,
And more than ever we must pay !

BEGGAR (*sings*). Good gentlemen and lovely ladies,

So red of cheek and fine of dress,

Behold, how needful here your aid is,

And see and lighten my distress !

Let me not vainly sing my ditty ;

He 's only glad who gives away :

A holiday, that shows your pity,

Shall be for me a harvest-day !

ANOTHER CITIZEN. On Sundays, holidays, there's naught
I take delight in,
Like gossiping of war, and war's array,
When down in Turkey, far away,
The foreign people are a-fighting.
One at the window sits, with glass and friends,
And sees all sorts of ships go down the river gliding :
And blesses then, as home he wends
At night, our times of peace abiding.

THIRD CITIZEN. Yes, Neighbour ! that's my notion, too :
Why, let them break their heads, let loose their passions,
And mix things madly through and through,
So, here, we keep our good old fashions !

OLD WOMAN (*to the Citizen's Daughter*). Dear me, how
fine ! So handsome, and so young !
Who wouldn't lose his heart, that met you ?
Don't be so proud ! I'll hold my tongue,
And what you'd like I'll undertake to get you.

CITIZEN'S DAUGHTER. Come, Agatha ! I shun the witch's
sight
Before folks, lest there be misgiving :
'Tis true, she showed me, on Saint Andrew's Night,[16]
My future sweetheart, just as he were living.

THE OTHER. She showed me mine, in crystal clear,[17]
With several wild young blades, a soldier-lover :
I seek him everywhere, I pry and peer,
And yet, somehow, his face I can't discover.

SOLDIERS.

Castles with lofty

Ramparts and towers,

Maidens disdainful

In Beauty's array,

Both shall be ours !

Bold is the venture,
Splendid the pay !
Lads, let the trumpets
For us be suing,—
Calling to pleasure,
Calling to ruin.
Stormy our life is ;
Such is its boon !
Maidens and castles
Capitulate soon.
Bold is the venture,
Splendid the pay !
And the soldiers go marching,
Marching away !

FAUST *and* WAGNER.

FAUST. Released from ice are brook and river
By the quickening glance of the gracious Spring ;
The colours of hope to the valley cling,
And weak old Winter himself must shiver,
Withdrawn to the mountains, a crownless king :
Whence, ever retreating, he sends again
Impotent showers of sleet that darkle
In belts across the green o' the plain.
But the sun will permit no white to sparkle !
Everywhere form in development moveth ;
He will brighten the world with the tints he loveth,
And, lacking blossoms, blue, yellow, and red,
He takes these gaudy people instead.
Turn thee about, and from this height
Back on the town direct thy sight.
Out of the hollow, gloomy gate,
The motley throngs come forth elate :
Each will the joy of the sunshine hoard,
To honour the Day of the Risen Lord !
They feel, themselves, their resurrection :
From the low, dark rooms, scarce habitable ;
From the bonds of Work, from Trade's restriction ;
From the pressing weight of roof and gable ;
From the narrow, crushing streets and alleys ;

From the churches' solemn and reverend night,
All come forth to the cheerful light.
How lively, see! the multitude sallies,
Scattering through gardens and fields remote,
While over the river, that broadly dallies,
Dances so many a festive boat;
And overladen, nigh to sinking,
The last full wherry takes the stream.
Yonder afar, from the hill-paths blinking,
Their clothes are colours that softly gleam.
I hear the noise of the village, even;
Here is the People's proper Heaven;
Here high and low contented see!
Here I am Man,—dare man to be!

WAGNER. To stroll with you, Sir Doctor, flatters;
'Tis honour, profit, unto me.
But I, alone, would shun these shallow matters,
Since all that's coarse provokes my enmity.
This fiddling, shouting, ten-pin rolling
I hate,—these noises of the throng:
They rave, as Satan were their sports controlling,
And call it mirth, and call it song!

PEASANTS *under the Linden-Tree.*

(*Dance and Song.*)

All for the dance the shepherd dressed,
In ribbons, wreath, and gayest vest
    Himself with care arraying:
Around the linden lass and lad
Already footed it like mad:
    Hurrah! hurrah!
    Hurrah—tarara-la!
The fiddle-bow was playing.

He broke the ranks, no whit afraid,
And with his elbow punched a maid,
    Who stood, the dance surveying:
The buxom wench, she turned and said
" Now, you I call a stupid-head!"

Hurrah ! hurrah !
Hurrah—tarara-la !
" Be decent while you're staying !"

Then round the circle went their flight,
They danced to left, they danced to right :
    Their kirtles all were playing.
They first grew red, and then grew warm,
And rested, panting, arm in arm—
    Hurrah ! hurrah !
    Hurrah—tarara-la !
    And hips and elbows straying.

Now, don't be so familiar here !
How many a one has fooled his dear,
    Waylaying and betraying !
And yet, he coaxed her soon aside,
And round the linden sounded wide :
    Hurrah ! hurrah !
    Hurrah—tarara-la !
    And the fiddle-bow was playing.

OLD PEASANT. Sir Doctor, it is good of you,
That thus you condescend, to-day,
Among this crowd of merry folk,
A highly-learned man, to stray.
Then also take the finest can,
We fill with fresh wine, for your sake :
I offer it, and humbly wish
That not alone your thirst it slake,—
That, as the drops below its brink,
So many days of life you drink !
    FAUST. I take the cup you kindly reach,
With thanks and health to all and each.
               [The People gather in a circle about him.
    OLD PEASANT. In truth, 'tis well and fitly timed,
That now our day of joy you share,
Who heretofore, in evil days,
Gave us so much of helping care.
Still many a man stands living here,

Saved by your father's skilful hand,
That snatched him from the fever's rage
And stayed the plague in all the land.
Then also you, though but a youth, [19]
Went into every house of pain :
Many the corpses carried forth,
But you in health came out again.
No test or trial you evaded :
A Helping God the helper aided.

    ALL. Health to the man, so skilled and **tried,**
That for our help he long may bide !

    FAUST. To Him above bow down, my friends,
Who teaches help, and succour sends !

                    [*He goes on with* WAGNER.

    WAGNER. With what a feeling, thou great man, must thou
Receive the people's honest veneration !
How lucky he, whose gifts his station
With such advantages endow !
Thou'rt shown to all the younger generation :
Each asks, and presses near to gaze ;
The fiddle stops, the dance delays.
Thou goest, they stand in rows to see,
And all the caps are lifted high ;
A little more, and they would bend the knee
As if the Holy Host came by.

    FAUST. A few more steps ascend, as far as yonder stone !—
Here from our wandering will we rest contented.
Here, lost in thought, I've lingered oft alone,
When foolish fasts and prayers my life tormented.
Here, rich in hope and firm in faith,
With tears, wrung hands and sighs, I've striven,
The end of that far-spreading death
Entreating from the Lord of Heaven !
Now like contempt the crowd's applauses seem :
Couldst thou but read, within mine inmost spirit,
How little now I deem
That sire or son such praises merit !
My father's was a sombre, brooding brain,
Which through the holy spheres of Nature groped **and**
        wandered,

And honestly, in his own fashion, pondered
With labour whimsical, and pain :
Who, in his dusky work-shop bending,
With proved adepts in company,
Made, from his recipes unending,
Opposing substances agree.
There was a Lion red, a wooer daring,[20]
Within the Lily's tepid bath espoused,
And both, tormented then by flame unsparing,
By turns in either bridal chamber housed.
If then appeared, with colours splendid,
The young Queen in her crystal shell,
This was the medicine—the patients' woes soon ended,
And none demanded—who got well?
Thus we, our hellish boluses compounding,
Among these vales and hills surrounding,
Worse than the pestilence, have passed.
Thousands were done to death from poison of my giving
And I must hear, by all the living,
The shameless murderers praised at last !

    WAGNER. Why, therefore, yield to such depression ?
A good man does his honest share
In exercising, with the strictest care,
The art bequeathed to his possession !
Dost thou thy father honour, as a youth ?
Then may his teaching cheerfully impel thee :
Dost thou, as man, increase the stores of truth ?
Then may thine own son afterwards excel thee.

    FAUST. O happy he, who still renews
The hope, from Error's deeps to rise for ever !
That which one does not know, one needs to use :
And what one knows, one uses never.
But let us not, by such despondence, so
The fortune of this hour embitter !
Mark how, beneath the evening sunlight's glow,
The green-embosomed houses glitter !
The glow retreats, done is the day of toil ;
It yonder hastes, new fields of life exploring ;
Ah, that no wing can lift me from the soil,
Upon its track to follow, follow soaring !

Then would I see eternal Evening gild
The silent world beneath me glowing,
On fire each mountain-peak, with peace each valley filled,
The silver brook to golden rivers flowing.
The mountain-chain, with all its gorges deep,
Would then no more impede my godlike motion ;
And now before mine eyes expands the ocean
With all its bays, in shining sleep !
Yet, finally, the weary god is sinking ;
The new-born impulse fires my mind,—
I hasten on, his beams eternal drinking,
The Day before me and the Night behind,
Above me heaven unfurled, the floor of waves beneath me,—
A glorious dream ! though now the glories fade.
Alas ! the wings that lift the mind no aid
Of wings to lift the body can bequeath me.
Yet in each soul is born the pleasure
Of yearning onward, upward and away,
When o'er our heads, lost in the vaulted azure,
The lark sends down his flickering lay,—
When over crags and piny highlands
The poising eagle slowly soars,
And over plains and lakes and islands
The crane sails by to other shores.

WAGNER. I've had, myself, at times, some odd caprices,
But never yet such impulse felt, as this is.
One soon fatigues, on woods and fields to look,
Nor would I beg the bird his wing to spare us :
How otherwise the mental raptures bear us
From page to page, from book to book !
Then winter nights take loveliness untold,
As warmer life in every limb had crowned you ;
And when your hands unroll some parchment rare and old,
All Heaven descends, and opens bright around you ;

FAUST. One impulse art thou conscious of, at best;
O, never seek to know the other !
Two souls, alas ! reside within my breast,
And each withdraws from, and repels, its brother.
One with tenacious organs holds in love
And clinging lust the world in its embraces ;

D

The other strongly sweeps, this dust above,
Into the high ancestral spaces.
If there be airy spirits near,
'Twixt Heaven and Earth on potent errands fleeing,
Let them drop down the golden atmosphere,
And bear me forth to new and varied being!
Yea, if a magic mantle once were mine,
To waft me o'er the world at pleasure,
I would not for the costliest stores of treasure—
Not for a monarch's robe—the gift resign.

    WAGNER. Invoke not thus the well-known throng,
Which through the firmament diffused is faring,
And danger thousand-fold, our race to wrong,
In every quarter is preparing.
Swift from the North the spirit-fangs so sharp[21]
Sweep down, and with their barbéd points assail you ;
Then from the East they come, to dry and warp
Your lungs, till breath and being fail you :
If from the Desert sendeth them the South,
With fire on fire your throbbing forehead crowning,
The West leads on a host, to cure the drouth
Only when meadow, field, and you are drowning.
They gladly hearken, prompt for injury,—
Gladly obey, because they gladly cheat us ;
From Heaven they represent themselves to be,
And lisp like angels, when with lies they meet us.
But, let us go ! 'Tis gray and dusky all :
The air is cold, the vapours fall.
At night, one learns his house to prize :—
Why stand you thus, with such astonished eyes ?
What, in the twilight, can your mind so trouble ?

    FAUST. Seest thou the black dog coursing there, through
       corn and stubble ?[22]

    WAGNER. Long since : yet deemed him not important in
       the least.

    FAUST. Inspect him close : for what tak'st thou the beast ?

    WAGNER. Why, for a poodle who has lost his master,
And scents about, his track to find.

    FAUST. Seest thou the spiral circles, narrowing faster,
Which he, approaching, round us seems to wind ?

A streaming trail of fire, if I see rightly,
Follows his path of mystery.

WAGNER. It may be that your eyes deceive you slightly ;
Naught but a plain black poodle do I see.

FAUST. It seems to me that with enchanted cunning
He snares our feet, some future chain to bind.

WAGNER. I see him timidly, in doubt, around us running,
Since, in his master's stead, two strangers doth he find.

FAUST. The circle narrows : he is near !

WAGNER. A dog thou seest, and not a phantom, here !
Behold him stop—upon his belly crawl—
His tail set wagging; canine habits, all !

FAUST. Come, follow us ! Come here, at least !

WAGNER. 'Tis the absurdest, drollest beast.
Stand still, and you will see him wait ;
Address him, and he gambols straight ;
If something's lost, he'll quickly bring it,—
Your cane, if in the stream you fling it.

FAUST. No doubt you're right : no trace of mind, I own,
Is in the beast : I see but drill, alone.

WAGNER. The dog, when he's well educated,
Is by the wisest tolerated.
Yes, he deserves your favour thoroughly,—
The clever scholar of the students, he !

[*They pass in the city-gate.*

———————

III.

THE STUDY.

FAUST (*entering with the poodle*).

Behind me, field and meadow sleeping,
I leave in deep, prophetic night,
Within whose dread and holy keeping
The better soul awakes to light.

The wild desires no longer win us,
The deeds of passion cease to chain ;
The love of Man revives within us,
The love of God revives again.

Be still, thou poodle ! make not such racket and riot!
Why at the threshold wilt snuffing be ?
Behind the stove repose thee in quiet !
My softest cushion I give to thee.
As thou, up yonder, with running and leaping
Amused us hast, on the mountain's crest,
So now I take thee into my keeping,
A welcome, but also a silent, guest.

Ah, when within our narrow chamber
The lamp with friendly lustre glows,
Flames in the breast each faded ember,
And in the heart, itself that knows.
Then Hope again lends sweet assistance,
And Reason then resumes her speech :
One yearns, the rivers of existence,
The very founts of Life to reach.

Snarl not, poodle ! To the sound that rises,
The sacred tones that my soul embrace,
This bestial noise is out of place.
We are used to see that Man despises
What he never comprehends,
And the Good and the Beautiful vilipends,
Finding them often hard to measure :
Will the dog, like Man, snarl *his* displeasure ?

But ah ! I feel, though will thereto be stronger,
Contentment flows from out my breast no longer.
Why must the stream so soon run dry and fail us,
And burning thirst again assail us ?
Therein I've borne so much probation !
And yet this want may be supplied us ;
We call the Supernatural to guide us ;
We pine and thirst for Revelation,

Which nowhere worthier is, more nobly sent,
Than here, in our New Testament.
I feel impelled, its meaning to determine,—
With honest purpose, once for all,
The hallowed Original
To change to my beloved German.

           [*He opens a volume and commences.*

'Tis written; "In the Beginning was the *Word.*"[3]
Here am I balked: who, now, can help afford?
The *Word?*—impossible so high to rate it;
And otherwise must I translate it,
If by the Spirit I am truly taught.
Then thus: "In the Beginning was the *Thought.*"
This first line let me weigh completely,
Lest my impatient pen proceed too fleetly.
Is it the *Thought* which works, creates, indeed?
"In the Beginning was the *Power*," I read.
Yet, as I write, a warning is suggested,
That I the sense may not have fairly tested.
The Spirit aids me: now I see the light!
"In the Beginning was the *Act*," I write.

If I must share my chamber with thee,
Poodle, stop that howling, prithee!
Cease to bark and bellow!
Such a noisy, disturbing fellow
I'll no longer suffer near me.
One of us, dost hear me!
Must leave, I fear me.
No longer guest-right I bestow;
The door is open, art free to go.
But what do I see in the creature?
Is that in the course of nature?
Is't actual fact? or Fancy's shows?
How long and broad my poodle grows?
He rises mightily:
A canine form that cannot be!
What a spectre I've harboured thus!
He resembles a hippopotamus

With fiery eyes, teeth terrible to see :
O, now am I sure of thee !
For all of thy half-hellish brood
The Key of Solomon is good.[24]

SPIRITS (*in the corridor*). Some one, within, is caught !
                Stay without, follow him not !
                Like the fox in a snare,
                Quakes the old hell-lynx there.
                Take heed—look about !
                Back and forth hover.
                Under and over,
                And he'll work himself out.
                If your aid can avail him,
                Let it not fail him ;
                For he, without measure,
                Has wrought for our pleasure.

FAUST. First to encounter the beast,
                The Words of the Four be addressed : [25]
                Salamander, shine glorious !
                Wave, Undine, as bidden !
                Sylph, be thou hidden !
                Gnome, be laborious !

Who knows not their sense
(These elements),—
Their properties
And power not sees,—
No mastery he inherits
Over the Spirits.

                Vanish in flaming ether,
                Salamander !
                Flow foamingly together,
                Undine !
                Shine in meteor-sheen,
                Sylph ;
                Bring help to hearth and shelf,
                Incubus ! Incubus !
                Step forward, and finish thus !

Of the Four, no feature
Lurks in the creature.
Quiet he lies, and grins disdain :
Not yet, it seems, have I given him pain.

Now, to undisguise thee, [26]
Hear me exorcise thee !
Art thou, my gay one,
Hell's fugitive stray-one ?
The sign witness now,
Before which they bow,
The cohorts of Hell !

With hair all bristling, it begins to swell.

> Base Being, hearest thou ?
> Knowest and fearest thou
> The One, unoriginate, [27]
> Named inexpressibly,
> Through all Heaven impermeate,
> Pierced irredressibly !

Behind the stove still banned,
See it, an elephant, expand !
It fills the space entire,
Mist-like melting, ever faster.
'Tis enough : ascend no higher,—
Lay thyself at the feet of the Master !
Thou seest, not vain the threats I bring thee :
With holy fire I'll scorch and sting thee !
Wait not to know
The threefold dazzling glow !
Wait not to know
The strongest art within my hands !

MEPHISTOPHELES, [28] *while the vapour is dissipating, steps forth*
from behind the stove, in the costume of a Travelling Scholar.

Why such a noise ?   What are my lord's commands ?
   FAUST. This was the poodle's real core,
A travelling scholar, then ?   The *casus* is diverting.
   MEPHIS. The learned gentleman I bow before :
You've made me roundly sweat, that's certain !

FAUST. What is thy name?

MEPHIS. A question small it seems,
For one whose mind the Word so much despises;
Who, scorning all external gleams,
The depths of being only prizes.

FAUST. With all you gentlemen, the name's a test,
Whereby the nature usually is expressed.
Clearly the latter it implies
In names like Beelzebub, Destroyer, Father of Lies.[29]
Who art thou, then?

MEPHIS. Part of that Power, not understood,
Which always wills the Bad, and always works the Good.

FAUST. What hidden sense in this enigma lies?

MEPHIS. I am the Spirit that Denies![30]
And justly so: for all things, from the Void
Called forth, deserve to be destroyed:
'Twere better, then, were naught created.
Thus, all which you as Sin have rated,—
Destruction,—aught with Evil blent,—
That is my proper element.

FAUST. Thou nam'st thyself a part, yet show'st complete
to me?

MEPHIS. The modest truth I speak to thee.
If Man, that microcosmic fool, can see
Himself a whole so frequently,
Part of the Part am I, once All, in primal Night,—
Part of the Darkness which brought forth the Light,
The haughty Light, which now disputes the space,
And claims of Mother Night her ancient place.
And yet, the struggle fails; since Light, howe'er it weaves,
Still, fettered, unto bodies cleaves:
It flows from bodies, bodies beautifies;
By bodies is its course impeded;
And so, but little time is needed,
I hope, ere, as the bodies die, it dies!

FAUST. I see the plan thou art pursuing:
Thou canst not compass general ruin,
And hast on smaller scale begun.

MEPHIS. And truly 'tis not much, when all is done,
That which to Naught is in resistance set,—

The Something of this clumsy world,—has yet,
With all that I have undertaken,
Not been by me disturbed or shaken :
From earthquake, tempest, wave, volcano's brand,
Back into quiet settle sea and land !
And that damned stuff, the bestial, human brood,—
What use, in having that to play with ?
How many have I made away with !
And ever circulates a newer, fresher blood.
It makes me furious, such things beholding :
From Water, Earth, and Air unfolding,
A thousand germs break forth and grow,
In dry, and wet, and warm, and chilly ;
And had I not the Flame reserved, why, really,
There's nothing special of my own to show !

   Faust. So, to the actively eternal
Creative force, in cold disdain
You now oppose the fist infernal,
Whose wicked clench is all in vain !
Some other labour seek thou rather,
Queer Son of Chaos, to begin !

   Mephis. Well, we'll consider : thou canst gather
My views, when next I venture in.
Might I, perhaps, depart at present ?

   Faust. Why thou shouldst ask, I don't perceive.
Though our acquaintance is so recent,
For further visits thou hast leave.
The window's here, the door is yonder ;
A chimney, also, you behold.

   Mephis. I must confess that forth I may not wander,
My steps by one slight obstacle controlled,—
The wizard's-foot, that on your threshold made is.[31]

   Faust. The pentagram prohibits thee ?
Why, tell me now, thou Son of Hades,
If that prevents, how cam'st thou in to me ?
Could such a spirit be so cheated ?

   Mephis. Inspect the thing : the drawing's not completed.
The outer angle, you may see,
Is open left—the lines don't fit it.

FAUST. Well,—Chance, this time, has fairly hit it!
And thus, thou'rt prisoner to me?
It seems the business has succeeded.

MEPHIS. The poodle naught remarked, as after thee he
        speeded;
But other aspects now obtain:
The Devil can't get out again.

FAUST. Try, then, the open window-pane!

MEPHIS. For Devils and for spectres this is law:
Where they have entered in, there also they withdraw.
The first is free to us; we're governed by the second.

FAUST. In Hell itself, then, laws are reckoned?
That's well! So might a compact be
Made with you gentlemen—and binding,—surely?

MEPHIS. All that is promised shall delight thee purely;
No skinflint bargain shalt thou see.
But this is not of swift conclusion;
We'll talk about the matter soon.
And now, I do entreat this boon—
Leave to withdraw from my intrusion.

FAUST. One moment more I ask thee to remain,
Some pleasant news, at least, to tell me.

MEPHIS. Release me, now! I soon shall come again;
Then thou, at will, may'st question and compel me.

FAUST. I have not snares around thee cast;
Thyself hast led thyself into the meshes.
Who traps the Devil, holds him fast!
Not soon a second time he'll catch a prey so precious.

MEPHIS. An't please thee, also I'm content to stay,
And serve thee in a social station;
But stipulating, that I may
With arts of mine afford thee recreation.

FAUST. Thereto I willingly agree,
If the diversion pleasant be.

MEPHIS. My friend, thou'lt win, past all pretences,
More in this hour to soothe thy senses,
Than in the year's monotony.
That which the dainty spirits sing thee,
The lovely pictures they shall bring thee,
Are more than magic's empty show.

Thy scent will be to bliss invited ;
Thy palate then with taste delighted,
Thy nerves of touch ecstatic glow !
All unprepared, the charm I spin :
We're here together, so begin !

SPIRITS.[32]   Vanish, ye darkling
    Arches above him !
    Loveliest weather,
    Born of blue ether,
    Break from the sky !
    O that the darkling
    Clouds had departed !
    Starlight is sparkling,
    Tranquiller-hearted
    Suns are on high.
    Heaven's own children
    In beauty bewildering,
    Waveringly bending,
    Pass as they hover ;
    Longing unending
    Follows them over.
    They, with their glowing
    Garments, out-flowing,
    Cover, in going,
    Landscape and bower,
    Where, in seclusion,
    Lovers are plighted,
    Lost in illusion.
    Bower on bower !
    Tendrils unblighted !
    Lo ! in a shower
    Grapes that o'ercluster
    Gush into must, or
    Flow into rivers
    Of foaming and flashing
    Wine, that is dashing
    Gems, as it boundeth
    Down the high places,
    And spreading, surroundeth
    With crystalline spaces,

In happy embraces,
Blossoming forelands,
Emerald shore-lands !
And the winged races
Drink, and fly onward—
Fly ever sunward
To the enticing
Islands, that flatter,
Dipping and rising
Light on the water !
Hark, the inspiring
Sound of their quiring !
See, the entrancing
Whirl of their dancing !
All in the air are
Freer and fairer.
Some of them scaling
Boldly the highlands,
Others are sailing,
Circling the islands ;
Others are flying ;
Life-ward all hieing,—
Ail for the distant
Star of existent
Rapture and Love !

MEPHIS. He sleeps !   Enough, ye fays ! your airy number
Have sung him truly into slumber :
For this performance I your debtor prove.—
Not yet art thou the man, to catch the Fiend and hold him !—
With fairest images of dreams infold him,
Plunge him in seas of sweet untruth !
Yet, for the threshold's magic which controlled him,
The Devil needs a rat's quick tooth.
I use no lengthened invocation :
Here rustles one that soon will work my liberation.

The lord of rats and eke of mice,
Of flies and bed-bugs, frogs and lice,
Summons thee hither to the door-sill,
To gnaw it where, with just a morsel

Of oil, he paints the spot for thee:—
There com'st thou, hopping on to me!
To work, at once! The point which made me craven
Is forward, on the ledge, engraven.
Another bite makes free the door:
So, dream thy dreams, O Faust, until we meet once more i
    FAUST (*awaking*). Am I again so foully cheated?
Remains there naught of lofty spirit-sway,
But that a dream the Devil counterfeited,
And that a poodle ran away?

IV.

THE STUDY.

FAUST. MEPHISTOPHELES.

FAUST. A knock? Come in! Again my quiet broken!
MEPHIS. 'Tis I!
FAUST. Come in!
MEPHIS. Thrice must the words be spoken.
FAUST. Come in, then!
MEPHIS. Thus thou pleasest me.
I hope we'll suit each other well;
For now, thy vapours to dispel,
I come, a squire of high degree,[33]
In scarlet coat, with golden trimming,
A cloak in silken lustre swimming,
A tall cock's-feather in my hat,
A long, sharp sword for show or quarrel,—
And I advise thee, brief and flat,
To don the self-same gay apparel,
That, from this den released, and free,
Life be at last revealed to thee!
    FAUST. This life of earth, whatever my attire,
Would pain me in its wonted fashion.[34]
Too old am I to play with passion;

Too young, to be without desire.
What from the world have I to gain?
Thou shalt abstain—renounce—refrain!
Such is the everlasting song
That in the ears of all men rings,—
That unrelieved, our whole life long,
Each hour, in passing, hoarsely sings.
In very terror I at morn awake,
Upon the verge of bitter weeping,
To see the day of disappointment break,
To no one hope of mine—not one—its promise keeping :—
That even each joy's presentiment
With wilful cavil would diminish,
With grinning masks of life prevent
My mind its fairest work to finish !
Then, too, when night descends, how anxiously
Upon my couch of sleep I lay me :
There, also, comes no rest to me,
But some wild dream is sent to fray me.
The God that in my breast is owned
Can deeply stir the inner sources;
The God, above my powers enthroned,
He cannot change external forces.
So, by the burden of my days oppressed,
Death is desired, and Life a thing unblest !
    MEPHIS. And yet is never Death a wholly welcome guest.
    FAUST. O fortunate, for whom, when victory glances,
The bloody laurels on the brow he bindeth !
Whom, after rapid, maddening dances,
In clasping maiden-arms he findeth !
O would that I, before that spirit-power,
Ravished and rapt from life, had sunken !
    MEPHIS. And yet, by some one, in that nightly hour,
A certain liquid was not drunken.
    FAUST. Eavesdropping, ha ! thy pleasure seems to be.
    MEPHIS. Omniscient am I not ! yet much is known to me.
    FAUST. Though some familiar tone, retrieving
My thoughts from torment, led me on,
And sweet, clear echoes came, deceiving
A faith bequeathed from Childhood's dawn,

Yet now I curse whate'er entices
And snares the soul with visions vain ;
With dazzling cheats and dear devices
Confines it in this cave of pain !
Cursed be, at once, the high ambition
Wherewith the mind itself deludes !
Cursed be the glare of apparition
That cn the finer sense intrudes !
Cursed be the lying dream's impression
Of name, and fame, and laurelled brow !
Cursed, all that flatters as possession,
As wife and child, as knave and plough !
Cursed Mammon be, when he with treasures
To restless action spurs our fate !
Cursed when, for soft, indulgent leisures,
He lays for us the pillows straight !
Cursed be the vine's transcendent nectar,—
The highest favour Love lets fall !
Cursed, also, Hope !—cursed Faith, the spectre !
And cursed be Patience most of all !

   CHORUS OF SPIRITS (*invisible*).[35] Woe! woe!
       Thou hast it destroyed,
       The beautiful world,
       With powerful fist :
       In ruin 'tis hurled,
       By the blow of a demigod shattered !
       The scattered
       Fragments into the Void we carry,
       Deploring
       The beauty perished beyond restoring.
       Mightier
       For the children of men,
       Brightlier
       Build it again,
       In thine own bosom build it anew !
       Bid the new career
       Commence,
       With clearer sense,
       And the new songs of cheer
       Be sung thereto !

MEPHIS. These are the small dependants
Who give me attendance.
Hear them, to deeds and passion
Counsel in shrewd old-fashion !
Into the world of strife,
Out of this lonely life
That of senses and sap has betrayed thee,
They would persuade thee.
This nursing of the pain forego thee,
That, like a vulture, feeds upon thy breast !
The worst society thou find'st will show thee
Thou art a man among the rest.
But 'tis not meant to thrust
Thee into the mob thou hatest !
I am not one of the greatest,
Yet, wilt thou to me entrust
Thy steps through life, I'll guide thee,—
Will willingly walk beside thee,—
Will serve thee at once and for ever
With best endeavour,
And, if thou art satisfied,
Will as servant, slave, with thee abide.

   FAUST. And what shall be my counter-service therefor ?
   MEPHIS. The time is long : thou need'st not now insist.
   FAUST. No—no ! The Devil is an egotist,
And is not apt, without a why or wherefore,
" For God's sake," others to assist.
Speak thy conditions plain and clear !
With such a servant danger comes, I fear.

   MEPHIS. *Here*, an unwearied slave, I'll wear thy tether,
And to thine every nod obedient be :
When *There* again we come together,
Then shalt thou do the same for me.

   FAUST. The *There* my scruples naught increases.
When thou hast dashed this world to pieces,
The others, then, its place may fill.
Here, on this earth, my pleasures have their sources ;
Yon sun beholds my sorrows in his courses ;
And when from these my life itself divorces,
Let happen all that can or will !

I'll hear no more : 'tis vain to ponder
If there we cherish love or hate,
Or, in the spheres we dream of yonder,
A High and Low our souls await.

MEPHIS. In this sense, even, canst thou venture.
Come, bind thyself by prompt indenture,
And thou mine arts with joy shalt see :
What no man ever saw, I'll give to thee

FAUST. Canst thou, poor Devil, give me whatsoever?
When was a human soul, in its supreme endeavour,
E'er understood by such as thou?
Yet, hast thou food which never satiates, now,—
The restless, ruddy gold hast thou,
That runs, quicksilver-like, one's fingers through,—
A game whose winnings no man ever knew,—
A maid that, even from my breast,
Beckons my neighbour with her wanton glances,
And Honour's god-like zest,
The meteor that a moment dances,—
Show me the fruits that, ere they're gathered, rot,
And trees that daily with new leafage clothe them !

MEPHIS. Such a demand alarms me not :
Such treasures have I, and can show them.
But still the time may reach us, good my friend,
When peace we crave and more luxurious diet.

FAUST. When on an idler's bed I stretch myself in quiet,
There let, at once, my record end !
Canst thou with lying flattery rule me,
Until, self-pleased, myself I see,—
Canst thou with rich enjoyment fool me,
Let that day be the last for me !
The bet I offer.

MEPHIS. Done !
FAUST. And heartily !
When thus I hail the Moment flying :
" Ah, still delay—thou art so fair ! " [36]
Then bind me in thy bonds undying,
My final ruin then declare !
Then let the death-bell chime the token,
Then art thou from thy service free !

E

The clock may stop, the hand be broken,
Then Time be finished unto me !

    MEPHIS. Consider well : my memory good is rated.

    FAUST. Thou hast a perfect right thereto.
My powers I have not rashly estimated :
A slave am I, whate'er I do—
If thine, or whose ? 'tis needless to debate it.

    MEPHIS. Then at the Doctors'-banquet I, to-day,[37]
Will as a servant wait behind thee.
But one thing more ! Beyond all risk to bind thee,
Give me a line or two, I pray.

    FAUST. Demand'st thou, Pedant, too, a document ?
Hast never known a man, nor proved his word's intent ?
Is't not enough, that what I speak to-day
Shall stand, with all my future days agreeing ?
In all its tides sweeps not the world away,
And shall a promise bind my being ?
Yet this delusion in our hearts we bear :
Who would himself therefrom deliver ?
Blest he, whose bosom Truth makes pure and fair !
No sacrifice shall he repent of ever.
Nathless a parchment, writ and stamped with care,
A spectre is, which all to shun endeavour.
The word, alas ! dies even in the pen,
And wax and leather keep the lordship then.
What wilt from me, Base Spirit, say ?—
Brass, marble, parchment, paper, clay ?
The terms with graver, quill, or chisel, stated ?
I freely leave the choice to thee.

    MEPHIS. Why heat thyself, thus instantly,
With eloquence exaggerated ?
Each leaf for such a pact is good ;
And to subscribe thy name thou'lt take a drop of blood.

    FAUST. If thou therewith art fully satisfied,
So let us by the farce abide.

    MEPHIS. Blood is a juice of rarest quality.

    FAUST. Fear not that I this pact shall seek to sever !
The promise that I make to thee
Is just the sum of my endeavour.
I have myself inflated all too high :

My proper place is thy estate :
The Mighty Spirit deigns me no reply,
And Nature shuts on me her gate.
The thread of Thought at last is broken,
And knowledge brings disgust unspoken.
Let us the sensual deeps explore,
To quench the fervours of glowing passion !
Let every marvel take form and fashion
Through the impervious veil it wore !
Plunge we in Time's tumultuous dance,
In the rush and roll of Circumstance !
Then may delight and distress,
And worry and success,
Alternately follow, as best they can :
Restless activity proves the man !

MEPHIS. For you no bound, no term is set.
Whether you everywhere be trying,
Or snatch a rapid bliss in flying,
May it agree with you, what you get !
Only fall to, and show no timid balking.

FAUST. But thou hast heard, 'tis not of joy we're talking.
I take the wildering whirl, enjoyment's keenest pain.
Enamoured hate, exhilarant disdain.
My bosom, of its thirst for knowledge sated,
Shall not, henceforth, from any pang be wrested,
And all of life for all mankind created
Shall be within mine inmost being tested :
The highest, lowest forms my soul shall borrow,
Shall heap upon itself their bliss and sorrow,
And thus, my own sole self to all their selves expanded,
I too, at last, shall with them all be stranded !

MEPHIS. Believe me, who for many a thousand year
The same tough meat have chewed and tested,
That from the cradle to the bier
No man the ancient leaven has digested !
Trust one of us, this Whole supernal
Is made but for a God's delight !
He dwells in splendour single and eternal,
But *us* he thrusts in darkness, out of sight,
And *you* he dowers with Day and Night.

FAUST. Nay, but I will!
MEPHIS.   A good reply!
One only fear still needs repeating :
The art is long, the time is fleeting.
Then let thyself be taught, say I !
Go, league thyself with a poet,
Give the rein to his imagination,
Then wear the crown, and show it,
Of the qualities of his creation,—
The courage of the lion's breed,
The wild stag's speed,
The Italian's fiery blood,
The North's firm fortitude !
Let him find for thee the secret tether
That binds the Noble and Mean together,
And teach thy pulses of youth and pleasure
To love by rule, and hate by measure !
I'd like, myself, such a one to see :
Sir Microcosm his name should be.

FAUST. What am I, then, if 'tis denied my part
The crown of all humanity to win me,
Whereto yearns every sense within me ?
MEPHIS. Why, on the whole, thou'rt—what thou art.
Set wigs of million curls upon thy head, to raise thee,
Wear shoes an ell in height,—the truth betrays thee,
And thou remainest—what thou art.

FAUST. I feel, indeed, that I have made the treasure
Of human thought and knowledge mine, in vain ;
And if I now sit down in restful leisure,
No fount of newer strength is in my brain :
I am no hair's-breadth more in height,
Nor nearer to the Infinite,
MEPHIS. Good Sir, you see the facts precisely
As they are seen by each and all.
We must arrange them now, more wisely,
Before the joys of life shall pall.
Why, Zounds !   Both hands and feet are, truly—
And head and virile forces—thine :
Yet all that I indulge in newly,
Is 't thence less wholly mine ?

If I've six stallions in my stall,
Are not their forces also lent me?
I speed along, completest man of all,
As though my legs were four-and-twenty.
Take hold, then ! let reflection rest,
And plunge into the world with zest !
I say to thee, a speculative wight
Is like a beast on moorlands lean,
That round and round some fiend misleads to evil plight,
While all about lie pastures fresh and green.

    FAUST. Then how shall we begin?

    MEPHIS.   We'll try a wider sphere.
What place of martyrdom is here !
Is't life, I ask, is't even prudence,
To bore thyself and bore the students?
Let Neighbour Paunch to that attend !
Why plague thyself with threshing straw for ever !
The best thou learnest, in the end
Thou dar'st not tell the youngsters—never !
I hear one's footsteps, hither steering.

    FAUST. To see him now I have no heart.

    MEPHIS. So long the poor boy waits a hearing,
He must not unconsoled depart.
Thy cap and mantle straightway lend me !
I'll play the comedy with art.   [*He disguises himself.*
My wits, be certain, will befriend me.
But fifteen minutes' time is all I need ;
For our fine trip, meanwhile, prepare thyself with speed !
                               [*Exit* FAUST.

    MEPHIS. (*in* FAUST's *long mantle*). Reason and Knowledge
        only thou despise,
The highest strength in man that lies !
Let but the Lying Spirit bind thee
With magic works and shows that blind thee,
And I shall have thee fast and sure !—
Fate such a bold, untrammelled spirit gave him,
As forwards, onwards, ever must endure ;
Whose over-hasty impulse drave him
Past earthly joys he might secure.
Dragged through the wildest life, will I enslave him,

Through flat and stale indifference ;
With struggling, chilling, checking, so deprave him
That, to his hot, insatiate sense,
The dream of drink shall mock, but never lave him :
Refreshment shall his lips in vain implore—
Had he not made himself the Devil's, naught could save him
Still were he lost for evermore !

A STUDENT *enters.*

STUD. A short time, only, am I here,
And come, devoted and sincere,
To greet and know the man of fame,
Whom men to me with reverence name.

MEPHIS. Your courtesy doth flatter me :
You see a man, as others be.
Have you, perchance, elsewhere begun ?

STUD. Receive me now, I pray, as one
Who comes to you with courage good,
Somewhat of cash, and healthy blood :
My mother was hardly willing to let me ;
But knowledge worth having I fain would get me.

MEPHIS. Then you have reached the right place now.

STUD. I'd like to leave it, I must avow ;
I find these walls, these vaulted spaces
Are anything but pleasant places.
'Tis all so cramped and close and mean ;
One sees no tree, no glimpse of green,
And when the lecture-halls receive me,
Seeing, hearing, and thinking leave me.

MEPHIS. All that depends on habitude.
So from its mother's breasts a child
At first, reluctant, takes its food,
But soon to seek them is beguiled.
Thus, at the breasts of Wisdom clinging,
Thou'lt find each day a greater rapture bringing.

STUD. I'll hang thereon with joy, and freely drain them ;
But tell me, pray, the proper means to gain them.

MEPHIS. Explain, before you further speak,
The special faculty you seek.

STUD. I crave the highest erudition ;

And fain would make my acquisition
All that there is in Earth and Heaven,
In Nature and in Science too.

    MEPHIS. Here is the genuine path for you ;
Yet strict attention must be given.

    STUD. Body and soul thereon I'll wreak ;
Yet, truly, I've some inclination
On summer holidays to seek
A little freedom and recreation.

    MEPHIS. Use well your time ! It flies so swiftly from
    us ;
But time through order may be won, I promise.
So, Friend, (my views to briefly sum,)
First, the *collegium logicum.*
There will your mind be drilled and braced,
As if in Spanish boots 'twere laced,
And thus, to graver paces brought,
'Twill plod along the path of thought,
Instead of shooting here and there,
A will-o'-the-wisp in murky air.
Days will be spent to bid you know,
What once you did at a single blow,
Like eating and drinking, free and strong,—
That one, two, three ! thereto belong.
Truly the fabric of mental fleece
Resembles a weaver's masterpiece,
Where a thousand threads one treadle throws,
Where fly the shuttles hither and thither,
Unseen the threads are knit together,
And an infinite combination grows.
Then, the philosopher steps in
And shows, no otherwise it could have been :
The first was so, the second so,
Therefore the third and fourth are so ;
Were not the first and second, then
The third and fourth had never been.
The scholars are everywhere believers,
But never succeed in being weavers.
He who would study organic existence,
First drives out the soul with rigid persistence ;

Then the parts in his hand he may hold and class,
But the spiritual link is lost, alas !
Encheiresin naturæ, this Chemistry names,[38]
Nor knows how herself she banters and blames !
   STUD. I cannot understand you quite.
   MEPHIS. Your mind will shortly be set aright,
When you have learned, all things reducing,
To classify them for your using.
   STUD. I feel as stupid, from all you've said,
As if a mill-wheel whirled in my head !
   MEPHIS. And after—first and foremost duty—
Of Metaphysics lean the use and beauty !
See that you most profoundly gain
What does not suit the human brain !
A splendid word to serve, you'll find
For what goes in—or won't go in—your mind.
But first, at least this half a year,
To order rigidly adhere ;
Five hours a day, you understand,
And when the clock strikes, be on hand !
Prepare beforehand for your part
With paragraphs all got by heart,
So you can better watch, and look
That naught is said but what is in the book :
Yet in thy writing as unwearied be,
As did the Holy Ghost dictate to thee !
   STUD. No need to tell me twice to do it !
I think, how useful 'tis to write ;
For what one has, in black and white,
One carries home and then goes through it.
   MEPHIS. Yet choose thyself a faculty !
   STUD. I cannot reconcile myself to Jurisprudence.
   MEPHIS. Nor can I therefore greatly blame you students
I know what science this has come to be.
All rights and laws are still transmitted
Like an eternal sickness of the race,—
From generation unto generation fitted,
And shifted round from place to place.
Reason becomes a sham, Beneficence a worry :
Thou art a grandchild, therefore woe to thee !

The right born with us, ours in verity,
This to consider, there's, alas! no hurry.

STUD. My own disgust is strengthened by your speech :
O lucky he, whom you shall teach !
I've almost for Theology decided.

MEPHIS. I should not wish to see you here misguided :
For, as regards this science, let me hint
'Tis very hard to shun the false direction ;
There's so much secret poison lurking in 't,
So like the medicine, it baffles your detection.
Hear, therefore, one alone, for that is best, in sooth
And simply take your master's words for truth.
On *words* let your attention centre !
Then through the safest gate you'll enter
The temple-halls of Certainty.

STUD. Yet in the word must some idea be.

MEPHIS. Of course ! But only shun too over-sharp a
tension,
For just where fails the comprehension,
A word steps promptly in as deputy.
With words 'tis excellent disputing ;
Systems to words 'tis easy suiting ;
On words 'tis excellent believing ;
No word can ever lose a jot from thieving.

STUD. Pardon ! With many questions I detain you,
Yet must I trouble you again.
Of Medicine I still would fain
Hear one strong word that might explain you.
Three years is but a little space,
And, God ! who can the field embrace ?
If one some index could be shown,
'Twere easier groping forward, truly.

MEPHIS. (*aside*). I'm tired enough of this dry tone,—
Must play the Devil again, and fully.   [*Aloud*
To grasp the spirit of Medicine is easy :
Learn of the great and little world your fill,
To let it go at last, so please ye,
Just as God will !
In vain that through the realms of science you **may drift** ;
Each one learns only—just what learn he can :

Yet he who grasps the Moment's gift,
He is the proper man.
Well-made you are, 'tis not to be denied
The rest a bold address will win you ;
If you but in yourself confide,
At once confide all others in you.
To lead the women, learn the special feeling !
Their everlasting aches and groans,
In thousand tones,
Have all one source, one mode of healing ;
And if your acts are half discreet,
You'll always have them at your feet.
A title first must draw and interest them,
And show that yours all other arts exceeds ;
Then, as a greeting, you are free to touch and test them,
While, thus to do, for years another pleads.
You press and count the pulse's dances,
And then, with burning sidelong glances,
You clasp the swelling hips, to see
If tightly laced her corsets be.

    STUD. That's better, now ! The How and Where, one sees

    MEPHIS. My worthy friend, gray are all theories,
And green alone Life's golden tree.

    STUD. I swear to you, 'tis like a dream to me.
Might I again presume, with trust unbounded,
To hear your wisdom thoroughly expounded?

    MEPHIS. Most willingly, to what extent I may.

    STUD. I cannot really go away :
Allow me that my album first I reach you,—
Grant me this favour, I beseech you !

    MEPHIS. Assuredly.   [*He writes, and returns the book.*

    STUD. (*reads*). *Eritis sicut Deus, scientes bonum et malum.*
                [*Closes the book with reverence, and withdraws.*

    MEPHIS. Follow the ancient text, and the snake thou wast
      ordered to trample !
With all thy likeness to God, thou'lt yet be a sorry example !

              FAUST *enters.*

    FAUST. Now, whither shall we go ?

    MEPHIS.   As best it pleases thee

The little world, and then the great, we'll see.[39]
With what delight, what profit winning,
Shalt thou sponge through the term beginning!

FAUST. Yet with the flowing beard I wear,
Both ease and grace will fail me there.
The attempt, indeed, were a futile strife;
I never could learn the ways of life.
I feel so small before others, and thence
Should always find embarrassments.[40]

MEPHIS. My friend, thou soon shalt lose all such misgiving:
Be thou but self-possessed, thou hast the art of living!

FAUST. How shall we leave the house, and start?
Where hast thou servant, coach and horses?

MEPHIS. We'll spread this cloak with proper art,
Then through the air direct our courses.
But only, on so bold a flight,
Be sure to have thy luggage light.
A little burning air, which I shall soon prepare us,
Above the earth will nimbly bear us,
And, if we're light, we'll travel swift and clear:
I gratulate thee on thy new career!

V.

AUERBACH'S CELLAR IN LEIPZIG.[41]

Carousal of Jolly Companions.

FROSCH. Is no one laughing? no one drinking?
I'll teach you how to grin, I'm thinking.
To-day you're like wet straw, so tame;
And usually you're all aflame.

BRANDER. Now that's your fault; from you we nothing see,
No beastliness and no stupidity.

FROSCH. (*Pours a glass of wine over* BRANDER'S *head*).
There's both together!

BRANDER.   Twice a swine !

FROSCH. You wanted them : I 've given you mine.

SIEBEL. Turn out who quarrels—out the door !
With open throat sing chorus, drink and roar !
Up ! holla ! ho !

ALTMAYER.   Woe's me, the fearful bellow !
Bring cotton, quick !   He's split my ears, that fellow.

SIEBEL. When the vault echoes to the song,
One first perceives the bass is deep and strong.

FROSCH. Well said ! and out with him that takes the
    least offence !

> *Ah, tara, lara, da !*

ALTMAYER.   *Ah, tara, lara, da !*

FROSCH. The throats are tuned, commence !   [*Sings.*

> *The dear old holy Roman realm,*
> *How does it hold together ?*

BRANDER. A nasty song ! Fie ! a political song—
A most offensive song ! Thank God, each morning, there-
    fore,
That you have not the Roman realm to care for !
At least, I hold it so much gain for me,
That I nor Chancellor nor Kaiser be.
Yet also we must have a ruling head, I hope,
And so we 'll choose ourselves a Pope.
You know the quality that can
Decide the choice, and elevate the man.

FROSCH (*sings*). Soar up, soar up, Dame Nightingale ! [43]
> *Ten thousand times my sweetheart hail !*

SIEBEL. No, greet my sweetheart not ! I tell you, I 'll
    resent it.

FROSCH. My sweetheart greet and kiss ! I dare you to
    prevent it !   [*Sings.*

> *Draw the latch ! the darkness makes :*
> *Draw the latch ! the lover wakes.*
> *Shut the latch ! the morning breaks.*

SIEBEL. Yes, sing away, sing on, and praise, and brag of
    her !
I 'll wait my proper time for laughter :
Me by the nose she lead, and now she 'll lead you after.
Her paramour should be an ugly gnome,

Where four roads cross, in wanton play to meet her:
An old he-goat, from Blocksberg coming home,
Should his good-night in lustful gallop bleat her!
A fellow made of genuine flesh and blood
Is for the wench a deal too good.
Greet her? Not I: unless, when meeting,
To smash her windows be a greeting!

    BRANDER (*pounding on the table*). Attention! Hearken
      now to me!
Confess, Sirs, I know how to live.
Enamoured persons here have we,
And I, as suits their quality,
Must something fresh for their advantage give.
Take heed! 'Tis of the latest cut, my strain,
And all strike in at each refrain!   [*He sings.*

        There was a rat in the cellar-nest,
        Whom fat and butter made smoother:
        He had a paunch beneath his vest
        Like that of Doctor Luther.
        The cook laid poison cunningly,
        And then as sore oppressed was he
        As if he had love in his bosom.

CHORUS (*shouting*). As if he had love in his bosom!
BRANDER. He ran around, he ran about,
        His thirst in puddles laving;
        He gnawed and scratched the house throughout,
        But nothing cured his raving.
        He whirled and jumped, with torment mad,
        And soon enough the poor beast had,
        As if he had love in his bosom.

CHORUS. As if he had love in his bosom!
BRANDER. And driven at last, in open day,
        He ran into the kitchen,
        Fell on the hearth, and squirming lay,
        In the last convulsion twitching.
        Then laughed the murderess in her glee:
        "Ha! ha! he's at his last gasp," said she,
        "As if he had love in his bosom!"

CHORUS. As if he had love in his bosom!
SIEBEL. How the dull fools enjoy the matter!

To me it is a proper art
Poison for such poor rats to scatter.

BRANDER. Perhaps you'll warmly take their part?

ALTMAYER. The bald-pate pot-belly I have noted:
Misfortune tames him by degrees;
For in the rat by poison bloated
His own most natural form he sees.

FAUST *and* MEPHISTOPHELES.

MEPHIS. Before all else, I bring thee hither
Where boon companions meet together,
To let thee see how smooth life runs away.
Here, for the folk, each day's a holiday:
With little wit, and ease to suit them,
They whirl in narrow, circling trails,
Like kittens playing with their tails;
And if no headache persecute them,
So long the host may credit give,
They merrily and careless live.

BRANDER. The fact is easy to unravel,
Their air's so odd, they've just returned from travel:
A single hour they 've not been here.

FROSCH. You 've verily hit the truth! Leipzig to me is
dear;
Paris in miniature, how it refines its people!

SIEBEL. Who are the strangers, should you guess?

FROSCH. Let me alone! I'll set them first to drinking,
And then, as one a child's tooth draws, with cleverness,
I'll worm their secret out, I'm thinking.
They're of a noble house, that's very clear:
Haughty and discontented they appear.

BRANDER. They're mountebanks, upon a revel.

ALTMAYER. Perhaps.

FROSCH.   Look out, I'll smoke them now

MEPHIS. (*to* FAUST). Not if he had them by the neck, I vow,
Would e'er these people scent the Devil!

FAUST. Fair greeting, gentlemen!

SIEBEL.   Our thanks: we give the same.

           [*Murmurs, inspecting* MEPHIS. *from the side,*
In one foot is the fellow lame?

MEPHIS. Is it permitted that we share your leisure ?
In place of cheering drink, which one seeks vainly here,
Your company shall give us pleasure.

    ALTMAYER. A most fastidious person you appear.

    FROSCH. No doubt 'twas late when you from Rippach
        started ? [43]
And supping there with Hans occasioned your delay ?

    MEPHIS. We passed, without a call, to-day.
At our last interview, before we parted
Much of his cousins did he speak, entreating
That we should give to each his kindly greeting.

                      [He bows to FROSCH.

    ALTMAYER (*aside*). You have it now ! he understands.

    SIEBEL.   A knave sharp-set !

    FROSCH. Just wait awhile : I'll have him yet.

    MEPHIS. If I am right, we heard the sound
Of well-trained voices, singing chorus ;
And truly, song must here rebound
Superbly from the arches o'er us.

    FROSCH. Are you, perhaps, a virtuoso ?

    MEPHIS. O no ! my wish is great, my power is only so-so.

    ALTMAYER. Give us a song !

    MEPHIS.   If you desire, a number.

    SIEBEL. So that it be a bran-new strain !

    MEPHIS. We've just retraced our way from Spain,
The lovely land of wine, and song, and slumber.   *[Sings.*

        There was a king once reigning,
          Who had a big black flea—

    FROSCH. Hear, hear ! A flea ! D'ye rightly take the jest ?
I call a flea a tidy guest.

    MEPHIS. (*sings*). There was a king once reigning,
          Who had a big black flea,
          And loved him past explaining,
          As his own son were he.
          He called his man of stitches ;
          The tailor came straightway :
          Here, measure the lad for breeches,
          And measure his coat, I say !

    BRANDER. But mind, allow the tailor no caprices ;
Enjoin upon him, as his head is dear,

To most exactly measure, sew and shear,
So that the breeches have no creases !
   MEPHIS. In silk and velvet gleaming
           He now was wholly drest—
           Had a coat with ribbons streaming,
           A cross upon his breast.
           He had the first of stations,
           A minister's star and name ;
           And also all his relations
           Great lords at court became.

           And the lords and ladies of honour
           Were plagued, awake and in bed ;
           The queen she got them upon her,
           The maids were bitten and bled.
           And they did not dare to brush them,
           Or scratch them, day or night :
           We crack them and we crush them,
           At once, whene'er they bite.
  CHORUS (*shouting*). We crack them and we crush them,
           At once, whene'er they bite !
  FROSCH. Bravo ! bravo ! that was fine.
  SIEBEL. Every flea may it so befal !
  BRANDER. Point your fingers and nip them all !
  ALTMAYER. Hurrah for Freedom ! Hurrah for wine !
  MEPHIS. I fain would drink with you, my glass to Free-
      dom clinking,
If 'twere better wine that here I see you drinking.
  SIEBEL. Don't let us hear that speech again !
  MEPHIS. Did I not fear the landlord might complain,
I'd treat these worthy guests, with pleasure,
To some from out our cellar's treasure.
  SIEBEL. Just treat, and let the landlord me arraign !
  FROSCH. And if the wine be good, our praises shall be ample.
But do not give too very small a sample ;
For, if its quality I decide,
With a good mouthful I must be supplied.
  ALTMAYER (*aside*). They're from the Rhine ! I guessed as
      much, before.
  MEPHIS. Bring me a gimlet here !

BRANDER. What shall therewith be done ?
You've not the casks already at the door ?

ALTMAYER. Yonder, within the landlord's box of tools,
    there's one !

MEPHIS. (*takes the gimlet*). (*To* FROSCH.) Now, give me of
    your taste some intimation.

FROSCH. How do you mean ? Have you so many kinds ?

MEPHIS. The choice is free : make up your minds.

ALTMAYER (*to* FROSCH). Aha ! you lick your chops, from
    sheer anticipation.

FROSCH. Good ! if I have the choice, so let the wine be
    Rhenish !
Our Fatherland can best the sparkling cup replenish.

MEPHIS. (*boring a hole in the edge of the table, at the place
    where* FROSCH *sits*). Get me a little wax, to make the
    stoppers, quick !

ALTMAYER. Ah ! I perceive a juggler's trick.

MEPHIS. (*to* BRANDER). And you?

BRANDER.   Champagne shall be my wine,
And let it sparkle fresh and fine !

        [MEPHIS. *bores : in the mean time one has made the*
                wax stoppers and plugged the holes with them.

What's foreign one can't always keep quite clear of,
For good things, oft, are not so near ;
A German can't endure the French to see or hear of,
Yet drinks their wines with hearty cheer.

SIEBEL. (*as* MEPHIS. *approaches his seat*). For me, I grant,
    sour wine is out of place ;
Fill up my glass with sweetest, will you ?

MEPHIS. (*boring*). Tokay shall flow at once, to fill you !

ALTMAYER. No—look me, Sirs, straight in the face !
I see you have your fun at our expense.

MEPHIS. O no ! with gentlemen of such pretence,
That were to venture far, indeed.
Speak out, and make your choice with speed !
With what a vintage can I serve you ?

ALTMAYER. With any—only satisfy our need.

        [*After the holes have been bored and plugged*
MEPHIS. (*with singular gestures*). Grapes the vine-stem bears,
Horns the he-goat wears !

                                            F

The grapes are juicy, the vines are wood,
The wooden table gives wine as good !
Into the depths of Nature peer,—
Only believe, there's a miracle here !
Now draw the stoppers, and drink your fill !

> ALL (*as they draw out the stoppers, and the wine which has been desired flows into the glass of each*). O beautiful fountain, that flows at will !
>
> MEPHIS. But have a care, that you nothing spill !
>
>   [*They drink repeatedly.*
>
> ALL (*sing*). As 'twere five hundred hogs, we feel

So cannibalic jolly !

> MEPHIS. See, now, the race is happy—it is free !
>
> FAUST. To leave them is my inclination.
>
> MEPHIS. Take notice, first ! their bestiality

Will make a brilliant demonstration.

> SIEBEL (*drinks carelessly : the wine spills upon the earth, and turns to flame*). Help ! Fire ! Help ! Hell-fire is sent !
>
> MEPHIS. (*charming away the flame*). Be quiet, friendly element !   [*To the revellers.*

A bit of purgatory 'twas for this time, merely.

> SIEBEL. What mean you ? Wait !—you'll pay for't dearly !

You'll know us, to your detriment.

> FROSCH. Don't try that game a second time upon us !
>
> ALTMAYER. I think we'd better send him packing quietly.
>
> SIEBEL. What, Sir ! you dare to make so free,

And play your hocus-pocus on us !

> MEPHIS. Be still, old wine-tub.
>
> SIEBEL.   Broomstick, you !

You face it out, impertinent and heady ?

> BRANDER. Just wait ! a shower of blows is ready.
>
> ALTMAYER (*draws a stopper out of the table : fire flies in his face*). I burn ! I burn !
>
> SIEBEL.   'Tis magic ! Strike—

The knave is outlawed ! Cut him as you like !

>   [*They draw their knives, and rush upon* MEPHIS.
>
> MEPHIS. (*with solemn gestures*). False word and form of air,

Change place, and sense ensnare !
Be here—and there !

>   [*They stand amazed, and look at each other*

ALTMAYER. Where am I ?   What a lovely land !

FROSCH. Vines ?   Can I trust my eyes ?

SIEBEL. And purple grapes at hand !

BRANDER. Here, over this green arbour bending,
See, what a vine ! what grapes depending !

> [*He takes* SIEBEL *by the nose : the others do the same
> reciprocally, and raise their knives.*

MEPHIS. (*as above*). Loose, Error, from their eyes the
band,
And how the Devil jests, be now enlightened !

> [*He disappears with* FAUST : *the revellers start and
> separate.*

SIEBEL. What happened ?

ALTMAYER.   How ?

FROSCH.   Was that your nose I tightened ?

BRANDER (*to* SIEBEL). And yours that still I have in
hand ?

ALTMAYER. It was a blow that went through every limb !
Give me a chair !   I sink ! my senses swim.

FROSCH. But what has happened, tell me now ?

SIEBEL. Where is he ?   If I catch the scoundrel hiding,
He shall not leave alive, I vow.

ALTMAYER. I saw him with these eyes upon a wine-cask
riding
Out of the cellar-door, just now.
Still in my feet the fright like lead is weighing.

> [*He turns towards the table.*

Why !   If the fount of wine should still be playing ?

SIEBEL. 'Twas all deceit, and lying, false design !

FROSCH. And yet it seemed as I were drinking wine.

BRANDER. But with the grapes how was it, pray ?

ALTMAYER. Shall one believe no miracles, just say !

VI.

WITCHES' KITCHEN.[44]

*Upon a low hearth stands a great caldron, under which a fire
is burning. Various figures appear in the vapours which
rise from the caldron. An ape sits beside it, skims it, and
watches lest it boil over. The he-ape, with the young ones,
sits near and warms himself. Ceiling and walls are covered
with the most fantastic witch-implements.*

FAUST. MEPHISTOPHELES.

FAUST. These crazy signs of witches' craft repel me !
I shall recover, dost thou tell me,
Through this insane, chaotic play ?
From an old hag shall I demand assistance ?
And will her foul mess take away
Full thirty years from my existence ?[45]
Woe's me, canst thou naught better find !
Another baffled hope must be lamented :
Has Nature, then, and has a noble mind
Not any potent balsam yet invented ?
MEPHIS. Once more, my friend, thou talkest sensibly.
There is, to make thee young, a simpler mode and apter ;
But in another book 'tis writ for thee,
And is a most eccentric chapter.
FAUST. Yet will I know it.
MEPHIS.   Good ! the method is revealed
Without or gold or magic or physician.
Betake thyself to yonder field,
There hoe and dig, as thy condition ;
Restrain thyself, thy sense and will
Within a narrow sphere to flourish ;
With unmixed food thy body nourish ;
Live with the ox as ox, and think it not a theft

That thou manur'st the acre which thou reapest ;—
That, trust me, is the best mode left,
Whereby for eighty years thy youth thou keepest !

FAUST. I am not used to that ; I cannot stoop to try it—
To take the spade in hand, and ply it.
The narrow being suits me not at all.

MEPHIS. Then to thine aid the witch must call.

FAUST. Wherefore the hag, and her alone ?
Canst thou thyself not brew the potion ?

MEPHIS. That were a charming sport, I own :
I'd build a thousand bridges meanwhile, I've a notion.
Not Art and Science serve, alone ;
Patience must in the work be shown.
Long is the calm brain active in creation ;
Time, only, strengthens the fine fermentation.
And all, belonging thereunto,
Is rare and strange, howe'er you take it :
The Devil taught the thing, 'tis true,
And yet the Devil cannot make it.   [*Perceiving the Animals.*
See, what a delicate race they be !
That is the maid ! the man is he !   [*To the Animals.*
It seems the mistress has gone away ?

THE ANIMALS.   Carousing, to-day !
              Off and about,
                By the chimney out !

MEPHIS. What time takes she for dissipating ?

THE ANIMALS. While we to warm our paws are waiting.

MEPHIS. (*to* FAUST). How findest thou the tender
    creatures ?

FAUST. Absurder than I ever yet did see.

MEPHIS. Why, just such talk as this, for me,
Is that which has the most attractive features !
                              [*To the Animals.*
But tell me now, ye curséd puppets,
Why do ye stir the porridge so ?

THE ANIMALS. We're cooking watery soup for beggars.

MEPHIS. Then a great public you can show.

THE HE-APE (*comes up and fawns on* MEPHIS.).
              O cast thou the dice !
              Make me rich in a trice,

Let me win in good season !
Things are badly controlled,
And had I but gold,
So had I my reason.

MEPHIS. How would the ape be sure his luck enhances,
Could he but try the lottery's chances !

*[In the mean time the young apes have been playing
with a large ball, which they now roll forward.*

THE HE-APE. The world's the ball :
Doth rise and fall,
And roll incessant :
Like glass doth ring,
A hollow thing,—
How soon will't spring,
And drop, quiescent ?
Here bright it gleams,
Here brighter seems :
I live at present !
Dear son, I say,
Keep thou away !
Thy doom is spoken !
'Tis made of clay,
And will be broken.

MEPHIS. What means the sieve ?

THE HE-APE (*taking it down*). Wert thou the thief,"*
I 'd know him and shame him.

*[He runs to the SHE-APE, and lets her look through
it.*

Look through the sieve !
Know'st thou the thief,
And darest not name him ?

MEPHIS. (*approaching the fire*). And what's this pot ?

HE-APE AND SHE-APE. The fool knows it not !
He knows not the pot,
He knows not the kettle !

MEPHIS. Impertinent beast !

THE HE-APE. Take the brush here, at least,
And sit down on the settle !

[He invites MEPHIS. to sit down

Faust (*who during all this time has been standing before a
mirror, now approaching and now retreating from it*).

What do I see?   What heavenly form revealed
Shows through the glass from Magic's fair dominions!
O lend me, Love, the swiftest of thy pinions,
And bear me to her beauteous field!
Ah, if I leave this spot with fond designing,
If I attempt to venture near,
Dim, as through gathering mist, her charms appear!—
A woman's form, in beauty shining!
Can woman, then, so lovely be?
And must I find her body, there reclining,
Of all the heavens the bright epitome?
Can Earth with such a thing be mated?

    Mephis. Why, surely, if a God first plagues Himself six
        days,

Then, self-contented, *Bravo!* says,
Must something clever be created.
This time, thine eyes be satiate!
I'll yet detect thy sweetheart and ensnare her,
And blest is he, who has the lucky fate,
Some day, as bridegroom, home to bear her.

        [**Faust** *gazes continually in the mirror.* **Mephis.**
          stretching himself out on the settle, and playing
          with the brush, continues to speak.

So sit I, like the King upon his throne:
I hold the sceptre, here,—and lack the crown alone.

    The Animals (*who up to this time have been making all
kinds of fantastic movements together, bring a crown to* **Mephis.**
with great noise).   O be thou so good
               With sweat and with blood
               The crown to belime!

        [*They handle the crown awkwardly and break it into
          two pieces, with which they spring around.*

               'Tis done, let it be!
               We speak and we see,
               We hear and we rhyme!

    Faust (*before the mirror*). Woe's me!   I fear to lose my
    wits.

MEPHIS. (*pointing to the Animals*). My own head, now, is
    really nigh to sinking.
THE ANIMALS. If lucky our hits,
            And everything fits,
              'Tis thoughts, and we're thinking !
FAUST (*as above*). My bosom burns with that sweet vision ;
Let us, with speed, away from here !
MEPHIS. (*in the same attitude*).   One must, at least, make
    this admission—
They 're poets, genuine and sincere.

> [*The caldron, which the* SHE-APE *has up to this time
> neglected to watch, begins to boil over: there ensues
> a great flame which blazes up the chimney. The
> WITCH comes careering down through the flame,
> with terrible cries.*

THE WITCH. Ow ! ow ! ow ! ow !
          The damnéd beast—the curséd sow !
          To leave the kettle, and singe the Frau !
          Accurséd fere !
                 [*Perceiving* FAUST *and* MEPHIS.
          What is that here ?
          Who are you here ?
          What want you thus ?
          Who sneaks to us ?
          The fire pain
          Burn bone and brain !

> [*She plunges the skimming-ladle in the caldron, and
> scatters flames towards* FAUST, MEPHISTOPHELES,
> *and the Animals.   The Animals whimper.*

MEPHIS. (*reversing the brush, which he has been holding in
his hand, and striking among the jars and glasses*).
          In two ! in two !
          There lies the brew !
          There lies the glass !
          The joke will pass,
          As time, foul ass !
          To the singing of thy crew.
       [*As the* WITCH *starts back, full of wrath and horror*
Ha ! knows't thou me ?   Abomination, thou !

Know'st thou, at last, thy Lord and Master?
What hinders me from smiting now
Thee and thy monkey-sprites with fell disaster?
Hast for the scarlet coat no reverence?
Dost recognize no more the tall cock's-feather?
Have I concealed this countenance?—
Must tell my name, old face of leather?

THE WITCH. O pardon, Sir, the rough salute!
Yet I perceive no cloven foot;
And both your ravens, where are *they* now?

MEPHIS. This time, I'll let thee 'scape the debt;
For since we two together met,
'Tis verily full many a day now.
Culture, which smooth the whole world licks,
Also unto the Devil sticks.
The days of that old Northern phantom now are over:
Where canst thou horns and tail and claws discover?
And, as regards the foot, which I can't spare, in truth,
'Twould only make the people shun me;
Therefore I've worn, like many a spindly youth,
False calves these many years upon me.

THE WITCH (*dancing*). Reason and sense forsake my
          brain,
Since I behold Squire Satan here again!

MEPHIS. Woman, from such a name refrain!

THE WITCH. Why so? What has it done to thee?

MEPHIS. It's long been written in the Book of Fable;
Yet, therefore, no whit better men we see:
The Evil One has left, the evil ones are stable.
Sir Baron call me thou, then is the matter good;
A cavalier am I, like others in my bearing.
Thou hast no doubt about my noble blood:
See, here's the coat-of-arms that I am wearing!
                    [*He makes an indecent gesture.*

THE WITCH (*laughs immoderately*). Ha! ha! That's just
          your way, I know:
A rogue you are, and you were always so.

MEPHIS. (*to* FAUST). My friend, take proper heed, I pray!
To manage witches, this is just the way.

THE WITCH. Wherein, Sirs, can I be of use?

MEPHIS. Give us a goblet of the well-known juice !
But, I must beg you, of the oldest brewage ;
The years a double strength produce.

THE WITCH. With all my heart !   Now, here's a bottle,
Wherefrom, sometimes, I wet my throttle,
Which, also, not the slightest, stinks ;
And willingly a glass I'll fill him.   [*Whispering.*
Yet, if this man without due preparation drinks,
As well thou know'st, within an hour 'twill kill him.

MEPHIS. He is a friend of mine, with whom it will agree,
And he deserves thy kitchen's best potation :
Come, draw thy circle, speak thine adjuration,
And fill thy goblet full and free !

> [*The* WITCH *with fantastic gestures draws a circle
> and places mysterious articles therein; meanwhile
> the glasses begin to ring, the caldron to sound, and
> make a musical accompaniment. Finally she brings
> a great book, and stations in the circle the Apes,
> who are obliged to serve as reading-desk, and to hold
> the torches.   She then beckons* FAUST *to approach.*

FAUST (*to* MEPHIS.).   Now, what shall come of this ? the
    creatures antic,
The crazy stuff, the gestures frantic,—
All the repulsive cheats I view,—
Are known to me, and hated, too.

MEPHIS. O, nonsense !   That's a thing for laughter ;
Don't be so terribly severe !
She juggles you as doctor now, that, after,
The beverage may work the proper cheer.

> [*He persuades* FAUST *to step into the circle.*

THE WITCH (*begins to declaim, with much emphasis from
    the book*). See, thus it's done !

> Make ten of one,
> And two let be,
> Make even three,
> And rich thou'lt be.
> Cast o'er the four !
> From five and six
> (The witch's tricks)
> Make seven and eight,

'Tis finished straight !
And nine is one,
And ten is none.
This is the witch's once-one's-one !"

FAUST. She talks like one who raves in fever.

MEPHIS. Thou'lt hear much more before we leave her
'Tis all the same : the book I can repeat,
Such time I've squandered o'er the history :
A contradiction thus complete
Is always for the wise, no less than fools, a mystery.
The art is old and new, for verily
All ages have been taught the matter,—
By Three and One, and One and Three,
Error instead of Truth to scatter.
They prate and teach, and no one interferes ;
All from the fellowship of fools are shrinking.
Man usually believes, if only words he hears,
That also with them goes material for thinking !

THE WITCH (*continues*). The lofty skill
               Of Science, still
               From all men deeply hidden !
               Who takes no thought,
               To him 'tis brought,
               'Tis given unsought, unbidden !

FAUST. What nonsense she declaims before us !
My head is nigh to split, I fear :
It seems to me as if I hear
A hundred thousand fools in chorus.

MEPHIS. O Sibyl excellent, enough of adjuration !
But hither bring us thy potation,
And quickly fill the beaker to the brim !
This drink will bring my friend no injuries :
He is a man of manifold degrees,
And many draughts are known to him.

[*The* WITCH, *with many ceremonies, pours the drink
into a cup ; as* FAUST *sets it to his lips, a light
flame arises.*

Down with it quickly ! Drain it off !
'Twill warm thy heart with new desire :

Art with the Devil hand and glove,
And wilt thou be afraid of fire?

[*The* WITCH *breaks the circle:* FAUST *steps forth.*

MEPHIS. And now, away! Thou dar'st not rest.

THE WITCH. And much good may the liquor do thee!

MEPHIS. (*to the* WITCH). Thy wish be on Walpurgis Night
  expressed;
What boon I have, shall then be given unto thee.

THE WITCH. Here is a song, which, if you sometimes sing,
You'll find it of peculiar operation.

MEPHIS. (*to* FAUST). Come, walk at once!   A rapid
  occupation
Must start the needful perspiration,
And through thy frame the liquor's potence fling.
The noble indolence I'll teach thee then to treasure,
And soon thou'lt be aware, with keenest thrills of pleasure,
How Cupid stirs and leaps, on light and restless wing.

FAUST. One rapid glance within the mirror give me,
How beautiful that woman-form!

MEPHIS. No, no! The paragon of all, believe me,
Thou soon shalt see, alive and warm.   [*Aside.*
Thou'lt find, this drink thy blood compelling,
Each woman beautiful as Helen!

VII.

A STREET.

FAUST.   MARGARET *passing by.*

FAUST. Fair lady, let it not offend you,
That arm and escort I would lend you!

MARG.[47] I'm neither lady, neither fair,
And home I can go without your care.

      [*She releases herself, and exit.*

FAUST. By Heaven, the girl is wondrous fair!
Of all I've seen, beyond compare;

So sweetly virtuous and pure,
And yet a little pert, be sure !
The lip so red, the cheek's clear dawn,
I'll not forget while the world rolls on !
How she cast down her timid eyes,
Deep in my heart imprinted lies :
How short and sharp of speech was she,
Why, 't was a real ecstasy !

MEPHISTO. *enters.*

FAUST. Hear, of that girl I'd have possession !
MEPHIS. Which, then?
FAUST.   The one who just went by.
MEPHIS. She, there ? She's coming from confession,
Of every sin absolved ; for I,
Behind her chair, was listening nigh,
So innocent is she, indeed,
That to confess she had no need.
I have no power o'er souls so green.

 FAUST. And yet, she's older than fourteen.

 MEPHIS. How now ! You're talking like Jack Rake,
Who every flower for himself would take,
And fancies there are no favours more,
Nor honours, save for him in store ;
Yet always doesn't the thing succeed.

 FAUST. Most Worthy Pedagogue, take heed !
Let not a word of moral law be spoken !
I claim, I tell thee, all my right ;
And if that image of delight
Rest not within mine arms to-night,
At midnight is our compact broken.

 MEPHIS. But think, the chances of the case !
I need, at least, a fortnight's space,
To find an opportune occasion.

 FAUST. Had I but seven hours for all,
I should not on the Devil call,
But win her by my own persuasion.

 MEPHIS. You almost like a Frenchman prate ;
Yet, pray, don't take it as annoyance !
Why, all at once, exhaust the joyance ?

Your bliss is by no means so great
As if you'd use, to get control,
All sorts of tender rigmarole,
And knead and shape her to your thought,
As in Italian tales 'tis taught.

FAUST. Without that, I have appetite.

MEPHIS. But now, leave jesting out of sight!
I tell you, once for all, that speed
With this fair girl will not succeed ;
By storm she cannot captured be ;
We must make use of strategy.

FAUST. Get me something the angel keeps!
Lead me thither where she sleeps !
Get me a kerchief from her breast,—
A garter that her knee has pressed !

MEPHIS. That you may see how much I'd fain
Further and satisfy your pain,
We will no longer lose a minute ;
I'll find her room to-day, and take you in it.

FAUST. And shall I see—possess her ?

MEPHIS.   No !
Unto a neighbour she must go,
And meanwhile thou, alone, mayst glow
With every hope of future pleasure,
Breathing her atmosphere in fullest measure.

FAUST. Can we go thither ?

MEPHIS.   'Tis too early yet.

FAUST A gift for her I bid thee get !   [*Exit.*

MEPHIS. Presents at once ? That's good : he's certain to
        get at her !
Full many a pleasant place I know,
And treasures, buried long ago :
I must, perforce, look up the matter.   [*Exit.*

VIII.

EVENING.

A SMALL, NEATLY KEPT CHAMBER.

MARGARET (*plaiting and binding up the braids of her hair*).
I'd something give, could I but say
Who was that gentleman, to-day.
Surely a gallant man was he,
And of a noble family ;
So much could I in his face behold,—
And he wouldn't, else, have been so bold !   [*Exit.*

MEPHISTOPHELES. FAUST.

MEPHIS.   Come in, but gently : follow me !
FAUST. (*after a moment's silence*).   Leave me alone, I beg
  of thee !
MEPHIS. (*prying about*).   Not every girl keeps things so
  neat.
FAUST (*looking around*).   O welcome, twilight soft and
  sweet,
That breathes throughout this hallowed shrine !
Sweet pain of love, bind thou with fetters fleet
The heart that on the dew of hope must pine !
How all around a sense impresses
Of quiet, order, and content !
This poverty what bounty blesses !
What bliss within this narrow den is pent !
        [*He throws himself into a leathern arm-chair near
        the bed.*
Receive me, thou, that in thine open arms
Departed joy and pain wert wont to gather !
How oft the children, with their ruddy charms,
Hung here, around this throne, where sat the father !
Perchance my love, amid the childish band,

Grateful for gifts the Holy Christmas gave her,
Here meekly kissed the grandsire's withered hand.
I feel, O maid ! thy very soul
Of order and content around me whisper,—
Which leads thee with its motherly control,
The cloth upon thy board bids smoothly thee unroll,
The sand beneath thy feet makes whiter, crisper.
O dearest hand, to thee 'tis given
To change this hut into a lower heaven !
And here !   [*He lifts one of the bed-curtains.*
              What sweetest thrill is in my blood !
Here could I spend whole hours, delaying :
Here Nature shaped, as if in sportive playing,
The angel blossom from the bud.

Here lay the child, with Life's warm essence
The tender bosom filled and fair,
And here was wrought, through holier, purer presence,
The form diviner beings wear !

And I ?   What drew me here with power ?
How deeply am I moved, this hour !
What seek I ?   Why so full my heart, and sore ?
Miserable Faust !   I know thee now no more.

Is there a magic vapour here ?
I came, with lust of instant pleasure,
And lie dissolved in dreams of love's sweet leisure !
Are we the sport of every changeful atmosphere ?

And if, this moment, came she in to me,
How would I for the fault atonement render !
How small the giant lout would be,
Prone at her feet, relaxed and tender !
    MEPHIS. Be quick !   I see her there, returning.
    FAUST. Go ! go ! I never will retreat.
    MEPHIS. Here is a casket, not unmeet,
Which elsewhere I have just been earning.
Here, set it in the press, with haste !
I swear, 'twill turn her head, to spy it :

Some baubles I therein had placed,
That you might win another by it.
True, child is child, and play is play.
   Faust. ┬ know not, should I do it?
   Mephis.   Ask you, pray?
Yourself, perhaps, would keep the bubble?
Then I suggest, 'twere fair and just
To spare the lovely day your lust,
And spare to me the further trouble.
You are not miserly, I trust?
I rub my hands, in expectation tender—
       [He places the casket in the press, and locks it again.
Now quick, away!
The sweet young maiden to betray,
So that by wish and will you bend her;
And you look as though
To the lecture-hall you were forced to go,—
As if stood before you, gray and loath,
Physics and Metaphysics both!
But away!   [Exeunt.
   Marg. (with a lamp). It is so close, so sultry, here!
                            [She opens the window
And yet 'tis not so warm outside.
I feel, I know not why, such fear!—
Would mother came!—where can she bide?
My body's chill and shuddering,—
I'm but a silly, fearsome thing!
              [She begins to sing, while undressing.

       There was a King in Thule,
       Was faithful till the grave,—
       To whom his mistress, dying,
       A golden goblet gave.

       Naught was to him more precious;
       He drained it at every bout:
       His eyes with tears ran over,
       As oft as he drank thereout.

       When came his time of dying,
       The towns in his land he told,

                                a

Naught else to his heir denying
Except the goblet of gold.

He sat at the royal banquet
With his knights of high degree,
In the lofty hall of his fathers
In the Castle by the Sea.

There stood the old carouser,
And drank the last life-glow ;
And hurled the hallowed goblet
Into the tide below.

He saw it plunging and filling,
And sinking deep in the sea :
Then fell his eyelids for ever,
And never more drank he !

[*She opens the press in order to arrange her clothes, and
perceives the casket of jewels.*

How comes that lovely casket here to me ?
I locked the press, most certainly.
'Tis truly wonderful !   What can within it be ?
Perhaps 'twas brought by some one as a pawn,
And mother gave a loan thereon ?
And here there hangs a key to fit :
I have a mind to open it. —
What is that ?   God in Heaven !   Whence came
Such things ?   Never beheld I aught so fair !
Rich ornaments, such as a noble dame
On highest holidays might wear !
How would the pearl-chain suit my hair ?
Ah, who may all this splendour own ?

[*She adorns herself with the jewellery, and steps before
the mirror.*

Were but the ear-rings mine, alone !
One has at once another air.
What helps one's beauty, youthful blood ?
One may possess them, well and good ;
But none the more do others care.

They praise us half in pity, sure ·
To gold still tends,
On gold depends.
All, all! Alas, we poor!

IX.

PROMENADE.

Faust, *walking thoughtfully up and down.* To him
Mephistopheles.

Mephis. By all love ever rejected! By hell-fire hot and
unsparing!
I wish I knew something worse, that I might use it for
swearing!
Faust. What ails thee? What is't gripes thee, elf?
A face like thine beheld I never.
Mephis. I would myself unto the Devil deliver,
If I were not a Devil myself!
Faust. Thy head is out of order, sadly:
It much becomes thee to be raving madly.
Mephis. Just think, the pocket of a priest should get
The trinkets left for Margaret!
The mother saw them, and, instanter,
A secret dread began to haunt her.
Keen scent has she for tainted air;
She snuffs within her book of prayer,
And smells each article, to see
If sacred or profane it be;
So here she guessed, from every gem,
That not much blessing came with them.
"My child," she said, "ill-gotten good
Ensnares the soul, consumes the blood.
Before the Mother of God we'll lay it;
With heavenly manna she'll repay it!"

But Margaret thought, with sour grimace,
" A gift-horse is not out of place,
And, truly ! godless cannot be
The one who brought such things to me."
A parson came, by the mother bidden :
He saw, at once, where the game was hidden,
And viewed it with a favour stealthy.
He spake : " That is the proper view,—
Who overcometh, winneth too.
The Holy Church has a stomach healthy :
Hath eaten many a land as forfeit,
And never yet complained of surfeit :
The Church alone, beyond all question,
Has for ill-gotten goods the right digestion."

FAUST. A general practice is the same,
Which Jew and King may also claim.

MEPHIS. Then bagged the spangles, chains, and rings,
As if but toadstools were the things,
And thanked no less, and thanked no more
Than if a sack of nuts he bore,—
Promised them fullest heavenly pay,
And deeply edified were they.

FAUST. And Margaret ?

MEPHIS.   Sits unrestful still,
And knows not what she should, or will ;
Thinks on the jewels, day and night,
But more on him who gave her such delight.

FAUST. The darling's sorrow gives me pain.
Get thou a set for her again !
The first was not a great display.

MEPHIS. O yes, the gentleman finds it all child's-play !

FAUST. Fix and arrange it to my will ;
And on her neighbour try thy skill !
Don't be a Devil stiff as paste,
But get fresh jewels to her taste !

MEPHIS. Yes, gracious Sir, in all obedience ! [*Exit* FAUST.
Such an enamoured fool in air would blow
Sun, moon, and all the starry legions,
To give his sweetheart a diverting show.   [*Exit.*

X.

THE NEIGHBOUR'S HOUSE.

MARTHA (*solus*).

MARTHA. God forgive my husband, yet he
Hasn't done his duty by me !
Off in the world he went straightway,—
Left me lie in the straw where I lay,
And, truly, I did naught to fret him :
God knows I loved, and can't forget him !   [*She weeps.*
Perhaps he's even dead !   Ah, woe !—
Had I a certificate to show !

MARG. (*comes*). Dame Martha !

MARTHA.   Margaret ! what's happened thee ?

MARG. I scarce can stand, my knees are trembling !
I find a box, the first resembling,
Within my press !   Of ebony,—
And things, all splendid to behold,
And richer far than were the old.

MARTHA. You mustn't tell it to your mother !
'Twould go to the priest, as did the other.

MARG. Ah, look and see—just look and see !

MARTHA (*adorning her*). O, what a blessed luck for thee !

MARG. But, ah ! in the streets I dare not bear them,
Nor in the church be seen to wear them.

MARTHA. Yet thou canst often this way wander,
And secretly the jewels don,
Walk up and down an hour, before the mirror yonder,—
We'll have our private joy thereon.
And then a chance will come, a holiday,
When, piece by piece, can one the things abroad display,
A chain at first, then other ornament :
Thy mother will not see, and stories we'll invent.

MARG. Whoever could have brought me things so precious !

That something's wrong, I feel suspicious.   [*A knock.*
Good Heaven! My mother can that have been?

   MARTHA (*peeping through the blind*). 'Tis some strange
     gentleman.—Come in!

MEPHISTOPHELES enters.

   MEPHIS. That I so boldly introduce me,
I beg you, ladies, to excuse me.
         [*Steps back reverently, on seeing* MARG.
   For Martha Schwerdtlein I'd inquire!
   MARTHA. I'm she: what does the gentleman desire?
   MEPHIS. (*aside to her*). It is enough that you are she:
You've a visitor of high degree.
Pardon the freedom I have ta'en,—
Will after noon return again.
   MARTHA (*aloud*). Of all things in the world! Just hear—
He takes thee for a lady, dear!
   MARG. I am a creature young and poor:
The gentleman's too kind, I'm sure.
The jewels don't belong to me.
   MEPHIS. Ah, not alone the jewelry!
The look, the manner, both betray—
Rejoiced am I that I may stay!
   MARTHA. What is your business? I would fain—
   MEPHIS. I would I had a more cheerful strain!
Take not unkindly its repeating:
Your husband's dead, and sends a greeting.
   MARTHA. Is dead? Alas, that heart so true!
My husband dead! Let me die, too!
   MARG. Ah, dearest dame, let not your courage fail!
   MEPHIS. Hear me relate the mournful tale!
   MARG. Therefore I'd never love, believe me!
A loss like this to death would grieve me.
   MEPHIS. Joy follows woe, woe after joy comes flying.
   MARTHA. Relate his life's sad close to me!
   MEPHIS. In Padua buried, he is lying
Beside the good Saint Antony,[43]
Within a grave well consecrated,
For cool, eternal rest created.
   MARTHA. He gave you, further, no commission?

MEPHIS. Yes, one of weight, with many sighs :
Three hundred masses buy, to save him from perdition !
My hands are empty, otherwise.

MARTHA. What ! Not a pocket-piece ? no jewelry ?
What every journeyman within his wallet spares,
And as a token with him bears,
And rather starves or begs, than loses ?

MEPHIS. Madam, it is a grief to me ;
Yet, on my word, his cash was put to proper uses.
Besides, his penitence was very sore,
And he lamented his ill fortune all the more.

MARG. Alack, that men are so unfortunate !
Surely for his soul's sake full many a prayer I'll proffer.

MEPHIS. You well deserve a speedy marriage-offer :
You are so kind, compassionate.

MARG. O, no ! As yet, it would not do.

MEPHIS. If not a husband, then a beau for you !
It is the greatest heavenly blessing,
To have a dear thing for one's caressing.

MARG. The country's custom is not so.

MEPHIS. Custom, or not ! It happens, though.

MARTHA. Continue, pray !

MEPHIS. I stood beside his bed of dying.
'Twas something better than manure,—
Half-rotten straw : and yet, he died a Christian, sure,
And found that heavier scores to his account were lying.
He cried : " I find my conduct wholly hateful !
To leave my wife, my trade, in manner so ungrateful !
Ah, the remembrance makes me die !
Would of my wrong to her I might be shriven !"

MARTHA (*weeping*). The dear, good man ! Long since was
    he forgiven.

MEPHIS. "Yet she, God knows ! was more to blame
    than I."

MARTHA. He lied ! What ! On the brink of death he
    slandered ?

MEPHIS. In the last throes his senses wandered,
If I such things but half can judge.
He said : " I had no time for play, for gaping freedom :
First children, and then work for bread to feed 'em,—

For bread, in the widest sense, to drudge,
And could not even eat my share in peace and quiet ! "

MARTHA. Had he all love, all faith forgotten in his not !
My work and worry, day and night ?

MEPHIS. Not so : the memory of it touched him quite.
Said he : " When I from Malta went away
My prayers for wife and little ones were zealous,
And such a luck from Heaven befell us,
We made a Turkish merchantman our prey,
That to the Soldan bore a mighty treasure.
Then I received, as was most fit,
Since bravery was paid in fullest measure,
My well-apportioned share of it."

MARTHA. Say, how ?   Say, where ?   If buried, did he
own it ?

MEPHIS. Who knows, now, whither the four winds have
blown it ?
A fair young damsel took him in her care,
As he in Naples wandered round, unfriended ;
And she much love, much faith to him did bear,
So that he felt it till his days were ended.

MARTHA. The villain !   From his children thieving
Even all the misery on him cast
Could not prevent his shameful way of living !

MEPHIS. But see!   He's dead therefrom, at last.
Were I in *your* place, do not doubt me,
I'd mourn him decently a year,
And for another keep, meanwhile, my eyes about me.

MARTHA. Ah, God ! another one so dear
As was my first, this world will hardly give me.
There never was a sweeter fool than mine,
Only he loved to roam and leave me,
And foreign wenches and foreign wine,
And the damned throw of dice, indeed.

MEPHIS. Well, well !   That might have done, however,
If he had only been as clever,
And treated *your* slips with as little heed.
I swear, with this condition, too,
I would, myself, change rings with you.

MARTHA. The gentleman is pleased to jest.

MEPHIS. (*aside*). I'll cut away, betimes, from here :
She'd take the Devil at his word, I fear.   [*To* MARGARET.
How fares the heart within your breast ?

MARG. What means the gentleman?

MEPHIS. (*aside*).   Sweet innocent, thou art !
                                         [*Aloud.*

Ladies, farewell !

MARG.   Farewell !

MARTHA.   A moment, ere we part !
I'd like to have a legal witness,
Where, how, and when he died, to certify with fitness.
Irregular ways I've always hated ;
I want his death in the weekly paper stated.

MEPHIS. Yes, my good dame, a pair of witnesses
Always the truth establishes.
I have a friend of high condition,
Who'll also add his deposition.
I'll bring him here.

MARTHA.   Good Sir, pray do !

MEPHIS. And this young lady will be present, too !
A gallant youth ! has travelled far :
Ladies with him delighted are.

MARG. Before him I should blush, ashamed.

MEPHIS. Before no king that could be named !

MARTHA. Behind the house, in my garden, then,
This eve we'll expect the gentlemen.

XI.

STREET.

FAUST. MEPHISTOPHELES.

FAUST. How is it ? under way ? and soon complete !

MEPHIS. Ah, bravo ! Do I find you burning ?
Well, Margaret soon will still your yearning :
At Neighbour Martha's you'll this evening meet.

A fitter woman ne'er was made
To ply the pimp and gipsy trade !

FAUST. 'Tis well.

MEPHIS. Yet something is required from us.

FAUST. One service pays the other thus.

MEPHIS. We've but to make a deposition valid
That now her husband's limbs, outstretched and pallid,
At Padua rest, in consecrated soil.

FAUST. Most wise ! And first, of course, we'll make the
   journey thither ?

MEPHIS. *Sancta simplicitas !* no need of such a toil ;
Depose, with knowledge or without it, either !

FAUST. If you've naught better, then, I'll tear your pretty
   plan !

MEPHIS. Now, there you are ! O holy man !
Is it the first time in your life you're driven
To bear false witness in a case ?
Of God, the world and all that in it has a place,
Of Man, and all that moves the being of his race,
Have you not terms and definitions given
With brazen forehead, daring breast ?
And, if you'll probe the thing profoundly,
Knew you so much—and you'll confess it roundly !—
As here of Schwerdtlein's death and place of rest ?

FAUST. Thou art, and thou remain'st, a sophist, liar.

MEPHIS. Yes, knew I not more deeply thy desire.
For wilt thou not, no lover fairer,
Poor Margaret flatter, and ensnare her,
And all thy soul's devotion swear her ?

FAUST. And from my heart.

MEPHIS.   'Tis very fine !
Thine endless love, thy faith assuring,
The one almighty force enduring,—
Will that, too, prompt this heart of thine ?

FAUST. Hold ! hold ! It will !—If such my flame,
And for the sense and power intense
I seek, and cannot find, a name ;
Then range with all my senses through creation,
Craving the speech of inspiration,
And call this ardour, so supernal,

Endless, eternal and eternal,—
Is that a devilish lying game?

    MEPHIS. And yet I'm right!

    FAUST.   Mark this, I beg of thee
And spare my lungs henceforth : whoever
Intends to have the right, if but his tongue be clever,
Will have it, certainly.
But come : the further talking brings disgust,
For thou art right, especially since I must.[49]

XII.

GARDEN.

MARGARET on FAUST'S arm. MARTHA and MEPHISTOPHELES
walking up and down.

    MARG. I feel, the gentleman allows for me,
Demeans himself, and shames me by it ;
A traveller is so used to be
Kindly content with any diet
I know too well that my poor gossip can
Ne'er entertain such an experienced man.

    FAUST. A look from thee, a word, more entertains
Than all the lore of wisest brains.   [*He kisses her hand.*

    MARG. Don't incommode yourself ! How could you ever
      kiss it !
It is so ugly, rough to see !
What work I do,—how hard and steady is it !
Mother is much too close with me.   [*They pass.*

    MARTHA. And you, Sir, travel always, do you not ?

    MEPHIS. Alas, that trade and duty us so harry !
With what a pang one leaves so many a spot,
And dares not even now and then to tarry !

    MARTHA.   In young wild years it suits your ways,
This round and round the world in freedom sweeping ;

But then come on the evil days,
And so, as bachelor, into his grave a-creeping,
None ever found a thing to praise.

MEPHIS. I dread to see how such a fate advances.

MARTHA. Then, worthy Sir, improve betimes your
        chances !   [*They pass*

MARG. Yes, out of sight is out of mind !
Your courtesy an easy grace is ;
But you have friends in other places,
And sensibler than I, you'll find.

FAUST. Trust me, dear heart ! what men call sensible
Is oft mere vanity and narrowness.

MARG.   How so ?

FAUST. Ah, that simplicity and innocence ne'er know
Themselves, their holy value, and their spell !
That meekness, lowliness, the highest graces
Which Nature portions out so lovingly—

MARG. So you but think a moment's space on me,
All times I'll have to think on you, all places !

FAUST. No doubt you're much alone ?

MARG. Yes, for our household small has grown,
Yet must be cared for, you will own.
We have no maid : I do the knitting, sewing, sweeping,
The cooking, early work and late, in fact ;
And mother, in her notions of housekeeping,
Is so exact !
Not that she needs so much to keep expenses down :
We, more than others, might take comfort, rather ·
A nice estate was left us by my father,
A house, a little garden near the town.
But now my days have less of noise and hurry ;
My brother is a soldier,
My little sister's dead.
True, with the child a troubled life I led,
Yet I would take again, and willing, all the worry,
So very dear was she.

FAUST. An angel, if like thee !

MARG. I brought it up, and it was fond of me.
Father had died before it saw the light,
And mother's case seemed hopeless quite,

So weak and miserable she lay ;
And she recovered, then, so slowly, day by day.
She could not think, herself, of giving
The poor wee thing its natural living ;
And so I nursed it all alone
With milk and water : 'twas my own.
Lulled in my lap with many a song,
It smiled, and tumbled, and grew strong.

    FAUST. The purest bliss was surely then thy dower.

    MARG. But surely, also, many a weary hour.
I kept the baby's cradle near
My bed at night: if't even stirred, I'd guess it,
And waking, hear.
And I must nurse it, warm beside me press it,
And oft, to quiet it, my bed forsake,
And dandling back and forth the restless creature take,
Then at the washtub stand, at morning's break ;
And then the marketing and kitchen-tending,
Day after day, the same thing, never-ending.
One's spirits, Sir, are thus not always good,
But then one learns to relish rest and food.   [*They pass.*

    MARTHA. Yes, the poor women are bad off, 'tis true ;
A stubborn bachelor there's no converting.

    MEPHIS. It but depends upon the like of you,
And I should turn to better ways than flirting.

    MARTHA. Speaks plainly, Sir, have you no one detected ?
Has not your heart been anywhere subjected ?

    MEPHIS. The proverb says : One's own warm hearth
And a good wife, are gold and jewels worth.

    MARTHA. I mean, have you not felt desire, though ne'er
    so slightly ?

    MEPHIS. I've everywhere, in fact, been entertained
    politely.

    MARTHA. I meant to say, were you not touched in
    earnest, ever ?

    MEPHIS. One should allow one's self to jest with ladies
    never.

    MARTHA. Ah, you don't understand !

    MEPHIS.   I'm sorry I'm so blind :
But I am sure—that you are very kind.   [*They pass.*

FAUST. And me, thou angel! didst thou recognize,
As through the garden-gate I came?

MARG. Did you not see it? I cast down my eyes.

FAUST. And thou forgiv'st my freedom, and the blame
To my impertinence befitting,
As the Cathedral thou wert quitting?

MARG. I was confused, the like ne'er happened me;
No one could ever speak to my discredit.
Ah, thought I, in my conduct has he read it—
Something immodest or unseemly free?
He seemed to have the sudden feeling
That with this wench 'twere very easy dealing.
I will confess, I knew not what appeal
On your behalf, here, in my bosom grew;
But I was angry with myself, to feel
That I could not be angrier with you.

FAUST. Sweet darling!

MARG.   Wait a while!

> [*She plucks a star-flower,*[50] *and pulls off the leaves,
> one after the other.*

FAUST.   Shall that a nosegay be?

MARG. No, it is just in play.

FAUST.   How?

MARG.   Go! you'll laugh at me.

> [*She pulls off the leaves and murmurs.*

FAUST. What murmurest thou?

MARG. (*half aloud*).   He loves me—loves me not.

FAUST. Thou sweet, angelic soul!

MARG. (*continues*). Loves me—not—loves me—not—

> [*plucking the last leaf, she cries with frank delight:*

He loves me!

FAUST.   Yes, child! and let this blossom-word
For thee be speech divine! He loves thee!
Ah, know'st thou what it means? He loves thee!

> [*He grasps both her hands.*

MARG. I'm all a-tremble!

FAUST.   O tremble not! but let this look,
Let this warm clasp of hands declare thee
What is unspeakable!
To yield one wholly, and to feel a rapture

In yielding, that must be eternal !
Eternal !—for the end would be despair.
No, no,—no ending ! no ending !
   MARTHA *(coming forward)*. The night is falling.
   MEPHIS.   Ay ! we must away.
   MARTHA. I'd ask you, longer here to tarry,
But evil tongues in this town have full play.
It's as if nobody had nothing to fetch and carry,[51]
Nor other labour,
But spying all the doings of one's neighbour :
And one becomes the talk, do whatsoe'er one may.
Where is our couple now ?
   MEPHIS.   Flown up the alley yonder,
The wilful summer-birds !
   MARTHA.   He seems of her still fonder.
   MEPHIS. And she of him. So runs the world away

XIII.

A GARDEN-ARBOUR.

MARGARET *comes in, conceals herself behind the door, puts her finger to her lips, and peeps through the crack.*

   MARG. He comes !
   FAUST *(entering)*. Ah, rogue ! a tease thou art :
I have thee !   [*He kisses her.*
   MARG. *(clasping him, and returning the kiss)*. Dearest man !
    I love thee from my heart.
                       [MEPHIS. *knocks.*
   FAUST *(stamping his foot)*. Who's there ?
   MEPHIS.   A friend !
   FAUST.   A beast !
   MEPHIS.   'Tis time to separate.
   MARTHA *(coming)*. Yes, Sir, 'tis late.
   FAUST.   May I not, then, upon you wait !

MARG. My mother would—farewell!

FAUST.   Ah, can I not remain!
Farewell!

MARTHA. Adieu!

MARG.   And soon to meet again!

[*Exeunt* FAUST *and* MEPHISTOPHELES.

MARG. Dear God! However is it, such
A man can think and know so much?
I stand ashamed and in amaze,
And answer "Yes" to all he says,
A poor, unknowing child! and he—
I can't think what he finds in me!   [*Exit.*

XIV.

FOREST AND CAVERN.

FAUST (*solus*).

FAUST. Spirit sublime, thou gav'st me, gav'st me all
For which I prayed.   Not unto me in vain
Hast thou thy countenance revealed in fire.
Thou gav'st me Nature as a kingdom grand,
With power to feel and to enjoy it.   Thou
Not only cold, amazed acquaintance yield'st,
But grantest, that in her profoundest breast
I gaze, as in the bosom of a friend.
The ranks of living creatures thou dost lead
Before me, teaching me to know my brothers
In air and water and the silent wood.
And when the storm in forests roars and grinds,
The giant firs, in falling, neighbour boughs
And neighbour trunks with crushing weight near down,
And falling, fill the hills with hollow thunders,—
Then to the cave secure thou leadest me,
Then show'st me mine own self, and in my breast

The deep, mysterious miracles unfold.
And when the perfect moon before my gaze
Comes up with soothing light, around me float
From every precipice and thicket damp
The silvery phantoms of the ages past,
And temper the austere delight of thought.

That nothing can be perfect unto Man
I now am conscious. With this ecstacy,
Which brings me near and nearer to the Gods,
Thou gav'st the comrade, whom I now no more
Can do without, though, cold and scornful, he
Demeans me to myself, and with a breath,
A word, transforms thy gifts to nothingness.
Within my breast he fans a lawless fire,
Unwearied, for that fair and lovely form:
Thus in desire I hasten to enjoyment,
And in enjoyment pine to feel desire.

MEPHISTOPHELES enters.

MEPHIS. Have you not led this life quite long enough ?
How can a further test delight you ?
'Tis very well, that once one tries the stuff,
But something new must then requite you.
FAUST. Would there were other work for thee !
To plague my day auspicious thou returnest.
MEPHIS. Well ! I'll engage to let thee be :
Thou darest not tell me so in earnest.
The loss of thee were truly very slight,—
A comrade crazy, rude, repelling :
One has one's hands full all the day and night ;
If what one does, or leaves undone, is right,
From such a face as thine there is no telling.
FAUST. There is, again, thy proper tone !—
That thou hast bored me, I must thankful be !
MEPHIS. Poor Son of Earth, how couldst thou thus alone
Have led thy life, bereft of me ?
I, for a time, at least, have worked thy cure ;
Thy fancy's rickets plague thee not at all :
Had I not been, so hadst thou, sure,

Walked thyself off this earthly ball.
Why here to caverns, rocky hollows slinking,
Sit'st thou, as 'twere an owl a-blinking ?
Why suck'st, from sodden moss and dripping stone,
Toad-like, thy nourishment alone ?
A fine way, this, thy time to fill !
The Doctor's in thy body still.

FAUST. What fresh and vital forces, canst thou guess,
Spring from my commerce with the wilderness ?
But, if thou hadst the power of guessing,
Thou wouldst be devil enough to grudge my soul the blessing

MEPHIS. A blessing drawn from supernatural fountains !
In night and dew to lie upon the mountains ;
All Heaven and Earth in rapture penetrating ;
Thyself to Godhood haughtily inflating ;
To grub with yearning force through Earth's dark marrow,
Compress the six days' work within thy bosom narrow,—
To taste, I know not what, in haughty power,
Thine own ecstatic life on all things shower,
Thine earthly self behind thee cast,
And then the lofty instinct, thus—   [*With a gesture:*
                                        at last,—
I daren't say how—to pluck the final flower !

FAUST. Shame on thee !

MEPHIS.   Yes, thou findest that unpleasant !
Thou hast the moral right to cry me " shame ! " at present.
One dares not that before chaste ears declare,
Which chaste hearts, notwithstanding, cannot spare ;
And, once for all, I grudge thee not the pleasure
Of lying to thyself in moderate measure.
But such a course thou wilt not long endure ;
Already art thou o'er-excited,
And, if it last, wilt soon be plighted
To madness and to horror, sure.
Enough of that !   Thy love sits lonely yonder,
By all things saddened and oppressed ;
Her thoughts and yearnings seek thee, tenderer, fonder,—
A mighty love is in her breast.
First came thy passion's flood and poured around her
As when from melted snow a streamlet overflows ;

Thou hast therewith so filled and drowned her,
That now *thy* stream all shallow shows.
Methinks, instead of in the forests lording,
The noble Sir should find it good,
The love of this young silly blood
At once to set about rewarding.
Her time is miserably long ;
She haunts her window, watching clouds that stray
O'er the old city-wall, and far away.
"Were I a little bird ! " so runs her song,
Day long, and half night long.
Now she is lively, mostly sad.
Now, wept beyond her tears ;
Then again quiet she appears,—
Always love-mad.

    Faust. Serpent ! serpent !

    Mephis *(aside)*. Ha ! do I trap thee !

    Faust. Get thee away with thine offences,
Reprobate ! Name not that fairest thing,
Nor the desire for her sweet body bring
Again before my half-distracted senses !

    Mephis. What wouldst thou, then ? She thinks that
        thou art flown ;
And half and half thou art, I own.

    Faust. Yet am I near, and love keeps watch and ward ;
Though I were ne'er so far, it cannot falter :
I envy even the Body of the Lord
The touching of her lips, before the altar.

    Mephis. 'Tis very well ! *My* envy oft reposes
On your twin-pair, that feed among the roses.

    Faust. Away, thou pimp !

    Mephis.   You rail, and it is fun to me.
The God, who fashioned youth and maid,
Perceived the noblest purpose of His trade,
And also made their opportunity.
Go on ! It is a woe profound !
'Tis for your sweetheart's room you're bound,
And not for death, indeed.

    Faust. What are, within her arms, the heavenly blisses ?
Though I be glowing with her kisses,

Do I not always share her need?
I am the fugitive, all houseless roaming,
The monster without aim or rest,
That like a cataract, down rocks and gorges foaming,
Leaps, maddened, into the abyss's breast!
And side-wards she, with young unwakened senses,
Within her cabin on the Alpine field
Her simple, homely life commences,
Her little world therein concealed.
And I, God's hate flung o'er me,
Had not enough, to thrust
The stubborn rocks before me
And strike them into dust!
She and her peace I yet must undermine:
Thou, Hell, hast claimed this sacrifice as thine!
Help, Devil! through the coming pangs to push me;
What must be, let it quickly be!
Let fall on me her fate, and also crush me,—
One ruin whelm both her and me!

    MEPHIS. Again it seethes, again it glows!
Thou fool, go in and comfort her!
When such a head as thine no outlet knows,
It thinks the end must soon occur.
Hail him, who keeps a steadfast mind!
Thou, else, dost well the devil-nature wear:
Naught so insipid in the world I find
As is a devil in despair.

XV.

MARGARET'S ROOM.

MARGARET *at the spinning-wheel alone.*

My peace is gone,
My heart is sore :
I never shall find it,
Ah, nevermore !

Save I have him near,
The grave is here ;
The world is gall
And bitterness all.

My poor weak head
Is racked and crazed ;
My thought is lost,
My senses mazed.

My peace is gone,
Mv heart is sore :
I never shall find it,
Ah, nevermore !

To see him, him only,
At the pane I sit ;
To meet him, him only,
The house I quit.

His lofty gait,
His noble size,
The smile of his mouth,
The power of his eyes,

And the magic flow
Of his talk, the bliss
In the clasp of his hand,
And, ah ! his kiss !

My peace is gone,
My heart is sore :
I never shall find it,
Ah, nevermore !

My bosom yearns
For him alone ;
Ah, dared I clasp him,
And hold, and own !

And kiss his mouth,
To heart's desire,
And on his kisses
At last expire !

XVI.

MARTHA'S GARDEN.

MARGARET. FAUST.

MARG. Promise me, Henry !—

FAUST.   What I can !

MARG. How is't with thy religion, pray ?
Thou art a dear, good-hearted man,
And yet, I think, dost not incline that way.

FAUST. Leave that, my child !   Thou knowest my love is
          tender ;
For love, my blood and life would I surrender,
And as for Faith and Church, I grant to each his own.

MARG. That's not enough : we must believe thereon.

FAUST. Must we ?

MARG. Would that I had some influence !
Then, too, thou honourest not the Holy Sacraments.
FAUST. I honour them.
MARG.   Desiring no possession.
'Tis long since thou hast been to mass or to confession.
Believest thou in God ?
FAUST. My darling, who shall dare
" I believe in God ! " to say ?
Ask priest or sage the answer to declare,
And it will seem a mocking play,
A sarcasm on the asker.
MARG.   Then thou believest not !
FAUST. Hear me not falsely, sweetest countenance !
Who dare express Him ?
And who profess Him,
Saying : I believe in Him !
Who, feeling, seeing,
Deny His being,
Saying : I believe Him not !
The All-enfolding,
The All-upholding,
Folds and upholds he not
Thee, me, Himself ?
Arches not there the sky above us ?
Lies not beneath us, firm, the earth ?
And rise not, on us shining,
Friendly, the everlasting stars ?
Look I not, eye to eye, on thee,
And feel'st not, thronging
To head and heart, the force,
Still weaving its eternal secret,
Invisible, visible, round thy life ?
Vast as it is, fill with that force thy heart,
And when thou in the feeling wholly blessed art,
Call it, then, what thou wilt,—
Call it Bliss ! Heart ! Love ! God !
I have no name to give it !
Feeling is all in all :
The Name is sound and smoke,
Obscuring Heaven's clear glow.

MARG. All that is fine and good, to hear it so:
Much the same way the preacher spoke,
Only with slightly different phrases.

FAUST. The same thing, in all places,
All hearts that beat beneath the heavenly day —
Each in its language—say ;
Then why not I, in mine, as well ?

MARG. To hear it thus, it may seem passable ;
And yet, some hitch in't there must be
For thou hast no Christianity.

FAUST. Dear love !

MARG.   I've long been grieved to see
That thou art in such company.

FAUST. How so ?

MARG.   The man who with thee goes, thy mate,
Within my deepest, inmost soul I hate.
In all my life there's nothing
Has given my heart so keen a pang of loathing,
As his repulsive face has done.

FAUST. Nay, fear him not, my sweetest one !

MARG. I feel his presence like something ill.
I've else, for all, a kindly will,
But, much as my heart to see thee yearneth,
The secret horror of him returneth ;
And I think the man a knave, as I live !
If I do him wrong, may God forgive !

FAUST. There must be such queer birds, however.

MARG. Live with the like of him, may I never !
When once inside the door comes he,
He looks around so sneeringly,
And half in wrath :
One sees that in nothing no interest he hath :
'Tis written on his very forehead
That love, to him, is a thing abhorréd.
I am so happy on thine arm,
So free, so yielding, and so warm,
And in his presence stifled seems my heart.

FAUST. Foreboding angel that thou art !

MARG. It overcomes me in such degree,
That wheresoe'er he meets us, even,

I feel as though I'd lost my love for thee.
When he is by, I could not pray to Heaven.
That burns within me like a flame,
And surely, Henry, 'tis with thee the same.

FAUST. There, now, is thine antipathy!

MARG. But I must go.

FAUST.   Ah, shall there never be
A quiet hour, to see us fondly plighted,
With breast to breast, and soul to soul united?

MARG. Ah, if I only slept alone!
I'd draw the bolts to-night, for thy desire;
But mother's sleep so light has grown,
And if we were discovered by her,
'Twould be my death upon the spot!

FAUST. Thou angel, fear it not!
Here is a phial: in her drink
But three drops of it measure,
And deepest sleep will on her senses sink.

MARG. What would I not, to give thee pleasure?
It will not harm her, when one tries it?

FAUST. If 't would, my love, would I advise it?

MARG. Ah, dearest man, if but thy face I see,
I know not what compels me to thy will:
So much have I already done for thee,
That scarcely more is left me to fulfil.   [*Exit*

Enter MEPHISTOPHLES.

MEPHIS. The monkey! Is she gone?

FAUST.   Hast played the spy again!

MEPHIS. I've heard, most fully, how she drew thee.
The Doctor has been catechised, 'tis plain;
Great good, I hope, the thing will do thee.
The girls have much desire to ascertain
If one is prim and good, as ancient rules compel:
If there he's led, they think, he'll follow them as well.

FAUST. Thou, monster, wilt not see nor own
How this pure soul, of faith so lowly,
So loving and ineffable,—
The faith alone

That her salvation is,—with scruples holy
Pines, lest she hold as lost the man she loves so well!
    MEPHIS. Thou, full of sensual, super-sensual desire,
A girl by the nose is leading thee.
    FAUST. Abortion, thou, of filth and fire!
    MEPHIS. And then, how masterly she reads physiognomy!
When I am present she's impressed, she knows not how;
She in my mask a hidden sense would read:
She feels that surely I'm a genius now,—
Perhaps the very Devil, indeed!
Well, well,—to-night—?
    FAUST.   What's that to thee?
    MEPHIS. Yet my delight 'twill also be!

XVII.

AT THE FOUNTAIN.

MARGARET *and* LISBETH, *with pitchers.*

    LISBETH. Hast nothing heard of Barbara?
    MARG. No, not a word. I go so little out.
    LISBETH. It's true, Sibylla said, to-day.
She's played the fool at last, there's not a doubt.
Such taking-on of airs!
    MARG.   How so?
    LISBETH.   It stinks!
She's feeding two, whene'er she eats and drinks.
    MARG. Ah!
    LISBETH.   And so, at last, it serves her rightly.
She clung to the fellow so long and tightly!
That was a promenading!
At village and dance parading!
As the first they must everywhere shine,
And he treated her always to pies and wine,
And she made a to-do with her face so fine;

So mean and shameless was her behaviour,
She took all the presents the fellow gave her.
'Twas kissing and coddling, on and on !
So now, at the end, the flower is gone.

    MARG. The poor, poor thing !

    LISBETH.   Dost pity her, at that ?
When one of us at spinning sat,
And mother, nights, ne'er let us out the door
She sported with her paramour.
On the door-bench, in the passage dark,
The length of the time they'd never mark.
So now her head no more she'll lift,
But do church-penance in her sinner's shift !

    MARG. He'll surely take her for his wife.

    LISBETH. He'd be a fool !   A brisk young blade
Has room, elsewhere, to ply his trade.
Besides, he's gone.

    MARG.   That is not fair !

    LISBETH. If him she gets, why let her beware !
The boys shall dash her wreath on the floor,
And we'll scatter chaff before her door ! [53]   [*Exit.*

    MARG. (*returning home*). How scornfully I once reviled,
When some poor maiden was beguiled !
More speech than any tongue suffices
I craved, to censure others' vices.
Black as it seemed, I blackened still,
And blacker yet was in my will ;
And blessed myself, and boasted high,—
And now—a living sin am I !
Yet—all that drove my heart thereto,
God ! was so good, so dear, so true !

XVIII.

DONJON.[54]

In a niche of the wall a shrine, with an image of the Mater
Dolorosa.   Pots of flowers before it.

MARGARET (*putting fresh flowers in the pots*).

MARG. Incline, O Maiden,
Thou sorrow-laden,
Thy gracious countenance upon my pain !

The sword Thy heart in,
With anguish smarting,
Thou lookest up to where Thy Son is slain !

Thou seest the Father ;
Thy sad sighs gather,
And bear aloft Thy sorrow and His pain !

Ah, past guessing,
Beyond expressing,
The pangs that wring my flesh and bone !
Why this anxious heart so burneth,
Why it trembleth, why it yearneth,
Knowest Thou, and Thou alone !

Where'er I go, what sorrow,
What woe, what woe and sorrow
Within my bosom aches !
Alone, and ah ! unsleeping,
I'm weeping, weeping, weeping,
The heart within me breaks.

The pots before my window,
Alas! my tears did wet,
As in the early morning
For thee these flowers I set.

Within my lonely chamber
The morning sun shone red :
I sat, in utter sorrow,
Already on my bed.

Help! rescue me from death and stain !
O Maiden !
Thou sorrow-laden,
Incline Thy countenance upon my pain

XIX.

NIGHT.

STREET BEFORE MARGARET'S DOOR.

VALENTINE (*a soldier*, MARGARET's *brother*).

VALENTINE. When I have sat at some carouse,
Where each to each his brag allows,
And many a comrade praised to me
His pink of girls right lustily,
With brimming glass that spilled the toast,
And elbows planted as in boast :
I sat in unconcerned repose,
And heard the swagger as it rose.
And stroking then my beard, I'd say,
Smiling, the bumper in my hand :
"Each well enough in her own way,
But is there one in all the land
Like sister Margaret, good as gold,—
One that to her can a candle hold?"
Cling! clang! "Here's to her!" went around

The board : " He speaks the truth ! " cried some ;
" In her the flower o' the sex is found ! "
And all the swaggerers were dumb.
And now !—I could tear my hair with vexation,
And dash out my brains in desperation !
With turned-up nose each scamp may face me,
With sneers and stinging taunts disgrace me,
And, like a bankrupt debtor sitting,
A chance-dropped word may set me sweating !
Yet, though I thresh them all together,
I cannot call them liars, either.

But what comes sneaking, there, to view ?
If I mistake not, there are two.
If *he's* one, let me at him drive !
He shall not leave the spot alive.

FAUST.　MEPHISTOPHELES.

FAUST. How from the window of the sacristy
Upward th' eternal lamp sends forth a glimmer,
That, lessening side-wards, fainter grows and dimmer,
Till darkness closes from the sky !
The shadows thus within my bosom gather.

MEPHIS. I'm like a sentimental tom-cat, rather,
That round the tall fire-ladders sweeps,
And stealthy, then, along the coping creeps :
Quite virtuous, withal, I come,
A little thievish and a little frolicsome.
I feel in every limb the presage
Forerunning the grand Walpurgis-Night :
Day after to-morrow brings its message,
And one keeps watch then with delight.

FAUST. Meanwhile, may not the treasure risen be,
Which there, behind, I glimmering see ?

MEPHIS. Shalt soon experience the pleasure,
To lift the kettle with its treasure.
I lately gave therein a squint—
Saw splendid lion-dollars in't.[55]

FAUST. Not even a jewel, not a ring,
To deck therewith my darling girl ?

MEPHIS. I saw, among the rest, a thing
That seemed to be a chain of pearl.

FAUST. That's well, indeed! For painful is it
To bring no gift when her I visit.

MEPHIS. Thou shouldst not find it so annoying,
Without return to be enjoying.
Now, while the sky leads forth its starry throng,
Thou'lt hear a masterpiece, no work completer:
I'll sing her, first, a moral song,
The surer, afterwards, to cheat her. [*Sings to the cither*

> What dost thou here
> In daybreak clear,
> Kathrina dear,
> Before thy lover's door?
> Beware! the blade
> Lets in a maid,
> That out a maid
> Departeth nevermore!

> The coaxing shun
> Of such an one!
> When once 'tis done
> Good-night to thee, poor thing!
> Love's time is brief:
> Unto no thief
> Be warm and lief,
> But with the wedding-ring!

VALENTINE (*comes forward*). Whom wilt thou lure? God's
element!
Rat-catching piper, thou!—perdition! [56]
To the Devil, first, the instrument!
To the Devil, then, the curst musician!

MEPHIS. The cither's smashed! For nothing more 'tis
fitting.

VALENTINE. There's yet a skull I must be splitting!

MEPHIS. (*to* FAUST). Sir Doctor, don't retreat, I pray!
Stand by: I'll lead, if you'll but tarry:
Out with your spit, without delay!
You've but to lunge, and I will parry.

VALENTINE. Then parry that !

MEPHIS.   Why not ? 'tis light.

VALENTINE. That, too !

MEPHIS.   Of course.

VALENTINE.   I think the Devil must fight !
How is it, then ? my hand's already lame.

MEPHIS. (*to* FAUST). Thrust home !

VALENTINE (*falls*).   O God !

MEPHIS.   Now is the lubber tame !
But come, away ! 'Tis time for us to fly ;
For there arises now a murderous cry.
With the police 'twere easy to compound it,
But here the penal court will sift and sound it.

                                        [*Exit with* FAUST.

MARTHA (*at the window*). Come out ! come out !

MARG. (*at the window*).   Quick, bring a light !

MARTHA (*as above*). They swear and storm, they yell and
        fight !

PEOPLE. Here lies one dead already—see !

MARTHA (*coming from the house*). The murderers, whither
        have they run ?

MARG. (*coming out*). Who lies here ?

PEOPLE.   'Tis thy mother's son

MARG. Almighty God ! what misery !

VALENTINE. I'm dying !   That is quickly said,
And quicker yet 'tis done.
Why howl, you women there ?   Instead,
Come here and listen, every one !

                                        [*All gather around him.*
My Margaret, see ! still young thou art,
But not the least bit shrewd or smart,
Thy business thus to slight :
So this advice I bid thee heed—
Now that thou art a w—— indeed,
Why, be one then, outright !

MARG. My brother ! God ! such words to me ?

VALENTINE. In this game let our Lord God be !
What's done's already done, alas !
What follows it, must come to pass.
With one begin'st thou secretly,

Then soon will others come to thee,
And when a dozen thee have known,
Thou'rt also free to all the town.
When Shame is born and first appears,
She is in secret brought to light,
And then they draw the veil of night
Over her head and ears ;
Her life, in fact, they're loath to spare her.
But let her growth and strength display,
She walks abroad unveiled by day,
Yet is not grown a whit the fairer.
The uglier she is to sight,
The more she seeks the day's broad light.
The time I verily can discern
When all the honest folk will turn
From thee, thou jade ! and seek protection
As from a corpse that breeds infection.
Thy guilty heart shall then dismay thee,
When they but look thee in the face :—
Shalt not in a golden chain array thee,
Nor at the altar take thy place !
Shalt not, in lace and ribbons flowing,
Make merry when the dance is going !
But in some corner, woe betide thee !
Among the beggars and cripples hide thee ;
And so, though even God forgive,
On earth a damned existence live !

MARTHA. Commend your soul to God for pardon,
That you your heart with slander harden !

VALENTINE. Thou pimp most infamous, be still !
Could I thy withered body kill,
'Twould bring, for all my sinful pleasure,
Forgiveness in the richest measure.

MARG. My brother ! This is Hell's own pain !

VALENTINE. I tell thee, from thy tears refrain !
When thou from honour didst depart
It stabbed me to the very heart.
Now through the slumber of the grave
I go to God as a soldier brave.   [Dies.

XX.

CATHEDRAL.

SERVICE, ORGAN, AND ANTHEM.

MARGARET, *among much people: the* EVIL SPIRIT *behind* MARGARET.

EVIL SPIRIT. How otherwise was it, Margaret,
When thou, still innocent,
Here to the altar cam'st,
And from the worn and fingered book
Thy prayers didst prattle,
Half sport of childhood,
Half God within thee!
Margaret!
Where tends thy thought?
Within thy bosom
What hidden crime?
Pray'st thou for mercy on thy mother's soul,
That fell asleep to long, long torment, and through thee?
Upon thy threshold whose the blood?
And stirreth not and quickens
Something beneath thy heart,
Thy life disquieting
With most foreboding presence?

MARG. Woe! woe!
Would I were free from the thoughts
That cross me, drawing hither and thither,
Despite me!

CHORUS.   *Dies iræ, dies illa,*[57]
                Solvet sæclum in favilla!

                              [*Sound of the organ.*

EVIL SPIRIT.   Wrath takes thee!
                The trumpet peals!

	The graves tremble !
	And thy heart
	From ashy rest
	To fiery torments
	Now again requickened,
	Throbs to life !
MARG.	Would I were forth !
	I feel as if the organ here
	My breath takes from me,
	My very heart
	Dissolved by the anthem !
CHORUS.	*Judex ergo cum sedebit,*
	Quidquid latet adparebit,
	Nil inultum remanebit.
MARG.	I cannot breathe !
	The massy pillars
	Imprison me !
	The vaulted arches
	Crush me !—Air !
EVIL SPIRIT.	Hide thyself ! Sin and shame
	Stay never hidden.
	Air ? Light ?
	Woe to thee !
CHORUS.	*Quid sum miser tunc dicturus,*
	Quem patronum rogaturus,
	Cum vix justus sit securus !
EVIL SPIRIT.	They turn their faces,
	The glorified, from thee :
	The pure, their hands to offer,
	Shuddering, refuse thee !
	Woe !
CHORUS.	*Quid sum miser tunc dicturus !*
MARG.	Neighbour ! your cordial ![58]

[She falls in a swoon

I 2

XXI.

WALPURGIS NIGHT."

THE HARTZ MOUNTAINS. *District of Schierke and Elend.*

FAUST. MEPHISTOPHELES.

MEPHIS. Dost thou not wish a broomstick-steed's assist-
ance ?
The sturdiest he-goat I would gladly see:
The way we take, our goal is yet some distance.
FAUST. So long as in my legs I feel the fresh existence,
This knotted staff suffices me.
What need to shorten so the way ?
Along this labyrinth of vales to wander,
Then climb the rocky ramparts yonder,
Wherefrom the fountain flings eternal spray,
Is such delight, my steps would fain delay.
The spring-time stirs within the fragrant birches,
And even the fir-tree feels it now :
Should then our limbs escape its gentle searches ?
MEPHIS. I notice no such thing, I vow !
'Tis winter still within my body :
Upon my path I wish for frost and snow.
How sadly rises, incomplete and ruddy,
The moon's lone disk, with its belated glow.
And lights so dimly, that, as one advances,
At every step one strikes a rock or tree !
Let us, then, use a Jack-o'-lantern's glances :
I see one yonder, burning merrily.
Ho, there ! my friend ! I'll levy thine attendance :
Why waste so vainly thy resplendence ?
Be kind enough to light us up the steep !
WILL-O'-THE-WISP. My reverence, I hope, will me enable

To curb my temperament unstable ;
For zigzag courses we are wont to keep.
MEPHIS. Indeed ? he'd like mankind to imitate !
Now, in the Devil's name, go straight,
Or I'll blow out his being's flickering spark !
WILL-O'-THE-WISP. You are the master of the house, I mark,
And I shall try to serve you nicely.
But then, reflect : the mountain's magic-mad to-day,
And if a will-o'-the-wisp must guide you on the way,
You mustn't take things too precisely.
FAUST, MEPHISTOPHELES, WILL-O'-THE-WISP (*in alternating
     song*). We, it seems, have entered newly
          In the sphere of dreams enchanted.
          Do thy bidding, guide us truly,
          That our feet be forwards planted
          In the vast, the desert spaces !
          See them swiftly changing places,
          Trees on trees beside us trooping,
          And the crags above us stooping,
          And the rocky snouts, outgrowing,—
          Hear them snoring, hear them blowing !
          O'er the stones, the grasses, flowing
          Stream and streamlet seek the hollow.
          Hear I noises ? songs that follow ?
          Hear I tender love-petitions ?
          Voices of those heavenly visions ?
          Sounds of hope, of love undying ?
          And the echoes, like traditions
          Of old days, come faint and hollow.

          Hoo-hoo ! Shoo-hoo ! Nearer hover
          Jay and screech-owl, and the plover,—
          Are they all awake and crying ?
          Is't the salamander pushes,
          Bloated-bellied, through the bushes ?
          And the roots, like serpents twisted,
          Through the sand and boulders toiling,
          Fright us, weirdest links uncoiling
          To entrap us, unresisted :
          Living knots and gnarls uncanny

Feel with polypus-antennæ
For the wanderer. Mice are flying,
Thousand-coloured, herd-wise hieing
Through the moss and through the heather!
And the fire-flies wink and darkle,
Crowded swarms that soar and sparkle,
And in wildering escort gather!

Tell me, if we still are standing,
Or if further we're ascending?
All is turning, whirling, blending,
Trees and rocks with grinning faces,
Wandering lights that spin in mazes,
Still increasing and expanding!

MEPHIS. Grasp my skirt with heart undaunted!
Here a middle-peak is planted,
Whence one sceth, with amaze,
Mammon in the mountain blaze.

FAUST. How strangely glimmers through the hollows
A dreary light, like that of dawn!
Its exhalation tracks and follows
The deepest gorges, faint and wan.
Here steam, there rolling vapour sweepeth;
Here burns the glow through film and haze:
Now like a tender thread it creepeth,
Now like a fountain leaps and plays.
Here winds away, and in a hundred
Divided veins the valley braids:
There, in a corner pressed and sundered,
Itself detaches, spreads and fades.
Here gush the sparkles incandescent
Like scattered showers of golden sand;—
But, see! in all their height, at present,
The rocky ramparts blazing stand.

MEPHIS. Has not Sir Mammon grandly lighted
His palace for this festal night?
'Tis lucky thou hast seen the sight;
The boisterous guests approach that were invited.

FAUST. How raves the tempest through the air!
With what fierce blows upon my neck 'tis beating!

MEPHIS. Under the old ribs of the rock retreating,
Hold fast, lest thou be hurled down the abysses there!
The night with the mist is black ;
Hark ! how the forests grind and crack !
Frightened, the owlets are scattered :
Hearken ! the pillars are shattered,
The evergreen palaces shaking !
Boughs are groaning and breaking,
The tree-trunks terribly thunder,
The roots are twisting asunder !
In frightfully intricate crashing
Each on the other is dashing,
And over the wreck-strewn gorges
The tempest whistles and surges !
Hear'st thou voices higher ringing ?
Far away, or nearer singing ?
Yes, the mountain's sides along,
Sweeps an infuriate glamouring song !

   WITCHES (*in chorus*). The witches ride to the Brocken's top,
     The stubble is yellow, and green the crop.
     There gathers the crowd for carnival :
     Sir Urian sits over all.[61]
     And so they go over stone and stock ;
     The witch she ——s, and ——s the buck.
   A VOICE. Alone, old Baubo's coming now ;[62]
     She rides upon a farrow-sow.
   CHORUS. Then honour to whom the honour is due !
     Dame Baubo's first, to lead the crew !
     A tough old sow and the mother thereon,
     Then follow the witches, every one.
   A VOICE. Which way com'st thou hither ?
   VOICE.   O'er the Ilsen-stone,
I peeped at the owl in her nest alone :
How she stared and glared !
   VOICE. Betake thee to Hell !
Why so fast and so fell ?
   VOICE. She has scored and has flayed me :
See the wounds she has made me !
   WITCHES (*chorus*). The way is wide, the way is long ;
     See, what a wild and crazy throng !

The broom it scratches, the fork it thrusts,
The child is stifled, the mother bursts.

WIZARDS (*semichorus*). As doth the snail in shell, we
crawl:
Before us go the women all.
When towards the Devil's House we tread,
Woman's a thousand steps ahead.

OTHER SEMICHORUS. We do not measure with such care:
Woman in thousand steps is there,
But howsoe'er she hasten may,
Man in one leap has cleared the way.

VOICE (*from above*). Come on, come on, from Rocky
Lake!

VOICE (*from below*). Aloft we'd fain ourselves betake.
We've washed, and are bright as ever you will,
Yet we're eternally sterile still.

BOTH CHORUSES. The wind is hushed, the star shoots by,
The dreary moon forsakes the sky;
The magic notes, like spark on spark,
Drizzle, whistling through the dark.

VOICE (*from below*). Halt, there! Ho, there!

VOICE (*from above*). Who calls from the rocky cleft below
there?

VOICE (*below*). Take me, too! take me, too!
I'm climbing now three hundred years,
And yet the summit cannot see:
Among my equals I would be.

BOTH CHORUSES. Bears the broom and bears the stock,
Bears the fork and bears the buck:
Who cannot raise himself to-night
Is evermore a ruined wight.

HALF-WITCH (*below*). So long I stumble, ill bestead,
And the others are now so far ahead!
At home I've neither rest nor cheer,
And yet I cannot gain them here.

CHORUS OF WITCHES. To cheer the witch will salve
avail;
A rag will answer for a sail!
Each trough a goodly ship supplies;
He ne'er will fly, who now not flies.

BOTH CHORUSES. When round the summit whirls our
    flight,
    Then lower, and on the ground alight;
    And far and wide the heather press
    With witchhood's swarms of wantonness!

                           [They settle down.

MEPHIS. They crowd and push, they roar and clatter!
They whirl and whistle, pull and chatter!
They shine, and spirt, and stink, and burn!
The true witch-element we learn.
Keep close! or we are parted, in our turn.
Where art thou?

    FAUST (*in the distance*). Here!

    MEPHIS.   What! whirled so far astray!
Then house-right I must use, and clear the way.
Make room! Squire Voland comes![63] Room, gentle rabble,
    room!
Here, Doctor, hold to me: in one jump we'll resume
An easier space, and from the crowd be free:
It's too much, even for the like of me.
Yonder, with special light, there's something shining clearer
Within those bushes; I've a mind to see.
Come on! we'll slip a little nearer.

    FAUST. Spirit of Contradiction! On! I'll follow straight.
'Tis planned most wisely, if I judge aright:
We climb the Brocken's top in the Walpurgis-Night,
That arbitrarily, here, ourselves we isolate.

    MEPHIS. But see, what motley flames among the heather!
There is a lively club together:
In smaller circles one is not alone.

    FAUST. Better the summit, I must own:
There fire and whirling smoke I see.
They seek the Evil One in wild confusion:
Many enigmas there might find solution.

    MEPHIS. But there enigmas also knotted be.
Leave to the multitude their riot!
Here will we house ourselves in quiet.
It is an old, transmitted trade,
That in the greater world the little worlds are made.
I see stark-nude young witches congregate,

And old ones, veiled and hidden shrewdly :
On my account be kind, nor treat them rudely !
The trouble's small, the fun is great.
I hear the noise of instruments attuning,—
Vile din ! yet one must learn to bear the crooning.
Come, come along ! It *must* be, I declare !
I'll go ahead and introduce thee there,
Thine obligation newly earning.
That is no little space : what say'st thou, friend ?
Look yonder ! thou canst scarcely see the end :
A hundred fires along the ranks are burning.
They dance, they chat, they cook, they drink, they court ;
Now where, just tell me, is there better sport ?

FAUST. Wilt thou, to introduce us to the revel,
Assume the part of wizard or of devil ?

MEPHIS. I'm mostly used, 'tis true, to go incognito,
But on a gala-day one may his orders show.
The Garter does not deck my suit,
But honoured and at home is here the cloven foot.
Perceiv'st thou yonder snail ?   It cometh, slow and steady ;
So delicately its feelers pry,
That it hath scented me already :
I cannot here disguise me, if I try.
But come ! we'll go from this fire to a newer :
I am the go-between, and thou the wooer.

[*To some, who are sitting around dying embers* :
Old gentlemen, why at the outskirts ?   Enter !
I'd praise you if I found you snugly in the centre,
With youth and revel round you like a zone :
You each, at home, are quite enough alone.

GENERAL. Say, who would put his trust in nations,
Howe'er for them one may have worked and planned ?
For with the people, as with women,
Youth always has the upper hand.

MINISTER. They're now too far from what is just and
      sage.
I praise the old ones, not unduly :
When we were all-in-all, then, truly,
Then was the real golden age.

PARVENU. We also were not stupid, either,

And what we should not, often did ;
But now all things have from their bases slid,
Just as we meant to hold them fast together.

AUTHOR. Who, now, a work of moderate sense will read?
Such works are held as antique and mossy ;
And as regards the younger folk, indeed,
They never yet have been so pert and saucy.

MEPHIS. (*who all at once appears very old*).[64] I feel that men
      are ripe for Judgment-Day,
Now for the last time I've the witches'-hill ascended :
Since to the lees *my* cask is drained away,
The world's, as well, must soon be ended.

HUCKSTER-WITCH. Ye gentlemen, don't pass me thus !
Let not the chance neglected be !
Behold my wares attentively :
The stock is rare and various.
And yet, there's nothing I've collected—
No shop, on earth, like this you'll find !—
Which has not, once, sore hurt inflicted
Upon the world, and on mankind.
No dagger's here, that set not blood to flowing ;
No cup, that hath not once, within a healthy frame
Poured speedy death, in poison glowing :
No gems, that have not brought a maid to shame ;
No sword, but severed ties for the unwary,
Or from behind struck down the adversary.

MEPHIS. Gossip ! the times thou badly comprehendest :
What's done has happed—what haps, is done !
'Twere better if for novelties thou sendest :
By such alone can we be won.

FAUST. Let me not lose myself in all this pother !
This is a fair, as never was another !

MEPHIS. The whirlpool swirls to get above :
Thou'rt shoved thyself, imagining to shove.

FAUST. But who's that ?

MEPHIS.   Note her especially,
'Tis Lilith.

FAUST.   Who ?

MEPHIS.   Adam's first wife is she."[65]
Beware the lure within her lovely tresses,

The splendid sole adornment of her hair !
When she succeeds therewith a youth to snare,
Not soon again she frees him from her jesses.

FAUST. Those two, the old one with the young one sitting,
They've danced already more than fitting.

MEPHIS. No rest to-night for young or old !
They start another dance : come now, let us take hold !

FAUST (*dancing with the young witch*). A lovely dream once
   came to me ;
  I then beheld an apple-tree,
   And there two fairest apples shone :
   They lured me so, I climbed thereon.

THE FAIR ONE. Apples have been desired by you,
   Since first in Paradise they grew ;
   And I am moved with joy, to know
   That such within my garden grow.

MEPHIS. (*dancing with the old one*). A dissolute dream once
   came to me :
   Therein I saw a cloven tree,
   Which had a ——— ——— ;
   Yet, ——— as 'twas, I fancied it.

THE OLD ONE. I offer here my best salute
   Unto the knight with cloven foot !
   Let him a ——— ——— prepare,
   If him ——— ——— ——— does not scare.

PROKTOPHANTASMIST.[66] Accursèd folk ! How dare you
 venture thus ?
Had you not, long since, demonstration
That ghosts can't stand on ordinary foundation ?
And now you even dance, like one of us !

THE FAIR ONE (*dancing*). Why does he come, then, to our
  ball ?

FAUST (*dancing*). O, everywhere on him you fall !
When others dance, he weighs the matter :
If he can't every step bechatter,
Then 'tis the same as were the step not made ;
But if you forwards go, his ire is most displayed.
If you would whirl in regular gyration
As he does in his dull old mill,

He'd show, at any rate, good-will,—
Especially if you heard and heeded his hortation.

PROKTOPHANTASMIST. You still are here? Nay, 'tis a
  thing unheard !
Vanish, at once ! We've said the enlightening word.
The pack of devils by no rules is daunted :
We are so wise, and yet is Tegel haunted.[67]
To clear the folly out, how have I swept and stirred !
'Twill ne'er be clean : why, 'tis a thing unheard !

THE FAIR ONE. Then cease to bore us at our ball !

PROKTOPHANTASMIST. I tell you, spirits, to your face,
I give to spirit-despotism no place ;
My spirit cannot practise it at all.   [*The dance continues.*
Naught will succeed, I see, amid such revels ;
Yet something from a tour I always save,
And hope, before my last step to the grave,
To overcome the poets and the devils.

MEPHIS. He now will seat himself in the nearest puddle ;
The solace this, whereof he's most assured ;
And when upon his rump the leeches hang and fuddle,
He'll be of spirits and of Spirit cured.

     [*To* FAUST, *who has left the dance :*
Wherefore forsakest thou the lovely maiden,
That in the dance so sweetly sang?

FAUST. Ah ! in the midst of it there sprang
A red mouse from her mouth—sufficient reason ![68]

MEPHIS. That's nothing ! One must not so squeamish
  be ;
So the mouse was not gray, enough for thee.
Who'd think of that in love's selected season ?

FAUST. Then saw I—

MEPHIS.   What ?

FAUST.   Mephisto, seest thou there,
Alone and far, a girl most pale and fair ?
She falters on, her way scarce knowing,
As if with fettered feet that stay her going.
I must confess, it seems to me
As if my kindly Margaret were she.

MEPHIS. Let the thing be ! All thence have evil drawn :
It is a magic shape, a lifeless eidolon.

Such to encounter is not good :
Their blank, set stare benumbs the human blood,
And one is almost turned to stone.
Medusa's tale to thee is known.

FAUST. Forsooth, the eyes they are of one whom, dying,
No hand with loving pressure closed ;
That is the breast whereon I once was lying,—
The body sweet, beside which I reposed !

MEPHIS. 'Tis magic all, thou fool, seduced so easily !
Unto each man his love she seems to be.

FAUST. The woe, the rapture, so ensnare me,
That from her gaze I cannot tear me !
And, strange ! around her fairest throat
A single scarlet band is gleaming,
No broader than a knife-blade seeming !

MEPHIS. Quite right ! The mark I also note.
Her head beneath her arm she'll sometimes carry ;
'Twas Perseus lopped it, her old adversary.
Thou crav'st the same illusion still !
Come, let us mount this little hill ;
The Prater shows no livelier stir,[69]
And, if they've not bewitched my sense,
I verily see a theatre.
What's going on ?

SERVIBILIS.[70]　　　'Twill shortly recommence :
A new performance—'tis the last of seven.
To give that number is the custom here :
'Twas by a Dilettante written,
And Dilettante in the parts appear.
That now I vanish, pardon, I entreat you !
As Dilettante I the curtain raise.

MEPHIS. When I upon the Blocksberg meet you,
I find it good : for that's your proper place.

XXII.

WALPURGIS-NIGHT'S DREAM.

OBERON AND TITANIA'S GOLDEN WEDDING.[71]

Intermezzo.

MANAGER. Sons of Mieding, rest to-day ![72]
Needless your machinery :
Misty vale and mountain gray,
That is all the scenery.

HERALD. That the wedding golden be,
Must fifty years be rounded :
But *the Golden* give to me,
When the strife's compounded.

OBERON. Spirits, if you're here, be seen—
Show yourselves, delighted !
Fairy king and fairy queen,
They are newly plighted.

PUCK. Cometh Puck, and, light of limb,
Whisks and whirls in measure :
Come a hundred after him,
To share with him the pleasure.

ARIEL.[73] Ariel's song is heavenly-pure,
His tongues are sweet and rare ones :
Though ugly faces he allure,
Yet he allures the fair ones.

OBERON. Spouses, who would fain agree,
Learn how we were mated !
If your pairs would loving be,
First be separated !

TITANIA. If her whims the wife control,
And the man berate her,
Take him to the Northern Pole,
And her to the Equator !

ORCHESTRA. TUTTI. *Fortissimo.*
Snout of fly, mosquito-bill,
And kin of all conditions,
Frog in grass, and cricket-trill,—
These are the musicians !

SOLO. See the bagpipe on our track !
'Tis the soap-blown bubble :
Hear the *schnecke-schnicke-schnack*
Through his nostrils double !

[*Spirit just growing into form.*
Spider's foot and paunch of toad,
And little wings—we know 'em !
A little creature 'twill not be,
But yet, a little poem.

A LITTLE COUPLE.[74] Little step and lofty leap
Through honey-dew and fragrance :
You'll never mount the airy steep
With all your tripping vagrance.

INQUISITIVE TRAVELLER.[75] Is't but masquerading play
See I with precision ?
Oberon, the beauteous fay,
Meets, to-night, my vision !

ORTHODOX.[76] Not a claw, no tail I see !
And yet, beyond a cavil,
Like "the Gods of Greece," must he
Also be a devil.

NORTHERN ARTIST.[77] I only seize, with sketchy air,
Some outlines of the tourney ;
Yet I betimes myself prepare
For my Italian journey.

PURIST. My bad luck brings me here, alas !
How roars the orgy louder !
And of the witches in the mass,
But only two wear powder.

YOUNG WITCH. Powder becomes, like petticoat,
A gray and wrinkled noddy ;
So I sit naked on my goat,
And show a strapping body.

Matron. We've too much tact and policy
To rate with gibes a scolder ;
Yet, young and tender though you be,
I hope to see you moulder.

Leader of the Band. Fly-snout and mosquito-bill,
Don't swarm so round the Naked !
Frog in grass and cricket-trill,
Observe the time, and make it !

Weathercock (*towards one side*).[78] Society to one's desire '
Brides only, and the sweetest !
And bachelors of youth and fire,
And prospects the completest !

Weathercock (*towards the other side*). And if the Earth
        don't open now
To swallow up each ranter,
Why, then will I myself, I vow,
Jump into hell instanter !

Xenies.[79] Us as little insects see !
With sharpest nippers flitting,
That our Papa Satan we
May honour as is fitting.

Hennings.[80] How, in crowds together massed,
They are jesting, shameless !
They will even say, at last,
That their hearts are blameless.

Musagetes. Among this witches' revelry
His way one gladly loses ;
And, truly, it would easier be
Than to command the Muses.

Ci-Devant Genius of the Age. The proper folks one's
        talents laud :
Come on, and none shall pass us !
The Blocksberg has a summit broad,
Like Germany's Parnassus.

Inquisitive Traveller. Say, who's the stiff and pompous
        man ?
He walks with haughty paces :
He snuffles all he snuffle can :
    " He scent's the Jesuits' traces "

K

CRANE.[31] Both clear and muddy streams, for me
Are good to fish and sport in :
And thus the pious man you see
With even devils consorting.

WORLDLING.[32] Yes, for the pious, I suspect,
All instruments are fitting ;
And on the Blocksberg they erect
Full many a place of meeting.

DANCER. A newer chorus now succeeds !
I hear the distant drumming.
" Don't be disturbed ! 'tis, in the reeds,
The bittern's changeless booming."

DANCING-MASTER. How each his legs in nimble trip
Lifts up, and makes a clearance !
The crooked jump, the heavy skip,
Nor care for the appearance.

GOOD FELLOW. The rabble by such hate are held,
To maim and slay delights them :
As Orpheus' lyre the brutes compelled,
The bagpipes here unites them.

DOGMATIST. I'll not be led by any lure
Of doubts or critic-cavils :
The Devil must be something, sure,—
Or how should there be devils ?

IDEALIST.[33] This once, the fancy wrought in me
Is really too despotic :
Forsooth, If I am all I see,
I must be idiotic !

REALIST. This racking fuss on every hand,
It gives me great vexation ;
And, for the first time, here I stand
On insecure foundation.

SUPERNATURALIST. With much delight I see the play,
And grant to these their merits,
Since from the devils I also may
Infer the better spirits.

SCEPTIC. The flame they follow, on and on,
And think they're near the treasure :
But *Devil* rhymes with *Doubt* alone,
So I am here with pleasure.

LEADER OF THE BAND. Frog in green, and cricket-trill,
Such dilettants !—perdition !
Fly-snout and mosquito-bill,—
Each one's a fine musician !

THE ADROIT. *Sanssouci*, we call the clan
Of merry creatures so, then ;
Go a-foot no more we can,
And on our heads we go, then.

THE AWKWARD. Once many a bit we sponged ; but now,
God help us ! that is done with :
Our shoes are all danced out, we trow,
We've but naked soles to run with.

WILL-O'-THE-WISPS. From the marshes we appear,
Where we originated ;
Yet in the ranks, at once, we're here
As glittering gallants rated.

SHOOTING-STAR. Darting hither from the sky,
In star and fire light shooting,
Cross-wise now in grass I lie :
Who'll help me to my footing ?

THE HEAVY FELLOWS. Room ! and round about us, room !
Trodden are the grasses :
Spirits also, spirits come,
And they are bulky masses.

PUCK. Enter not so stall-fed quite,
Like elephant-calves about one !
And the heaviest weight to-night
Be Puck, himself, the stout one !

ARIEL. If loving Nature at your back,
Or Mind, the wings uncloses,
Follow up my airy track
To the mount of roses !

ORCHESTRA. (*Pianissimo*). Cloud and trailing mist o'erhead
Are now illuminated :
Air in leaves, and wind in reed,
And all is dissipated.[84]

XXIII.

DREARY DAY.

A FIELD.

FAUST. MEPHISTOPHELES.

FAUST. In misery! In despair! Long wretchedly astray on the face of the earth, and now imprisoned! That gracious, ill-starred creature shut in a dungeon as a criminal, and given up to fearful torments! To this has it come! to this!—Treacherous, contemptible spirit, and thou hast concealed it from me!—Stand, then,—stand! Roll the devilish eyes wrathfully in thy head! Stand and defy me with thine intolerable presence! Imprisoned! In irretrievable misery! Delivered up to evil spirits, and to condemning, unfeeling Man! And thou hast lulled me, meanwhile, with the most insipid dissipations, hast concealed from me her increasing wretchedness, and suffered her to go helplessly to ruin!

MEPHIS. She is not the first.

FAUST. Dog! Abominable monster! Transform him, thou Infinite Spirit! transform the reptile again into his dog-shape, in which it pleased him often at night to scamper on before me, to roll himself at the feet of the unsuspecting wanderer, and hang upon his shoulders when he fell! Transform him again into his favourite likeness, that he may crawl upon his belly in the dust before me,—that I may trample him, the outlawed, under foot! Not the first! O woe! woe which no human soul can grasp, that more than one being should sink into the depths of this misery,—that the first, in its writhing death-agony under the eyes of the Eternal Forgiver, did not expiate the guilt of all others! The misery of this single one pierces to the very marrow of my life; and thou art calmly grinning at the fate of thousands!

MEPHIS. Now we are already again at the end of our wits, where the understanding of you men runs wild. Why didst thou enter into fellowship with us, if thou canst not carry it out? Wilt fly, and art not secure against dizziness? Did we thrust ourselves upon thee, or thou thyself upon us?

FAUST. Gnash not thus thy devouring teeth at me! It fills me with horrible disgust. Mighty, glorious Spirit, who hast vouchsafed to me Thine apparition, who knowest my heart and my soul, why fetter me to the felon-comrade, who feeds on mischief and gluts himself with ruin?

MEPHIS. Hast thou done?

FAUST. Rescue her, or woe to thee! The fearfullest curse be upon thee for thousands of ages!

MEPHIS. I cannot loosen the bonds of the Avenger, nor undo his bolts. Rescue her? Who was it that plunged her into ruin? I, or thou? [FAUST *looks around wildly.*

Wilt thou grasp the thunder? Well, that it has not been given to you, miserable mortals! To crush to pieces the innocent respondent—that is the tyrant-fashion of relieving one's self in embarrassments.

FAUST. Take me thither! She shall be free!

MEPHIS. And the danger to which thou wilt expose thyself! Know that the guilt of blood, from thy hand, still lies upon the town! Avenging spirits hover over the spot where the victim fell, and lie in wait for the returning murderer.

FAUST. That, too, from thee? Murder and death of a world upon thee, monster! Take me thither, I say, and liberate her!

MEPHIS. I will convey thee there; and hear, what I can do! Have I all the power in Heaven and on Earth? I will becloud the jailer's senses: get possession of the key, and lead her forth with human hand! I will keep watch: the magic steeds are ready, I will carry you off. So much is in my power.

FAUST. Up and away!

XXIV.

NIGHT.

OPEN FIELD.

FAUST *and* MEPHISTOPHELES *speeding onward on black horses.*

FAUST. What weave they there round the raven-stone ?[86]
MEPHIS. I know not what they are brewing and doing.
FAUST. Soaring up, sweeping down, bowing and bending!
MEPHIS. A witches'-guild.
FAUST. They scatter, devote and doom!
MEPHIS. On! on!

XXV.

DUNGEON.

FAUST, *with a bunch of keys and a lamp, before an iron door.*

A shudder, long unfelt, comes o'er me ;
Mankind's collected woe o'erwhelms me, here.
She dwells within the dark, damp walls before me,
And all her crime was a delusion dear !
What ! I delay to free her ?
I dread, once again to see her ?
On ! my shrinking but lingers Death more near.
        [*He grasps the lock: the sound of singing is heard*
                inside.
                My mother, the harlot [86]
                Who put me to death ;
                My father, the varlet,
                Who eaten me hath !

Little sister, so good,
Laid my bones in the wood,
In the damp moss and clay:
Then was I a beautiful bird o' the wood;
Fly away!   Fly away!

FAUST (*unlocking*). She does not dream her lover listens
near;
That he the rattling chain, the rustling straw, can hear.

[*He enters.*

MARG. (*hiding herself on the pallet*). Woe! woe! They
come.   O death of bitterness!

FAUST (*whispering*). Hush! hush!   The hour is come that
frees thee.

MARG. (*throwing herself before him*). Art thou a man, then
pity my distress!

FAUST. Thy cries will wake the guards, and they will seize
thee!   [*He takes hold of the fetters to unlock them.*

MARG. (*on her knees*). Who, headsman! unto thee such
power
Over me could give?
Thou'rt come for me at midnight hour:
Have mercy on me, let me live!
Is't not soon enough when morning chime has rung?

[*She rises.*

And I am yet so young, so young!
And now Death comes, and ruin!
I, too, was fair, and that was my undoing.
My love was near, but now he's far;
Torn lies the wreath, scattered the blossoms are.
Seize me not thus so violently!
Spare me!   What have I done to thee?
Let me not vainly entreat thee!
I never chanced, in all my days, to meet thee!
    FAUST. Shall I outlive this misery?
    MARG. Now am I wholly in thy might.
But let me suckle, first, my baby!
I blessed it all this livelong night;
They took't away, to vex me, maybe,
And now they say I killed the child outright,
And never shall I be glad again.

They sing songs about me! 'tis bad of the folk to do it!
There's an old story has the same refrain;
Who bade them so construe it?

    FAUST (*falling upon his knees*). Here lieth one who loves
      thee ever.
The thraldom of thy woe to sever.

    MARG. (*flinging herself beside him*). O let us kneel, and
      call the Saints to hide us!
Under the steps beside us,
The threshold under,
Hell heaves in thunder!
The Evil One
With terrible wrath
Seeketh a path
His prey to discover!

    FAUST (*aloud*). Margaret! Margaret!

    MARG. (*attentively listening*). That was the voice of my
      lover!   [*She springs to her feet: the fetters fall off.*
Where is he? I heard him call me.
I am free! No one shall enthrall me.
To his neck will I fly,
On his bosom lie!
On the threshold he stood, and *Margaret!* calling,
Midst of Hell's howling and noises appalling,
Midst of the wrathful, infernal derision,
I knew the sweet sound of the voice of the vision!

    FAUST. 'Tis I!

    MARG.   'Tis thou! O, say it once again!
                                [*Clasping him*
'Tis he! 'tis he! Where now is all my pain?
The anguish of the dungeon, and the chain?
'Tis thou! Thou comest to save me,
And I am saved!—
Again the street I see
Where first I looked on thee;
And the garden, brightly blooming,
Where I and Martha wait thy coming.

    FAUST (*struggling to leave*). Come! Come with me!

    MARG.   Delay, now!
So fain I stay, when thou delayest!   [*Caressing him*

FAUST. Away, now!
If longer here thou stayest,
We shall be made to dearly rue it.

MARG. Kiss me!—canst no longer do it?
My friend, so short a time thou'rt missing,
And hast unlearned thy kissing?
Why is my heart so anxious, on thy breast?
Where once a heaven thy glances did create me,
A heaven thy loving words expressed,
And thou didst kiss, as thou wouldst suffocate me—
Kiss me!
Or I'll kiss thee!   [*She embraces him.*
Ah, woe! thy lips are chill!
And still.
How changed in fashion
Thy passion!
Who has done me this ill?   [*She turns away from him.*

FAUST. Come, follow me! My darling, be more bold:
I'll clasp thee, soon, with warmth a thousand-fold;
But follow now! 'Tis all I beg of thee.

MARG. (*turning to him*). And is it thou? Thou, surely,
        certainly?

FAUST. 'Tis I! Come on!

MARG.   Thou wilt unloose my chain,
And in thy lap wilt take me once again.
How comes it that thou dost not shrink from me?—
Say, dost thou know, my friend, whom thou mak'st free?

FAUST. Come! come! The night already vanisheth

MARG. My mother have I put to death;
I've drowned the baby born to thee.
Was it not given to thee and me?
Thee, too!—'Tis thou! It scarcely true doth seem—
Give me thy hand! 'Tis not a dream!
Thy dear, dear hand!—But, ah, 'tis wet!
Why, wipe it off! Methinks that yet
There's blood thereon.
Ah, God! what hast thou done?
Nay, sheathe thy sword at last!
Do not affray me!

FAUST. O, let the past be past !
Thy words will slay me !
    MARG. No, no !   Thou must outlive us.
Now I'll tell thee the graves to give us :
Thou must begin to-morrow
The work of sorrow !
The best place give to my mother,
Then close at her side my brother,
And me a little away,
But not too very far, I pray !
And here, on my right breast, my baby lay !
Nobody else will lie beside me !—
Ah, within thine arms to hide me,
That was a sweet and a gracious bliss,
But no more, no more can I attain it !
I would force myself on thee and constrain it,
And it seems thou repellest my kiss :
And yet 'tis thou, so good, so kind to see !
    FAUST. If thou feel'st it is I, then come with me !
    MARG. Out yonder ?
    FAUST. To freedom.
    MARG.   If the grave is there,
Death lying in wait, then come !
From here to eternal rest :
No further step—no, no !
Thou goest away !   O Henry, if I could go !
    FAUST. Thou canst !   Just will it !   Open stands the door!
    MARG. I dare not go : there's no hope any more.
Why should I fly ?   They'll still my steps waylay !
It is so wretched, forced to beg my living,
And a bad conscience sharper misery giving !
It is so wretched, to be strange, forsaken,
And I'd still be followed and taken !
    FAUST. I'll stay with thee.
    MARG. Be quick !   Be quick !
Save thy perishing child !
Away !   Follow the ridge
Up by the brook,
Over the bridge,
Into the wood,

To the left, where the plank is placed
In the pool!
Seize it in haste!
'Tis trying to rise,
'Tis struggling still!
Save it!   Save it!

FAUST. Recall thy wandering will!
One step, and thou art free at last!

MARG. If the mountain we had only passed!
There sits my mother upon a stone,—
I feel an icy shiver!
There sits my mother upon a stone,
And her head is wagging ever.
She beckons, she nods not, her heavy head falls o'er;
She slept so long that she wakes no more.
She slept while we were caressing:
Ah, those were the days of blessing!

FAUST. Here words and prayers are nothing worth;
I'll venture, then, to bear thee forth.

MARG. No—let me go!   I'll suffer no force!
Grasp me not so murderously!
I've done, else, all things for the love of thee.

FAUST. The day dawns: Dearest!   Dearest!

MARG. Day?   Yes, the day comes,—the last day breaks
      for me!
My wedding-day it was to be!
Tell no one thou hast been with Margaret!
Woe for my garland!   The chances
Are over—'tis all in vain!
We shall meet once again.
But not at the dances!
The crowd is thronging, no word is spoken.
The square below
And the streets overflow:
The death-bell tolls, the wand is broken.
I am seized, am bound, and delivered—
Shoved to the block—they give the sign
Now over each neck has quivered
The blade that is quivering over mine.
Dumb lies the world like the grave!

FAUST. O had I ne'er been born !

MEPHIS. (*appears outside*). Off! or you're lost ere morn.
Useless talking, delaying and praying !
My horses are neighing :
The morning twilight is near.

MARG. What rises up from the threshold here ?
He ! he ! suffer him not !
What does he want in this holy spot ?
He seeks me !

FAUST.   Thou shalt live.

MARG. Judgment of God ! myself to thee I give.

MEPHIS. (*to* FAUST). Come ! or I 'll leave her in the lurch,
        and thee !

MARG. Thine am I, Father ! rescue me !
Ye angels, holy cohorts, guard me,
Camp around, and from evil ward me !
Henry !   I shudder to think of thee.

MEPHIS. She is judged !

VOICE (*from above*).   She is saved !

MEPHIS. (*to* FAUST)   Hither to me !

                        [*He disappears with* FAUST.

VOICE (*from within, dying away*).   Henry !   Henry !

SECOND PART OF THE TRAGEDY.

IN FIVE ACTS.

INTRODUCTION

TO THE SECOND PART.

Eleusin servat quod ostendat revisentibus.
SENECA, *Quœst. Nat.* vii. 31.

I KNOW how much prepossession I encounter, in claiming for the Second Part of Faust a higher intellectual character, if a lower dramatic and poetical value, than the First Part. In Mr. Hayward's Appendix, and Mr. Lewes' *Life of Goethe*, the Second Part is virtually declared to be a secondary, unimportant work, chaotic in detail and without any consistent design as a whole ; in short, the mistake of Goethe's old age, instead of being, as it really is, the conception of his prime, partly written, and entirely planned, before the publication of the First Part.

The first mistake which many of the critics have made is in attempting any comparison of the two parts. While the moral and intellectual problem, which is first stated in the *Prologue in Heaven*, advances through richer and broader phases of development to its final solution, the story which comes to an end in Margaret's dungeon is not resumed. The Second Part opens abruptly in a broad, bright, crowded world ; we not only breathe a new atmosphere, but we come back to Faust and Mephistopheles as if after a separation of many years, and find that our former acquaintances have changed in the interval, even as ourselves. "It must be remembered," says Goethe, "that the First Part is the development of a somewhat obscure individual condition. It is almost wholly subjective; it is the expression of a confused, restricted, and passionate nature." On the other hand, we learn from the study of Goethe's life that the wealth of the material which he had accumulated for the Second Part occasioned an embarrassment in regard to the form, which partly accounts for the long postponement of the work. He expressly declares that the Second Part of the drama must be performed upon a different, a broader, and more elevated stage of action; that one who has not lived in the world and acquired some experience will not know how to comprehend it; and that, like an unsolved riddle, it will repeatedly allure the reader to the renewed study of its secret meanings.

The early disparagement which the Second Part of *Faust* received is only in our day beginning to give way to an intelligent recognition of its grand design, its wealth of illustration, and the almost inexhaustible variety and beauty of its rhythmical forms.

The reader to whom this part is a new land must, however, of necessity be furnished with a compass and an outline chart before he enters it. He may, otherwise, lose his way in its tropical jungles, before reaching that "peak in Darien," from which Keats, like Balboa, beheld a new side of the world. I consider that a brief previous statement of the argument is absolutely required.

We must forget the tragical story of the First Part, and return to the compact between Faust and Mephistopheles, where the latter declares: "The little world and then the great, we'll see." The former world is at an end, and, after an opening scene which symbolizes the healing influences of Time and Nature, Faust and his companion appear at the Court of the German Emperor. The ruined condition of the realm gives Mephistopheles a chance of acquiring place and power for Faust, through the introduction of a new financial system. While this is in progress, the days of the Carnival furnish the occasion for a Masquerade, crowded with allegorical figures, representing Society and Government. Goethe found that no detached phases of life were adequate to his purpose. Faust, in the First Part, is an individual, in narrow association with other individuals : here he is thrown into the movement of the world, the phenomena of human development, and becomes, to a certain extent, typical of Man. Hence the allegorical character of the Masquerade, which is confusing, from the great range and mixture of its symbolism.

The Emperor's wish to have Paris and Helena called from the Shades (as in the original Legend) is expressed when Faust is already growing weary of the artificial life of the Court. Mephistopheles sends him to the mysterious Mothers, that he may acquire the means of evoking the models of Beauty ; and at this point the artistic, or æsthetic element—the sense of the Beautiful in the human mind—is introduced as a most important agent of human culture, gradually refining and purifying Faust's nature, and lifting it for ever above all the meanness and littleness of the world. Mephistopheles is bound by his compact to serve, even in fulfilling this aspiration which he cannot comprehend ; but he obeys unwillingly, and with continual attempts to regain his diminishing power. After the apparition of Helena, and Faust's rash attempt to possess at once the Ideal of the Beautiful, the scene changes to the latter's old Gothic chamber, where we meet the Student of the First Part as a Baccalaureus, and find Wagner, in his laboratory, engaged in creating a Homunculus. This whimsical sprite guides Faust and Mephistopheles to the Classical Walpurgis-Night, where the former continues his pilgrimage towards Helena (the Beautiful), while the latter, true to his negative character, finally reaches his ideal of Ugliness in the Phorkyads. The allegory of the Classical Walpurgis-Night is also difficult to be unravelled, but it is not simply didactic, like that of the Carnival Masquerade. A purer strain of poetry breathes through it, and the magical moonlight which shines upon its closing Festals of the Sea prepares us for the sunbright atmosphere of the *Helena.*

This interlude, occupying the Third Act, is another allegory, complete in itself, and only lightly attached to the course of the drama. While it exhibits, in the latter connection, the æsthetic purification of Faust's nature, its leading motive is the reconciliation of the Classic and Romantic elements in Art and Literature. Euphorion, the child of Faust and Helena, who vanishes in flame, leaving only his garments and lyre behind him, is then presented to us as Byron, and the Act closes with a transmigration of "the fair humanities of old religion into the spirit and sentiment of Modern Poetry.

The Fourth Act exhibits Faust to us, enlightened and elevated above his former self, and anxious for a grand and worthy sphere of activity. His aim is, to bend Nature to the service of Man,—to bar the ocean from a great stretch of half-submerged land, and thus conquer the aimless force of the unruly elements. Mephistopheles takes advantage of the political dissensions of the Empire, and the appearance of a new claimant for the crown, at the head of an army, to proffer his own and Faust's services to the Emperor. A battle takes place ; the rebels are defeated, through the magic arts of Mephistopheles, and Faust receives the sea-shore in feoff for ever.

The Fifth Act opens on the accomplished work. Faust, a hundred years old, inhabits a palace, in the midst of a green, thickly-peopled land, diked from the sea. But he has not yet found the one moment of supreme happiness. A pestilential marsh still remains to be drained ; and he has not succeeded in gaining the coveted possession of a sand-hill near his palace, the residence of an old couple who have charge of a little chapel on the downs. Mephistopheles endeavours to implicate him in the guilty seizure of this Naboth's vineyard, but is again baffled. Faust, become blind, finds a clearer light dawning upon his spirit : while the workmen are employed upon the canal which completes his great work, he perceives that he has created free and happy homes for the coming generations of men, and the fore-feeling of satisfied achievement impels him to say to the passing Moment : "Ah, still delay, — thou art so fair !" When the words are uttered, he sinks upon the earth, dead.

The struggle of Mephistopheles with the angels for the possession of Faust's soul, and a scene in Heaven, where Margaret appears, like Beatrice in Dante's *Paradiso*, as the spiritual guide of her redeemed lover, close the drama. Although the condition of the compact has been fulfilled, Mephistopheles loses his wager. In willing the Bad, he has worked the Good : the "obscure aspiration" in Faust's nature has lifted itself, through Love, Experience, the refining power of the Beautiful, and beneficent activity, to more than an instinct, to a knowledge of "the one true way." The Epilogue in

Heaven carries us back to the Prologue, and indicates to us, through a wondrous, mystic symbolism, the victorious vitality of Good and the omnipotence of the Divine Love.

Briefly, then, Act I. represents Society and Government; Acts II. and III. the development of the Idea of the Beautiful as the highest human attribute, with almost a saving power; Act IV., War; and Act V., Beneficent Activity, crowned by Grace and Redemption. The financial scheme, the discussion of geological theories, the union of the Classic and Romantic, and the intro duction of those three tricksy spirits, the Boy Charioteer, Homunculus, and Euphorion (whom I interpret as different personifications of Goethe's own Poetic Genius), must be considered as digressions from the direct course of the plot.

In concluding this labour of years, I venture to express the hope that, however I may have fallen short of reproducing the original in another, though a kindred language, I may, at least, have assisted in naturalizing the masterpiece of German literature among us, and to that extent have explained the supreme place which has been accorded to Goethe among the poets of the world. Where I have differed from the German critics and commentators, I would present the plea, that the laws of construction are similar, whether one builds a cottage or a palace; and the least of authors, to whom metrical expression is a necessity, may have some natural instinct of the conceptions of the highest.

B. T.

ACT I.

I.

A PLEASANT LANDSCAPE.

TWILIGHT.

FAUST, bedded on flowery turf, fatigued, restless, endeavouring to sleep. Circle of hovering spirits in motion: graceful diminutive figures.

ARIEL.[1] (*Chant accompanied by Æolian harps.*)
> When the Spring returns serener
> Raining blossoms over all;
> When the fields with blessing greener
> On the earth-born children call;
> Then the craft of elves propitious
> Hastes to help where help it can:
> Be he holy, be he vicious,
> Pity they the luckless man.

Who round this head in airy circles hover,
Yourselves in guise of noble Elves discover!
The fierce convulsions of his heart compose;
Remove the burning barbs of his remorses,
And cleanse his being from the suffered woes!
Four pauses makes the Night upon her courses,[2]
And now, delay not, let them kindly close!
First on the coolest pillow let him slumber,
Then sprinkle him with Lethe's drowsy spray!
His limbs no more shall cramps and chills encumber
When sleep has made him strong to meet the day.

Perform, ye Elves, your fairest rite :
Restore him to the holy Light !

CHORUS[3] (*singly, by two or more, alternately and collectively*).

When around the green-girt meadow
Balm the tepid winds exhale,
Then in fragrance and in shadow
Twilight spreads her misty veil :
Whispers peace in accents cheery,
Rocks the heart in childhood's play,
And upon these eyelids weary
Shuts the golden gates of Day.

Now the Night already darkles,
Holy star succeeds to star ;
Dazzling lights and fainter sparkles
Glimmer near and gleam afar ;
Glimmer here, the lake reflecting,
Gleam in cloudless dark aboon ;
While, the bliss of rest protecting,
Reigns in pomp the perfect moon.

Now the Hours are cancelled for thee,
Pain and bliss have fled away :
Thou art whole : let faith restore thee !
Trust the new, the rising Day !
Vales grow green, and hills are lifting
Through the shadow-rest of morn ;
And in waves of silver, drifting
On to harvest, rolls the corn.

Wouldst thou win desires unbounded,
Yonder see the glory burn !
Lightly is thy life surrounded—
Sleep's a shell, to break and spurn !
When the crowd sways, unbelieving,
Show the daring will that warms !
He is crowned with all achieving,
Who perceives and then performs.

[*A tremendous tumult announces the approach of the Sun.*

ARIEL.   Hearken ! Hark !—the Hours careering !
          Sounding loud to spirit-hearing,
          See the new-born day appearing !
          Rocky portals jarring shatter,
          Phœbus' wheels in rolling clatter,
          With a crash the Light draws near !
          Pealing rays and trumpet-blazes,—
          Eye is blinded, ear amazes :
          The Unheard can no one hear !
          Slip within each blossom-bell,
          Deeper, deeper, there to dwell,—
          In the rocks, beneath the leaf !
          If it strikes you, you are deaf.

FAUST. Life's pulses now with fresher force awaken
To greet the mild ethereal twilight o'er me ;
This night, thou, Earth ! hast also stood unshaken,
And now thou breathest new-refreshed before me,
And now beginnest, all thy gladness granting,
A vigorous resolution to restore me,
To seek that highest life for which I 'm panting.—
The world unfolded lies in twilight glimmer,
A thousand voices in the grove are chanting ;
Vale in, vale out, the misty streaks grow dimmer ;
The deeps with heavenly light are penetrated ;
The boughs, refreshed, lift up their leafy shimmer
From gulfs of air where sleepily they waited ;
Colour on colour from the background cleareth,
Where flower and leaf with trembling pearls are freighted
And all around a Paradise appeareth.

Look up !—The mountain summits, grand, supernal,
Herald, e'en now, the solemn hour that neareth ;
They earliest enjoy the light eternal
That later sinks, till here below we find it.
Now to the Alpine meadows, sloping vernal,
A newer beam descends ere we divined it,
And step by step unto the base hath bounded :
The sun comes forth ! Alas, already blinded,
I turn away, with eyesight pierced and wounded !

'T is thus, when, unto yearning hope's endeavour
Its highest wish on sweet attainment grounded,
The portals of fulfilment widely sever :
But if there burst from those eternal spaces
A flood of flame, we stand confounded ever ;
For Life's pure torch we sought the shining traces,
And seas of fire—and what a fire ! —surprise us.
Is 't love ?   Is 't Hate ? that burningly embraces,
And that with pain and joy alternate tries us ?
So that, our glances once more earthward throwing,
We seek in youthful drapery to disguise us.

Behind me, therefore, let the sun be glowing !
The cataract, between the crags deep-riven,
I thus behold with rapture ever-growing.
From plunge to plunge in thousand streams 't is given,
And yet a thousand, to the valleys shaded
While foam and spray in air are whirled and driven.
Yet how superb, across the tumult braided,
The painted rainbow's changeful life is bending,
Now clearly drawn, dissolving now and faded,
And evermore the showers of dew descending !
Of human striving there's no symbol fuller :
Consider, and 't is easy comprehending—
Life is not light, but the refracted colour.

II.

THE EMPEROR'S CASTLE.

HALL OF THE THRONE.

COUNCIL OF STATE AWAITING THE EMPEROR.

Trumpets.

Enter COURT RETAINERS *of all kinds, splendidly dressed. The* EMPEROR *advances to the throne: the* ASTROLOGER *on his right hand.*

EMPEROR. I greet you, Well-beloved and Trusty,
Assembled here from far and wide !
I see the Wise Man at my side ;
But where's the Fool, his rival lusty ?

SQUIRE. Behind thy mantle's flowing swell
Suddenly on the stairs he fell :
They bore away the weight of fat ;
If dead, or drunk ? none knoweth that.

SECOND SQUIRE. As quick as thought, through all the pother
Him to replace there came another,
Adorned and prinked with wondrous art,
Yet so grotesque that all men start.
The guards their halberds cross-wise hold
To bar him—them he thrusts apart :
Lo ! here he comes, the Fool so bold !

MEPHIS. (*kneeling before the throne*). What's cursed and
       welcomely expected ?
What is desired, yet always chased ?
What evermore with care protected ?
What is accused, condemned, disgraced ?
To whom darest thou not give a hearing ?
Whose name hears each man willingly ?

What is 't, before thy throne appearing?
What keeps itself away from thee?

EMPEROR. Spare us thy words! the time is pressing;
This is no place for riddle guessing:
These gentlemen such things explain.
Solve it thyself! to hear I'm fain.
My old Fool went, I fear, an endless distance:
Take thou his place, come here and lend assistance!

[MEPHIS. *goes up and stations himself on the* EMPEROR'S *left hand.*

MURMURS OF THE CROWD. Another fool—for worries new!—
        Whence came he?—how did he get through?
        The old one fell—he's walked his path.—
        He was a barrel—this a lath!

EMPEROR. So now, my Well-beloved and Loyal,
Be welcome all, from near and far!
You meet beneath a fortunate star;
Welfare and luck are now the aspects royal.
But tell me why, in days so fair,
When we've withdrawn ourselves from care,
And beards of beauty masquerading wear,—
When gay delights for us are waiting,
Why should we plague ourselves, deliberating?
Yet, since the task you think we cannot shun,
'T is settled, then, so be it done!

CHANCELLOR. The highest virtue, like a halo-zone
Circles the Emperor's head; and he alone
Is worthy validly to exercise it.
'T is justice!—all men love and prize it,
None can forego, but all require and want it:
The people look to him, that he should grant it.
But, ah! what help can human wit impart
Or readiness of hand, or kindly heart,
When lies the State, as if in fever fretting,
And brooded Evil evil is begetting?
Who looks abroad from off this height supreme
Throughout the realm, 't is like a weary dream,
Where one deformity another mouldeth,
Where lawlessness itself by law upholdeth,
And 't is an age of Error that unfoldeth!

One plunders flocks, a woman one,
Cup, cross, and candlestick from altar,
And then to boast it does not palter,
Of limb or life nowise undone.
To Court behold the plaintiffs urging,
Where puffs the judge on cushions warm,
And swells, meanwhile, with fury surging,
Rebellion's fast-increasing storm !
His easy way through crime is broken,
Who his accomplices selects ;
And " Guilty ! " hears one only spoken
Where Innocence itself protects.
They all pull down what they should care for,—
Destroy their weal, in self-despite :
How can the sense develop, therefore,
Which, only, leads us to the Right ?
At last, the man of good intent
To flatterer and briber bendeth ;
The judge, debarred from punishment,
Mates with the felon, ere he endeth.
I 've painted black, but denser screen
I 'd rather draw before the scene.   [*Pause*
Here measures cannot be evaded ;
When all offend, and none are aided,
His Majesty a victim stands.

    GENERAL-IN-CHIEF. In these wild days, how discords
      thicken !
Each strikes and in return is stricken,
And they are deaf to all commands.
The burgher in his fortifications,
The knight upon his rocky nest,
Have sworn to worry out our patience
And keep their strength with stubborn crest.
The mercenaries, no whit better,
Impatiently demand their pay,
And, if we were not still their debtor,
They 'd start forthwith and march away.
Let one forbid what all would practise
And in a hornet's nest he stands :
The realm which they should guard, the fact is,

'T is devasted by their hands.
They give the rein to wild disorder,
And half the world is wasted now ;
There still are kings beyond our border,
But none thinks it concerns him anyhow.

   TREASURER. Trust allies, and we soon shall rue us
The subsidies they promised to us—
Like water in leaky pipes—don't come.
Then, Sire, in all thy states extended
To whom hath now the rule descended ?
Where'er one goes, a new lord is at home,
And hopes to live in independence ;
He takes his course and we look on :
Such rights we 've given to our attendants
That all *our* right to anything is gone.
On parties, too, whate'er the name be,
Our trust, to-day, is far from great ;
Though loud their praise or fierce their blame be,
Indifferent is their love and hate.
The Ghibellines and Guelfs from labour
Are resting—both laid on the shelf.
Who, therefore, now will help his neighbour ?
Each has enough, to help himself.
The gate of gold no more unlatches,
And each one gathers, digs, and scratches,
While our strong-box is void indeed.

   LORD HIGH STEWARD. What evil I, as well, am having !
We 're always trying to be saving,
And ever greater is our need :
Thus daily grows this task of mine.
The cooks have all they want at present,—
Wild-boar and deer, and hare and pheasant
Duck, peacock, turkey, goose, and chicken :
These, paid in kind, are certain picking,
And do not seriously decline ;
Yet, after all, we 're short of wine.
Where casks on casks were once our cellars filling,
Rare vintages of flavours finely thrilling,
The noble lords' eternal swilling
Has drained them off, till not a drop appears.

The City Council, too, must tap their liquor ;
They drink from mug, and jug, and beaker,
Till no one longer sees or hears.
'T is I must pay for all the dances ;
The Jew will have me, past all chances ;
His notes of hand and his advances
Will soon eat up the coming years.
Before they 're fat the swine are taken ;
Pawned is the pillow, ere one waken ;
The bread is eaten ere the board it sees.

 EMPEROR (*after some reflection, to* MEPHIS.). Say, Fool,
canst thou not add a want to these?

 MEPHIS. I? Not at all! I see the circling splendour—
Thyself, and thine! Should one his trust surrender,
Where Majesty thus unopposed commands,
Where ready power the hostile force disbands,
Where loyal wills, through understanding strong,
And mixed activities, around thee throng?
What powers for evil could one see combining,—
For darkness, where such brilliant stars are shining?

 MURMURS. He is a scamp—who comprehends.—
  He lies his way—until it ends.—
  I know it now—what 's in his mind.—
  What then?—A project lurks behind!

 MEPHIS. Where, in this world, doth not some lack appear?
Here this, here that,—but money 's lacking here.
True, from the floor you can't at once collect it,
But, deepliest hidden, wisdom may detect it.
In veins of mountains, under building-bases,
Coined and uncoined, there 's gold in many places :
And ask you who shall bring it to the light?
A man endowed with Mind and Nature's might.

 CHANCELLOR. Nature and Mind—to Christians we don't
  speak so.
Thence to burn Atheists we seek so,
For such discourses very dangerous be.
Nature is Sin, and Mind is Devil :
Doubt they beget in shameless revel,
Their hybrid in deformity.
Not so with us !—Two only races

Have in the Empire kept their places,
And prop the throne with worthy weight.
The Saints and Knights are they : together
They breast each spell of thunder-weather,
And take for pay the Church and State.
The vulgar minds that breed confusion
Are met with an opposing hand :
They 're wizards !—heretics !   Delusion
Through them will ruin town and land.
And these will you, with brazen juggle,
Within this high assembly smuggle ?
For hearts corrupt you scheme and struggle ;
The Fool's near kin are all the band.

    Mephis. By that, I know the learned lord you are :
What you don't touch, is lying leagues afar ;
What you don't grasp, is wholly lost to you ;
What you don't reckon, think you, can't be true ;
What you don't weigh, it has no weight, alas !
What you don't coin, you 're sure it will not pass.

    Emperor. Therewith to help our needs you naught deter-
        mine.
What wilt thou, here, with such a Lenten sermon ?
I 'm tired of the eternal If and How :
Money we want : good, then, procure it now !

    Mephis. I 'll furnish what you wish, and more : 't is, true,
A light task, but light things are hard to do.
The gold 's on hand,—yet, skilfully to win it,
That is the art : who knows how to begin it ?
Consider only, in those days of blood
When o'er the Empire poured a human flood,
How many men, such deadly terror steeled them,
Took their best goods, and here and there concealed them ?
'T was so beneath the mighty Roman sway,
And ever so repeated till our day.
All that was buried in the earth, to save it :
The Emperor owns the earth, and he should have it.

    Treasurer. Now, for a Fool, his words are rather bright :
That is indeed the old Imperial right.

    Chancellor. Satan has laid his golden snares, to try us ;
Such things as these are neither right nor pious.

LORD HIGH STEWARD. Let him but bring his gifts to
    Court, and share them,
And if things were a little wrong, I'd bear them!

    GENERAL-IN-CHIEF. The Fool is shrewd, to promise each
      his needs;
Whence it may come the soldier never heeds.

    MEPHIS. And should you think, perchance, I overreach
      you,
Here's the Astrologer—ask him to teach you!
The spheres of Hour and House are in his ken,[5]
What are the heavenly aspects!—tell us, then?

    MURMURS. Two rogues are they,—in league they've grown,
      Dreamer and Fool—so near the throne!
      The song is old—and flatly sung.—
      The Fool he prompts—the Wise Man's tongue!

    ASTROLOGER (*speaks:* MEPHIS. *prompts*). The Sun himself
      is gold of purest ray;
The herald, Mercury, serves for love and pay;
Dame Venus has bewitched you all, for she,
Early and late, looks on you lovingly;
Chaste Luna has her whims, no two alike;
Mars threatens you, although he may not strike,
And Jupiter is still the splendid star.
Saturn is great, though seeming small and far;
As metal, him we don't much venerate,
Of value slight, though heavy in his weight.
Now, when of Sol and Luna union's had,—
Silver with gold,—then is the world made glad:
All else, with them, is easy to attain,—
Palaces, gardens, cheeks of rosy stain;
And these procures this highly learned man,
Who that can do which none of us e'er can.

    EMPEROR. Two meanings in his words I find,
And yet they don't convince my mind.

    MURMURS. Why tell us that?—stuff stale and flat
      'T is quackery!—'t is chemistry!
      I've heard the strain—and hoped in vain,--
      And though it come—'t is all a hum.

    MEPHIS. They stand around, amazed, unknowing
They do not trust the treasure-spell:

One dreams of mandrake, nightly growing,
The other of the dog of Hell.
Why, then, should one suspect bewitching,
And why the other jest and prate,
When in their feet, they, too, shall feel the itching,
When they shall walk with tottering gait?
All feel the secret operation
Of Nature's ever-ruling might,
And from the bases of Creation
A living track winds up to light.
In every limb when something twitches
In any place uncanny, old,—
Decide at once, and dig for riches!
There lies the fiddler, there the gold![6]

MURMURS. It hangs like lead my feet about.—
    I 've cramp i' the arm—but that is gout.—
    I 've tickling in the greater toe.—
    Down all my back it pains me so.—
    From signs like these 't is very clear
    The richest treasure-ground is here.

EMPEROR. Haste then! Thou 'lt not again make off!
Test now thy frothy, lying graces,
And show at once the golden places!
My sword and sceptre I will doff,
Mine own imperial hands I 'll lend thee,
If thou liest not, therein befriend thee,
But, if thou liest, to Hell will send thee!

MEPHIS. I 'd find, in any case, the pathway there!—
Yet I cannot enough declare
What, ownerless, waits everywhere.
The farmer, following his share,
Turns out a gold-crock with the mould:
He seeks saltpetre where the clay-walls stand,[7]
And findeth rolls of goldenest gold,
With joyful fright, in his impoverished hand.
What vaults there are to be exploded,
Along what shafts and mines corroded,
The gold-diviner's steps are goaded,
Until the Under-world is nigh!
In cellars vast he sees the precious

Cups, beakers, vases, plates, and dishes,
Row after row, resplendent lie :
Rich goblets, cut from rubies, stand there,
And, would he use them, lo ! at hand there
Is ancient juice of strength divine.
Yet, trust to him who 's knowledge gotten,
The wood o' the staves has long been rotten,
A cask of tartar holds the wine.[8]
Not only gold and gems are hiding,
But of proud wines the heart abiding,
In terror and in night profound :
Herein assiduously explore the wise ;
It is a farce, by day to recognize,
But mysteries are with darkness circled round.

EMPEROR. See thou to them ! What profits the Obscure ?
Whate'er has value comes to daylight, sure.
At dead of night who can the rogue betray ?
Then all the cows are black, the cats are gray.
If pots are down there, full of heavy gold,
Drive on thy plough, and turn them from the mould.

MEPHIS. Take hoe and spade thyself, I pray thee,—
Thou shalt be great through peasant-toil !
A herd of golden calves, to pay thee,
Will loose their bodies from the soil.
And then at once canst thou, with rapture,
Gems for thyself and for thy mistress capture :
Their tints and sparkles heighten the degree
Of Beauty as of Majesty.

EMPEROR. Then quick ! at once ! how long will it require ?

ASTROLOGER (*prompted by* MEPHIS.). Sire, moderate such
urgence of desire !
Let first the gay, the motley pastime end !
Not to the goal doth such distraction tend.
First self-command must quiet and assure us ;
The upper things the lower will procure us.
Who seeks for Good, must first be good ;
Who seeks for joy, must moderate his blood ;
Who wine desires, let him the ripe grapes tread ;
Who miracles, by stronger faith be led !

EMPEROR. Let us the time in merriment efface !

And, to our wish, Ash-Wednesday comes apace.
Meanwhile, we'll surely celebrate withal
More jovially the maddening Carnival.

[*Trumpets.* *Exeut.*

MEPHIS. How closely linked are Luck and Merit,
Doth never to these fools occur :
Had they the Philosopher's Stone, I swear it,
The stone would lack the Philosopher !

III.

SPACIOUS HALL,

WITH ADJOINING APARTMENTS,

Arranged and Decorated for the Carnival Masquerade.[9]

HERALD. Think not, as in our German bounds, your
   chance is
Of Death's or Fools' or Devils' dances ;
Here cheerful revels you await.
Our Ruler, on his Roman expedition,
Hath for his profit, your fruition,
Crossed o'er the Alpine high partition,
And won himself a gayer State.
He to the holy slipper bowed him
And first the right of power besought ;
Then, as he went to get the Crown allowed him,
For us the Fool's-cap he has also brought.
Now are we all new-born, to wear it ;
Each tactful and experienced man,
Drawn cosily o'er head and ears, doth bear it ;
A fool he seems, yet he must share it,
And be, thereby, as sober as he can.
They crowding come, I see already,
Close coupling, or withdrawn unsteady,—

The choruses, like youth from school.
Come in or out, bring on your ranks !
Before or after—'tis the rule—
With all its hundred thousand pranks,
The World is one enormous Fool !

GARDEN-GIRLS. (*Song, accompanied with mandolines.*)
>   That we win your praises tender
>   We are decked in festal gear ;
>   At the German Court of splendour,
>   Girls of Florence, we appear.
>
>   On our locks of chestnut glosses
>   Wear we many a flowery bell ;
>   Silken threads and silken flosses
>   Here must play their parts, as well.
>
>   Our desert, not over-rated,
>   Seems to us assured and clear,
>   For by art we've fabricated
>   Flowers that blossom all the year.
>
>   Every sort of coloured snipping
>   Won its own symmetric right :
>   Though your wit on each be tripping,
>   In the whole you take delight.
>
>   We are fair to see and blooming,
>   Garden-girls, and gay of heart :
>   For the natural way of woman
>   Is so near akin to art.

HERALD.   Let us see the wealth of blossoms
>   Basket-crowning heads that bear them,
>   Garlanding your arms and bosoms !
>   Each select, and lightly wear them.
>   Haste ! and bosky arbours dressing,
>   Let a garden here enring us !
>   Worthy they of closer pressing,
>   Hucksters and the wares they bring us.

GARDEN-GIRLS. Now in cheerful places chaffer,
>   But no marketing be our ?

Briefly, clearly, let each laugher
Know the meaning of his flowers.

OLIVE BRANCH, WITH FRUIT.[10] Flowery sprays I do not
    covet ;
Strife I shun, or branch above it,
Foe of conflict I remain.
Yet am I the marrow of nations,
Pledge of happy consummations,
Sign of peace on every plain.
Be, to-day, my lucky fate
Worthy head to decorate !

WREATH OF EARS (*golden*). You to crown, the gifts of Ceres
Here their kindly grace have sent ;
Unto Use what chiefly dear is
Be your fairest ornament !

FANCY WREATH. Gayest blossoms, like to mallows,—
From the moss a marvel grew !
Fashion calls to light, and hallows,
That which Nature never knew.

FANCY NOSEGAY. What our name is, Theophrastus[11]
Would not dare to say : contrast us !
Yet we hope to please you purely,
If not all, yet many, surely,—
Such as fain we'd have possess us,
Braiding us in shining tresses,
Or, a fairer fate deciding,
On the heart find rest abiding.

CHALLENGE. Motley fancies blossom may
For the fashion of the day,
Whimsical and strangely moulded,
Such as Nature ne'er unfolded :
Bells of gold and stems of green
In the plenteous locks be seen !—
Yet we

ROSEBUDS   lie concealed behind ;
Lucky, who shall freshly find !
When the summer-time returneth,
And the rosebud, bursting, burneth,
Who such blisses would surrender !
Promise sweet, and yielding tender,

They, in Flora's realm, control
Swiftly eyes and sense and soul.
[*Under green, leafy arcades, the* GARDEN-GIRLS
adorn and gracefully exhibit their wares.

GARDENERS. (*Song, accompanied with theorbos.*)
Blossoms there, that sprout in quiet,
Round your heads their charms are weaving;
But the fruits are not deceiving,
One may try the mellow diet.

Sunburnt faces tempt with glowing
Cherries, peaches, plums, your vision:
Buy! for vain the eye's decision
To the tongue's and palate's showing.

Ripest fruit from sunniest closes
Eat, with taste and pleasure smitten!
Poems one may write on roses,
But the apple must be bitten.

Then permit that we be mated
With your youth, so flowery-fair:
Thus is also decorated,
Neighbour-like, our riper ware.

Under wreaths of flowery tether,
As the leafy arbours suit,
All may then be found together,
Buds and leaves, and flower and fruit!
[*With alternating songs, accompanied with mandolines
and theorbos, both Choruses continue to set forth
their wares upon steps rising aloft, and to offer
them to the spectators.*

MOTHER *and* DAUGHTER.

MOTHER. Maiden, when thou cam'st to light,
Tiny caps I wrought thee;
Body tender, soft, and white,
Lovely face I brought thee.
As a bride I thought thee, led

To the richest, wooed and wed,
As a wife I thought thee.

Ah! already many a year,
Profitless, is over:
None of all the wooers here
Now around thee hover;
Though with one was wont to dance,
Gav'st another nudge and glance,—
Hast not found thy lover!

I to feast and revel thee
Vainly took, to match one:
Pawns, and hindmost man of three,
Would not help thee snatch one.
Every fool now wears his cap:
Sweetheart, open thou thy lap!
Still, perchance, mayst catch one!

[*Other maiden-playmates, young and beautiful, join
the garden-girls: the sound of familiar gossip is
heard. Fishers and bird-catchers, with nets,
fishing-rods, limed twigs, and other implements,
appear, and disperse themselves among the maidens.
Reciprocal attempts to win, to catch, to escape, and
to hold fast, give opportunity for the most agreeable
dialogues.*

WOOD-CUTTERS [12] (*Enter, boisterously and boorishly*).

Room! make a clearing!
Room in your revel!
The trees we level
That tumble cracking:
Where we're appearing
Look out for whacking.
Our praise adjudging,
Make clear this fable!
Save Coarse were drudging
Within your borders,
Would Fine be able
To build their orders,
Howe'er they fretted?

Be taught in season,
For you'd be freezing
Had we not sweated !

PULCINELLI (*uncouth, almost idiotic*). You, Fools, are
trooping,
Since birth so stooping ;
The wise ones we are,
From burdens freer.
Our caps, though sleazy,
And jackets breezy
To wear are easy :
It gives us pleasure
To go with leisure,
With slippered shuffles
Through market-scuffles,
To gape at the pother,
Croak at each other !
Through crowded places
You always trace us,
Eel-like gliding,
Skipping and hiding,
Storming together :
Moreover, whether
You praise—reprove us,
It does n't move us.

PARASITES (*fawningly lustful*). Ye woodland bandsmen,
And they, your clansmen,
The charcoal-burners,
To you we turn us :
For all such plodding,
Affirmative nodding,
Tortuous phrases,
Blowing both ways—is
Warming or chilling,
Just as you 're feeling :
What profit from it ?
There might fall fire,
Enormous, dire,
From heaven's summit,
Were there not billets

And coal in waggons,
To boil your skillets
And warm your flagons.
It roasts and frizzles;
It boils and sizzles!
The taster and picker,
The platter-licker,
He sniffs the roasting,
Suspects the fishes,
And clears, with boasting,
His patron's dishes.

Drunken Man [13] (*unconsciously*). Naught, to-day, bring
melancholy!
Since I feel so frank and free:
Fresh delight and songs so jolly,
And I brought them both with me!
Thus I 'm drinking, drinking, drinking!
Clink your glasses, clinking, clinking!
You behind there, join the rout!
Clink them stout, and then it 's out!

Though my wife assailed me loudly,
Rumpled me through thin and thick;
And, howe'er I swaggered proudly,
Called me "masquerading stick":
Yet I 'm drinking, drinking, drinking!
Clink your glasses! clinking, clinking!
Masking sticks, another bout!
When you 've clinked them, drink them out!

Say not mine a silly boast is!
I am here in clover laid:
Trusts the host not, trusts the hostess,—
She refusing, trusts the maid.
Still I 'm drinking, drinking, drinking!
Come, ye others, clinking, clinking!
Each to each! keep up the rout;
We, I 'm thinking, drink them out.

How and where my fun I 'm spying,
Let me have it as I planned!

Let me lie where I am lying,
For I cannot longer stand.
CHORUS. Every chum be drinking, drinking !
 Toast afresh, with clinking, clinking !
 Bravely keep your seats, and shout !
 Under the table *he* 's drunk out.
 [*The* HERALD *announces various Poets—Poets of Na-*
  ture, Courtly and Knightly Minstrels, Sentimentalists
  as well as Enthusiasts. In the crowd of competi-
  tors of all kinds, no one allows another to commence
  his declamation. One slips past with a few words.
SATIRIST. Know ye what myself, the Poet,
 Would the most rejoice and cheer ?
 If I dared to sing, and utter,
 That which no one wants to hear.
 [*The Night and Churchyard Poets excuse themselves,*
  because they have just become engaged in a most
  interesting conversation with a newly-arisen vam-
  pire, and therefrom a new school of poetry may
  possibly be developed. The HERALD *is obliged to*
  accept their excuses, and meanwhile calls forth the
  Grecian Mythology, which, even in modern masks,
  loses neither its character nor its power to charm.

THE GRACES.[14]

AGLAIA. Life we bless with graces living ;
 So be graceful in your giving !
HEGEMONE. Graceful be in your receival ;
 Wish attained is sweet retrieval.
EUPHROSYNE. And in days serene and spacious,
 In your thanks be chiefly gracious !

THE PARCÆ.[15]

ATROPOS. I, the eldest, to the spinning
 Have received the invitation ;
 When the thread of Life 's beginning
 There is need of meditation.

 Finest flax I winnow featly
 That your thread be softly given ;

Draw it through my fingers neatly,
Make it thin, and smooth, and even.

If too wanton your endeavour,
Grasping here of joy each token,
Think the thread won't stretch for ever !
Have a care ! it might be broken.

CLOTHO. Know that, given to me for wearing,
Lately were the shears supplied ;
Since men were not by the bearing
Of our eldest edified.

Useless webs she long untangled,
Dragging them to air and light ;
Dreams of fortune, hope-bespangled,
Clipped and buried out of sight.

Also I, in ignorance idle,
Made mistakes in younger years,
But to-day, myself to bridle,
In their sheath I stick the shears.

Thus restrained in proper measure,
Favour I this cheerful place :
You these hours of liberal pleasure
Use at will, and run your race !

LACHESIS. In my hands, the only skilful,
Was the ordered twisting placed ;
Active are my ways, not wilful,
Erring not through over-haste.

Threads are coming, threads are reeling ;
In its course I each restrain :
None, from off the circle wheeling,
Fails to fit within the skein.

If I once regardless gadded,
For the world my hopes were vain :
Hours are counted, years are added,
And the weaver takes the chain.

HERALD. You would not recognize who now appear,
Though ne'er so learned you were in ancient writing;
To look at them, in evil so delighting,
You'd call them worthy guests, and welcome here.

They are THE FURIES,[16] no one will believe us,—
Fair, well-proportioned, friendly, young in years:
But make acquaintance, and straightway appears
How snake-like are such doves to wound, deceive us.

Though they are spiteful, yet on this occasion,
When every fool exults in all his blame,
They also do not crave angelic fame,
But own themselves the torments of the nation.

ALECTO. What good of that, for you will trust us still !—
Each of us young and fair, a wheedling kitten,
Hath one of you a girl with whom he's smitten,
We'll rub and softly stroke his ears, until

'T is safe to tell him, spite of all his loathing,
That she has also this and the other flame,—
A blockhead he, or humpbacked, squint and lame,
And if betrothed to him, she's good-for-nothing !

We're skilled, as well, the bride to vex and sever:
Why scarce a week ago, her very lover
Contemptuous things *to her* was saying of her !
Though they make up, there's something rankles ever.

MEGÆRA. That's a mere jest ! For, let them once be
                married,
I go to work, and can, in every case,
The fairest bliss by wilful whims displace.
Man has his various moods, the hours are varied,

And, holding the Desired that once did charm him,
Each for the More-desired, a yearning fool,
Leaves the best fortune, use has rendered cool:
He flies the sun, and seeks the frost to warm him.

Of ills for all I understand the brewing,
And here Asmodi as my follower lead,[17]
To scatter mischief at the proper need,
And send the human race, in pairs, to ruin.

    TISIPHONE. Steel and poison I, not malice,
        Mix and sharpen for the traitor :
        Lov'st thou others, soon or later,
        Ruin pours for thee the chalice.

        Through the moment's sweet libation
        See the gall and wormwood stealing !
        Here no bargaining, no dealing !
        Like the act and retaliation.

        No one babble of forgiving !
        To the rocks I cry : *Revenge !* is
        Echo's answer : he who changes
        Shall be missed among the living.

    HERALD. Do me the favour, now, to stand aside,
For that which comes is not to you allied.
You see a mountain pressing through the throng,[19]
The flanks with brilliant housings grandly hung,
A head with tusks, a snaky trunk below,—
A mystery, yet I the key will show.
A delicate woman sits upon his neck,
And with a wand persuades him to her beck ;
The other, throned aloft, superb to see,
Stands in a glory, dazzling, blinding me.
Beside him walk two dames in chains ; one fearful
And sore depressed, the other glad and cheerful.
One longs for freedom and one feels she 's free :
Let each declare us who she be !

    FEAR. Smoky torches, lamps are gleaming
        Through the festal's wildering train ;
        Ah ! amid these faces scheming
        I am fastened by my chain.

        Off, ridiculously merry !
        I mistrust your grinning spite :
        Each relentless adversary
        Presses nearer in the night.

Friend would here as foe waylay me,
But I know the masking shapes ;
Yonder 's one that wished to slay me,—
Now, discovered, he escapes.

From the world I fain would wander
Through whatever gate I find ;
But perdition threatens yonder,
And the horror holds my mind.

HOPE. Good my sisters, I salute you !
Though to-day already suit you
Masquerading thus demurely,
Yet I know your purpose surely
To reveal yourselves to-morrow.
And if we, by torches lighted,
Fail to feel a special pleasure,
Yet in days of cheerful leisure,
At our will, delight we 'll borrow,
Or alone or disunited
Free through fairest pastures ranging,
Rest and action interchanging,
And in life no cares that fetter
Naught forego, but strive for better.
Welcome guests are all around us,
Let us mingle with the rest !
Surely, what is best hath found us,
Or we 'll somewhere find the best.

PRUDENCE. Two of human foes, the greatest,
Fear and Hope, I bind the faster,
Thus to save you at the latest :
Clear the way for me, their master.

I conduct the live colossus,
Turret-crowned with weighty masses ;
And unweariedly he crosses,
Step by step, the steepest passes.

But aloft the goddess planted,
With her broad and ready pinions,

Turns to spy where gain is granted
Everywhere in Man's dominions.

Round her all is bright and glorious ;
Splendour streams on all her courses :
Victory is she—the victorious
Goddess of all active forces.

ZOÏLO-THERSITES.[19] Ho ! ho ! I 've hit the time of day.
You 're all together bad, I say !
But what appeared my goal to me
Is she up there, Dame Victory.
She, with her snowy wings spread out,
Thinks she 's an eagle, past a doubt ;
And, wheresoever she may stir,
That land and folk belong to her ;
But when a famous thing is done
I straightway put my harness on,
To lift the low, the high upset,
The bent to straighten, bend the straight,—
That, only, gives my heart a glow,
And on this earth I 'll have it so.

HERALD. Then take, thou beggar-cur, the blow,
This magic baton's stroke of skill !—
So, twist and wriggle at thy will !
See how the double dwarfish ape
Rolls to a hideous ball in shape !—
A marvel ! 'T is an egg we view ;
It puffs itself and cracks in two :
A pair of twins come forth to-day,
The Adder and the Bat are they.
Forth in the dust one winds and creeps ;
One darkly round the ceiling sweeps.
They haste to join in company :
The third therein I would not be !

MURMURS. Come ! the dance is yonder gay.—
No ! I would I were away.—
Feel'st thou how the phantom race
Flits about us in this place ?—
Something whizzes past my hair.—
Round my feet I saw it fare.—

None of us are injured, though.—
But we all are frightened so.—
Wholly spoiled is now the fun.—
Which the vermin wanted done.

HERALD. Since, as Herald, I am aiding
At your merry masquerading,
At the gate I'm watching, fearful
Lest within your revels cheerful
Something slips of evil savour ;
And I neither shrink nor waver.
Yet, I fear, the airy spectres
Enter, baffling all detectors,
And from goblins that deceive you
I'm unable to relieve you.
First, the dwarf became suspicious ;
Now a mightier pageant issues
Yonder, and it is my duty
To explain those forms of beauty :
But the thing I comprehend not,
How can I its meaning mention ?
Help me to its comprehension !
Through the crowd you see it wend not ?
Lo ! a four-horse chariot wondrous,
Hither drawn, the tumult sunders ;
Yet the crowd seems not to share in 't—
Nowhere is a crush apparent.
Coloured lights, in distance dimmer,
Motley stars around it shimmer ;
Magic-lantern-like they glimmer.
On it storms, as to assault.
Clear the way ! I shudder !

BOY CHARIOTEER.   Halt !
Steeds, restrain the eager pinion,
Own the bridle's old dominion,
Check yourselves, as I desire you,
Sweep away, when I inspire you !—
Honour we these festal spaces !
See, the fast increasing faces,
Circles, full of admiration !
Herald, come ! and in thy fashion,

Ere we take from here our glories,
Name us, and describe and show us !
For we 're naught but allegories,
Therefore 't is thy place to know us.

HERALD. No, thy name from me is hidden,—
I could describe thee, were I bidden.

BOY CHARIOTEER. Try it !

HERALD.   Granted, at the start,
Young and beautiful thou art,—
A half-grown boy ; and yet the woman-nature
Would rather see thee in completed stature.
To me thou seem'st a future fickle wooer,
Changing the old betrayed love for a newer.

BOY CHARIOTEER. Go on !   So far, 't is very fine :
Make the enigma's gay solution thine !

HERALD. Black lightning of the eyes, the dark locks
glowing,[20]
Yet bright with jewelled anadem,
And light thy robe as flower on stem,
From shoulder unto buskin flowing
With tinsel-braid and purple hem !
One for a maiden might surmise thee,
Yet, good or ill, as it might be,
The maids, e'en now, would take and prize thee :
They 'd teach thee soon thy A B C.

BOY CHARIOTEER. And he, who like a splendid vision,
Sits proudly on the chariot's throne ?

HERALD. He seems a king, of mien Elysian ;
Blest those, who may his favour own !
No more has he to earn or capture ;
His glance detects where aught 's amiss,
And to bestow his perfect rapture
Is more than ownership and bliss.

BOY CHARIOTEER. Thou darest not at this point desist
Describe him fully, I insist !

HERALD. But undescribed is Dignity,
The healthy, full-moon face I see,
The ample mouth, the cheeks that fresher
Shine out beneath his turban's pressure,

Rich comfort in the robe he's wearing,—
What shall I say of such a bearing?
He seems, as ruler, known to me.

BOY CHARIOTEER. Plutus, the God of Wealth, is he
He hither comes in proud attire ;
Much doth the Emperor him desire.

HERALD. Of thee the *What* and *How* declare to me !

BOY CHARIOTEER. I am Profusion, I am Poesy.
The Poet I, whose perfect crown is sent
When he his own best goods hath freely spent.
Yet, rich in mine unmeasured pelf,
Like Plutus I esteem myself :
I prank and cheer his festal show
And whatsoe'er he lacks bestow.

HERALD. Fresh charm to thee thy brag imparts,
But let us now behold thine arts !

BOY CHARIOTEER. Just see me fillip with my fingers !
What brilliance round the chariot lingers,
And there a string of pearls appears !
    [*continuing to fillip and snap his fingers in all
      directions :*
Take golden spangles for neck and ears,
Combs, and diadems free of flaw,
And jewelled rings as ne'er ye saw !
I also scatter flamelets bright,
Awaiting where they may ignite.

HERALD. How strives the crowd with eager longing,
Almost upon the giver thronging !
As in a dream he snaps the toys ;
All catch and snatch with crush and noise.
But now new tricks have I detected :
What each has zealously collected
His trouble doth but poorly pay ;
The gifts take wings and fly away.
The pearls are loosened from their band,
And beetles crawl within his hand ;
He shakes them off, and then instead,
Poor dolt, they hum around his head !
The others find their solid things
Are butterflies with gaudy wings.

N

How much the scamp to promise seems,
And only gives what golden gleams !
BOY CHARIOTEER. Masks to announce, I grant, thou'rt
    worthy ;
But 'neath the shell of Being to bestir thee
Is not a herald's courtly task :
A sharper sight for that we ask.
Yet every quarrel I evade ;
To thee, my Chief, be speech and question made !
                      [Turning to PLUTUS.
Didst thou not unto me confide
The tempest of the steeds I guide ?
Canst thou not on my guidance reckon ?
Am I not there, where thou dost beckon ?
And have I not, on pinions boldest,
Conquered for thee the palm thou holdest ?
When in thy battles I have aided,
I ever have been fortunate ;
Thy brow when laurels decorate,
Have I not them with hand and fancy braided ? "
PLUTUS. If there be need that I bear witness now,
I'm glad to say : soul of my soul art thou !
Thine acts are always to my mind,
And thou the richer art, I find.
Thy service to reward, I hold
The green bough higher than my crowns of gold.
To all a true word spoken be :
Dear Son, I much delight in thee.
BOY CHARIOTEER (*to the Crowd*). The greatest gifts my
    hand flings out,
See ! I have scattered round about.
On divers heads there glows the tongue
Of flame which I upon them flung,—
Leaps back and forth among the shapes,
On this remains, from that escapes,
But very seldom upward streams
In transient flush of mellow beams ;
And unto many, ere they mark,
It is extinct and leaves them dark.
CHATTER OF WOMEN. Upon the chariot that man

Is certainly a charlatan :
There, perched behind, the clown is seen,
From thirst and hunger grown so lean
As one ne'er saw him ; if you'd pinch,
He has n't flesh to feel and flinch.

THE STARVELING. Disgusting women, off ! I know
That when I come, you'd have me go.
When woman fed her own hearth-flame,
Then *Avaritia* was my name ;[23]
Then throve the household fresh and green,
For naught went out and much came in.
To chest and press I gave good heed,
And that you'd call a vice, indeed !
But since in later years, the fact is,
Economy the wife won't practise,
And, like the host of spendthrift scholars,
Has more desires than she has dollars,
The husband much discomfort brooks,
For there are debts where'er he looks.
She spends what spoil she may recover
Upon her body, or her lover ;
In luxury eats, and to excess
Drinks with the flirts that round her press ;
For me that raises money's price ;
Male is my gender, Avarice !

LEADER OF THE WOMEN. With dragons, mean may be
the dragon ;
It's all, at best, but lying stuff !
He comes, the men to spur and egg on,
And now they 're troublesome enough.

CROWD OF WOMEN. The scarecrow ! Knock him from
the waggon !
What means the fag, to threaten here ?
As if his ugly face we'd fear !
Of wood and pasteboard is each dragon :
Come on—his words shall cost him dear !

HERALD. Now, by my wand ! Be still—let none stir !
Yet for my help there's scarcely need ;
See how each grim and grisly monster,
Clearing the space around with speed,

Unfolds his fourfold wings of dread !
The dragons shake themselves in anger,
With flaming throats, and scaly clangour;
The place is clear, the crowd has fled.

[PLUTUS *descends from the chariot.*

HERALD. How kingly comes he from above !
Ile beckons, and the dragons move ;
Then from the chariot bring the chest
With gold, and Avarice thereon.
See, at his feet the load they rest !
A marvel 'tis, how it was done.

PLUTUS (*to the* CHARIOTEER). Now thou hast left the
onerous burden here,
Thou'rt wholly free : away to thine own sphere !
Here it is not ! Confused and wild, to-day,
Distorted pictures press around our way.
Where clear thy gaze in sweet serenity,
Owning thyself, confiding but in thee,
Thither, where Good and Beauty are unfurled,
To Solitude !—and there create thy world !

BOY CHARIOTEER. Thus, as an envoy, am I worthy of
thee ;
Thus, as my next of kindred, do I love thee.
Where thou art, is abundance ; where I go
Each sees a splendid profit round him grow.
In inconsistent life each often wavers,
Whether to seek from thee, or me, the favours.
Thy followers may be indolent, 'tis true ;
Who follows me, has always work to do.
My deeds are never secret and concealed ;
I only breathe, and I'm at once reveal:d.
Farewell, then ! Thou the bliss hast granted me ;
But whisper low, and I return to thee !

[*Exit, as he came.*

PLUTUS 'Tis time, now to unchain the precious metals !
The padlocks with the herald's wand I smite :
The chest is opened : look ! from iron kettles
It pours like golden blood before your sight.
It boils, and threatens to devour, as fuel,
Melting them, crown and ring and chain and jewel !

ALTERNATE CRIES OF THE CROWD. See here, and there !
     they boil and swim ;
     The chest is filling to the brim !—
     Vessels of gold are filling there,
     And minted rolls are turning there.
     And ducats jingle as they jump !—
     O, how my heart begins to thump !—
     All my desire I see, and more.
     They're rolling now along the floor.—
     'Tis offered you : don't be a dunce,
     Stoop only, and be rich at once !—
     Then, quick as lightning we, the rest,
     Will take possession of the chest.

HERALD. What ails ye, fools ? What mean ye all !
     'Tis but a joke of Carnival.
     To-night be your desires controlled ;
     Think you we'd give you goods and gold ?
     Why, in this game there come to view
     Too many counters even, for you.
     A pleasant cheat, ye dolts ! forsooth
     You take at once for naked truth.
     What's truth to you ? Illusion bare
     Surrounds and rules you everywhere.
     Thou Plutus-mask, Chief unrevealed,
     Drive thou this people from the field !

PLUTUS. Thy wand thereto is fit and free ;
     Lend it a little while to me !
     I dip it in the fiery brew,—
     Look out, ye maskers ! all of you.
     It shines, and snaps, and sparkles throws ;
     The burning wand already glows.
     Who crowdeth on, too near to me,
     Is burned and scorched relentlessly.—
     And now my circuit I'll commence.

CRIES AND CROWDING. Woe's me ! We're lost—there's
     no defence !—
     Let each one fly, if fly he can !—
     Back ! clear the way, you hindmost man !—
     It sparkles fiercely in mine eyes.—
     The burning wand upon me lies.—

We all are lost, we all are lost!—
Back, back ! ye maskers, jammed and tossed !—
Back, senseless crowd, away from there !—
O, had I wings, I'd take the air.

PLUTUS. Now is the circle crowded back,
And none, I think, scorched very black.
The throng retires,
Scared by the fires.
As guaranty for ordered law,
A ring invisible I draw.

HERALD. A noble work is thine, to-night :
I thank thy wisdom and thy might.

PLUTUS. Preserve thy patience, noble friend,
For many tumults yet impend.

AVARICE. Thus, if one pleases, pleasantly
May one survey this circle stately ;
For, ever foremost, crowd the women greatly,
If aught to stare at, or to taste, there be.
Not yet entirely rusty are my senses !
A woman fair is always fair to me :
And since, to-day, it makes me no expenses,
We'll go a courting confidently.
But in a place so populate
All words to every ear don't penetrate ;
So, wisely I attempt, and hope success,
Myself by pantomime distinctly to express.
Hand, foot, and gesture will not quite suffice,
So I employ a jocular device.
Like clay will I the gold manipulate ;
One may transform it into any state.

HERALD. What will the lean fool do ? Has he,
So dry a starveling, humour ? See,
He kneads the gold as it were dough !
Beneath his hands 'tis soft ; yet, though
He roll and squeeze it, for his pains
Disfigured still the stuff remains.
He turns to the women there, and they
All scream, and try to get away,
With gestures of disgust and loathing :
The ready rascal stops at nothing.

I fear he takes delight to see
He has offended decency.
I dare not silently endure it :
Give me my wand, that I may cure it !

PLUTUS. The danger from without he does not see :
Let him alone ; his Fool's-hour fast is waning.
There'll be no space for his mad pranks remaining ;
Mighty is Law, mightier Necessity.

TUMULT AND SONG. The savage hosts, with shout and
hail,
From mountain-height and forest-vale
Come, irresistibly as Fate :
Their mighty Pan they celebrate.
They know, forsooth, what none can guess,
And in the empty circle press.

PLUTUS. I know you well, and your illustrious Pan !
Boldly together you've performed your plan.
Full well I know what every one does not,
And clear for you, as duty bids, the spot.
Be Fortune still her favour lending !
The strangest things may here be bred :
They know not whitherward they're wending,
Because they have not looked ahead.

SAVAGE SONG. Furbished people, tinsel-stuff !
They're coming rude, they're coming rough ;
In mighty leap, in wildest race,
Coarse and strong they take their place.

FAUNS. Fauns, pair on pair,
Come dancing down,
With oaken crown
On crispy hair ;
The fine and pointed ear is seen,
Leaf-like, the clustering curls between:
A stubby nose, face broad and flat,
The women don't object to that ;
For when his paw holds forth the Faun,
The fairest to the dance is drawn.

SATYR. See now, behind, the Satyr skip,
With foot of goat, lean leg and hip,—
Lean and sinewy must they be :

For, chamois-like, on mountains he
Loveth to stand or scamper free.
Then, strong in freedom of the skies
Child, wife, and man doth he despise,
Who, deep in the valley's smoke and steam
That they live also, snugly dream ;
While, pure and undisturbed, alone
The upper world is all his own.

GNOMES. [24] The little crowd comes tripping there :
They don't associate pair by pair.
In mossy garb, with lantern bright,
They move commingling, brisk and light,
Each working on his separate ground,
Like firefly-emmets swarming round ;
And press and gather here and there,
Always industrious everywhere.
With the " Good People " kin we own ;
As surgeons of the rocks we're known.
Cupping the mountains, bleeding them
From fullest veins, depleting them
Of store of metals, which we pile,
And merrily greet : " Good cheer ! " the while.
Well-meant the words, believe us, then !
We are the friends of all good men.
Yet we the stores of gold unseal
That men may pander, pimp, and steal ;
Nor iron shall fail his haughty hand
Who universal murder planned :
And who these three Commandments breaks
But little heed o' the others takes.
For that we're not responsible :
We're patient—be you, too, as well !

GIANTS. The wild men of the woods they're named,
And in the Hartz are known and famed
In naked nature's ancient might
They come, each one a giant wight,
With fir-tree trunk in brawny hand,
Around the loins a puffy band,
The merest apron of leaf and bough —
The Pope hath no such guards, I trow.

N**ymphs** **in** **chorus.** (*They surround the great* Pan.) He
  comes ! We scan
   The world's great All,
   Whose part doth fall
   To mighty Pan.
  Ye gayest ones, advance to him,
  Your maddest measures dance to him!
  Since serious and kind is he,
  He wills that we should joyous be.
  Under the blue, o'er-vaulting roof,
  Ever he seemeth slumber-proof ;
  Yet murmurs of the brooks he knows,
  And soft airs lull him to repose.
  At midday sleeping, o'er his brow
  The leaf is moveless on the bough :
  Of healthy buds the balsam there
  Pervades the still, suspended air :
  The nymph no longer dares to leap,
  And where she stands, she falls asleep.
  But when, all unexpected, he
  Maketh his voice heard terribly,
  Like rattling thunder, roar of wave,
  Then each one seeks himself to save ;
  The serried ranks disperse in fright,
  The hero trembles in the fight.
  Then honour to whom the honour is due,
  And hail to him who led us to you !
D**eputation** **of** G**nomes** (*to the great* Pan). When the
  rich possession, shining
   Through the rocks in thread and vein,
   To the skilful wand's divining
   Shows its labyrinthine chain,

   We in vaults and caverns spacious,
   Troglodytes, contented bide ;
   While in purest daylight, gracious
   Thou the treasures dost divide.

   Now we see, wilt thou believe us,
   Here a wondrous fountain run

> Promising with ease to give us
> What was hardly to be won.
>
> Lo! It waits for thy attaining:
> Then be moved to break the spell!
> All the wealth which thou art gaining
> Profits all the world as well.

PLUTUS (*to the* HERALD). We, in the highest sense, must
    be collected,
> And let what *may* come, come, though unexpected.
> Thy courage has not yet been counted short:
> The fearful thing we now shall see will try it;
> The world and History will both deny it,
> So write it faithfully in thy report!

HERALD (*grasping the wand which* PLUTUS *holds in his
    hand*). The dwarfs conduct the great Pan nigher,
> Yet gently, to the fount of fire.
> It bubbles from the throat profound,
> Then sinks, retreating to the ground,
> And dark the open crater shows;
> And then again it boils and glows.
> Great Pan in cheerful mood stands by,
> Rejoiced the wondrous things to spy,
> And right and left the foam-pearls fly.
> How can he in the cheat confide?
> He bends and stoops, to look inside.—
> But now, behold! his beard falls in:
> Whose is that smoothly-shaven chin?
> His hand conceals it from our sight.
> What follows is a luckless plight;
> The beard, on fire, flies back to smite
> His wreath and head and breast with flame:
> To pain is turned the merry game.
> They haste to quench the fire, but none
> The swiftly-kindling flames can shun,
> That flash and dart on other heads
> Till wide the conflagration spreads:
> Wrapped in the element, in turn
> The masking groups take fire and burn.

But hark ! what news is bruited here
From mouth to mouth, from ear to ear ?
O evermore ill-fated night,
That brings to us such woe and blight !
To-morrow will proclaim to all
What no one wishes to befall,
For everywhere the cry I hear :
" The Emperor suffers pain severe ! "
O were the proclamation wrong !
The Emperor burns and all his throng.
Accurst be they who him misled,
With resinous twigs on breast and head,
To rave and bellow hither so,
To general, fatal overthrow.
O Youth ! O Youth ! wilt never thou
Limit thy draught of joy, in season ?—
O Majesty, wilt never thou,
Omnipotent, direct with reason ?
The mimic woods enkindled are ;
The pointed tongues lick upward far
To where the rafters interlace :
A fiery doom hangs o'er the place.
Our cup of misery overflows,
For who shall save us no one knows,
The ash-heap of a night shall hide,
To-morrow, this imperial pride.

PLUTUS.   Terror is enough created ;
Now be help inaugurated !
Smite, thou hallowed wand, and make
Earth beneath thee peal and quake !
Thou, the spacious breadth of air,
Cooling vapours breathe and bear !
Hither speed, around us growing,
Misty films and belts o'erflowing,
And the fiery tumult tame !
Trickle, whisper, clouds, be crisper,
Roll in masses, softly drenching,
Mantling everywhere, and quenching !
Ye, the moist, the broadly bright'ning.

Change to harmless summer lightning
All this empty sport of flame !—
When by spirits we're molested,
Then be Magic manifested.

————————

IV.

PLEASURE GARDEN.

THE MORNING SUN.

The EMPEROR, *his Court, Gentlemen and Ladies :* FAUST, MEPHISTOPHELES, *becomingly, according to the mode, not showily dressed : both kneel.*

FAUST. Sire, pardon'st thou the jugglery of flame ?
EMPEROR (*beckoning him to rise*). I wish more exhibitions
        of the same.
A sudden stood I in a glowing sphere ;
It almost seemed as if I Pluto were.
There lay, like night, with little fires besprent,
A rocky bottom.   Out of many a vent,
Whirling, a thousand savage flames ascended,
Till in a single vault their streamers blended.
The tongues even to the highest dome were shot,
That ever was, and ever then was not.
Through the far space of spiral shafts of flame
The long processions of the people came ;
Crowding, till all the circle was o'errun,
They did me homage, as they've ever done.
Some from my Court I knew : to speak with candour,
A Prince I seemed o'er many a salamander.
    MEPHIS. That art thou, Sire !   Because each element
Fully accepts thy Majesty's intent.
Obedient Fire is tested now by thee :
Where wildest heaving, leap into the Sea,
And scarce the pearly floor thy foot shall tread,
A grand rotunda rises o'er thy head :

Thou seest the green, translucent billows swelling,
With purple edge, for thy delightful dwelling,
Round thee, the central point.   Walk thou at will,
The liquid palaces go with thee still !
The very walls rejoice in life, disporting
In arrowy flight, in chasing and consorting :
Sea-marvels crowd around the glory new and fair,
Shoot from all sides, yet none can enter there.
There gorgeous dragons, golden-armoured, float ;
There gapes the shark, thou laughest in his throat.
However much this Court thy pride may please,
Yet hast thou never seen such throngs as these.
Nor from the loveliest shalt thou long be parted ;
The curious Nereids come, the wild, shy-hearted,
To thy bright dwelling in the endless waters,—
Timid and sly, as fish the youngest daughters,
The elder cunning : Thetis hears the news
And will, at once, her second Peleus choose.
The seat, then, on Olympus high and free—

   EMPEROR. The spaces of the air I leave to thee :
One all too early must ascend that throne.

   MEPHIS. And Earth, high Prince ! already is thine own.

   EMPEROR. What fortune brought thee here, for our
      delights,
Directly from the One and Thousand Nights ?
If thou like Scheherazade art rich in stories,
My favour shall insure thee higher glories.
Be ready always, when your world of day,
As often haps, disgusts me every way !

   LORD HIGH STEWARD (*enters hastily*). Highness Serene, I
      never dared expect
To trumpet forth a fortune so select
As this, supremely blessing me,
Which I announce with joy to thee :
Reckoning on reckoning's balanced squarely ;
The usurer's claws are blunted rarely ;
I'm from my hellish worry free :
Things can't in Heaven more cheerful be.

   GENERAL-IN-CHIEF (*follows hastily*). Arrears of pay are
      settled duly,

The army is enlisted newly ;
The trooper's blood is all alive,
The landlords and the wenches thrive.

    EMPEROR. How breathe your breasts in broader spaces !
How cheerful are your furrowed faces !
How ye advance with nimble speed !

      TREASURER (*appearing*). Ask these, 'tis they have done
        the deed !

      FAUST. It is the Chancellor's place the matter to present.

      CHANCELLOR (*who comes forward slowly*). In my old days
        I'm blest, and most content.
So hear and see the fortune-freighted leaf
Which has transformed to happiness our grief.   [*He reads.*
"To all to whom this cometh, be it known ;
A thousand crowns in worth this note doth own.
It to secure, as certain pledge, shall stand
All buried treasure in the Emperor's land :
And 'tis decreed, perfecting thus the scheme,
The treasure, soon as raised, shall this redeem."

    EMPEROR. A most enormous cheat—a crime, I fear !
Who forged the Emperor's sign-manual here ?
Has there not been a punishment condign ?

      TREASURER. Remember ! Thou the note didst undersign ;
Last night, indeed. Thou stood'st as mighty Pan,
And thus the Chancellor's speech, before thee, ran :
" Grant to thyself the festal pleasure, then
The People's good—a few strokes of the pen ! "
These didst thou give : they were, ere night retreated,
By skilful conjurers thousandfold repeated ;
And, that a like advantage all might claim,
We stamped at once the series with thy name :
Tens, Thirties, Fifties, Hundreds, are prepared.
Thou canst not think how well the folk have fared.
Behold thy town, half-dead once, and decaying,
How all, alive, enjoying life, are straying !
Although thy name long since the world made glad,
Such currency as now it never had.
No longer needs the alphabet thy nation,
For in this sign each findeth his salvation.

    EMPEROR. And with my people does it pass for gold ?

For pay in court and camp, the notes they hold?
Then I must yield, although the thing's amazing.

LORD HIGH STEWARD. 'Twas scattered everywhere, like
  wild-fire blazing,
As currency, and none its course may stop.
A crowd surrounds each money-changer's shop,
And every note is there accepted duly
For gold and silver's worth—with discount, truly.
Thence it is spread to landlords, butchers, bakers:
One half the people feast as pleasure-takers;
In raiment new the others proudly go,—
The tradesmen cut their cloth, the tailors sew,
The crowd "The Emperor's health!" in cellars wishes,
Midst cooking, roasting, rattling of the dishes.

MEPHIS. If one along the lonely terrace stray,
He sees the lady, in superb array,
With brilliant peacock-fan, before one eye;
A note she looks for, as she simpers by,
And readier than by wit or eloquence
Before Love's favour falls the last defence.
One is not plagued his purse or sack to carry:
Such notes one lightly in his bosom bears,
Or them with fond epistles neatly pairs:
The priest devoutly in his breviary
Bears his: the soldier would more freely trip,
And lightens thus the girdle round his hip.
Your Majesty will pardon, if my language
Seems as it might the lofty work disparage.

FAUST. The overplus of wealth, in torpor bound,
Which in thy lands lies buried in the ground,
Is all unused; nor boldest thought can measure
The narrowest boundaries of such a treasure.
Imagination, in its highest flight,
Exerts itself, but cannot grasp it quite;
Yet minds, that dare explore the secrets soundless,
In boundless things possess a faith that's boundless.

MEPHIS. Such paper, stead of gold and jewelry,
So handy is—one knows one's property:
One has no need of bargains or exchanges,
But drinks of love or wine, as fancy ranges.

If one needs coin, the brokers ready stand,
And if it fail, one digs awhile the land.
Goblet and chain one then at auction sells,
And paper, liquidated thus, compels
The shame of doubters and their scornful wit.
The people wish naught else; they're used to it:
From this time forth, your borders, far and wide,
With jewels, gold, and paper are supplied.

EMPEROR. You've given our empire this prosperity;
The pay, then, equal to the service be!
The soil intrusted to your keeping, shall you
The best custodians be, to guard its value.
You know the hoards, well-kept, of all the land,
And when men dig, 'tis you must give command.
Unite then now, ye masters of our treasure,
This, your new dignity, to wear with pleasure,
And bring the Upper World, erewhile asunder,
In happiest conjunction with the Under!

TREASURER. No further strife shall shake our joint
　　position;
I like to have as partner the magician.　　[Exit, with FAUST.

EMPEROR. Man after man, the Court will I endow:
Let each confess for what he'll spend, and how!

PAGE (receiving). I'll lead a jolly life, enjoy good cheer.

A SECOND (the same). I'll buy at once some trinkets for
　　my dear.

CHAMBERLAIN (accepting). Wines twice as good shall down
　　my throat go trickling.

A SECOND (the same). I feel the dice within my pockets
　　tickling.

KNIGHT BANNERET (reflectively). My lands and castle
　　shall be free of debt.

ANOTHER (the same). I'll add to other wealth the wealth I
　　get.

EMPEROR. I hoped the gifts to bolder deeds would beckon;
But he who knows you, knows whereon to reckon.
I see that, spite of all this treasure-burst,
You stay exactly as you were at first.

FOOL (approaching). You scatter favours: grant me also
　　some!

EMPEROR. Thou'rt come to life ?   'Twould go at once for
   rum.

FOOL. The magic leaves ! I don't quite comprehend.

EMPEROR. That I believe ; for them thou'lt badly spend.

FOOL. There others drop : I don't know what to do.

EMPEROR. Just pick them up ! they fall to thy share, too.
                                                   [*Exit.*

FOOL. Five thousand crowns are mine?   How unexpected!

MEPHIS. Two-leggèd wine-skin, art thou resurrected ?

FOOL. Much luck I've had, but like this never yet.

MEPHIS. Thou'rt so rejoiced, it puts thee in a sweat.

FOOL. But look at this, is't money's-worth, indeed ?

MEPHIS. 'Twill bring thee what thy throat and belly need.

FOOL. And cattle can I buy, and house and land ?

MEPHIS. Of course ! just make an offer once, off-hand !

FOOL. Castle and wood, and chase, and fishing ?

MEPHIS.   All !
   I'd like upon Your Worship then to call.

FOOL. To-night as landed owner I shall sit.   [*Exit.*

MEPHIS (*solus*). Who now will doubt that this our Fool
   has wit ?

V.

A GLOOMY GALLERY.

FAUST. MEPHISTOPHELES.

MEPHIS. What wilt thou with me in this gloomy gallery ?
Is there not still enough of sport
There, in the crowded, motley Court,—
Not chance for tricks, and fun, and raillery ?

   FAUST. Don't tell me that !—In our old days the fun
   of it
Didst thou wear out, and I'll have none of it.
Thy wandering here and there is planned
Just to evade what I demand.

                                       9

But I'm tormented something to obtain ;
The Marshal drives me, and the Chamberlain.
The Emperor orders, he will instantly
Helen and Paris here before him see,—
The model forms of Man and Woman, wearing,
Distinctly shown, their ancient shape and bearing.
Now to the work !   I dare not break my word.

   MEPHIS. So thoughtlessly to promise was absurd.

   FAUST. Thou hast not, comrade, well reflected
What comes of having used thy powers :
We've made him rich ; 'tis now expected
That we amuse his idle hours.

   MEPHIS. Thou deem'st the thing is quickly fixed ;
Here before steeper ways we're standing ;
With strangest spheres would'st thou be mixed,
And, sinful, addest new debts to the old,—
Think'st Helen will respond to thy commanding
As freely as the paper-ghosts of gold !
With witches'-riches and with spectre-pictures,
And changeling-dwarfs, I'll give no cause for strictures ;
But Devil's darlings, though you may not scold 'em,
You cannot quite as heroines behold 'em.

   FAUST. The old hand-organ still I hear thee play !
From thee one always gets uncertain sense,
The father, thou, of all impediments :
For every means thou askest added pay.
A little muttering, and the thing takes place ;
Ere one can turn, beside us here her shade is.

   MEPHIS. I've no concern with the old heathen race ;
They house within their special Hades.[25]
Yet there's a way.

   FAUST. Speak, nor delay thy history !

   MEPHIS. Unwilling, I reveal a loftier mystery.—
In solitude are throned the Goddesses,
No space around them, Place and Time still less ;
Only to speak of them embarrasses.
They are THE MOTHERS ![26]

   FAUST (*terrified*). Mothers !

   MEPHIS. Hast thou dread ?

   FAUST. The Mothers ! Mothers ! —a strange word is said.

MEPHIS. It is so. Goddesses, unknown to ye,
The Mortals,—named by us unwillingly.
Delve in the deepest depths must thou, to reach them :
'Tis thine own fault that we for help beseech them.

FAUST. Where is the way ?

MEPHIS. No way !—To the Unreachable,
Ne'er to be trodden ! A way to the Unbeseechable,
Never to be besought ! Art thou prepared ?
There are no locks, no latches to be lifted ;
Through endless solitudes shalt thou be drifted.
Hast thou through solitudes and deserts fared ?

FAUST. I think 'twere best to spare such speeches ;
They smell too strongly of the witches,
Of cheats that long ago insnared.
Have I not known all earthly vanities ?
Learned the inane, and taught inanities ?
When as I felt I spake, with sense as guide,
The contradiction doubly shrill replied ;
Enforced by odious tricks, have I not fled
To solitudes and wildernesses dread,
And that I might not live alone, unheeded,
Myself at last unto the Devil deeded !

MEPHIS. And hadst thou swum to farthest verge of ocean,
And there the boundless space beheld,
Still hadst thou seen wave after wave in motion,
Even though impending doom thy fear compelled.
Thou hadst seen something,—in the beryl dim
Of peace-lulled seas the sportive dolphins swim ;
Hadst seen the flying clouds, sun, moon, and star :
Naught shalt thou see in endless Void afar,—
Not hear thy footstep fall, nor meet
A stable spot to rest thy feet.

FAUST. Thou speak'st, as of all mystagogues the chief,
Who e'er brought faithful neophytes to grief ;
Only reversed :— I to the Void am sent,
That Art and power therein I may augment :
To use me like the cat is thy desire,
To scratch for thee the chestnuts from the fire.
Come on, then ! we'll explore, whate'er befall ;
In this, thy Nothing, may I find my All !

MEPHIS. I'll praise thee, ere we separate: I see
Thou knowest the Devil thoroughly.
Here, take this key ! [27]

  FAUST.   That little thing ?

  MEPHIS. Take hold of it, not undervaluing !

  FAUST. It glows, it shines,—increases in my hand !

  MEPHIS. How much 'tis worth, thou soon shalt under-
   stand.
The Key will scent the true place from all others :
Follow it down !—'twill lead thee to the Mothers.

  FAUST (*shuddering*). The Mothers ! Like a blow it strikes
  me still !
What is the word, to hear which makes me chill ?

  MEPHIS. Art thou so weak, disturbed by each new word ?
Wilt only hear what thou'st already heard ?
To wondrous things art thou so used already,
Let naught, howe'er it sound, make thee unsteady ?

  FAUST. Nathless in torpor lies no good for me ;
The chill of dread is Man's best quality.
Though from the feeling oft the world may fend us,
Deeply we feel, once smitten, the Tremendous.

  MEPHIS. Descend, then ! I could also say : Ascend !
'Twere all the same. Escape from the Created
To shapeless forms in liberated spaces !
Enjoy what long ere this was dissipated !
There whirls the press, like clouds on clouds unfolding ;
Then with stretched arm swing high the key thou'rt hold-
   ing !

  FAUST (*inspired*). Good ! grasping firmly, fresher strength
  I win :
My breast expands, let the great work begin !

  MEPHIS. At last a blazing tripod tells thee this,
That there the utterly deepest bottom is.
Its light to thee will then the Mothers show,
Some in their seats, the others stand or go,
At their own will : Formation, Transformation,
The Eternal Mind's eternal recreation,
Forms of all creatures,—there are floating free.
They'll see thee not ; for only wraiths they see.
So pluck up heart,—the danger then is great,—

Go to the tripod ere thou hesitate,
And touch it with the key!

> [FAUST, *with the key, assumes a decidedly command-*
> *ing attitude.* MEPH:S. *observing him.*

So, that is right!
It will adhere, and follow thee to light.
Composedly mounting, by thy luck upborne,
Before they notice it, shalt thou return.
When thou the tripod hither hast conveyed,
Then call the hero, heroine, from the shade,—
The first that ever such a deed perfected:
'Tis done, and thou thereto hast been selected.
For instantly, by magic process warmed,
To gods the incense-mist shall be transformed.

FAUST. What further now?

MEPHIS. Downward thy being strain!
Stamp and descend, stamping thou'lt rise again.

> [FAUST *stamps, and sinks out of sight.*

If only, by the key, he something learn!
I'm curious to see if he return.

VI.

BRILLIANTLY LIGHTED HALLS.

EMPEROR AND PRINCES. THE COURT IN MOVEMENT.

CHAMBERLAIN (*to* MEPHISTOPHELES). The spirit scene
  you've promised, still you owe us;
Our Lord's impatient; come, the phantasm show us!

LORD HIGH STEWARD. Just now His Gracious Self did
  question me:
Delay not, nor offend His Majesty!

MEPHIS. My comrade's gone to set the work in motion;
How to begin, he has the proper notion.
In secret he the charms must cull,
Must labour with a fervour tragic:

Who would that treasure lift, the Beautiful,
Requires the highest Art, the sage's Magic.

LORD HIGH STEWARD. What arts you need, is all the
same to me ;
The Emperor wills that you should ready be.

A BLONDE (*to* MEPHIS.). One word, Sir! Here you see a
visage fair,—
In sorry summer I another wear !
There sprout a hundred brown and reddish freckles,
And vex my lily skin with ugly speckles.
A cure !

MEPHIS. 'Tis pity ! Shining fair, yet smitten,—
Spotted, when May comes, like a panther-kitten !
Take frog-spawn, tongues of toads, which cohobate,
Under the full moon deftly distillate,
And, when it wanes, apply the mixture :
Next spring, the spots will be no more a fixture.

A BRUNETTE. To sponge upon you, what a crowd's
advancing !
I beg a remedy : a frozen foot
Annoys me much, in walking as in dancing ;
And awkwardly I manage to salute.

MEPHIS. A gentle kick permit, then, from my foot !

THE BRUNETTE. Well,—that might happen, when the
two are lovers.

MEPHIS. My kick a more important meaning covers :
Similia similibus, when one is sick.
The foot cures foot, each limb its hurt can palliate ;
Come near ! Take heed ! and, pray you, don't retaliate !

THE BRUNETTE (*screaming*). Oh ! Oh ! it stings ! That
was a fearful kick,
Like hoof of horse.

MEPHIS. But it has cured you, quick.
To dance whene'er you please, you now are able ;
To press your lover's foot, beneath the table.

LADY (*pressing forwards*). Make room for me ! Too great
is my affliction,
My tortures worse than those described in fiction :
His bliss, till yesterday, was in *my* glances,
But now he turns his back, and spins with *her* romances.

MEPHIS. The matter's grave, but listen unto me!
Draw near to him with gentle, soft advances;
Then take this coal and mark him stealthily
On mantle, shoulder, sleeve,—though ne'er so slight,
Yet penitent at once his heart will be.
The coal thereafter you must straightway swallow,
And let no sip of wine or water follow:
He'll sigh before your door this very night.

     THE LADY. It is not poison sure?

     MEPHIS. (*offended*).   Respect, where it is due!
To get such coals, you'd travel many a mile:
They're from the embers of a funeral pile,
The fires whereof we once more hotly blew.

     PAGE. I love, yet still am counted adolescent.

     MEPHIS. (*aside*). I know not whom to listen to, at present.
                              [*To the Page.*

Let not the younger girls thy fancies fetter;
Those well in years know how to prize thee better.—
                 [*Others crowd around him.*

Already others? 'Tis a trial, sooth!
I'll help myself, at last, with naked truth—
The worst device!—so great my misery.
O Mothers! Mothers! let but Faust go free!
                     [*Gazing around him*

The lights are burning dimly in the hall,
The Court is moving onward, one and all:
I see them march, according to degrees,
Through long arcades and distant galleries.
Now they assemble in the ample space
Of the Knights' Hall; yet hardly all find place.
The breadth of walls is hung with arras rich,
And armour gleams from every nook and niche.
Here, I should think, there needs no magic word:
The ghosts will come, and of their own accord.

VII.

HALL OF THE KNIGHTS, DIMLY LIGHTED.

The Emperor and Court have entered.

HERALD. Mine ancient office, to proclaim the action,
Is by the spirits' secret influence thwarted :
One tries in vain ; such wildering distraction
Can't be explained, or reasonably reported.
The chairs are ranged, the seats are ready all :
The Emperor sits, fronting the lofty wall,
Where, on the tapestry the battles he
Of the great era may with comfort see.
Here now are all—Prince, Court, and their belonging,
Benches on benches in the background thronging ;
And lovers, too, in these dim hours enchanted,
Beside their loved ones lovingly are planted.
And now, since all have found convenient places,
We're ready : let the spirits show their faces !   [*Trumpets.*

ASTROLOGER. Begin the Drama ! 'Tis the Sire's command :
Ye walls, be severed straightway, and expand !
Naught hinders ; magic answers our desire :
The arras flies, as shrivelled up by fire ;
The walls are split, unfolded : in the gloom
A theatre appears to be created :
By mystic light are we illuminated,
And I ascend to the proscenium.

MEPHIS. (*rising to view in the prompter's box*). I hope to
          win, as prompter, general glory ;
For prompting is the Devil's oratory.   [*To the Astrologer*
Thou know'st the tune and time the stars that lead ;
Thou wilt my whispers like a master heed.

ASTROLOGER. By power miraculous, we here behold
A massive temple of the days of old.

Like Atlas, who erewhile the heavens upbore,
The serried columns stand, an ample store :
Well may they for the weight of stone suffice,
Since two might bear a mighty edifice.

    ARCHITECT.[29] That the antique ? As fine it can't be rated ;
I'd sooner style it awkward, over-weighted.
Coarse is called noble, and unwieldy, grand :
Give me the slender shafts that soar, expand !
To lift the mind, a pointed arch may boast ;
Such architecture edifies us most.

    ASTROLOGER. Receive with reverence the star-granted
      hours ;
Let magic words bind Reason's restless powers,
But in return unbind, to circle free,
The wings of splendid, daring Phantasy !
What you have boldly wished, see now achieved !
Impossible 'tis—therefore to be believed.

        [FAUST *rises to view on the other side of the*
         proscenium.

In priestly surplice, crowned, a marvellous man,
He now fulfils what he in faith began.
With him, a tripod from the gulf comes up :
I scent the incense-odours from the cup.
He arms himself, the work to consecrate,
And henceforth it can be but fortunate.

    FAUST (*sublimely*). Ye Mothers, in your name, who set
      your throne
In boundless Space, eternally alone,
And yet companioned ! All the forms of Being,
In movement, lifeless, ye are round you seeing.
Whate'er once was, there burns and brightens free
In splendour—for 'twould fain eternal be ;
And ye allot it, with all-potent might,
To Day's pavilions and the vaults of Night.
Life seizes some, along his gracious course ;
Others arrests the bold Magician's force ;
And he, bestowing as his faith inspires,
Displays the Marvellous, that each desires.

    ASTROLOGER. The glowing key has scarcely touched the
      cup,

And lo ! through all the space, a mist rolls up :
It creeps about, and like a cloudy train,
Spreads, rounding, narrowing, parting, closed again.
And now, behold a spirit-masterpiece !
Music is born from every wandering fleece.
The tones of air, I know not how they flow ;
Where'er they move all things melodious grow.
The pillared shaft, the triglyph even rings :
I think, indeed, the whole bright temple sings.
The vapours settle ; as the light film clears,
A beauteous youth, with rhythmic step, appears
Here ends my task ; his name I need not tell :
Who doth not know the gentle Paris well ?

  LADY. O, what a youthful bloom and strength I see !

  A SECOND. Fresh as a peach, and full of juice, is he !

  A THIRD. The finely drawn, the sweetly swelling lip !

  A FOURTH. From such a cup, no doubt, you'd like to
   sip ?

  A FIFTH. He's handsome, if a little unrefined.

  A SIXTH. He might be somewhat gracefuller, to my
   mind.

  KNIGHT. The shepherd I detect ; I find him wearing
No traces of the Prince, or courtly bearing.

  ANOTHER. O, yes ! half-naked is the youth not bad ;
But let us see him first in armour clad !

  LADY. He seats himself, with such a gentle grace !

  KNIGHT. You'd find his lap, perchance, a pleasant place ?

  ANOTHER. He lifts his arm so lightly o'er his head.

  CHAMBERLAIN. 'Tis not allowed : how thoroughly ill-
   bred !

  LADY. You lords find fault with all things evermore.

  CHAMBERLAIN. To stretch and yawn before the Emperor !

  LADY. He only acts : he thinks he's quite alone.

  CHAMBERLAIN. Even the play should be politely shown.

  LADY. Now sleep falls on the graceful youth so sweetly.

  CHAMBERLAIN. Now will he snore : 'tis natural, completely !

  YOUNG LADY. Mixed with the incense-steam, what odour
   precious
Steals to my bosom, and my heart refreshes ?

OLDER LADY. Forsooth, it penetrates and warms the
    feeling !
It comes from him.

    OLDEST LADY.   His flower of youth, unsealing,
It is : Youth's fine ambrosia, ripe, unfading,
The atmosphere around his form pervading.

                     [HELENA *comes forward.*

    MEPHIS. So, that is she ? *My* sleep she would not waste :
She's pretty, truly, but she's not my taste.

    ASTROLOGER. There's nothing more for me to do, I trow ;
As man of honour, I confess it now.
The Beauty comes, and had I tongues of fire,—
So many songs did Beauty e'er inspire,—
Who sees her, of his wits is dispossessed,
And who possessed her was too highly blessed.

    FAUST. Have I still eyes ? Deep in my being springs
The fount of Beauty, in a torrent pouring !
A heavenly gain my path of terror brings.
The world was void, and shut to my exploring,—
And, since my priesthood, how hath it been graced !
Enduring 'tis, desirable, firm-based.
And let my breath of being blow to waste,
If I for thee unlearn my sacred duty !
The form, that long erewhile my fancy captured,
That from the magic mirror so enraptured,
Was but a frothy phantom of such beauty !
'Tis Thou, to whom the stir of all my forces,—
The essence of my passion's courses,—
Love, fancy, worship, madness,—here I render !

    MEPHIS. (*from the box*). Be calm !—you lose your rôle, to
    be so tender !

    OLDER LADY. Tall and well-formed ! Too small the head,
    alone.

    YOUNGER LADY. Just see her foot ! A heavier ne'er was
    shown.

    DIPLOMATIST. Princesses of her style I've often seen :
From head to foot she's beautiful, I ween.

    COURTIER. She near the sleeper steals, so soft and sly.

    LADY. How ugly, near that youthful purity !

    POET. Her beauty's light is on him like a dawn.

LADY. Endymion and Luna—as they're drawn !

POET. Quite right !   The yielding goddess seems to sink,
And o'er him bend, his balmy breath to drink.
Enviable fate—a kiss !—the cup is full !

DUENNA. Before all people !—that is more than cool.

FAUST. A fearful favour to the boy !

MEPHIS.   Be still !
Suffer the shade to do whate'er it will !

COURTIER. She slips away, light-footed : he awakes.

LADY. Just as I thought !   Another look she takes.

COURTIER. He stares : what haps, to him a marvel is.

LADY. But none to her, what she before her sees !

COURTIER. She turns around to him with dignity.

LADY. I see, she means to put him through his paces :
All men, in such a case, act stupidly.
Then, too, he thinks that first he's won her graces.

KNIGHT. Majestically fine !—She pleases me.

LADY. The courtesan !   How very vulgar she !

PAGE. Just where he is, is where I'd like to be !

COURTIER. Who would not fain be caught in such sweet
            meshes ?

LADY. Through many a hand hath passed that jewel pre-
         cious ;
The gilding, too, is for the most part gone.

ANOTHER. She has been worthless from her tenth year
             on.

KNIGHT. Each takes the best that chance for him obtains :
I'd be content with these fair remains.

A LEARNÈD MAN. I freely own, though I distinctly see,
'Tis doubtful if the genuine one she be.
The Present leads us to exaggeration,
And I hold fast the written, old relation.
I read that, truly, ere her bloom was blighted,
The Trojan gray-beards greatly she delighted.
And here, methinks, it tallies perfectly :
I am not young, yet she delighteth me.

ASTROLOGER. No more a boy !   A bold, heroic form,
He clasps her, who can scarce resist the storm.
With arm grown strong he lifts her high and free :
Means he to bear her off ?

FAUST.   Rash fool, let be?
Thou dar'st?   Thou hear'st not!   Hold!—I'll be obeyed.

MEPHIS. The spectral drama thou thyself hast made

ASTROLOGER. A word more!   After all we've seen to-day,
I call the piece : *The Rape of Helena.*

FAUST. What!   Rape?   Am I nothing here?   To stead me,
Is not this key still shining in my hand?
Through realms of terror, wastes, and waves it led me,
Through solitudes, to where I firmly stand.
Here foothold is!   Realities here centre!
The strife with spirits here the mind may venture,
And on its grand, its double lordship enter!
How far she was, and nearer, how divine!
I'll rescue her, and make her doubly mine.
Ye Mothers! Mothers! crown this wild endeavour!
Who knows her once must hold her, and for ever!

ASTROLOGER. What art thou doing, Faust?   O, look at
him!
He seizes her : the form is growing dim.
He turns the key against the youth, and, lo!
It touches him— Woe's me!   Away now!   Woe on woe!

        [*Explosion.* FAUST *lies upon the earth. The Spirits*
            dissolve in vapour.

MEPHIS. (*taking* FAUST *upon his shoulders*). You have it
now!   One's self with fools to hamper,
At last even on the Devil puts a damper.

                       [*Darkness. Tumult*

ACT II.

I.

A HIGH-ARCHED, NARROW, GOTHIC CHAMBER, FORMERLY FAUST'S, UNCHANGED.

MEPHISTOPHELES *coming forth from behind a curtain. While he holds it up and looks behind him,* FAUST *is seen lying stretched out upon an antiquated bed.*

> MEPHIS. Lie there, ill-starred ! seduced, unwise,
> To bonds that surely hold the lover !
> Whom Helena shall paralyze
> Not soon his reason will recover.   [*Looking around him.*
> I look about, and through the glimmer
> Unchanged, uninjured, all appears :
> The coloured window-panes, methinks, are dimmer,
> The cobwebs have increased with years.
> The ink is dry, the paper old and brown,
> But each thing in its place I find :
> Even the quill is here laid down,
> Wherewith his compact with the Devil he signed.
> Yea, deeper in, the barrel's red
> With trace of blood I coaxed him then to shed.
> A thing so totally unique
> The great collectors would go far to seek.
> Half from its hook the old fur-robe is falling,
> That ancient joke of mine recalling,
> How once I taught the boy such truth
> As still, it may be, nourishes the youth.
> The wish returns, with zest acuter,

Aided by thee, thou rough disguise,
Once more to take on airs as college tutor,
As one infallible in one's own eyes.
The *savans* this assurance know :
The Devil lost it, long ago !

> [*He shakes the fur which he has taken down : moths,
> crickets, and beetles fly out.*

CHORUS OF INSECTS. Welcome, and hail to thee !
> Patron, to-day :
> We're flying and humming,
> We hear and obey.
> Singly and silently
> Us thou hast sown ;
> Hither, by thousands,
> Father, we've flown.
> The imp in the bosom
> Is snugly concealed ;
> But lice in the fur-coat
> Are sooner revealed.

MEPHIS. What glad surprise I feel, from this young life
> bestowed !
One reaps in time, if one has only sowed.
Once more I'll shake the ancient fleeces out :
Still here and there a chance one flies about.—
Off, and around ! in hundred thousand nooks
Hasten to hide yourselves—among the books,
There, in the pasteboard's wormy holes,
Here, in the smoky parchment scrolls,
In dusty jars, that broken lie,
And yonder skull with empty eye.
In all this trash and mould unmatched,
Crotchets for ever must be hatched.[31]

> [*He puts on the fur-mantle*

Come, once again upon my shoulders fall !
Once more am I the Principal.
But 'tis no good to ape the college ;
For where are those who will my claim acknowledge ?

> [*He pulls the bell, which gives out a shrill, penetrating
> sound, causing the halls to tremble and the doors to
> fly open.*

FAMULUS (*tottering hither down the long, dark gallery*)
    What a sound !   What dreadful quaking !
    Stairs are rocking, walls are shaking ;
    Through the coloured windows brightening
    I behold the sudden lightning ;
    Floors above me crack and rumble,
    Lime and lumber round me tumble,
    And the door, securely bolted,
    Is by magic force unfolded.—
    There !   How terrible ! a Giant
    Stands in Faust's old fur, defiant !
    As he looks, and beckons thither,
    I could fall, my senses wither.
    Shall I fly, or shall I wait ?
    What, O what shall be my fate !

MEPHIS. (*beckoning*). Come hither, Friend !   Your name is
    Nicodemus.

FAMULUS. Most honoured Sir, such is my name—*Oremus !*

MEPHIS. Dispense with that !

FAMULUS.   O joy, you know me yet.

MEPHIS. Old, and a student still,—I don't forget,
    Most mossy Sir !   Also a learned man
    Continues study, since naught else he can.
    'Tis thus one builds a moderate house of cards ;
    The greatest minds ne'er end them, afterwards.
    Your master is a skilful fellow, though ;
    The noble Doctor Wagner all must know.
    The first in all the learned world is he,
    Who now together holds it potently,
    Wisdom increasing, daily making clearer.
    How thirst for knowledge listener and hearer !
    A mighty crowd around him flocks.
    None for the rostrum e'er were meeter :
    The keys he holds as doth Saint Peter,
    The Under and the Upper he unlocks.
    His light above all others sparkles surer,
    No name or fame beside him lives :
    Even that of Faust has grown obscurer ;
    'T is he alone invents and gives.

FAMULUS. Pardon, most honoured Sir ! if I am daring

To contradict you, in declaring
All that upon the subject has no bearing ;
For modesty is his allotted part.
The incomprehensible disappearing
Of that great man to him is most uncheering ;
From his return he hopes new strength and joy of heart.
As in the days of Doctor Faust, the room,
Since he's away, all things unchanged,
Waits for its master, long estranged.
To venture in, I scarce presume.—
What stars must govern now the skies !
It seemed as if the basements quivered ;
The door-posts trembled, bolts were shivered :
You had not entered, otherwise.

MEPHIS. Where may his present dwelling be ?
Lead me to him !   Bring him to me !

FAMULUS. His prohibition is so keen !
I do not dare to intervene.
For months, his time unto the great work giving,
In most secluded silence he is living.
The daintiest of distinguished learners,
His face is like a charcoal-burner's,
From nose to ears all black and deadened ;
His eyes from blowing flames are reddened :
Thus he, each moment, pants and longs,
And music make the clattering tongs.

MEPHIS. And entrance why should he deny me !
I'll expedite his luck, if he'll but try me !

> [*The* FAMULUS *goes off :* MEPHISTOPHELES *seats him-*
> *self with gravity.*

Scarce have I taken my position here,
When there, behind, I see a guest appear.
I know him ; he is of the school new-founded,
And his presumption will be quite unbounded.

BACCALAUREUS [32] (*storming along the corridor*).
Doors and entrances are open !
Well,—at last there's ground for hoping
That no more, in mouldy lumber,
Death-like, doth the Living slumber,

P

To himself privations giving,
Till he dies of very living !

All this masonry, I'm thinking,
To its overthrow is sinking ;
And, unless at once we hurry,
Us will crush and ruin bury.
Daring though I be, 't were murther
Should I dare to venture further.

What is that I see before me ?
Here, (what years have since rolled o'er me !)
Shy and unsophisticated,
I as honest freshman waited ;
Here I let the gray-beards guide me,
Here their babble edified me !

Out of dry old volumes preaching,
What they knew, they lied in teaching ;
What they knew, themselves believed not,
Stealing life, that years retrieved not.
What ! —in yonder cell benighted
One still sits, obscurely lighted !

Nearer now, I see, astounded,
Still he sits, with furs surrounded,—
Truly, as I saw him last,
Roughest fleeces round him cast !
Then adroit he seemed to be,
Not yet understood by me :
But to-day 't will naught avail him—
O, I'll neither fear nor fail him !

If, ancient Sir, that bald head, sidewards bending
Hath not been dipped in Lethe's river cold,
See, hitherward, your grateful scholar wending,
Outgrown the academic rods of old.
You're here, as then when I began ;
But *I* am now another man.

MEPHIS. I 'm glad my bell your visit brought ma
Your talents, then, I rated high ;

The worm, the chrysalid soon taught me
The future brilliant butterfly.
Your curly locks and ruffle-laces
A childish pleasure gave ; you wooed the graces.
A queue, I think, you've never worn !
But now your head is cropped and shorn.
Quite bold and resolute you appear.
But don't go, *absolute*, home from here ! [33]

BACCALAUREUS. Old master, in your old place leaning,
Think how the time has sped, the while !
Spare me your words of double meaning !
We take them now in quite another style.
You teased and vexed the honest youth ;
You found it easy then, in truth,
To do what no one dares, to-day.

MEPHIS. If to the young the simple truth we say,
The green ones find it nowise pleasant play ;
But afterwards, when years are over,
And they the truth through their own hide discover,
Then they conceive, themselves have found it out :
" The master was a fool !" one hears them shout.

BACCALAUREUS. A rogue, perhaps ! What teacher will
        declare
The truth to us, exactly fair and square ?
Each knows the way to lessen or exceed it,
Now stern, now lively, as the children need it.

MEPHIS. Beyond a doubt, there is a time to learn ;
But you are skilled to teach, I now discern.
Since many a moon, some circles of the sun,
The riches of experience you have won.

BACCALAUREUS. Experience ! mist and froth alone ;
Nor with the mind at all coequal :
Confess, what one has always known
Is not worth knowing, in the sequel !

MEPHIS. (*after a pause*). It's long seemed so to me.   I
        was a fool :
My shallowness I now must ridicule.

BACCALAUREUS. I'm glad of that !   I hear some reason
    yet—
The first old man of sense I ever met !

MEPHIS. I sought for hidden treasures, grand and golden,
And hideous coals and ashes were my share.

BACCALAUREUS. Confess that now your skull, though bald
and olden,
Is worth no more than is yon empty, there !

MEPHIS. (*amiably*). Know'st thou, my friend, how rude
thou art to me ?

BACCALAUREUS. One lies, in German, would one courteous
be.

MEPHIS. (*wheeling his chair still nearer to the proscenium, to
the spectators*). Up here am I deprived of light and
air :
Shall I find shelter down among you there ?

BACCALAUREUS. It is presumptuous, that one will try
Still to be something, when the time 's gone by.
Man's life lives in his blood, and where, in sooth,
So stirs the blood as in the veins of youth ?
There living blood in freshest power pulsates,
And newer life from its own life creates.
Then something's done, then moves and works the man ;
The weak fall out, the sturdy take the van.
While half the world beneath *our* yoke is brought,
What, then, have you accomplished ?   Nodded—thought—
Dreamed, and considered—plan, and always plan !
Age is an ague-fever, it is clear,
With chills of moody want and dread ;
When one has passed his thirtieth year,
One then is just the same as dead.[34]
'T were best, betimes, to put you out o' the way.

MEPHIS. The Devil, here, has nothing more to say.

BACCALAUREUS. Save through my will, no Devil can there
be.

MEPHIS. (*aside*). The Devil, though, will trip thee presently !

BACCALAUREUS. This is Youth's noblest calling and most
fit !
The world was not, ere I created it ;
The sun I drew from out the orient sea :
The moon began her changeful course with me ;
The Day put on his shining robes, to greet me ;

The Earth grew green, and burst in flower to meet me,
And when I beckoned, from the primal night
The stars unveiled their splendours to my sight.
Who, save myself, to you deliverance brought
From commonplaces of restricted thought?
I, proud and free, even as dictates my mind,
Follow with joy the inward light I find,
And speed along, in mine own ecstasy,
Darkness behind, the Glory leading me !   [*Exit.*

  MEPHIS. Go hence, magnificent Original !—
What grief on thee would insight cast !
Who can think wise or stupid things at all,
That were not thought already in the Past?
Yet even from him we 're not in special peril ;
He will, ere long, to other thoughts incline :
The must may foam absurdly in the barrel,
Nathless it turns at last to wine.

        [*To the younger parterre, which does not applaud.*
My words, I see, have left you cold ;
For you, my children, it may fall so :
Cons.der now, the Devil 's old ;
To understand him, be old also !

II.

LABORATORY.

After the manner of the Middle Ages ; extensive, ponderous apparatus for fantastic purposes.

  WAGNER (*at the furnace*). The loud bell chimes with fearful clangour,
The sooty walls feel the vibration ;
Soon must the long suspense be ended
Of my most earnest expectation.
It shines, the darknesses are rended :

Within the phial's inmost chamber
It gleams, as doth a living ember,—
Yea, a carbuncle, burning, bright'ning,
It rays the darkness with its lightning.
Now white and clear the lustres blend !
O that I hold, nor lose it more !
Ah, God ! what rattles at the door ?

   Mephis. (*entering*). Welcome !   I mean it as a friend.

   Wagner (*anxiously*).   Be welcome to the planet of the
        hour ;   [*Whispering.*

Yet breath and speech suspend !   A work of power,
A splendid work, will soon be here displayed.

   Mephis. (*whispering*). What is it, then ?

   Wagner (*whispering*). A man is being made.

   Mephis. A man ?   And what enamoured pair
Have you within the chimney hidden ?

   Wagner. Nay, God forbid !   This procreation is most
      rare :

Of the old, senseless mode we're now well ridden.
The tender point, whence Life commenced its course,
The outward stress of gracious inward force,
Which took and gave 'tself delineating,
First near, then foreign traits assimilating,
We now of all its dignity divest :
The beast therein may further find a zest,
But Man must learn with his great gifts to win
Henceforth a purer, loftier origin.

              [*Turning towards the furnace.*

It brightens,—see !   Sure, now, my hopes increase
That if, from many hundred substances,
Through mixture—since on mixture all depends—
The human substance gently be compounded,
And by a closed retort surrounded,
Distilled, and fed, and slowly founded,
Then in success the secret labour ends.

            [*Again turning towards the furnace.*

'T will be ! the mass is working clearer !
Conviction gathers, truer, nearer !
The mystery which for Man in Nature lies
We dare to test, by knowledge led ;

And that which she was wont to organize
We crytallize, instead.

MEPHIS. Who lives, learns many secrets to unravel;
For him, upon this earth, there's nothing new can be:
I've seen already, in my years of travel,
Much crystallized humanity.

WAGNER (*up to this time continuously attentive to the phial*).
It mounts, it lightens, grows,—'t is won!
A moment more, and it is done!
Insane, at first, appears a great intent:
We yet shall laugh at chance in generation;
A brain like this, for genuine thinking meant,
Will henceforth be a thinker's sure creation.

[*Rapturously inspecting the phial.*

The glass vibrates with sweet and powerful tone;
It darkens, clears: it *must* arrive at being!
And now in delicate shape is shown
A pretty manikin, moving, living, seeing!
What more can we, what more the world demand?
The secret, solved, all men may reach:
Hark! as the ringing tones expand,
They form a voice, result in speech.

HOMUNCULUS [35] (*in the phial, to* WAGNER). How goes it,
  Daddy? It was then no jest!
Come, press me tenderly upon thy breast!
But not too hard, for fear the glass might shatter!
This is the quality of matter:
For what is natural, scarce the world has place;
What 's artificial, needs restricted space. [*To* MEPHIS.
Thou rogue, Sir Cousin! here I find thee, too?
And at the proper time! My thanks are due:
A lucky fortune led thee here to me;
Since I exist, then I must active be.
I'd fain begin my work without delay:
Thou art adroit in shortening my way.

WAGNER. But first, a word! I 'm shamed that answers
  fail me;
For old and young with problems so assail me.
Now, for example, none e'er comprehended
How soul and body wedded are and blended,

Hold fast, as if defying separation,
Yet never cease their mutual irritation.
Therefore—

   MEPHIS.   Desist ! I'd rather ask him why
The man and wife agree so wretchedly.
To thee, my friend, the thing will ne'er be clear :
There's work to do : for that the little fellow's here.

   HOMUNCULUS. What's to be done ?

   MEPHIS. (*pointing to a side-door*). Thy talents here employ!

   WAGNER (*still gazing at the phial*). Forsooth, thou art the
       very loveliest boy !

      [*The side-door opens :* FAUST *is seen stretched out upon*
      a couch.

   HOMUNCULUS (*astonished*). Significant !—

      [*The phial slips out of* WAGNER'S *hands, hovers over*
      FAUST, *and shines upon him.*

      Fair scenery ! [36]—Waters, moving
In forest shadows : women there, undressing,
The loveliest forms !—the picture is improving.
One, marked by beauty, splendidly expressing
Descent from Gods or high heroic races,
Now dips her foot in the translucent shimmer :
The living flame of her sweet form displaces
The yielding crystal, cool around the swimmer.
But what a sound of wings !   What rapid dashing
Across the glassy pool, what fluttering, splashing !
The maidens fly, alarmed ; but only she,
The queen, looks on, composed and terror-free,
And sees with proud and womanly delight
The swan-prince press her knee with plumage white,
Importunately tame : he grows acquainted.—
But all at once floats up a vapour pale,
And covers with its closely-woven veil
The loveliest picture ever dreamed or painted.

   MEPHIS. How much hast thou to tell,—what stories
      merry !
So small art thou, so great a visionary !
Nothing see I !—

   HOMUNCULUS.   Of course.   Thou, from the North
And in the age of mist brought forth,

In knighthood's and in priestcraft's murky den,
How should thy sight be clearer, then?
In gloom alone art thou at home.   [*Gazing around.*
Brown masonry, repellent, crumbling, slowly,
Arch-pointed, finical, fantastic, lowly!—
If this man wakes, another danger's nigh;
At once upon the spot he'll die.
Wood-fountains, swans, and naked beauties,
Such was his dream of presage fair:
How should these dark surroundings suit his
Desires, when them *I* scarce can bear?
Away with him!

   MEPHIS.   I hail the issue's chances.

   HOMUNCULUS. Command the warrior to the fight,
Conduct the maiden to the dances,
And all is finished, as is right.
Just now—there breaks on me a light—
'T is Classical Walpurgis-Night;
Whate'er may come, it is the best event,
So bring him to his proper element!

   MEPHIS. The like of that I never heard one mention.

   HOMUNCULUS. How should it have attracted your attention?
Only romantic ghosts are known to you;
A genuine phantom must be classic too.

   MEPHIS. But whitherward shall then we travel, tell me!
Your antique cronies in advance repel me.

   HOMUNCULUS. Northwestwards, Satan, is thy park and
         pale,
But we, this time, southeastwards sail.
Peneus, there, the great plain wanders through,
By thickets, groves, and silent coves, and meadow grasses;
The level stretches to the mountain passes,
And o'er it lies Pharsalus, old and new.

   MEPHIS. Alas! have done! Bring not that fell collision
Of tyrant and of slave before my vision!
I'm tired of that: for scarcely is it done
Than they the same thing have again begun;
And no one marks that he's the puppet blind
Of sly Asmōdi, lurking there behind.

They fight, we're told, their freedom's right to save;
But, clearlier seen, 't is slave that fights with slave.

HOMUNCULUS. Leave unto men their fractiousness and
        clatter:
Each must protect himself, as best he can,
From boyhood up, and thus becomes a man.
How this one shall recover, is our matter.
Hast thou a method, let it tested be!
But hast thou none, so leave the case to me!

MEPHIS. There's many a Brocken-method I might try,
But pagan bolts, I find, the way deny.
The Grecian race was little worth, alway;
It dazzles with the senses' freer play,
To cheerful sins the heart of man entices;
While ours are ever counted gloomy vices.
Now, what shall be?

HOMUNCULUS.   Shyness was ne'er thy blame.
When I to thee Thessalian witches name,
I've not said nothing, that I know.

MEPHIS. (*lustfully*). Thessalian witches! Well! The
        persons, those,
Whom I inquired for, long ago.
Night after night beside them to repose,
I think would hardly suit: but so,
A mere espial, trial,—

HOMUNCULUS.   Here! cast o'er
The knight your magic mantle, and infold him!
The rag will still, as heretofore,
Upon his airy course—and thine—uphold him.
I'll light the way.

WAGNER (*anxiously*). And I?

HOMUNCULUS.   Eh? You
Will stay at home, most weighty work to do.
Unfold your ancient parchments, and collect
Life's elements as your recipes direct,
One to the other with due caution fitting.
The *What* consider, more the *How* and *Why!*
Meanwhile, about the world at random flitting,
I may detect the dot upon the "I." [37]
The lofty aim will then accomplished be;

Such an endeavour merits such requital :
Gold, honour, glory, healthy forces vital,
And science, too, and virtue,—possibly.
Farewell !

   WAGNER (*sorrowfully*). Farewell ! It doth depress my
      heart :
I fear, already, we for ever part.

   MEPHIS. Down to Peneus, with his aid !
Sir Cousin is a deft attendant.   [*Ad spectatores*
Upon the creatures we have made
We are, ourselves, at last, dependent.

III.

CLASSICAL WALPURGIS-NIGHT.[38]

I.

THE PHARSALIAN FIELDS.

Darkness.

   ERICHTHO. To this night's awful festival, as oft before,
I enter here, Erichtho, I, the gloomy one :
Not so atrocious as the evil poets draw,
In most superfluous slander—for they never cease
Their blame or praises . . . Over-whitened I behold
The vale, with waves of tents that glimmer gray afar,
The after-vision of that fatal, fearful night.
How oft is it repeated !—will it for ever be
For ever re-enacted ! No one grants the realm
Unto another : unto him whose might achieved
And rules it, none ; for each, incompetent to rule
His own internal self, is all too fain to sway
His neighbour's will, even as his haughty mind inclines.
But here a lesson grand was battled to the end,
How force resists and grapples with the greater force,

The lovely, thousand-blossomed wreath of Freedom rends,
And bends the stubborn laurel round the Ruler's brow.
Here, of his days of early greatness Pompey dreamed :
Before the trembling balance Cæsar yonder watched !
It will be weighed : the world knows unto whom it turned.
The watch-fires flash and glow, spendthrift of ruddy flame ;
Reflections of the squandered blood the earth exhales,
And, lured by rare and marvellous splendour of the night,
The legion of Hellenic legends gathers here.
Round all the fires uncertain hover, or at ease
Sit near them, fabulous forms of ancient days. . . . .
The moon, imperfect, truly, but of clearest beam,
Arises, scattering mellow radiance everywhere :
Vanish the phantom tents, the fires are burning blue.

But o'er my head what unexpected meteor !
It shines, illuminates the sphere of earth below.
I scent the Living ! therefore it becomes me not
Them to approach, I being harmful unto them :
An evil name it brings me, and it profits naught.
Already now it sinks : discreetly I withdraw.   [*Exit.*

The Airy Travellers above.

HOMUNCULUS. Once again the circle follow,
                O'er the flames and horrors hover !
                Ghostly 't is in vale and hollow,
                Spectral all that we discover.
MEPHIS.   If, as through my window nightly,
                In the grewsome North, I see
                Spectres hideous and unsightly,
                Here is home, as there, to me.
HOMUNCULUS. See ! a tall one there is striding
                On before us in the shade.
MEPHIS.   Through the air she saw us gliding,
                And it seems she is afraid.
HOMUNCULUS. Let her stride ! The knight be taken
                Now, and set upon the strand :
                Here to life again he 'll waken,
                Seeking it in fable-land.
FAUST (*as he touches the earth*). Where is she ?—

HOMUNCULUS.   It's more than we can tell,
　　　But to inquire would here be well.
　　　Thou'rt free to hasten, ere the day,
　　　From flame to flame, and seek her so :
　　　Who to the Mothers found his way,
　　　Has nothing more to undergo.

MEPHIS. I also claim my share in the excursion ;
　　　Yet know no better plan for our diversion,
　　　Than that each one, amid these fires,
　　　Should seek such fortunes as he most desires.
　　　Then, as a sign to reunite us,
　　　Let, little one, thy lantern sound and light us !

HOMUNCULUS. Thus shall it shine, and thus shall ring !
　　　　　　　　　　　[*The glass shines and rings powerfully*

And now, away to many a marvellous thing !

FAUST (*solus*). Where is she ?—But no further question
　　　make !
If this were not the soil that bore her feet,
If not the wave that to her coming beat,
Yet 't is the air that knows the tongue she spake.
Here, by a marvel !　Here, on Grecian land ! [39]
I felt at once the earth whereon I stand.
Through me, the sleeper, fresher spirit stealing,
I rise refreshed, Antæus in my feeling.
Together here I find the strangest store ;
Let me this labyrinth of flames explore.　　　[*Goes away.*

MEPHIS. (*prying around*). And as among these fires I
　　　wander, aimless,
I find myself so strange, so disconcerted : [40]
Quite naked most, a few are only shirted ;
The Griffins insolent, the Sphinxes shameless,
And what not all, with pinions and with tresses,
Before, behind, upon one's eyesight presses !—
Indecency, 'tis true, is our ideal,
But the Antique is too alive and real ;
One must with modern thought the thing bemaster
And in the fashion variously o'erplaster :—
Disgusting race !　Yet I, perforce, must meet them,
And as new guest with due decorum greet them.—
Hail, then, Fair Ladies !　Graybeards wise, good cheer

GRIFFIN (*snarling*). Not graybeards! Graybeards? No
    one likes to hear
One call him *gray.* For in each word there rings
The source, wherefrom its derivation springs.[41]
Gray, growling, grewsome, grinning, graves, and grimly,
Etymologically accord, nor dimly,
And make us grim.

    MEPHIS.   And yet, why need you stiffen?
You like the *grif* in your proud title, "Griffin."

    GRIFFIN (*as above, and continuously so*). Of course! for
    this relation is found fit;
Though often censured, oftener praised was it.
Let one but *grip* at maidens, crowns, and gold:
Fortune is gracious to the Griper bold.

    ANTS (*of the colossal kind*). You speak of gold, much had
    ourselves collected;
In rocks and caverns secretly we trapped it:
The Arimaspean race our store detected,—
They're laughing now, so far away they've snapped it.

    THE GRIFFINS. We soon shall force them to confess.

    THE ARIMASPEANS.[42] But not in this free night of jubilee.
Before the morrow, all will squandered be;
This time our efforts will obtain success.

    MEPHIS. (*who has seated himself between the* SPHINXES). How
    soon I feel familiar here, among you!
I understand you, one and all.

    SPHINX. Our spirit-tones, when we have sung you,
Become, for you, material.
Now name thyself, till we shall know thee better.

    MEPHIS. With many names would men my nature fetter
Are Britons here? So round the world they wheel,
To stare at battle-fields, historic traces,
Cascades, old walls, and classic dreary places;
And here were something worthy of their zeal.
Their Old Plays also testify of me;
Men saw me there as "Old Iniquity."

    SPHINX. How did they hit on that?

    MEPHIS.   I know not, verily

    SPHINX. Perhaps! Hast thou in star-lore any power?
What say'st thou of the aspects of the hour?

Mephis. (*looking up*). Star shoots on star, the cloven moon
    doth ride
In brilliance ; in this place I'm satisfied :
I warm myself against thy lion's hide.
It were a loss to rise from out these shades :—
Propose enigmas, or at least charades !

Sphinx. Express thyself, and 't will a riddle be.[43]
Try once thine own analysis : 't were merry.
" To both Devout and Wicked necessary :
To those, a breast-plate for ascetic fighting ;
To these, boon-comrade, in their pranks uniting ;
And both amusing Zeus, the fun delighting."

First Griffin (*snarling*). I like not him !

Second Griffin (*snarling more gruffly*). What will the
    fellow here ?

Both. The Nasty One is not of us, t' is clear !

Mephis. (*brutally*). Think'st thou, perhaps, thy guest has
    nails to scratch,
That with thy sharper talons cannot match ?
Just try it once !

Sphinx (*gently*). Stay, should'st thou find it well ;
But from our ranks thou wilt thyself expel.
In thine own land thou'rt wont thyself to pamper,
Yet here, I think, thy spirits feel a damper.

Mephis. Thine upper part entices ; naught is fairer ;
But, further down, the beast excites my terror.

Sphinx. Bitter, False one, will be thy expiation ;
Our claws are sound and worthy proof,
But thou, with withered horse's-hoof,
Art ill at ease in our association. [*The* Sirens *prelude above*

Mephis. On yonder poplars by the river,
    What are the birds that swing above ?

Sphinx. Beware ! The very best that ever
    Existed, they have lured to love.

Sirens.[44] Ah, why vitiate your senses,
    Where those Uglinesses darken ?
    We, in crowds, come hither : hearken
    How the accordant strain commences,
    Meet for Sirens' soft pretences !

SPHINXES (*mocking them, in the same melody*). Let them to
    descend be bidden !
      In the branches they have hidden
      Hideous falcon-claws they're wearing,
      And you'll feel their cruel tearing,
      Once you lend them willing ear.
SIRENS. Banish hate and envy, rather !
      We the purest pleasures gather,
      Under Heaven's auspicious sphere !
      On the earth and on the ocean,
      We, with cheerful beckoning motion,
      Bid the wanderer welcome here.
MEPHIS. These are of novelties the neatest,
    Where from the throat and harp-string sweetest
    The tones around each other twine.
    They're lost on me, these tinkling trickles ;
    The sound my ear-drum pats and tickles,
    But cannot reach this heart of mine.
SPHINXES. Speak not of heart ! Fool, so to call it !
An old and wrinkled leathern wallet
Would better suit that face of thine.
    FAUST (*approaching*). How strange ! I, satisfied, behold
      these creatures,—
In the Repulsive, grand and solid features : [45]
A fate propitious I behold advance.
Whither transports me now this solemn glance ?
              [*Pointing to the* SPHINXES.
Once before these took Œdipus his stand :
              [*Pointing to the* SIRENS.
These made Ulysses writhe in hempen band :
              [*Pointing to the* ANTS.
By these the highest treasure was amassed :
              [*Pointing to the* GRIFFINS.
By these 't was held inviolate and fast :
Fresh spirit fills me, face to face with these—
Grand are the Forms, and grand the Memories !
    MEPHIS. Once thou hadst cursed such crude antiques,
But now, it seems, they've comfort given ;
For when a man his sweetheart seeks,
Welcome to him are monsters, even.

FAUST (*to the* SPHINXES). Ye woman-forms, give ear, and say
Hath one of you seen Helena?

SPHINXES. Before her day our line expired in Greece;
Our very last was slain by Hercules:
Yet ask of Chiron, if thou please.
He gallops round throughout this ghostly night,
And if he halt for thee, thy chance is bright.

SIRENS. Thou are not to failure fated!
How Ulysses, lingering, learned us,
Nor, regardless passing, spurned us,
Manifold hath he narrated:
All to thee shall be confided,
Seekest thou our meads, divided
By the dark-green arms of Ocean.

SPHINX. Let not thyself thus cheated be!
Not like Ulysses bound,—but we
Will with good counsel thee environ:
If thou canst find the noble Chiron,
Thou'lt learn what I have promised thee.

[FAUST *goes away.*

MEPHIS. (*ill-temperedly*). What croaks and flaps of wings
go past!
One cannot see, they fly so fast,
In single file, from first to last:
A hunter would grow tired of these.

SPHINX. The storm-wind like, that winter harrows,
Reached hardly by Alcides' arrows,
They are the swift Stymphalides;
And not ill-meant their greetings creak,
With goose's foot and vulture's beak.
They fain would join us in our places,
And show themselves as kindred races.

MEPHIS. (*as if intimidated*). Some other brute is hissing
shrill.

SPHINX. Be not afraid, though harsh the pæan!
They are the hydra-heads, the old Lernæan,
Cut from the trunk, yet think they're something still.
But say, what means your air distressed?
Why show your gestures such unrest?

Q

Where will you go? Then take your leave!
That chorus, there, I now perceive,
Turns like a weather-cock your neck. Advance!—
Greet as you will each lovely countenance!
They are the Lamiæ, wenches vile,
With brazen brows and lips that smile,
Such as the satyr-folk have found so fair:
A cloven foot may venture all things there.

    MEPHIS. But stay you here, that I again may find you!

    SPHINX. Yes! Join the airy rabble, there behind you!
From Egypt we, long since, with all our peers,
Accustomed were to reign a thousand years.
If for our place your reverence be won,
We rule for you the days of Moon and Sun.

        We sit before the Pyramids
        For the judgment of the Races,
        Inundation, War, and Peace,—
        With eternal changeless faces.

II.

PENEUS

(surrounded with NYMPHS *and Tributary Streams).*

    PENEUS.[46] Stir yourselves, ye whispering rushes,
        Rustle, slender willow-bushes,
        Sister reeds, breathe softer, crisper,
        Trembling poplar-branches, whisper
        To the interrupted dream!
        Fearful premonitions wake me,
        Secret shudders thrill and shake me
        In my rippling, sleeping stream.

    FAUST *(advancing to the river)*. Here, behind the vines
        that dangle
        O'er the thicket's bowery tangle,
        If I heard aright, were noises
        Similar to human voices.

Babbling seemed the wave to patter,
And the breeze in sport to chatter.
Nymphs (*to* Faust). For thee were it better
　　　　　To lie here, reviving
　　　　　In coolness thy body,
　　　　　Outwearied with striving,—
　　　　　The rest, that eludes thee,
　　　　　To taste, and be free:
　　　　　We'll rustle and murmur,
　　　　　And whisper to thee

Faust. I am awake! Let them delay me,
　　The incomparable Forms!—and sway me,
　　As yonder to my sight confessed!
　　How strangely am I moved, how nearly!
　　Are they but dreams? or memories, merely?
　　Already once was I so blest.
　　Beneath the swaying bushes hiding,
　　The full, fresh waves are softly gliding;
　　They scarcely rustle on their path:
　　A hundred founts from all sides hasten,
　　To fill a pure and sparkling basin,
　　The hollowed level of a bath.
　　The fair young limbs of women trouble
　　The watery glass that makes them double,
　　And doubles, thus, the eye's delight:
　　In joyous bath each other aiding,
　　Or boldly swimming, shyly wading,
　　Then cry, and splash, and foamy fight.
　　It were enough, the picture viewing,—
　　My healthy eyesight here renewing,—
　　Yet I desire the still unseen.
　　My gaze would pierce through yonder cove,
　　Whose leafy wealth is folded over
　　The vision of the stately Queen.

　　Strange! across the crystal skimming,
　　From the coves the swans are swimming,
　　Moving in majestic state:
　　Floating calmly and united,
　　But how proud and self-delighted,

Head and neck they lift elate ! . . .
One, his feathers proudly pluming,
Boldly on his grace presuming,
Leads the others in the race ;
With his whitest plumage showing
Wave-like on the wave he's throwing,
Speeds he to the sacred place. . .
The others back and forth together
Swim on with smoothly shining feather,
And soon, in mimic battle met,
Shall chase aside the maids affrighted,
Till, for their own protection slighted,
Their bounden service they forget.

NYMPHS. Sisters, bend and lay the ear
   On the turf beside the river !
   Sound of hoofs, if right I hear,
   Swift approaching, seems to shiver.
   Would I knew whose rapid flight
   Brings a message to the Night !

FAUST. As I think, the earth is ringing
  From a charger, hither springing.
    See there ! See there !
    A fortune comes, most fair :
    Shall I attain its blessing ?
    O, marvel past expressing !
  A rider trots towards us free :
  Spirit and strength in him I see,—
  Upon a snow-white steed careering. . . .
  I know him now, I hail with awe
  The famous son of Philyra !—
  Halt, Chiron, halt !   I've something for thy hearing.

CHIRON.[47] What then ?   What is it ?
FAUST.   Thy course delay !
CHIRON. I rest not.
FAUST.   Take me with thee, then, I pray !
CHIRON. Mount ! and I thus can ask, at leisure,
Whither thy way.   Thou standest on the shore ;
I'll bear thee through the flood, with pleasure,
  FAUST (*mounting*). Whither thou wilt.   I thank thee
  evermore. . . .

The mighty man, the pedagogue, whose place
And fame it was, to teach a hero-race,—
The splendid circle of the Argonauts,
And all whose deeds made quick the Poet's thoughts.

CHIRON. We will not further speak of these !
As Mentor even Pallas is not venerated ;
And, after all, they manage as they please,
As if they'd not been educated.

FAUST. The leech, who knoweth flower and fruit,
Whose lore can sound the deepest root,—
Who heals the sick, and soothes the wounded place,
Him, here, in mind and body I embrace !

CHIRON. When heroes, near me, felt the smart,
My helpful knowledge failed them seldom ;
But, at the last, I left mine art
To priest and simple-gathering beldam.

FAUST. Thy speech the true great man betrays,
Who cannot hear a word of praise ;
His modesty would fain confound us
To think his equals still were round us.

CHIRON. Thou seemest skilled to feign such matter—
People and Prince alike to flatter.

FAUST. But surely thou wilt grant to me
That thou the greatest of thy time didst see,
Upon their paths of proud achievement trod,
And lived thy days, a serious demigod.
Among those grand, heroic forms of all,
Whom didst thou for the best and worthiest hold ?

CHIRON. Of those beneath the Argonaut's bright banner,
Each worthy was in his peculiar manner,
And by the virtue of his strength selective
Sufficed therein, where others were defective.
Castor and Pollux were as victors hailed,
Where beauty and the grace of youth prevailed :
Decision, the swift deed for other's aid,
Gave the fair crown before the Boreads laid :
Reflective, prudent, strong, in council wise,
So Jason ruled, delight of women's eyes :
Then Orpheus, gentle, silent, brooding, lowering,
But when he struck the lyre, all-overpowering.

Sharp-sighted Lynceus, who by day and dark
Through shoreward breakers steered the sacred bark.
Danger is best endured where men are brothers;
When one achieves, then praise him all the others.

    FAUST. But Hercules thy speech is wronging—

      CHIRON. Ah, me! awaken not my longing! . . .
I had not seen, in Fields Elysian,
How Phœbus, Arês, Hermes, shine;
But there arose before my vision
A form that all men call divine.
A king by birth, as ne'er another,
A youth magnificent to view;
Though subject to his elder brother,
And to the loveliest women, too.
No second such hath Gæa granted,[48]
Or Hebe led to Heaven again;
For him the songs are vainly chanted,
The marble hewn for him in vain.

    FAUST. Though ever to his form addicted,
His grace the sculptors could not wreak.
The fairest Man hast thou depicted,
Now of the fairest Woman speak!

    CHIRON. What!—Little worth is woman's beauty,
So oft an image dumb we see:
I only praise, in loving duty,
A being bright and full of glee.
For beauty in herself delighteth;
And irresistibly she smiteth
When sweetly she with Grace uniteth,
Like Helena, when her I bore.

    FAUST. Her didst thou bear?

    CHIRON.   This back she pressed.

    FAUST. Was I not wild enough, before;
And now such seat, to make me blest!

    CHIRON. Just so she grasped me by the hair
As thou dost.

    FAUST.   O, I scarcely dare
To trust my senses!—tell me more!
She is my only aspiration!
Whence didst thou bear her—to what shore?

CHIRON. Not difficult is the relation.
'Twas then, when came the Dioscuri bold
To free their sister from the robbers' hold;
But these, accustomed not to be subdued,
Regained their courage and in rage pursued.
The swamps below Eleusis did impede
The brothers' and the sister's flying speed:
The brothers waded: splashing through the reed,
I swam: then off she sprang, and pressing me
On the wet mane, caressing me,
She thanked with sweetly-wise and conscious tongue.
How charming was she!—dear to age, so young!

FAUST. But seven years old!—

CHIRON.   Philologists, I see
Even as they cheat themselves, have cheated thee.
'Tis curious with your mythologic dame:
The Poet takes her when he needs her name;
She grows not old, stays ever young and warm,
And of the most enticing form;
Seduced in youth, in age enamouring still,—
Enough! no time can bind the Poet's will.

FAUST. Then let no bonds of Time be thrown around
    her!
Even as on Pheræ's isle Achilles found her,
Beyond the bounds of Time.   What blessing rare,
In spite of Fate such love to win and wear!
And shall not I, by mightiest desire,
Unto my life that sole fair form acquire,
That shape eternal, peer of Gods above,
Tender as grand, sublime as sweet with love?
Thou saw'st her once; to-day I saw her beam,
The dream of Beauty, beautiful as Dream!
My soul, my being, now is bound and chained;
I cannot live, unless she be attained.

CHIRON. Thou, Stranger! feel'st, as man, such ecstasy!
Among us, Spirits, mad thou seem'st to be.
Yet, as it haps, thy fortune now is omened;
For every year, though only for a moment,
It is my wont to call at Manto's dwelling,—

She, Esculapius' child, whose prayers are swelling
Unto her father, that, his fame to brighten,
The brains of doctors he at last enlighten,
And them from rashly dealing death may frighten.
I like her best of all the guild of Sibyls,—
Helpful and kind, with no fantastic fribbles ;
She hath the art, if thou the time canst borrow,
With roots of power to give thee healing thorough.

FAUST. But I will not be healed ! my aim is mighty !
I will not be, like others, meanly flighty !

CHIRON. The noble fountain's cure neglect thou not :
But quick dismount !   We've reached the spot.

FAUST. And whither, in this dreary night, hast thou
To land through pebbly rivers brought me now ?

CHIRON. Here Rome and Greece in battle tried their
          powers ;
Here flows Peneus, there Olympus towers,—
The greatest realm that e'er was lost in sand.
The monarch flies, the conquering burghers stand.
Look up and see, in moonlight shining clear,
The memorable, eternal Temple near !

MANTO[49] (*dreaming within*). From horse-hoofs tremble
The sacred steps of the Temple !
The Demigods draw near.

CHIRON. Quite right !
Open your eyes, and see who's here !

MANTO (*awaking*). Welcome ! Thou dost not fail, I see.

CHIRON. And still thy temple stands for thee !

MANTO. And speedest thou still unremitting ?

CHIRON. And thou in peaceful calm art sitting,
While I rejoice in restless heels ?

MANTO. I wait, and Time around me wheels.
And he ?

CHIRON.   The vortex of this night
Hath whirled him hither to thy sight.
Helen, with mad, distracted senses,
Helen, he'd win by all pretences,
And knows not how or where the task commences ;
But he deserves the Esculapian cure.

MANTO. To whom the Impossible is lure
I love.   [CHIRON *is already far away.*
          Rash one, advance ! there's joy for thee !
This dark way leads thee to Persephone.
Under Olympus' hollow foot,
Secret, she waits prohibited salute.
I smuggled Orpheus in to her, of old :
Use *thy* chance better !   On !—be bold !   [*They descend.*

III.

ON THE UPPER PENEUS, AS BEFORE.

SIRENS. Plunge in cool Peneus' wave !
There 'tis well to sport in swimming,
Songs with chorded voices hymning,
That the ill-starred folk we save.
Health is none where water fails !
Let our hosts, with sounding pæan,
Hasten to the blue Ægæan,
Where each joy shall swell our sails.   [*Earthquake*
Back the frothy wave is flowing,
Now no longer downward going ;
Shakes the bed, the waters roar,
Cracks and smokes the stony shore.
Let us fly !   Come, every one !
By this marvel profit none.
Leave, ye guests, this wild commotion
For the cheerful sports of Ocean,
Shining, where the quivering reaches,
Lightly heaving, bathe the beaches,—
There, where Luna's double splendour
Freshens us with night-dews tender.
There the freest life delights us ;
Here the threatening Earthquake frights us :
Who is prudent, haste away !
Fearful is it, here to stay.

Seismos[50] (*growling and jolting in the depths*). Once again
    the force applying,
    Bravely with the shoulders prying,
    We to get above are trying,
    Where to us must all give way.

Sphinxes. What a most repulsive shaking,
    Terrible and hideous quaking,
    What a quivering and shocking,
    Hither rolling, thither rocking !
    What vexation and dismay !
    But we shall not change our station,
    Were all Hell in agitation. . . .
    Now behold a dome upswelling,
    Wonderful ! 'Tis *he*, compelling,—
    He, the hoary antiquated,
    He who Delos' isle created,
    Bidding it from ocean break,
    For the childed woman's sake.
    He, with all his force expended,
    Rigid arms and shoulders bended,
    Like an Atlas in his gesture
    Pushes up the earth's green vesture,
    Loam and grit, and sand and shingle,
    Where the shore and river mingle :
    Thus our valley's bosom quiet
    Cross-wise tears he, in his riot.
    In unwearied force defiant,
    He, a caryatid-giant,
    Bears a fearful weight of boulders,
    Buried still below his shoulders ;
    But no further shall be granted,
    For the Sphinxes here are planted.

Seismos. The work alone I've undertaken :
    The credit will be given to me :
    Had I not jolted, shoved, and shaken,
    How should this world so beauteous be ?
    How stood aloft your mountains ever,
    In pure and splendid blue of air,
    Had I not heaved with huge endeavour
    Till they, like pictures, charm you there ?

When, where ancestral memory brightens,
Old Night and Chaos saw me sore betrayed,
And in the company of Titans
With Pelion and Ossa as with balls we played,
None could in ardent sport of youth surpass us,
Until, outwearied, at the last,
Even as a double cap, upon Parnassus
His summits wickedly we cast.
Apollo, now, upon that mount of wonder
Finds with the Muses his retreat :
For even Jove, and for his bolts of thunder,
I heaved and held the lofty seat.
Thus have I forced the fierce resistance
And struggled upward from the deep ;
And summon now to new existence
The joyous dwellers of the steep.

SPHINXES. 'Tis true, the hill would seem primeval,
And warranted of old to stand,
Had we not witnessed its upheaval,
Toiling and towering from the land.
A bushy forest, spreading, clothes its face,
And rocks on rocks are pressing to their place.
A Sphinx, therefrom, is by no fear o'ertaken :
We shall not let our sacred seats be shaken.

GRIFFINS.[51] Gold in spangle, leaf, and spark
Glimmers through the fissures dark.
Quick, lest others should detect it,
Haste, ye Emmets, and collect it !

CHORUS OF EMMETS. As they the giant ones,
Upward have thrown it,
Quick-footed, pliant ones,
Climb it and own it !
Rapidly in and out !
In each such fissure
Is every crumb about
Wealth for the wisher !
Seek for them greedily,
Even the slightest :
Everywhere speedily
Gather the brightest !

    Diligent be, and bold—
    Swarm to the fountain :
    Only bring in the Gold !
    Heed not the Mountain !

GRIFFINS. Come in ! come in !—the treasure heap ;
Our claws upon it we shall keep.
The most efficient bolts they are ;
The greatest wealth they safely bar.

  PYGMIES. Verily, here we sit securely ;
    How it happened, is not clear.
    Ask not whence we came ; for surely
    'Tis enough that we are here.
    Unto Life's delighted dwelling
    Suitable is every land ;
    Where a rifted rock is swelling,
    Also is the Dwarf at hand.
    Male and female, busy, steady,
    We as models would suffice :
    Who can tell if such already
    Laboured so in Paradise ?
    Here our lot as best we measure,
    And our star of fate is blest ;
    Mother Earth brings forth with pleasure,
    In the East as in the West.

  DACTYLS. If she, in a single night,
    The Pygmies brought to light,
    Pygmiest of all she'll create yet,
    And each find his mate yet !

PYGMY-ELDERS. Be ye, in haste,
    Conveniently placed !
    Labour, and lead
    Strength unto speed !
    Peace is yet with ye,
    Build now the smithy,—
    The host be arrayed
    With armour and blade !
    Emmets, laborious,
    Working victorious,
    Scorning to settle,
    Furnish us metal !

Dactyls, your host,
Smallest and most,
Hear the requiring,
Bring wood for firing !
Heap in the chambers
Fuel, untiring :
Furnish us embers !

GENERALISSIMO.
With arrow and bow,
Encounter the foe !
By yonder tanks
The heron-ranks,
The countless-nested,
The haughty-breasted,
At one quick blow
Shoot, and bring low !
All together,
That we may feather
Our helmets so.

EMMETS AND DACTYLS.
Who now will save us !
We bring the iron,
And chains enslave us.
To break our fetters
Were now defiant ;
We bide our season,—
Meanwhile, be pliant !

THE CRANES OF IBYCUS.[52]
Murder-cries and moans of
dying !
Startled wings that flap in flying !
What lament, what pain and fright
Pierces to our airy height !
All have fallen in the slaughter,
Reddening with their blood the water !
Pygmy-lust, misformed and cruel,
Robs the heron of his jewel.
On their helms the plumage waves,—
Yonder fat-paunched, bow-legged knaves !
Comrades of our files of motion,
Serried wanderers of ocean,
You we summon to requital
In a cause to you so vital.

Strength and blood let no one spare !
Endless hate to them we swear !

            [They disperse, croaking in the air.

MEPHIS. (*on the plain*). With ease the Northern witches I
    controlled,
But o'er these foreign sprites no power I hold.
The Blocksberg is a most convenient place ;
Howe'er one strays, one can his path retrace.
Dame Ilse watches for us from her stone,
And Henry sits upon his mountain-throne :
The Snorers snarl at Elend—snorting peers,—
And all is finished for a thousand years.
But here, who knows if, even where he stand,
Beneath his feet may not puff up the land ?
I cheerily wander through a level glade,
And, all at once, behind me heaved, is made
A mountain—scarcely to be called so, true ;
Yet high enough the Sphinxes from my view
To intercept. . . . Still many a fire flares out
Adown the vale, the mad concern about. . .
Still dance and hover, beckoning and retreating,
The gay groups round me, with their knavish greeting.
But gently now ! For, spoiled by stealthy pleasure,
One always seeks to snatch some dainty treasure.

   LAMIÆ.[53] (*drawing* MEPHIS. *after them*). Quicker and
           quicker !
        And further take him !
        Then hesitating,
        Chattering and prating !
        'Tis fun to make him—
        Old, sinful Tricker !—
        Follow behind us :
        To penance comes he
        With halt-foot clumsy ;
        He marches hobbling,
        And forwards wobbling ;
        His leg he trails
        In haste to find us ;
        We fly—he fails.

Mephis. (*standing still*). Accurséd fate! Deceived, as oft!
Since Adam's time seduced and scoffed!
Though old we grow, not wisely schooled:
Enough already I've been fooled!
We know, how wholly worthless is the race,
With body corseted and painted face;
Of health responsive own they not a tittle,
Where'er one grasps them, every limb is brittle.
The thing is known, and patent to our glances,
And yet, whene'er the trollops pipe, one dances.

Lamiæ (*pausing*). Halt! he reflects; his steps delay:
Turn back to meet him, lest he get away!

Mephis. (*striding forwards*). Forwards! the doubt, my
    strength benumbing,
I won't encourage foolishly;
For were the witches not forthcoming,
Why, who the devil would Devil be!

Lamiæ (*very graciously*). Round this hero lightly moving,
    Let his heart, the choice approving,
    One of us select for loving!

Mephis. True, in this uncertain lustre,
    Seem ye fair maids, in a cluster;
    Fain would I to you be juster.

Empusa (*pressing forwards*). Not me, too? I'm also
    fitted
In your train to be admitted!

Lamiæ. She's one too many; for, in short,
    She always ruins all our sport.

Empusa (*to* Mephis.). Empusa, with the ass's foot,[14]
    Thy cousin dear, gives thee salute!
    Only a horse's hoof is thine,
    And yet, Sir Cousin, greeting fine!

Mephis. Strangers I here anticipated,
    And, find, alas! my near-related:
    The old tale—instances by dozens—
    From Hartz to Hellas always cousins!

Empusa. I act with promptness and decision;
    In many forms could meet thy vision:
    Yet in thy honour now, instead,
    Have I put on the ass's head.

MEPHIS. Great things, I see, are here portended,
      Thus with the race as kinsman blended :
      Let come what may, since I have known her—
      The ass's head—I'd fain disown her.

LAMIÆ. Leave her, the Ugly ! She doth scare
      Whatever lovely seems and fair ;
      Whate'er was lovely, fair to see,
      When *she* comes, ceases so to be.

MEPHIS. These cousins also,—soft, delicious,
      Are one and all to me suspicious :
      I fear, beneath their cheeks of roses
      Some metamorphosis reposes.

LAMIÆ. But try—take hold ! For we are many,
      And if thou hast a lucky penny,
      Secure thyself the highest prize !
      What means thy wanton organ-grinding !
      A wretched wooer 'tis, we're finding,
      Yet swagger'st thus, and seem'st so wise ! . . .
      Now one of us will he lay hand on,
      So by degrees your masks abandon,
      And show your natures to his eyes !

MEPHIS. The fairest here have I selected. . . .

                        [Clasping her.

      O, what a broomstick, unexpected !

                       [Grasping another.
      And this one ? . . . Vilest countenance !

LAMIÆ. Think not thou'rt worth a better chance !

MEPHIS. That little one, she warms my gizzard. . . .
      But through my hand she slips, a lizard ;
      Her smooth braids, snaky-like, intwine.
      I try the tall one, yet she worse is,—
      I only grasp a Bacchic thyrsus,
      The head a scaly cone of pine.
      What follows next ? Behold a fat one :
      Perhaps I'll find delight in *that* one,
      So, once for all, the chance renew !
      The Turks, for one so puffy, flabby,
      Would pay a price by no means shabby . . .
      But ah ! the puff-ball bursts in two !

LAMIÆ. Now scatter widely, hovering, feigning,
 In lightning-like, dark flight enchaining
 The interloping witch's-son !
 Uncertain circles, awful, poiseless !
 Horrid bat-wings, flying noiseless !
 He 'scapes too cheaply, when it's done.
MEPHIS. (*shaking himself*). I've not become, it seems, a
  great deal shrewder ;
 The North's absurd, 'tis here absurder, ruder,
 The spectres here preposterous as there,
 People and poets shallow ware.
 This masquerade resembles quite—
 As everywhere—a dance of appetite.
 I sought a lovely masked procession,
 And caught such things, I stood aghast. ..
 I'd give myself a false impression,
 If this would only longer last.
     [*Losing himself among the rocks.*
 Where am I then ? and whither sped ?
 There was a path ; 'tis now a dread.
 By level ways I've wandered hither,
 Where rubble now is piled together.
 I clamber up and down in vain ;
 Where shall I find my Sphinx again ?
 I had not dreamed so mad a sight.—
 A mountain in a single night !
 A bold witch-journey, to my thought :
 Their Blocksberg with them they have brought.
OREAD (*from the natural rock*).[55] Come up to me ! My
  mountain old
 In its primeval form behold !
 Revere the steep and rocky stairs, ascending
 Where Pindus' offshoots with the plain are blending !
 Unshaken, thus I heaved my head
 When o'er my shoulders Pompey fled.
 Beside me this illusive rock
 Will vanish at the crow of cock.
 I see such fables oft upthrown,
 And suddenly again go down.
MEPHIS. Honour to thee, thou reverend Head,

With strength of oak engarlanded !
The clearest moonlight never cleaves
The darkness of your crowded leaves.
I see between the bushes go
A light, with unpretending glow.
How all things fit and balance thus !
'Tis verily Homunculus.
    Now whence thy way, thou little lover ?

HOMUNCULUS. From place to place I flit and hover,
And, in the best sense, I would fain exist,
And most impatient am, my glass to shatter :
But what till now I've witnessed, is't
Then strange if I mistrust the matter ?
Yet I'll be confidential, if thou list :
I follow two Philosophers this way.
'Twas " Nature !" " Nature !"—all I heard them say ;
I'll cling to them, and see what they are seeing,
For they must understand this earthly being,
And I shall doubtless learn, in season,
Where to betake me with the soundest reason.

MEPHIS. Then do it of thy own accord !
For here, where spectres from their hell come,
Is the philosopher also welcome.
That so his art and favour delectate you,
At once a dozen new ones he'll create you.
Unless thou errest, thou wilt ne'er have sense ;
Wouldst thou exist, thyself the work commence !

    HOMUNCULUS. Good counsel, also, is not to reject.

    MEPHIS. Then go thy way ! We further will inspect.
                                    [*They separate.*

ANAXAGORAS (*to* THALES).[56] Thy stubborn mind will not be
        rightened :
What else is needful, that thou be enlightened ?

    THALES. To every wind the billows yielding are ;
Yet from the cliff abrupt they keep themselves afar.

    ANAXAGORAS. By fiery vapours rose this rock you're seeing.

    THALES. In moisture came organic life to being.

    HOMUNCULUS (*between the two*). To walk with you may I
        aspire ?
To come to being is my keen desire.

ANAXAGORAS. Hast thou, O Thales? ever in a night
   Brought forth from mud such mountain to the light?

THALES. Nature, the living current of her powers,
   Was never bound to Day and Night and Hours;
   She makes each form by rules that never fail,
   And 'tis not force, even on a mighty scale.

ANAXAGORAS. But here it *was!*—Plutonic fire, the shaper!
   Explosive force of huge Æolian vapour
   Broke through the level Earth's old crust primeval,
   And raised the new hill with a swift upheaval!

THALES. What further shall therefrom result? The hill
   Is there: 'tis well!—so let it stand there still!
   In such a strife one loses leisure precious,
   Yet only leads the patient folk in leashes.

ANAXAGORAS. The Mountain's rocky clefts at once
   Are peopled thick with Myrmidons,
   With Pygmies, Emmets, Fingerlings,
   And other active little things.   [*To* HOMUNCULUS
   To greatness hast thou ne'er aspired,
   But lived an eremite retired;
   Canst thou persuade thy mind to govern,
   I'll have thee chosen as their sovereign.

HOMUNCULUS. What says my Thales?

THALES.   —Will not recommend:
   For small means only unto small deeds tend,
   But great means make the small man great.
   See there! The Cranes, with purpose heinous!—
   The troubled populace they menace,
   And they would menace thus the king.
   With pointed beak and talons ample
   The little men they pierce and trample:
   Doom comes already thundering.
   It was a crime, the heron-slaughter,
   Beset amid their peaceful water;
   But from that rain of arrows deadly
   A fell revenge arises redly,
   And calls the kindred o'er the flood
   To spill the Pygmies' guilty blood.
   What use for shield and helm and spear?

Or for the dwarfs the heron-feather?
Dactyl and Emmet hide together:
 Their cohorts scatter, seek the rear!
ANAXAGORAS (*after a pause, solemnly*). Though I the sub-
 terranean powers approve,
Yet help, in this case, must be sought above. . . .
O thou aloft, in grace and vigour vernal,
Tri-named, tri-featured, and eternal,
By all my people's woe I cry to thee,
Diana, Luna, Hecaté!
Thou breast-expanding One, thou deeply-pondering,
Thou calmly-shining One, majestic wandering.
The fearful craters of thy shade unseal,
And free from spells thine ancient might reveal!

          [*Pause.*

  Am I too swiftly heard?
  Has then my cry
  To yonder sky,
  The course of Nature from its orbit stirred?
And greater, ever greater, drawing near,
Behold the Goddess' orbéd throne appear,
Enormous, fearful in its grimness,
With fires that redden through the dimness! . . .
No nearer! Disk of dread, tremendous,
Lest thou, with land and sea, to ruin send us!
Then were it true, Thessalian Pythonesses [57]
With guilty spells, as Song confesses,
Once from thy path thy steps enchanted,
Till fatal gifts by thee were granted? . . .
The shield of splendour slowly darkles,
Then suddenly splits, and shines, and sparkles!
What rattling and what hissing follow,
With roar of winds and thunders hollow!—
Before thy throne I speak my error. . . .
O, pardon! *I* invoked the terror.

       [*Casts himself upon his face.*
THALES. How many things can this man see and hear?
 What happed, is not to me entirely clear;
 I've not, like him, experienced it.
 The Hours are crazy, we'll admit;

For Luna calmly shines, and free,
 In her high place, as formerly.
HOMUNCULUS. Look yonder where the Pygmies fled !
 The round Hill has a pointed head.
 I felt a huge rebound and shock ;
 Down from the moon had fallen the rock,
 And then, without the least ado,
 Both foe and friend it smashed and slew.
 I praise such arts as these, that show
 Creation in a night fulfilled ;
 That from above and from below
 At once this mountain-pile could build.
THALES. Be still ; 'Twas but imagined so.
 Farewell, then, to the ugly brood !
 That thou wast not their king, is good.
 Off to the cheerful festals of the Sea !
 There as a marvellous guest, they'll honour thee.

          [They depart.

MEPHIS. (*climbing up the opposite side*). Here must I
 climb by steep and rocky stairways,
 And roots of ancient oaks—the vilest rare ways !
 Upon my Hartz, the resinous atmosphere
 Gives hints of pitch, to me almost as dear
 As sulphur is,—but here, among these Greeks,
 For such a smell one long and vainly seeks ;
 And curious am I—for 'tis worth the knowing—
 To find wherewith they keep their fires of Hell a-going
DRYAD. At home, be wise as it befits thee there ;
 Abroad, thou hast no cleverness to spare.
 Thou shouldst not homeward turn thy mind, but here
 The honour of the ancient oaks revere.
MEPHIS. One thinks on all relinquished there ;
 Use made it Paradise, and keeps it fair.
 But say, what is't, in yonder cave
 Obscure, a crouching triple-shape resembling ?
DRYAD. The Phorkyads ! [58] Go there, if thou art brave,
 Address them, if thou canst, untrembling !
MEPHIS. Why not ! . . I something see, and am dumb-
 founded !
 Proud as I am, I must confess the truth :

I've never seen their like, in sooth,—
Worse than our hags, an Ugliness unbounded !
How can the Deadly Sins then ever be
Found ugly in the least degree,
When one this triple dread shall see ?
We would not suffer them to dwell
Even at the dreariest door of Hell ;
But here, in Beauty's land, the Greek,
They're famed, because they're called *antique*. . . .
They stir, they seem to scent my coming ;
Like vampire-bats, they're squeaking, twittering, humming.

THE PHORKYADS. Give me the eye, my sisters, that it
spy
Who to our temple ventures now so nigh.

MEPHIS. Most honoured Dame ! Approaching, by your
leave,
Grant that your triple blessing I receive.
I come, though still unknown, yet, be it stated,
If I mistake not, distantly related.
Old, reverend Gods, already did I see ;
To Ops and Rhea have I bowed the knee ;
The Parcæ even—your sisters—yesterday,
Or day before, they came across my way ;
And yet the like of you ne'er met my sight :
Silent am I, and ravished with delight.

THE PHORKYADS. This spirit seems to have intelligence.

MEPHIS. I am amazed no poet has the sense
To sing your praises,—say, how can it be
That we no pictures of your beauty see ?
Should not, through you, the chisel strive to wean us
From shapes like those of Juno, Pallas, Venus ?

THE PHORKYADS. Sunken in solitude and stillest night
The mind of us ne'er took so far a flight.

MEPHIS. How should it, then ? since here, concealed from
view,
None ever see you, none are seen by you !
But choose those dwelling-places, and be known,
Where Art and Splendour share an equal throne ;
Where swift, with double tread, day after day,

A marble block as hero walks away ;
Where—

THE PHORKYADS. Cease, and rouse in us no longer vision !
What profit, if we knew them with precision ?—
We, born in night, akin to gloom alone,
Unto ourselves almost, to others quite, unknown.

MEPHIS. In such a case there's little more to say,
But one one's self to others can convey.
One eye supplies you three, one tooth as well,
So were it mythologically possible
In two the being of the Three to cover,
And unto me the third fair form make over,
A short time, only.

ONE.   Will it do, forsooth ?

THE OTHERS. We'll try it !—but without or eye or tooth.

MEPHIS. Now just the best thing have you taken away.
How shall I then the image stern display ?

ONE. 'Tis easily done : just close one eye,
And let thy one side-tusk be seen thereby :
In profile thus, with not a trait diminished,
Thy sisterly resemblance will be finished.

MEPHIS. So be it, then !

THE PHORKYADS.   So be it !

MEPHIS. (as PHORKYAD in profile).   Me behold,
The much-beloved son of Chaos old !

THE PHORKYADS. Daughters of Chaos are we, by good
right.

MEPHIS. Disgrace !   They'll call me now hermaphrodite.

THE PHORKYADS. In our new sister-triad what a beauty !
Two eyes have we, two teeth, for further duty.

MEPHIS. Now from all eyes I'll hide this visage fell,
To fright the devils in the pool of Hell.   [Exit.

IV.

ROCKY COVES OF THE ÆGEAN SEA.

The Moon delaying in the Zenith. Sirens *couched upon the cliffs around, fluting and singing.*

Sirens. Though erewhile, by spells nocturnal,
Thee Thessalian hags infernal
Downward drew, with guilt intended,—
Look, from where thine arch is bended,
On the multitudinous, splendid
Twinkles of the billowy Ocean !
Shine upon the throngs in motion
O'er the waters, wild and free !
To thy service vowed are we :
Fairest Luna, gracious be !

Nereids and Tritons (*as wonders of the sea*). Call with
clearer, louder singing
Through the Sea's broad bosom ringing
Call the tenants of the Deep !
When the storm swept unimpeded
We to stillest depths receded ;
Forth at sound of song we leap.
See ! delighted and elated,
We ourselves have decorated,
With our golden crowns have crowned us,
With our spangled girdles bound us,
Chains and jewels hung around us !
Are all spoils which you purvey !
Treasures, here in shipwreck swallowed,
You have lured, and we have followed
You, the Dæmons of our bay.

Sirens. In the crystal cool, delicious,
Smoothly sport the happy fishes,
Pliant lives that nothing mar ;
Yet, ye festive crowds that gather,

    We, to-day, would witness, rather,
    That ye more than fishes are.

NEREIDS AND TRITONS. We, before we hither wandered,
    Thoroughly the question pondered :
    Sisters, Brothers, speed afar !
    Briefest travel, light endurance,
    Yield the validest assurance
    That we more than fishes are.   *[They depart.*

SIRENS. Off ! they have left the place,
    Steering away to Samothrace,
    Vanished with favouring wind.
    What is their purpose there, in the dreary
    Domain of the lofty Cabiri ?
    Gods are they, but the strangest crew,
    Ever begetting themselves anew,
    And unto their own being blind.

    In thy meridian stay,
    Luna !—graciously delay,
    That the Night still embrace us,
    And the Day not chase us !

THALES (*on the shore, to* HOMUNCULUS). I fain would lead
    thee unto Nereus old.
Not distant are we from his cavern cold,
But stubbornness is his delight,
The peevish and repulsive wight.
Howe'er the human race has tried,
The Grumbler's never satisfied :
Yet he the Future hath unsealed,
And men thereto their reverence yield,
And give him honour in his station.
Many his benefits have tasted.

    HOMUNCULUS. Then let us try, without more hesitation !
My glass and flame will not at once be wasted.

    NEREUS. Are human voices those that reach mine ear ?
At once my wrath is kindled, keen and clear.
Aspiring forms, that high as Gods would ramble,
Yet ever damned their own selves to resemble.
In ancient years could I divinely rest,
Yet was impelled to benefit the Best ;

And when, at last, I saw my deeds completed,
It fully seemed as were the work defeated.

THALES. And yet we trust thee, Graybeard of the Sea !
Thou art the Wise One : drive us not from thee !
Behold this Flame, in man's similitude :
It yields itself unto thy counsel good.

NEREUS. What ! Counsel ? When did ever men esteem it !
Wise words in hard ears are but lifeless lore.
Oft as the Act may smite them when they scheme it,
The People are as self-willed as before.
How warned I Paris, in paternal trust,
Before a foreign woman woke his lust !
Upon the Grecian strand he stood so bold ;
I saw in spirit, and to him foretold
The smoky winds, the overwhelming woe,
Beams all a-blaze, murder and death below,—
Troy's judgment-day, held fast in lofty rhyme,
A terror through a thousand years of time !
My words seemed sport unto the reckless one :
His lust he followed : fallen was Ilion,—
A giant carcass, stiff, and hacked with steel,
To Pindus' eagles 'twas a welcome meal.
Ulysses, too ! did I not him presage
The wiles of Circe and the Cyclops' rage ?
His paltering mind, his crew's inconstant strain,
And what not all ?—and did it bring him gain ?
Till him, though late, the favouring billow bore,
A much-tossed wanderer, to the friendly shore.

THALES. Such conduct, truly, gives the wise man **pain,**
And yet the good man once will try again.
An ounce of gratitude, his help repaying,
Tons of ingratitude he sees outweighing.
And nothing trifling now we beg of thee ;
The boy here wishes to be born, and be.

NEREUS. Let not my rarest mood be spoiled, I pray ;
Far other business waits for me to-day.
I've hither bidden, by the wave and breeze,
The Graces of the Sea, the Dorides.[60]
Olympus bears not, nor your lucent arch,
Such lovely forms, in such a lightsome march :

They fling themselves, in wild and wanton dalliance,
From the sea-dragons upon Neptune's stallions,
Blent with the element so freely, brightly,
That even the foam appears to lift them lightly.
In Venus' chariot-shell, with hues of morn,
Comes Galatea, now the fairest, borne;
Who, since that Cypris turned from us her face,
In Paphos reigns as goddess in her place.
Thus she, our loveliest, long since came to own,
As heiress, templed town and chariot-throne.
Away! the father's hour of rapture clips
Hate from the heart, and harshness from the lips.
Away to Proteus! Ask that wondrous man
Of Being's and of Transformation's plan!

[*He retires towards the sea.*

THALES. We, by this step, gain nothing: one may meet
Proteus, and straight he melts, dissolving fleet.
Though he remain, he only says
That which confuses and astonishes.
However, of such counsel thou hast need;
So, at a venture, let us thither speed!   [*They depart.*

SIRENS (*on the rocks above.*) What is't, that, far advancing,
        Glides o'er the billows dancing?
        As, when the winds are shifted,
        Shine snowy sails, uplifted,
        So shine they o'er the waters,
        Transfigured Ocean-daughters.
        We'll clamber down, and, near them,
        Behold their forms, and hear them.

NEREIDS AND TRITONS. What in our hands we bear you
        Much comfort shall prepare you.
        Chelone's buckler giant
        Shines with its forms defiant :—
        They're Gods that we are bringing;
        High songs must you be singing!

SIRENS. Small to the sight,
        Great in their might,—
        Saviours of the stranded,
        Ancient Gods, and banded.

NEREIDS AND TRITONS. We bring you the Cabir
   To festals calm and cheery ;
   For where their sway extendeth
   Neptune the realm befriendeth.

SIRENS. We yield to your claim ;
    When a shipwreck came,
    Irresistibly you
    Protected the crew.

NEREIDS AND TRITONS. Three have we brought hither,
   The fourth refused us altogether :
   He was the right one, said he,—
   Their only thinker ready.

SIRENS. One God the other God
    Smites with the scoffer's rod :
    Honour all grace they bring
    Fear all evil they fling !

NEREIDS AND TRITONS. Seven are they, really.

SIRENS. Where, then, stay the other three ?

NEREIDS AND TRITONS. The truth we cannot gather,
   Ask on Olympus, rather !
   There pines the eighth, forgotten,
   By no one ever thought on !
   In grace to us entreated,
   But not yet all completed.

    These incomparable, unchainable,
    Are always further yearning,
    With desire and hunger burning
    For the Unattainable !

SIRENS. These are our ways :
    The God that sways
    Sun, Moon, or other blaze,
    We worship : for it pays.

NEREIDS AND TRITONS. Highest glory for us behold,
   Leading these festals cheery !

SIRENS. The heroes of the ancient time
    Fail of their glory's prime,
    Where and howe'er it may unfold ;
    Though they have won the Fleece of Gold,—

       Ye, the Cabiri!   [*Repeated as full chorus.*
       Though they have won the Fleece of Gold,—
       We! Ye! the Cabiri!

           [*The* NEREIDS *and* TRITONS *move past.*

HOMUNCULUS. These Malformations, every one,
       Had earthern pots for models : [62]
       Against them now the wise men run,
       And break their stubborn noddles.

THALES. That is the thing one wishes, just !
       The coin takes value from its rust.

PROTEUS (*unperceived*). This pleases me, the old fable-ranger !
       The more respectable, the stranger.

THALES. Where art thou, Proteus ?

PROTEUS. (*speaking ventriloquially, now near, now at a distance*). Here ! and here !

THALES. I pardon thee thine ancient jeer.
       Cheat not a friend with vain oration :
       Thou speak'st, I know, from a delusive station.

PROTEUS (*as if at a distance*). Farewell !

THALES (*softly to* HOMUNCULUS).   He is quite near :
       shine brilliantly !
       For curious as a fish is he ;
And in whatever form he hide,
A flame will make him hither glide.

HOMUNCULUS. At once a flood of light I'll fling,
Yet softly, lest the glass should spring.

PROTEUS (*in the form of a giant tortoise*). What shines so
       fair, so graciously ?

THALES (*covering* HOMUNCULUS). Good ! If thou wishest,
       canst thou nearer see.
Be not annoyed to take a little trouble,
And show thyself on man's foundation double.
What we disclose, to whomsoe'er would see it,
With our will only, by our favour, be it !

PROTEUS (*in a noble form*). Still world-wise pranks thou
       failest to forget.

THALES. To change thy form remains thy pleasure yet.

           [*He uncovers* HOMUNCULUS.

PROTEUS (*astonished*). A shining dwarf ! The like I ne'er
       did see !

THALES. He asks thy counsel, he desires to be.
He is, as I myself have heard him say,
(The thing's a marvel!) only born half-way.
He has no lack of qualities ideal,
But far too much of palpable and real.
Till now the glass alone has given him weight,
And he would fain be soon incorporate.

PROTEUS. Thou art a genuine virgin's-son:
Finished, ere thou shouldst be begun!

THALES (*whispering*). Viewed from another side, the thing
    seems critical:
He is, methinks, hermaphroditical!

PROTEUS. Then all the sooner 'twill succeed:
Let him but start, 'twill be arranged with speed.
No need to ponder here his origin;
On the broad ocean's breast must thou begin!
One starts there first within a narrow pale,[63]
And finds, destroying lower forms, enjoyment:
Little by little, then, one climbs the scale,
And fits himself for loftier employment.

HOMUNCULUS. Here breathes and blows a tender air;
And I delight me in the fragrance rare.

PROTEUS. Yea, verily, my loveliest stripling!
And farther on, far more enjoyable.
Around yon narrow spit the waves are rippling,
The halo bright and undestroyable!
There to the host we'll nearer be,
Now floating hither o'er the sea.
Come with me there!

THALES.   I'll go along.

HOMUNCULUS. A spirit-purpose, triply strong!

V.

TELCHINES OF RHODES.[64]

On Sea-Horses and Sea-Dragons, wielding Neptune's Trident.

CHORUS. We've forged for old Neptune the trident that
        urges
To smoothness and peace the refractory surges
When Jove tears the cloud of the tempest asunder,
'Tis Neptune encounters the roll of the thunder :
The lightnings above may incessantly glow,
But wave upon wave dashes up from below,
And all that, between them, the terrors o'erpower,
Long tossed and tormented, the Deep shall devour ;
And thence he hath lent us his sceptre to-day.—
Now float we contented, in festal array.
    SIRENS. You, to Helios consecrated,
            To the bright Day's blessing fated,—
            You to this high Hour we hail :
            Luna's worship shall prevail !
    TELCHINES. O loveliest Goddess by night over-vaulted !
Thou hearest with rapture thy brother exalted :
To listen to Rhodes thou wilt lean from the skies :
To him, there, the pæans eternally rise.
When the day he begins, when he ends its career,
His beam is the brighest that falls on us here.
The mountains, the cities, the sea and the shore,
Are lovely and bright to the God they adore :
No mist hovers o'er us, and should one appear,
A beam and a breeze, and the Island is clear !
There Phœbus his form may by hundreds behold,—
Colossal, as youth, as the Gentle, the Bold ;
For we were the first whose devotion began
To shape the high Gods in the image of Man.
    PROTEUS. But leave them to their boasting, singing !
Beside the holy sunbeams, bringing

All life, their dead works are a jest.
They melt and cast, with zeal impassioned,
And what they once in bronze have fashioned,
They think it's something of the best.
There proud ones are at last made lowly:
The forms of Gods, that stood and shone,
Were by an earthquake overthrown,
And long since have been melted wholly.
This earthly toil, whate'er it be,
Is never else than drudgery:
A better life the waves declare thee,
And now to endless seas shall bear thee
Proteus-Dolphin.
                          [*He transforms himself*
              'Tis done ! Behold !
Unto thy fairest fortune waken :
Upon my back shalt thou be taken,
And wedded to the Ocean old.

 THALES. Yield to the wish so wisely stated,
  And at the source be thou created !
  Be ready for the rapid plan !
  There, by eternal canons wending,
  Through thousand, myriad forms ascending,
  Thou shalt attain, in time, to Man.
     [HOMUNCULUS *mounts the Proteus-Dolphin.*
 PROTEUS. In spirit seek the watery distance !
  Boundless shall there be thine existence,
  And where to move, thy will be free.
  But struggle not to higher orders !
  Once Man, within the human borders,
  Then all is at an end for thee.
 THALES. That's as it haps : 'tis no ill fate
  In one's own day to be true man and great.
 PROTEUS (*to* THALES). Some one, perchance, of thine own
   kind !
  Their lives continue long, I find ;
  For with thy pallid phantom-peers
  I've seen thee now for many hundred years.
 SIRENS (*on the rocks*). See ! what rings of cloudlets,
   gliding
   Round the moon, in circles play !

They are doves whom Love is guiding,
With their wings as white as day.
Paphos hither sends them fleetly,
All her ardent birds, to us,
And our festival completely
Crowns with purest rapture, thus !

NEREUS (*advancing to* THALES). Though some nightly
    wanderer's vision
Deem yon ring an airy spectre,
We, the spirits, with decision
Entertain a view correcter :
They are doves, whose convoy gathers
Round my daughter's chariot-shell,
With a flight of wondrous spell,
Learned in old days of the fathers.

THALES. That I also think is best,
Which the true man comfort gives,
When in warm and peaceful nest
Something holy for him lives.

PSYLLI AND MARSI [65] (*on sea-bulls, sea heifers and sea-
rams*). In hollow caves on Cyprus' shore,
By the Sea-God still unbattered,
Not yet by Seismos shattered,
By eternal winds breathed o'er,
And still, as in days that are measured,
Contented and silently pleasured,
The chariot of Cypris we've treasured.
By the murmurs, the nightly vibrations,
O'er the waves and their sweetest pulsations,
Unseen to the new generations,
The loveliest daughter we lead.
We fear not, as lightly we hie on,
Either Eagle or wing-lifted Lion,
Either Crescent or Cross,
Though the sky it emboss,—
Though it changefully triumphs and flashes,
In defeat to forgetfulness dashes,
Lays the fields and the cities in ashes !
Straightway, with speed,
The loveliest of mistresses forth we lead.

s

SIRENS. Lightly moved, with paces graver,
　　　　Circle round the car again ;
　　　　Line on line inwoven, waver
　　　　Snake-like in a linking chain.—
　　　　Stalwart Nereids, come, enring us,
　　　　Rudest women, wild and free ;
　　　　Tender Dorides, ye bring us
　　　　Her, the Mother of the Sea,—
　　　　Galatea, godlike woman,
　　　　Worthiest immortality,
　　　　Yet, like those of lineage human,
　　　　Sweet with loving grace is she.

DORIDES (*in chorus, mounted on dolphin, passing* NEREUS).
　　　　Lend us, Luna, light and shadow,
　　　　Show this youthful flower and fire !
　　　　For we bring beloved spouses,
　　　　Praying for them to our sire.　　　　[*To* NEREUS.
　　　　They are boys, whom we have rescued
　　　　From the breaker's teeth of dread ;
　　　　They, on reeds and mosses bedded,
　　　　Back to light and life we led :
　　　　Now must they, with glowing kisses,
　　　　Thank us for the granted blisses ;
　　　　On the youths thy favour shed !

NEREUS. Lo, now ! what double gains your deed requite !
　　　　You show compassion, and you take delight.

DORIDES. If thou praisest our endeavour,
　　　　Father, grant the fond request,
　　　　Let us hold them fast for ever
　　　　On each young, immortal breast.

NEREUS. Take joy in what you've finely captured,
　　　　And shape to men the youthful crew ;
　　　　I cannot grant the boon enraptured
　　　　Which only Zeus can give to you.
　　　　The billows, as they heave and rock you,
　　　　Allow to love no firmer stand,
　　　　So, when these fancies fade and mock you,
　　　　Send quietly the youths to land.

DORIDES. Fair boys, we must part, forsooth ;
　　　　Yet we love you, we vow it !

> We have asked for eternal truth,
> But the Gods will not allow it.

THE YOUTHS. We sailor-boys, if still you would
>> Give love, as first you gave it,
>> We've never had a life so good,
>> And would not better have it!

>>> [GALATEA *approaches on her chariot of shell.*[66]

NEREUS. 'Tis thou, O my darling!
GALATEA.   O, Sire! what delight!
Linger, ye dolphins! I cling to the sight.
NEREUS. Already past, they swiftly wander
On, in circling courses wheeling!
What care they for the heart's profoundest feeling!
Ah, would they took me with them yonder!
Yet a single glance can cheer
All the livelong barren year.

THALES. Hail! All hail! with newer voices:
How my spirit rejoices,
By the True and the Beautiful penetrated!
From Water was everything first created!
Water doth everything still sustain!
Ocean, grant us thine endless reign!
If the clouds thou wert sending not,
The swelling streams wert spending not,
The winding rivers bending not,
And all in thee were ending not,
Could mountains, and plains, and the world itself, be?
The freshest existence is nourished by thee!

ECHO (*chorus of the collective circles*). The freshest existence
>> flows ever from thee!

NEREUS. They turn and wheel again, afar;
No longer face to face they are.
In linking circles, wide extending,—
In their festive dances blending,—
The countless cohorts now appear.
But Galatea's chariot-shell
Still I see, and see it well:
It shines like a star
Through the crowds intwining.
Love from the tumult still is shining!

Though ne'er so far,
It shimmers bright and clear,
Ever true and near.

 HOMUNCULUS. This softly heaving brine on,
   Whatever I may shine on
   Is all with beauty crowned.

 PROTEUS. Within this moisture living,
   Thy lamp now first is giving
   A clear and splendid sound.

 NEREUS. What mystery new, 'mid the crowds that are
  wheeling,
Is now to our vision its wonders revealing?
What flames round the shell at the feet of the Queen?—
Now flaring in force, and now shining serene,
As if by the pulses of love it were fed.

 THALES. Homunculus is it, by Proteus misled! . . .
And these are the signs of imperious yearning,
The presage of swelling, impatiently spurning:
He'll shiver his glass on the glittering throne—
He glows and he flashes, and now he hath flown!

 SIRENS. What fiery marvel the billows enlightens,
As one on the other is broken and brightens?
It flashes, and wavers, and hitherward plays!
On the path of the Night are the bodies ablaze,
And all things around are with flames overrun:
Then Eros be ruler, who all things begun!

   Hail, ye Waves! Hail, Sea unbounded,
   By the holy Fire surrounded!
   Water, hail! Hail, Fire, the splendid!
   Hail, Adventure rarely ended!

 ALL TOGETHER. Hail, ye Airs that softly flow!
   Hail, ye caves of Earth below!
   Honoured now and evermore
   Be the Elemental Four!

ACT III.

—◆—

BEFORE THE PALACE OF MENELAUS IN SPARTA.

HELENA *enters, with the* CHORUS *of Captive Trojan Women.*
PANTHALIS, *Leader of the Chorus.*

HELENA.[67] I, much admired and much reviled,—I Helena,
Come from the strand where we have disembarked but now,
Still giddy from the restless rocking of the waves
Of Ocean, which from Phrygian uplands hitherwards
On high, opposing backs—Poseidon's favour won
And Euros' strength—have borne us to our native bay.
Below there, with the bravest of his warriors, now
King Menelaus feels the joy of his return;
But thou, O bid me welcome back, thou lofty House
Which Tyndarus, my father, on the gentle slope,
Returning from the Hill of Pallas, builded up;
And when I here with Clytemnestra sister-like,
With Castor and with Pollux gaily sporting, grew,
Before all Sparta's houses nobly was adorned.
Ye valves of yon dark iron portals, ye I hail!
Once through your festive and inviting opening
It happened that to me, from many singled out,
The coming of the bridegroom Menelaus shone.
Unfold again for me, that I the King's command
Fulfil with strictness, as unto a spouse is meet:
Give entrance now, and let all things be left behind
Which hitherto have stormed upon me, full of doom!
For, since this place all unsuspicious I forsook
For Cytheræa's fane, as holy duty called,

But there the robber seized me, he the Phrygian,—
Happened have many things, which people far and wide
So fain relate, but which so fain hears not the one
Of whom the legend rose, and to a fable grew.

CHORUS. Disdain thou not, O beautiful Dame,
            Possession proud of the highest estate!
            For the greatest fortune is thine alone,
            The fame of beauty that towers o'er all.
            The name of the hero heralds his path,
            Thence proudly he strides;
            Yet bends at once the stubbornest man,
                And yields to all-conquering Beauty's might.

HELENA. Enough, with mine own spouse have I been
            hither shipped,
And now by him beforehand to his city sent;
Yet what his purposes may be, I fail to guess.
Do I come here as wife? Or do I come as queen?
Or come, an offering for the Prince's bitter pain,
And for the long-endured misfortune of the Greeks?
For they, the Immortals, verily fixed my Fame and Fate
Ambiguously, attendants twain of doubtful worth
To Beauty, who upon this very threshold stand
With gloomy and with threatening presence at my side.
Then, even, in the hollow ship, but seldom looked
My spouse on me, nor ever word of comfort spake:
As if he brooded evil, fronting me he sat.
But now, when speeding towards the strand of that deep
            cove
Eurotas makes, scarce had the foremost vessels' prows
The land saluted, than he spake, as urged the Gods:
" Here, in their ordered rank, my warriors disembark;
Them shall I muster, ranged along the ocean-strand.
But thou go ever onwards, up the hallowed banks
Of fair Eurotas, dowered with gifts of plenteous fruit,
Guiding the stallions o'er the bloom of watery meads,
Till there, on that most lovely plain thy journey ends,
Where Lacedemon, once a fruitful spreading field,
Surrounded by austerest mountains, built its seat.
Set thou thy foot within the high-towered princely House,
And muster well the maids, whom there behind I left,

Together with the old and faithful Stewardess.
Let her display to thee the wealth of treasures stored,
Even as thy father them bequeathed, and I myself,
In war and peace accumulating, have amassed.
All things shalt thou in ancient order find : because
It is the Ruler's privilege, that he all things
In faithful keeping find, returning to his house,—
Where'er he may have left it, each thing in its place ;
For power to change in aught possesses not the slave."

 CHORUS. Let now the splendid, accumulate wealth
     Rejoice and cheer thee, in eye and heart !
     For the gleam of chain and the glory of crown
     Are lying idly in haughty repose :
     But enter thou in and challenge them all,
     And they will respond.
     I rejoice to witness Beauty compete
     With gold and pearl and the jewel-stone.

 HELENA. Thereafter further came my lord's imperious
     speech :
" Now when all things in order thou inspected hast,
Then take so many tripods as thou needful deem'st,
And vessels manifold, such as desires at hand
Who offers to the Gods, fulfilling holy use,—
The kettles, also bowls, the shallow basin's disk ;
The purest water from the sacred fountain fill
In lofty urns ; and further, also ready hold
The well-dried wood that rapidly accepts the flame ;
And let the knife, well-sharpened, fail not finally ;
Yet all besides will I relinquish to thy care."
So spake he, urging my departure ; but no thing
Of living breath did he, who ordered thus, appoint,
That shall, to honour the Olympian Gods, be slain.
'Tis critical ; and yet I banish further care,
And let all things be now to the high Gods referred,
Who that fulfil, whereto their minds may be disposed,
Whether by men 'tis counted good, or whether bad ;
In either case we mortals, we are doomed to bear.
Already lifted oft the Offerer the axe
In consecration o'er the bowed neck of the beast,

And could not consummate the act ; for enemies
Approaching, or Gods intervening, hindered him.

CHORUS. What shall happen, imagin'st thou not.
  Queen, go forwards
  With courage !
  Blessing and evil come
  Unexpected to men :
  Though announced, yet we do not believe.
  Burned not Ilion, saw we not also
  Death in the face, shamefullest death ?
  And are we not here,
  With thee companioned, joyously serving,
  Seeing the dazzling sun in the heavens,
  And the fairest of earth, too,—
  Kindest one, thee,—we, the happy ?

HELENA. Let come, what may ! Whate'er awaits me, it
  beseems
That I without delay go up in the Royal House,
Which, long my need and yearning, forfeited almost,
Once more hath risen on my sight, I know not how.
My feet no longer bear me with such fearlessness
Up the high steps, which as a child I sprang across.

CHORUS. Cast ye, O sisters ! ye
  Sorrowful captives,
  All your troubles far from ye !
  Your mistress's joy partake,
  Helena's joy partake,
  Who the paternal hearth
  Delightedly now is approaching,
  Truly with late-returning
  But with firmer and surer feet !

  Praise ye the sacredest,
  Still re-establishing
  And home-bringing Immortals !
  How the delivered one
  Soars as on lifted wings
  Over asperities, while in vain

The prisoned one, yearningly,
Over the fortress-parapet
Pineth with outspread arms!

But a God took hold of her,
The Expatriate,
And from Ilion's ruins
Hither hath born her again,
To the ancient, the newly embellished
Paternal house,
From unspeakable
Raptures and torments,
Early youthful days,
Now refreshed, to remember.

PANTHALIS (*as* LEADER OF THE CHORUS). Forsake ye now
　　　the joy-encompassed path of Song,
And towards the portal's open valves your glances turn!
What, Sisters, do I see?　Returneth not the Queen
With swift and agitated step again to us?
What is it now, great Queen, what could encounter thee
To move and shake thee so, within thy house's halls,
Instead of greeting?　Thou canst not conceal the thing;
For strong repulsion written on thy brow I see,
And noble indignation, struggling with amaze.

HELENA (*who has left the wings of the portal open, excitedly*).
A common fear beseemeth not the child of Zeus;
No lightly-passing hand of terror touches her;
But that fell Horror, which the womb of ancient Night
With first of things delivered, rolled through many forms,
Like glowing clouds that from the mountain's fiery throat
Whirl up expanding, even heroes' breasts may shake.
Thus terribly have here to-day the Stygian Gods
Mine entrance in the house betokened, and I fain,
Even as a guest dismissed, would take myself away
From this oft-trodden threshold I so longed to tread.
But, no! hither have I retreated to the light;
Nor further shall ye force me, Powers, be who ye may!
Some consecration will I muse: then, purified,
The hearth-fire may the wife so welcome, as the lord.

LEADER OF THE CHORUS. Discover, noble Dame, unto
    thy servants here,
Who reverently assist thee, what hath come to pass.

    HELENA. What I beheld, shall ye with your own eyes
    behold,
If now that shape the ancient Night hath not at once
Re-swallowed to the wonders of her deepest breast.
But I with words will yet declare it, that ye know.
When solemnly, my nearest duty borne in mind,
The Royal House's gloomy inner court I trod,
Amazed I saw the silent, dreary corridors.
No sound of diligent labour, going forwards, met
The ear, no signs of prompt and busy haste the eye;
And not a maid appeared to me, no stewardess
Such as is wont to greet the stranger, friendly-wise.
But when towards the ample hearth-stone I advanced,
I saw, beside the glimmering ashes that remained,
A veiled and giant woman seated on the ground,
Not like to one who sleeps, but one deep-sunk in thought.
With words of stern command I summoned her to work,
The stewardess surmising, who meanwhile, perchance,
My spouse with forethought there had stationed when he left,
But she, still crouched together, sat immovable.
Stirred by my threats at last, she lifted the right arm
As if from hearth and hall she beckoned me away.
I turned indignantly from her, and swiftly sped
Unto the steps whereon aloft the Thalamos
Adorned is set, and near thereto the treasure-room:
But suddenly from the floor the wondrous figure sprang,
Barring my way imperiously, and showed herself
In haggard height, with hollow, blood-discoloured eyes,
A shape so strange that eye and mind confounded are.
But to the winds I speak: for all in vain doth Speech
Fatigue itself, creatively to build up forms.
There look, yourselves! She even ventures forth to light!
Here are we masters, till the lord and king shall come.
The horrid births of Night doth Phœbus, Beauty's friend,
Drive out of sight to caverns, or he binds them fast.

       [PHORKYAS *appears on the threshold, between the*
      door-posts.

CHORUS.[68] Much my experience, although the tresses,
    Youthfully clustering, wave on my temples;
    Many the terrible things I have witnessed,
    Warriors lamenting, Ilion's night,
    When it fell.

Through the beclouded, dusty and maddened
Throngs of the combatants, heard I the Gods then
    Terribly calling, heard I the iron
    Accents of Discord clang through the field,
    City-wards.

Ah, yet stood they, Ilion's
    Ramparts; but ever the fiery glow
Ran from neighbour to neighbour walls,
    Ever extending from here and there,
    With the roar of its own storm,
    Over the darkening city.

Flying saw I, through smoke and flame,
    And the tongues of the blinding fire,
    Fearful angering presence of Gods,
    Stalking marvellous figures,
    Giant-great, through the gloomy
    Fire illuminate vapours.

    Saw I, or was it but
    Dread of the mind, that fashioned
    Forms so affrighting? Never can
    Justly I say it? Yet that I Her.
    Horrible, here with eyes behold,
    Is to me known and certain:
    Even to my hand were palpable,
    Did not the terror restrain me,
    Holding me back from the danger.

    Which one of Phorkys'
    Daughters then art thou!
    Since I compare thee
    Unto that family.

Art thou, perchance, of the Graiæ,
One of the dreaded gray-born,
One eye and tooth only
Owning alternately ?

Darest thou, Monster,
Here beside Beauty,
Unto high Phœbus'
Vision display thee ?
Step thou forth, notwithstasnding !
For the Ugly beholds he not,
Even as his hallowed glances
Never beheld the shadow.

Yet a sorrowful adverse fate,
Us mortals compelleth, alas !
To endure the unspeakable eye-pain
Which She, the accurst, reprehensible,
Provokes in the lovers of Beauty.

Yes, then hearken, if thou brazenly
Us shalt encounter, hear the curse,—
Hear the threat of every abuse
From the denouncing mouths of the Fortunate,
Whom the Gods themselves have fashioned !

PHORKYAS.[69] Old is the saw, and yet its sense is high and
    true,
That Shame and Beauty ne'er together, hand in hand,
Pursued their way across the green domains of Earth.
Deep-rooted dwells in both such force of ancient hate,
That wheresoever on their way one haps to meet
The other, each upon her rival turns her back :
Then forth again vehemently they hasten on,
Shame deep depressed, but Beauty insolent and bold,
Till her at last the hollow night of Orcus takes,
If Age hath not beforehand fully tamed her pride.
So now I find ye, shameless ones, come from abroad
With arrogance o'erflowing, as a file of cranes
That with their hoarse, far-sounding clangour high in air,
A cloudy line, slow-moving, send their creaking tones

Below, the loan, belated wanderer to allure
That he look up ; but, notwithstanding, go their way,
And he goes his : and likewise will it be, with us.
Who, then, are you, that round the Royal Palace high
Like Mænads wild, or like Bacchantes, dare to rave ?
Who, then, are you, that you the House's stewardess
Assail and howl at, as the breed of dogs the moon ?
Think ye from me 'tis hidden, of what race ye are ?
Ye brood, in war begotten and in battle bred,
Lustful of man, seducing no less than seduced,
Emasculating soldiers', burghers' strength alike !
Methinks, to see your crowd, a thick cicada-swarm
Hath settled on us, covering the green-sown fields.
Devourers ye of others' toil ! Ye snatch and taste,
Destroying in its bud the land's prosperity !
Wares are ye, plundered, bartered, and in market sold !

    HELENA. Who rates the servant-maids in presence of the
        Dame
Audaciously invades the Mistress' household-right :
Her only it becometh to commend what is
Praiseworthy, as to punish what is blamable.
Content, moreover, am I with the service which
They gave me, when the lofty strength of Ilion
Beleaguered stood, and fell in ruin : none the less
When we the sorrowful and devious hardships bore
Of errant travel, where each thinks but of himself.
Here, too, the like from this gay throng do I expect :
Not what the slave is, asks the lord, but how he serves.
Therefore, be silent, cease to grin and jeer at them !
If thou the Palace hitherto hast guarded well
In place of Mistress, so much to thy credit stands ;
But now that she herself hath come, shouldst thou retire
Lest punishment, in place of pay deserved, befall !

    PHORKYAS. To threaten the domestics is a right assured,
Which she, the spouse august of the God-prospered king,
By many years of wise discretion well hath earned.
Since thou, now recognised, thine ancient station here
Again assum'st, as Queen and Mistress of the House,
Grasp thou the reigns so long relaxed, be ruler now,
Take in thy keep the treasure, and ourselves thereto !

But first of all protect me, who the eldest am,
From this pert throng, who with thee, Swan of Beauty
    matched,
Are only stumpy-winged and cackling, quacking geese.

    LEADER OF THE CHORUS. How ugly, near to Beauty, showeth
        Ugliness !

    PHORKYAS. How silly, near to understanding, want of
        sense !

        [*Henceforth the* CHORETIDS *answer in turn, stepping
         singly forth from the* CHORUS.

    CHORETID I. Of Father Erebus relate, relate of Mother
        Night !

    PHORKYAS. Speak thou of Scylla, sister-children of one
        flesh !

    CHORETID II. Good store of hideous monsters shows thy
        family tree !

    PHORKYAS. Go down to Orcus !   There thy tribe and
        kindred seek !

    CHORETID III. Those who dwell there are all by far too
        young for thee.

    PHORKYAS. On old Tiresias try thy lascivious arts !

    CHORETID IV. Orion's nurse was great-great-grandchild
        unto thee !

    PHORKYAS. Thee harpies, I suspect, did nurse and feed on
        filth.

    CHORETID V. Wherewith dost thou such choice emaciation
        feed ?

    PHORKYAS. Not with the blood, for which thou all too
        greedy art.

    CHORETID VI. Thou, hungering for corpses, hideous corpse
        thyself !

    PHORKYAS. The teeth of vampires in thy shameless muzzle
        shine !

    LEADER OF THE CHORUS. Thine shall I stop, when I declare
        thee who thou art.

    PHORKYAS. Then name thyself the first !   The riddle thus
        is solved.

    HELENA. Not angered, but in sorrow, do I intervene,
Prohibiting the storm of this alternate strife !
For nothing more injurious meets the ruling lord

Than quarrels of his faithful servants, underhand.
The echo of his orders then returns no more
Accordantly to him in swiftly finished acts,
But, roaring wilfully, encompasses with storm
Him, self-confused and chiding to the empty air.
Nor this alone : in most unmannered anger ye
Have conjured hither pictures of the shapes of dread,
Which so surround me, that to Orcus now I feel
My being whirled, despite these well-known native fields.
Can it be memory? Was it fancy, seizing me?
Was all that, I? and am I, now? and shall I henceforth be
The dream and terror of those town-destroying ones?
I see the maidens shudder : but, the eldest, thou
Composedly standest—speak a word of sense to me !

PHORKYAS. Whoe'er the fortune manifold of years recalls,
Sees as a dream at last the favour of the Gods.
But thou, so highly dowered, so past all measure helped,
Saw'st in the ranks of life but love-desirous men,
To every boldest hazard kindled soon and spurred.
Thee early Theseus snatched, excited by desire,
Like Heraclês in strength, a splendid form of man.

HELENA. He bore me forth, a ten-year-old and slender
    roe,
And shut me in Aphidnus' tower, in Attica.

PHORKYAS. But then, by Castor and by Pollux soon
    released,
The choicest crowd of heroes, wooing, round thee pressed.

HELENA. Yet most my secret favour, freely I confess,
Patroclus won, the likeness of Pelides he.

PHORKYAS. Wed by thy father's will to Menelaus then,
The bold sea-rover, the sustainer of his house.

HELENA. My sire the daughter gave him, and the govern-
    ment :
Then from our wedded nearness sprang Hermione.

PHORKYAS. Yet when be boldly claimed the heritage of
    Crete,
To thee, the lonely one, too fair a guest appeared.

HELENA. Why wilt thou thus recall that semi-widow-
    hood,
And all the hideous ruin it entailed on me ?

PHORKYAS. To me, a free-born Cretan, did that journey
    bring
Imprisonment, as well,—protracted slavery.

HELENA. At once he hither ordered thee as stewardess,
Giving in charge the fortress and the treasure-stores.

PHORKYAS. Which thou forsookest, wending to the towered
    town
Of Ilion, and the unexhausted joys of love.

HELENA. Name not those joys to me! for sorrow all too stern
Unendingly was poured upon my breast and brain.

PHORKYAS. Nathless, they say, dost thou appear in double
    form ;
Beheld in Ilion,—in Egypt, too, beheld.

HELENA. Make wholly not confused my clouded, wandering
    sense !
Even in this moment, who I am I cannot tell.

PHORKYAS. And then, they say, from out the hollow
    Realm of Shades
Achilles yet was joined in passion unto thee,
Who earlier loved thee, 'gainst all ordinances of Fate !

HELENA. To him, the Vision, I, a Vision, wed myself :
It was a dream, as even the words themselves declare.
I vanish hence, and to myself a Vision grow.
           [*She sinks into the arms of the* SEMICHORUS

CHORUS. Silence ! silence !
    False-seeing one, false-speaking one !
    Out of the hideous, single-toothed
    Mouth, what should be exhaled from
    Such abominable horror-throat !
    For the Malevolent, seeming benevolent,—
    Wolf's wrath under the sheep's woolly fleece,—
    Fearfuller far is unto me than
    Throat of the three-headed dog.
    Anxiously listening stand we here.
    When ? how ? where shall break again forth
    Further malice
    From the deeply-ambushed monster ?

    Now, stead of friendly words and consoling,
    Lethe-bestowing, gratefully mild,

Stirrest thou up from all the Past
Evillest more than good things,
And darkenest all at once
Both the gleam of the Present
And also the Future's
Sweetly glimmering dawn of hope !

Silence ! silence !
That the Queen's high spirit,
Nigh to forsake her now,
Hold out, and upbear yet
The Form of all forms
Which the sun shone on ever.

> [HELENA *has recovered, and stands again in the*
> *centre.*

PHORKYAS. Forth from transient vapours comes the lofty
sun of this bright day,
That, obscured, could so delight us, but in splendour dazzles
now.
As the world to thee is lovely, thou art lovely unto us ;
Though as ugly they revile me, well I know the Beautiful.

HELENA. Tottering step I from the Void that—dizzy,
fainting,—round me closed ;
And again would fain be resting, for so weary are my limbs.
Yet to Queens beseemeth chiefly, as to all men it beseems,
Calm to be, and pluck up courage, whatsoe'er may menace
them.

PHORKYAS. Standing now in all thy greatness, and in all
thy beauty, here,
Says thine eye that thou commandest : what command'st
thou ? speak it out !

HELENA. Be prepared, for much neglected in your quarrel,
to atone !
Haste, a sacrifice to furnish, as the king hath ordered me !

PHORKYAS. All is ready in the palace—vessels, tripods,
sharpened axe,
For the sprinkling, fumigating : show to me the victim
now !

HELENA. This the king not indicated.

PHORKYAS.   Spake it not ? O word of woe !

T

HELENA. What distress hath overcome thee?

PHORKYAS.   Queen, the offering art thou!"

HELENA. I?

PHORKYAS.   And these.

CHORUS.   Ah, woe and sorrow!

PHORKYAS.   Thou shalt fall beneath the axe.

HELENA. Fearful, yet foreboded!   I, alas!

PHORKYAS.   There seemeth no escape.

CHORUS. Ah! and what to us will happen?

PHORKYAS.   She will die a noble death;

But upon the lofty beam, upholding rafter-frame and roof,

As in birding-time the throstles, ye in turn shall struggling
  hang!

> [HELENA *and the* CHORUS *stand amazed and alarmed,*
> *in striking, well-arranged groups.*

PHORKYAS. Ye Phantoms!—like to frozen images ye
  stand,

In terror thus from Day to part, which is not yours.

Men, and the race of spectres like you, one and all,

Renounce not willingly the bright beams of the sun;

But from the end may none implore or rescue them.

All know it, yet 'tis pleasant unto very few.

Enough! ye all are lost: now speedily to work!

> [*She claps her hands: thereupon appear in the door-*
> *way muffled dwarfish forms, which at once carry*
> *out with alacrity the commands expressed.*

This way, ye gloomy, sphery-bodied monster throng!

Roll hitherwards! ye here may damage as ye will.

The altar portable, the golden-horned, set up!

The axe let shimmering lie across the silver rim!

The urns of water fill!   For soon, to wash away,

Shall be the black blood's horrible and smutching stains.

Here spread the costly carpets out upon the dust,

That so the offering may kneel in queenly wise,

And folded then, although with severed head, at once

With decent dignity be granted sepulture!

LEADER OF THE CHORUS. The Queen is standing, sunk in
  thought, beside us here,

The maidens wither like the late-mown meadow grass;

Methinks that I, the eldest, in high duty bound,

Should words exchange with thee, primeval eldest thou !
Thou art experienced, wise, and seemest well-disposed,
Although this brainless throng assailed thee in mistake.
Declare then, if thou knowest, possible escape !

PHORKYAS. 'Tis easy said. Upon the Queen it rests
    alone,
To save herself, and ye appendages with her.
But resolution, and the swiftest, needful is.

CHORUS. Worthiest and most reverend of the Parcæ, wisest
    sibyl thou,
Hold the golden shears yet open, then declare us Day and
    Help !
We already feel discomfort of the soaring, swinging, strug-
    gling ;
And our limbs in dances first would rather move in joyous
    cadence,
Resting afterwards on lovers' breasts.

HELENA. Let these be timid ! Pain I feel, but terror
    none ;
Yet if thou know'st of rescue, grateful I accept !
Unto the wise, wide-seeing mind is verily shown
The Impossible oft as possible. Then speak, and say !

CHORUS. Speak and tell us, tell us quickly, how escape we
    now the fearful,
Fatal nooses, that so menace, like the vilest form of necklace,
Wound about our tender throats ? Already, in anticipation,
We can feel the choking, smothering—if thou, Rhea, lofty
    Mother
Of the Gods, to mercy be not moved.

PHORKYAS. Have you then patience, such long-winded
    course of speech
To hear in silence ? Manifold the stories are.

CHORUS. Patience enough ! Meanwhile, in hearing, still
    we live.

PHORKYAS. Whoso, to guard his noble wealth, abides at
    home,
And in his lofty dwelling well cements the chinks
And also from the pelting rain secures the roof,
With him, the long days of his life, shall all be well :
But whosoe'er his threshold's holy square-hewn stone

T 2

Lightly with flying foot and guilty oversteps,
Finds, when he comes again, the ancient place indeed,
But all things altered, if not utterly o'erthrown.

HELENA. Wherefore declaim such well-known sayings here,
    as these?

Thou wouldst narrate: then stir not up annoying themes!

PHORKYAS. It is historic truth, and nowise a reproach.
Sea-plundering, Menelaus steered from bay to bay!
He skirted as a foe the islands and the shores,
Returning with the booty, which in yonder rusts.
Then ten long years he passed in front of Ilion;
But for the voyage home how many know I not.
And now how is it, where we stand by Tyndarus'
Exalted House? How is it with the regions round?

HELENA. Has then Abuse become incarnated in thee,
That canst not open once thy lips, except to blame?

PHORKYAS. So many years deserted stood the valley-hills
That in the rear of Sparta northwards rise aloft,
Behind Taygetus; whence, as yet a nimble brook,
Eurotas downward rolls, and then, along our vale
By reed-beds broadly flowing, nourishes your swans.
Behind there in the mountain-dells a daring breed
Have settled, pressing forth from the Cimmerian Night,
And there have built a fortress inaccessible,
Whence land and people now they harry, as they please.

HELENA. Have they accomplished that? Impossible it
    seems.

PHORKYAS. They had the time: it may be twenty years,
    in all.

HELENA. Is one a Chief? and are they robbers many—
    leagued?

PHORKYAS. Not robbers are they! yet of many one is
    Chief;

I blame him not, although on me he also fell.
He might, indeed, have taken all; yet was content
With some *free-gifts*, he said: tribute he called it not.

HELENA. How looked the man?

PHORKYAS.   By no means ill: he pleased me well.
Cheerful and brave and bold, and nobly-formed is he,
A prudent man and wise, as few among the Greeks.

They call the race Barbarians ; yet I question much
If one so cruel be, as there by Ilion
In man-devouring rage so many heroes were ;
His greatness I respected, did confide in him.
And then, his fortress !   That should ye yourself behold !
'Tis something other than unwieldy masonry,
The which your fathers, helter-skelter tumbling, piled,—
Cyclopean like the Cyclops, stones undressed at once
On stones undressed upheaving : there, however, there
All plumb and balanced is, conformed to square and rule.
Behold it from without !   It rises heavenward up
So hard, so tight of joint, and mirror-smooth as steel.
To climb up there—nay, even your Thought itself slide
        off !
And mighty courts of ample space within, enclosed
Around with structures of all character and use.
There you see pillars, pillarets, arches great and small,
Balconies, galleries for looking out and in,
And coats of arms.

    CHORUS.   What are they ?

    PHORKYAS.   Ajax surely bore
A twisted serpent on his shield, as ye have seen.
The Seven also before Thebes had images,
Each one upon his shield, with many meanings rich.
One saw there moon and star on the nocturnal sky,
And goddesses, and heroes, ladders, torches, swords,
And whatsoe'er afflicting threateneth good towns.
Such symbols also bore our own heroic band,
In shining tints, bequeathed from eldest ancestry.
You see there lions, eagles, likewise claws and beaks,
Then buffalo-horns, with wings and roses, peacocks' tails,
And also bars—gold, black and silver, blue and red.
The like of these in halls are hanging, row on row,—
In halls unlimited and spacious as the world :
There might ye dance !

    CHORUS.   But tell us, are there dancers there !

    PHORKYAS. Ay, and the best !—a blooming, gold-haired
        throng of boys,
Breathing ambrosial youth !   So only Paris breathed,
When he approached too nearly to the Queen.

HELENA. Thou fall'st
Entirely from thy part : speak now the final word !

PHORKYAS. 'Tis thou shalt speak it : say with grave
distinctness, Yes !
Then straight will I surround thee with that fortress.

CHORUS. Speak,
O speak the one brief word, and save thyself and us !

HELENA. What ! Shall I fear King Menelaus may
transgress
So most inhumanly, as thus to smite myself ?

PHORKYAS. Hast thou forgotten how he thy Deiphobus,
Brother of fallen Paris, who with stubborn claim
Took thee, the widow, as his fere, did visit with
Unheard-of mutilation ? Nose and ears he cropped,
And otherwise disfigured : 'twas a dread to see.

HELENA. That did he unto him : he did it for my sake.

PHORKYAS. Because of him he now will do the like to
thee.
Beauty is indivisible : who once possessed
Her wholly, rather slays than only shares in part.

> [*Trumpets in the distance: the* CHORUS *starts in
> terror.*

Even as the trumpet's piercing clangour gripes and tears
The ear and entrail-nerves, thus Jealousy her claws
Drives in the bosom of the man, who ne'er forgets
What once was his, but now is lost, possessed no more.

CHORUS. Hear'st thou not the trumpets pealing? see'st
thou not the shine of swords ?

PHORKYAS. King and Lord, be welcome hither ! willing
reckoning will I give.

CHORUS. What of us ?

PHORKYAS. You know it 'clearly, see her death before
your eyes ;
There, within, your own shall follow : nay, there is no help
for you ! [*Pause.*

HELENA. What I may venture first to do, have I devised.
A hostile Dæmon art thou, that I feel full well,
And much I fear thou wilt convert the Good to Bad,
But first to yonder fortress now I follow thee ;
What then shall come, I know : but what the Queen thereby

Às mystery in her deepest bosom may conceal,
Remain unguessed by all! Now, Ancient, lead the way!

CHORUS. O how gladly we go,
             Hastening thither!
             Chasing us, Death,
             And, rising before us,
             The towering castle's
             Inaccessible ramparts.
             Guard us as well may they
             As Ilion's citadel-fort,
             Which at last alone
             Fell, through comtemptible wiles!

[*Mists arise and spread, obscuring the background,
    also the nearer portion of the scene, at pleasure.*

             How is it? how?
             Sisters, look around!
             Was it not cheerfullest day?
             Banded vapours are hovering up
             Out of Eurotas' holy stream;
             Vanished e'en now hath the lovely
             Reed-engarlanded shore from the sight;
             Likewise the free, gracefully proud,
             Silently floating swans,
             Mated in joy of their swimming,
             See I, alas! no more.

             Still—but still
             Crying, I hear them,
             Hoarsely crying afar!
             Ominous, death presaging!
             Ah, may to us the tones not also,
             Stead of deliverance promised,
             Ruin announce at the last!—
             Us, the swan-like and slender,
             Long white-throated, and She,
             Our fair swan-begotten.
             Woe to us, Woe!

All is covered and hid
Round us with vapour and cloud :
Each other behold we not !
What happens ? do we advance ?
Hover we only with
Skipping footstep along the ground ?
Seest thou naught ? Soars not even, perchance.
Hermes before us ? Shines not the golden wand,
Bidding, commanding us back again
To the cheerless, gray-twilighted,
Full of impalpable phantoms,
Over-filled, eternally empty Hades ?

Yes, at once the air is gloomy, sunless vanish now the
    vapours,
Gray and darkly, brown as buildings. Walls present them-
    selves before us,
Blank against our clearer vision. Is't a court ? a moat, or
    pitfall ?
Fear-inspiring, any way ! and Sisters, ah, behold us
    prisoned,—
Prisoned now, as ne'er before !

> [*Inner court-yard of a Castle, surrounded with rich,
> fantastic buildings of the Middle Ages.*

LEADER OF THE CHORUS. Precipitate and foolish, type of
    women ye !
Dependent on the moment, sport of every breeze
That blows mischance or luck ! and neither ever ye
Supported calmly. One is sure to contradict
The others fiercely, and cross-wise the others her :
Only in joy and pain ye howl and laugh alike.
Be silent now, and hearken what the Mistress here,
High-thoughted, may determine for herself and us !

HELENA. Where art thou, Pythoness ? Whatever be thy
    name.
Step forth from out these arches of the gloomy keep !
If thou didst go, unto the wondrous hero-lord
Me to announce, preparing thus reception fit,
Then take my thanks, and lead me speedily to him !
I wish the wandering closed, I wish for rest alone.

LEADER OF THE CHORUS. In vain thou lookest, Queen, all
   ways around thee here ;
That fatal shape hath vanished hence, perhaps remained
There in the mists, from out whose bosom hitherwards—
I know not how—we came, swiftly, without a step.
Perhaps, indeed, she strays, lost in the labyrinth
Of many castles wondrously combined in one,
Seeking august and princely welcome from the lord.
But see ! up yonder moves in readiness a crowd :
In galleries, at windows, through the portals, comes
A multitude of servants, hastening here and there ;
And this proclaims distinguished welcome to the guest.

 CHORUS. My heart is relieved ! O, yonder behold
How so orderly downward with lingering step
The crowd of the youths in dignity comes,
In regular march ! Who hath given command
That they marshal in ranks, and so promptly disposed,
The youthfullest boys of the beautiful race ?
What shall most I admire ? Is't the delicate gait,
Or the curls of the hair on the white of the brow,
Or the twin-rounded cheeks, blushing red like the peach,
And also, like them, with the silkiest down ?
Fain therein would I bite, yet I fear me to try ;
For, in similar case, was the mouth thereupon
Filled—I shudder to tell it !—with ashes.

    But they, the fairest,
    Hither they come :
    What do they bear ?
    Steps to the throne
    Carpet and seat,
    Curtain and tent,
    Or similar gear ;
    Waving around, and
    Cloudy wreaths forming
    O'er the head of our Queen
    For she already ascendeth,
    Invited, the sumptuous couch.
    Come, forward, now,
    Step by step,

Solemnly ranged !
Worthy, O, threefold worthy her,
May such a reception be blessed ?

[*All that is described by the* CHORUS *takes place by
degrees. After the boys and squires have descended
in a long procession,* FAUST *appears above, at the
head of the staircase, in knightly Court costume of
the Middle Ages, and then comes down slowly and
with dignity.*

LEADER OF THE CHORUS (*observing him intently*).

If now, indeed, the Gods to this man have not lent,
As oft they do to men—a brave, transcendent form,
A winning presence, stately dignity of mien,
For temporary service, all he undertakes
Will always bring him triumph, whether in fight with men,
Or in the minor wars with fairest ladies waged.
Him, verily, to hosts of others I prefer,
Whom highly-famed withal, I have myself beheld.
With slow and solemn step, by reverence restrained,
I see the Prince approach : turn thou thy head, O Queen !

FAUST (*approaching: a man in fetters at his side*).

Instead of solemn greeting, as beseems,
Or reverential welcome, bring I thee,
Fast-bound in welded fetters, here, the knave
Whose duty slighted cheated me of mine.
Kneel down, thou Culprit, that this lofty Dame
May hear the prompt confession of thy guilt !
This, Sovereign Mistress, is the man select
For piercing vision, on the turret high
Stationed to look around, the space of heaven
And breadth of earth to read with sharpest glance,
If here or there perchance come aught to view,—
Between the stronghold and the circling hills
If aught may move, whether the billowy herds
Or waves of armèd men : those we protect,
Encounter these. To-day—what negligence !
Thou comest, he proclaims it not : we fail
In honourable reception, most deserved,
Of such high guest. Now forfeited hath he
His guilty life, and should have shed the blood

Of death deserved; but only thou shalt mete
Pardon or punishment, at thy good will.

    HELENA. So high the power, which thou has granted me,
As Mistress and as Judge, although it were
(I may conjecture) meant but as a test,—
Yet now I use the Judge's bounden right
To give the Accused a hearing: speak then, thou!

    LYNCEUS, THE WARDER OF THE TOWER. Let me kneel
                and let me view her,
    Let me live, or let me die!
    For enslaved, devoted to her,
    This God-granted Dame, am I.

    Watching for the Morn's advancing
    Where her pathways eastward run,
    All at once, a sight entrancing,
    In the South arose the sun.

    There to look, the Wonder drew me:
    Not the glens, the summits cold,
    Space of sky or landscape gloomy,—
    Only Her did I behold.

    Beam of sight to me was given,
    Like the lynx on highest tree;
    But in vain I've urged and striven,
    'Twas a dream that fettered me.

    Could I know, or how be aided?
    Think of tower or bolted gate?
    Vapours rose and vapours faded,
    And the Goddess came in state!

    Eye and heart did I surrender
    To the softly-shining spell:
    Blinding all with Beauty's splendour,
    She hath blinded me, as well.

    I forgot the warder's duty
    And the trumpet's herald-call:
    Threaten to destroy me! Beauty
    Bindeth anger, frees her thrall.

HELENA. The Evil which I brought, I dare no more
Chastise. Ah, woe to me! What fate severe
Pursues me, everywhere the breasts of men
So to infatuate, that nor them, nor aught
Besides of worth, they spare? Now plundering,
Seducing, fighting, hurried to and fro,
Heroes and Demigods, Gods, Demons even,
Hither and thither led me, sore-perplexed.
Sole, I the world bewildered, doubly more;
Now threefold, fourfold, woe on woe I bring.
Remove this guiltless man, let him go free!
The God-deluded merits no disgrace.

FAUST. Amazed, O Queen, do I behold alike
The unerring archer and the stricken prey.
I see the bow, wherefrom the arrow sped
That wounded him. Arrows on arrows fly,
And strike me. I suspect the feathered hum
Of bolts cross-fired through all the courts and towers.
What am I now? At once rebellious thou
Makest my faithfullest, and insecure
My walls. Thence do I fear that even my hosts
Obey the conquering and unconquered Dame.
What else remains, but that I give to thee
Myself, and all I vainly fancied mine?
Let me, before thy feet, in fealty true,
Thee now acknowledge, Lady, whose approach
Won thee at once possession and the throne!

LYNCEUS (*with a chest, and men who follow, bearing others*)
                Thou seest me, Queen, returned and free!
                The wealthy begs a glance from thee:
                Thee he beheld, and feeleth, since,
                As beggar poor, yet rich as prince.

                What was I erst! What now am I?
                What shall I will?—what do, or try?
                What boots the eyesight's sharpest ray?
                Back from thy throne it bounds away.

                Forth from the East we hither pressed,[n]
                And all was over with the West:

So long and broad the people massed,
The foremost knew not of the last.

The foremost fell, the second stood ;
The third one's lance was prompt and good ;
Each one a hundred's strength supplied :
Unnoted, thousands fell and died.

We onward pressed, in stormy chase ;
The lords were we from place to place ;
And where, to-day, *I* ruled as chief,
The morrow brought another thief.

We viewed the ground, but viewed in haste :
The fairest woman one embraced,
One took the oxen from the stall ;
The horses followed one and all.

But my delight was to espy
What rarest was, to mind and eye ;
And all that others might amass
To me was so much withered grass.

I hunted on the treasure-trail
Where'er sharp sight could me avail :
In every pocket did I see,
And every chest was glass to me.

And heaps of gold I came to own,
With many a splendid jewel-stone :
The emeralds only worthy seem
Greenly upon thy breast to gleam.

'Twixt lip and ear let swaying sleep
The pearly egg of Ocean's deep ;
Such place the rubies dare not seek,
They're blanched beside the rosy cheek.

And thus, the treasure's offering
I here before thy presence bring :
Laid at thy feet, be now revealed
The spoils of many a bloody field !

Though I have brought of chests a store,
Yet iron caskets have I more.
Let me attend thee, do thy will,
And I thy treasure-vaults will fill.

For scarcely didst thou mount the throne,
Than bowed to own and bent to own
Thy Beauty's sway, that very hour,
Wisdom, and Wealth, and sovereign Power.

All such I held secure, as mine ;
Now freed therefrom, behold it thine !
I deemed its worth and value plain ;
Now see I, it was null and vain.

What I possessed from me doth pass,
Dispersed like mown and withered grass.
One bright and beauteous glance afford,
And all its worth is straight restored !

FAUST. Remove with speed the burden boldly won,
Not blamed, indeed, but neither with reward.
All is her own already, which the keep
Within it holds ; and special offer thus
Is useless.   Go, and pile up wealth on wealth
In order fit !   Present the show august
Of splendours yet unseen !   The vaulted halls
Make shine like clearest heaven !   Let Paradise
From lifeless pomp of life created be !
Hastening, before her footsteps be unrolled
The flower-embroidered carpets !   Let her tread
Fall on the softest footing, and her glance,
Gods only bear undazed, on proudest pomp !
LYNCEUS. What the lord commands is slight :
        For the servants, labour light :
        Over wealth and blood and breath

> This proud Beauty governeth.
> Lo ! thy warrior-throngs are tame ;
> All the swords are blunt and lame ;
> Near the bright form we behold
> Even the sun is pale and cold ;
> Near the riches of her face
> All things empty, shorn of grace.

HELENA (*to* FAUST). Fain to discourse with thee, I bid
  thee come
Up hither to my side ! The empty place
Invites its lord, and thus secure me mine.

FAUST. First, kneeling, let the dedication be
Accepted, lofty Lady ! Let me kiss
The gracious hand that lifts me to thy side.
Confirm me as co-regent of thy realm,
Whose borders are unknown, and win for thee
Guard, slave and worshipper, and all in one !

HELENA. I hear and witness marvels manifold ;
Amazement takes me, much would I inquire.
Yet now instruct me wherefore spake the man
With strangely-sounding speech, friendly and strange :
Each sound appeared as yielding to the next,[72]
And, when a word gave pleasure to the ear,
Another came, caressing then the first.

FAUST. If thee our people's mode of speech delight,
O thou shalt be enraptured with our song,
Which wholly satisfies both ear and mind !
But it were best we exercise it now :
Alternate speech entices, calls it forth.

HELENA. Canst thou to me that lovely speech impart ?

FAUST. 'Tis easy : it must issue from the heart ;
And if the breast with yearning overflow,
One looks around, and asks—

HELENA.   Who shares the glow ?

FAUST. Nor Past nor Future shades an hour like this ;
But wholly in the Present—

HELENA.   Is our bliss.

FAUST. Gain, pledge, and fortune in the Present stand :
What confirmation does it ask ?

HELENA.   My hand.

CHORUS. Who would take it amiss, that our Princess
     Granteth now to the Castle's lord
     Friendliest demonstration?
     For, indeed, collectively are we
     Captives, as ofttimes already,
     Since the infamous downfall
     Of Ilion, and the perilous,
     Labyrinthine, sorrowful voyage.

     Women, to the love of men accustomed,
     Dainty choosers are they not,
     But proficients skilful;
     And unto golden-haired shepherds,
     Perchance black, bristly Fauns, too,
     Even as comes opportunity,
     Unto the limbs in their vigour
     Fully award they an equal right.

     Near, and nearer already sit
     They, to each other drawn,
     Shoulder to shoulder, knee to knee;
     Hand in hand, they bend and sway
     Over the throne's
     Softly-pillowed, luxurious pomp
     Majesty here not withholds its
     Secretest raptures,
     Wilfully, boldly revealed
     Thus to the eyes of the people.

HELENA. I feel so far away, and yet so near;
And am so fain to say: "Here am I! here."

FAUST. I scarcely breathe; I tremble; speech is dead.
It is a dream, and day and place have fled.

HELENA. I seem as life were done, and yet so new,
Blent thus with thee,—to thee, the Unknown, true!

FAUST. To probe this rarest fate be not impelled!
Being is duty, though a moment held.

PHORKYAS (*violently entering*).

     Spell in lovers' primers sweetly!
     Probe and dally, cosset featly,

Test your wanton sport completely!
But there is not time, nor place.
Feel ye not the gloomy presage?
Hear ye not the trumpet's message?
For the ruin comes apace.
Menelaus with his legions
Storms across the hither regions;
Call to battle all your race!
By the victors execrated,
Like Deiphobus mutilated,
Thou shalt pay for woman's grace:
First shall dangle every light one,
At the altar, then, the Bright One
Find the keen axe in its place!

FAUST. Disturbance rash! repulsively she presses in;
Not even in danger meet is senseless violence.
Ill message makes the fairest herald ugly seem;
Thou, Ugliest, delightest but in evil news.
Yet this time shalt thou not succeed; with empty breath
Stir, shatter thou the air! There is no danger here,
And unto us were danger but an idle threat.

[*Signals, explosions from the towers, trumpets and
cornets, martial music. A powerful armed force
marches past.*

No! hero-bands, none ever braver,
At once shalt thou assembled see:
He, sole, deserves the ladies' favour,
Whose arm defends them gallantly.

[*To the leaders of the troops, who detach themselves
from the columns, and come forwards.*

With rage restrained, in silence banded,
And certain of the victory-feast,
Ye, Northern blossoms, half expanded,
Ye, flowery fervours of the East!

The light upon their armour breaking,
They plundered realm on realm, at will:
They come, and lo! the earth is quaking;
They march away, it thunders still!

ʊ

In Pylos we forsook the waters;
The ancient Nestor is no more,
And soon our lawless army scatters
The troops of kings on Grecian shore.

Back from these walls, no more delaying,
Drive Menelaus to the sea!
There let him wander, robbing, slaying,
As was his wish and destiny.

I hail you Dukes, as forth ye sally
Beneath the rule of Sparta's Queen!
Now lay before her mount and valley,
And you shall share the kingdom green!

Thine, German, be the hand that forges
Defence for Corinth and her bays:
Achaïa, with its hundred gorges,
I give thee, Goth, to hold and raise.

Towards Elis, Franks, direct your motion;
Messene be the Saxon's state:
The Norman claim and sweep the ocean,
And Argolis again made great!

Then each shall dwell in homes well-dowered,
And only outer foemen meet;
Yet still by Sparta over-towered,
The Queen's ancestral, ancient seat.

Each one shall she behold, abiding
In lands that lack no liberal light;
And at her feet ye'll seek, confiding,
Your confirmation, law and light!

    [FAUST *descends from the throne: the Princes form*
       a circle around him, in order to receive special
       commands and instructions.

CHORUS. Who for himself the Fairest desires,
        First of all things, let him

Bravely and wisely a weapon acquire!
Flattering, indeed, he may conquer
What on earth is the highest;
But he quietly may not possess.
Wily sneaks entice her away,
Robbers boldly abduct her from him:
This to hinder be he prepared!

Therefore now our Prince I praise,
Holding him higher than others,
Since he wisdom and strength combines,
So that the strong men obedient stand,
Waiting his every beckon.
They his orders faithfully heed,
Each for the profiting of himself
As for the Ruler's rewarding thanks,
And for the highest renown of both.

For who shall tear her away,
Now, from the mighty possessor?
His is she, and to him be she granted,
Doubly granted by us, whom he,
Even as her, within by sure walls hath surrounded,
And without by a powerful host.

FAUST. The gifts they've won by our concession,—
In fee to each a wealthy land,—
Are grand and fair: grant them possession!
We in the midst will take our stand.

And they in rivalry protect thee,
Half-Island, girdled by the sea
With whispering waves,—whose soft hill-chains connect thee
With the last branch of Europe's mountain-tree!

This land, before all lands in splendour,
On every race shall bliss confer,—
Which to my queen in glad surrender
Yields, as it first looked up to her,

When, 'mid Eurotas' whispering rushes
She burst from Leda's purple shell,
So blinding in her beauty's flushes,
That mother, brothers, felt the spell!

This land which seeks thy sole direction
Its brightest bloom hath now unfurled:
Prefer thy fatherland's affection
To what is wholly thine, the world!

And though upon its ridgy backs of mountains
The Sun's cold arrow smites each cloven head,
Yet, where the rock is greened by falling fountains,
The wild-goat nibbles and is lightly fed.

The springs leap forth, the streams united follow;
Green are the gorges, slopes, and meads below:
On hundred hillsides, cleft with many a hollow,
Thou seest the woolly herds like scattered snow.

Divided, cautious, graze with measured paces
The cattle onward to the dizzy edge,
Yet for them all are furnished sheltered places,
Where countless caverns arch the rocky ledge.

Pan guards them there, and nymphs of life are dwelling
In bushy clefts, that moist and freshest be;
And yearningly to higher regions swelling,
The branches crowd aloft of tree on tree.

Primeval woods? the strong oak there is regnant,
And bough crooks out from bough in stubborn state;
The maple mild, with sweetest juices pregnant,
Shoots cleanly up, and dallies with its weight.

And motherly, in that still realm of shadows,
The warm milk flows, for child's and lambkin's lips:
At hand is fruit, the food of fertile meadows,
And from the hollow trunk the honey drips.

Here comfort is in birth transmitted;
To cheek and lip here joy is sent:
Each is immortal in his station fitted,
And all are healthy and content.

And thus the child in that bright season gaineth
The father-strength, as in a dream:
We wonder; yet the question still remaineth,
If they are men, when Gods they seem.

So was Apollo shepherd-like in feature,
That other shepherds were as fair and fleet;
For where in such clear orbit moveth Nature,
All worlds in inter-action meet.[73]

                [*Taking his seat beside her*

Thus hath success my fate and thine attended;
Henceforth behind us let the Past be furled!
O, feel thyself from highest God descended!
For thou belongest to the primal world.

Thy life shall circumscribe no fortress frowning!
Still, in eternal youth, stands as it stood,
For us, our stay with every rapture crowning,
Arcadia in Sparta's neighbourhood.

To tread this happy soil at last incited,
Thy flight was towards a joyous destiny!
Now let our throne become a bower unblighted,
Our bliss become Arcadian and free!

        [*The scene of action is completely transformed.
           Against a range of rocky caverns close bowers are
           constructed. A shadowy grove extends to the foot of
           the rocks which rise on all sides. FAUST and
           HELENA are not seen: the CHORUS lies scattered
           about, sleeping.*

   PHORKYAS. How long these maidens have been sleeping,
     know I not:
If they allowed themselves to dream what now mine eyes
So clearly saw, is equally unknown to me.

Therefore, I wake them. They, the Young, shall be
    amazed,—

Ye also, Bearded Ones, who sit below and wait,—

Solution of these marvels finally to see.

Awake! arise! and shake from off your locks the dew,

The slumber from your eyes! Listen, and cease to blink!

    CHORUS. Speak and tell us, quickly tell us, all the wonders
        that have happened!

We shall hear with greater pleasure, if belief we cannot give
    it,

For both eye and mind are weary, to behold these rocks
    alone.

    PHORKYAS. Children, you have hardly rubbed your eyes,
        and are you weary now?

Hear me, then! Within these caverns, in the grottos and
    the arbours,

Screen and shelter have been lent, as unto twain idyllic
    lovers,

To our Lord and to our Lady.

    CHORUS.   How? within there?

    PHORKYAS.   Separated

From the world, me only did they summon to their quiet
    service.

Honoured thus, I stood beside them, but, as fit in one so
    trusted,

Looked around at something other, turning here and there at
    random,—

Seeking roots, and bark, and mosses, being skilled in healing
    simples,—

And the twain were left alone.

    CHORUS. Speakest thou as if within were spaces roomy as
        the world is:

Wood and meadow, lakes and rivers,—what a fable dost thou
    spin!

    PHORKYAS. Certainly, ye Inexperienced! Those are
        unexplored recesses:

Hall on hall, and court on court succeeding, musingly I
    tracked.

All at once a laughter echoes through the spaces of the
    caverns;

As I look, a Boy is leaping from the mother's lap to
     father's,
From the father to the mother: the caressing and the
     dandling,
Teasing pranks of silly fondness, cry of sport and shout of
     rapture,
They, alternate, deafen me.
He, a Genius naked, wingless, like a Faun without the
     beasthood,
Leaps upon the solid pavement; yet the pavement now re-
     acting,
Sends him flying high in air, and at the second bound or
     third, he
Seems to graze the vaulted roof.
Cries, disquieted, the mother: " Leap repeatedly, at pleasure,
But beware of flying! for prohibited is flight to thee."
And thus warns the faithful father: " Dwells in earth the
     force elastic
Which thee upwards thus impelleth; touch but with thy toe
     the surface,
Like the son of Earth, Antæus, straightway art thou strong
     again."
So he springs upon the rocky masses, from a dizzy cornice
To another, and around, as springs a ball when sharply
     struck.
Yet, a-sudden, in a crevice of the hollow gulf he's vanished,
And it seemeth we have lost him! Mother mourns, and
     father comforts,
Shoulder-shrugging, anxiously I stand. But now, again,
     what vision!
Are there treasures yonder hidden? Garments striped with
     broidered blossoms
Hath he worthily assumed.
Tassels from his shoulders swaying, fillets flutter round his
     bosom,
In his hand the golden lyre, completely like a little Phœbus,
Cheerily to the brink he steps, the jutting edge: we stand
     astounded,
And the parents in their rapture clasp each other to the
     heart.

What around his head is shining? What it is, were hard to
  warrant,
Whether golden gauds, or flame of all-subduing strength of
  soul.
So he moves with stately gesture, even as boy himself pro-
  claiming
Future Master of all Beauty, all the melodies eternal
Throbbing in his flesh and blood; and you shall thus, delighted,
  hear him,—
Thus shall you behold him, with a wonder never felt before

CHORUS. Call'st thou a marvel this,
   Creta's begotten? [74]
   Poetic-didactical word
   Hast thou listened to never?
   Never yet hearkened Ionia's,
   Never received also Hellas'
   Godlike, heroical treasure
   Of ancient, primitive legends?

   All that ever happens
   Now in the Present
   Mocks like a mournful echo
   The grander days of the Fathers.
   Not comparable is thy story
   Unto that loveliest falsehood,
   Than Truth more credible,
   Sung of the Son of Maia!

   This strong and delicate, yet
   Scarcely delivered suckling,
   Swathe ye in purest downy bands,
   Bind ye in precious diapered stuffs,
   As is the gossiping nurse's
   Unreasonable notion!
   Strongly and daintily draws, no less,
   Now the rogue the flexible,
   Firm yet elastic body
   Cunningly out, and leaveth the close,
   Purple, impeding shell
   Quietly there in its place,

Like the completed butterfly,
Which from the chilly chrysalid
Nimbly, pinion-unfolding, slips,
Boldly and wilfully fluttering through
Sunshine-pervaded ether.
So he, too, the sprightliest :
That unto thieves and jugglers—
All the seekers of profit, as well,—
He the favourable Dæmon was,
Did he speedily manifest
By the skilfullest artifice.
Straight from the Ruler of Ocean stole
He the trident,—from Arês himself
Slyly the sword from the scabbard ;
Arrows and bow from Phœbus, and then
Tongs that Hephæstos was using.
Even from Zeus, the Father, bolts had he
Filched, had the fire not scared him.
Eros, also, he overcame
In leg-tripping wrestling match ;
Then from Cypris, as she caressed him,
Plundered the zone from her bosom.

[*An exquisite, purely melodious music of stringed
    instruments resounds from the cavern. All become
    attentive, and soon appear to be deeply moved.
    From this point to the pause designated, there is a
    full musical accompaniment.*

PHORKYAS. Hark ! the music, pure and golden ;
        Free from fables be at last !
        All your Gods, the medley olden,
        Let depart ! their day is past.

        You no more are comprehended ;
        We require a higher part :
        By the heart must be expended
        What shall work upon the heart.
                            [*She retires towards the rocks.*

CHORUS. If the flattering music presses,
        Fearful Being, to thine ears,

We, restored to health, confess us
Softened to the joy of tears.

Let the sun be missed from heaven,
When the soul is bright with morn !
What the world has never given
Now within our hearts is born.

HELENA. FAUST. EUPHORION *in the costume already described.*

EUPHORION.[75] Hear ye songs of childish pleasure,
      Ye are moved to playful glee ;
      Seeing me thus dance in measure,
      Leap your hearts parentally.

HELENA. Love, in human wise to bless us,
      In a noble Pair must be ;
      But divinely to possess us,
      It must form a precious Three.

FAUST. All we seek has therefore found us ;
      I am thine and thou art mine !
      So we stand as Love hath bound us ;
      Other fortune we resign.

CHORUS. Many years shall they, delighted,
      Gather from the shining boy
      Double bliss for hearts united :
      In their union what a joy !

EUPHORION. Let me be skipping,
      Let me be leaping !
      To soar and circle,
      Through ether sweeping,
      Is now the passion
      That me hath won.

FAUST. But gently ! gently !
      Not rashly faring ;
      Lest plunge and ruin
      Repay thy daring,
      Perchance destroy thee,
      Our darling son !

EUPHORION. I will not longer
      Stagnate below here !
      Let go my tresses,

My hands let go, here!
Let go my garments!
They all are mine.

HELENA. O think! Bethink thee
To whom thou belongest!
How it would grieve us,
And how thou wrongest
The fortune fairest,—
Mine, His, and Thine!

CHORUS. Soon shall, I fear me,
The sweet bond untwine!

HELENA AND FAUST. Curb, thou Unfortunate!
For our desiring,
Thine over-importunate
Lofty aspiring!
Rurally quiet,
Brighten the plain!

EUPHORION. Since you will that I try it,
My flight I restrain.
[*Winding in dance through the* CHORUS, *and
drawing them with him.*
Round them I hover free;
Gay is the race:
Is this the melody?
Move I with grace?

HELENA. Yes, that is featly done:
Lead them through, every one,
Mazes of art!

FAUST. Soon let it ended be!
Sight of such jugglery
Troubles my heart.

CHORUS (*with* EUPHORION *dancing nimbly and singing, in
interlinking ranks*). When thou thine arms so fair
Charmingly liftest,
The curls of thy shining hair
Shakest and shiftest;
When thou, with foot so light,
Brushest the earth in flight,
Hither and forth again
Leading the linkéd chain,

Then is thy goal in sight,
Loveliest Boy?
All of our hearts in joy
Round thee unite.

EUPHORION. Not yet repose,
Ye light-footed roes !
Now to new play
Forth, and away !
I am the hunter,
You are the game.

[Pause.

CHORUS. Wouldst thou acquire us,
Be not so fast !
We are desirous
Only, at last,
Clasping thy beauty,
Kisses to claim !

EUPHORION. Through groves and through hedges !
O'er cliffs and o'er ledges !
Lightly what fell to me,
That I detest :
What I compel to me
Pleases me best.

HELENA AND FAUST. How perverse, how wild he's
growing !
Vain to hope for moderation ;
Now it sounds like bugles blowing,
Over vale and forest pealing :
What disorder !   What a brawl !

CHORUS (*entering singly, in haste*). Forth from us with
swiftness ran he !
Spurning us with scornful feeling,
Now he drags from out the many
Here, the wildest one of all.

EUPHORION (*bearing a young* MAIDEN). Here I drag the
little racer,
And by force will I embrace her ;
For my bliss and for my zest
Press the fair, resisting breast,
Kiss the mouth, repellent still,—
Manifest my strength and will.

MAIDEN. Let me go !   This frame infoldeth
Also courage, strength of soul :
Strong as thine, our will upholdeth,
When another would control.
I am in a strait, thou deemest ?
What a force thine arm would claim !
Hold me, Fool, and ere thou dreamest
I will scorch thee, in my game.
       [*She turns to flame and flashes up in the air*
To the airy spaces follow,
Follow me to caverns hollow,
Snatch and hold thy vanished aim !

EUPHORION (*shaking off the last flames*). Rocks all around
     me here,
Over the forests hung !
Why should they bound me here ?
Still am I fresh and young.
Tempests are waking now,
Billows are breaking now :
Both far away I hear ;
Fain would be near.
       [*He leaps ever farther up the rocks.*

HELENA, FAUST, AND CHORUS. Chamois-like, dost thou
     aspire ?
Fearful of the fall are we.

EUPHORION. I must clamber ever higher,
Ever further must I see.

Now, where I am, I spy ?
Midst of the Isle am I :
Midst of Pelops' land,
Kindred in soul I stand ![75]

CHORUS. Bide thou by grove and hill,
Peacefully, rather !
We from the vineyards will
Grapes for thee gather,—
Grapes from the ridges tanned,
Figs, and the apple's gold :
Ah ! yet the lovely land,
Loving, behold !

EUPHORION. Dream ye the peaceful day ?
                 Dream, then, who may !
                 War ! is the countersign :
                 Victory—word divine !
CHORUS.   Who peace and unity
                 Scorneth, for war's array,
                 With impunity
                 Slays his hope of a better day.
EUPHORION. They, who this land have led
                 Through danger and dread,
                 Free, boundlessly brave,
                 Lavish of blood they gave,—
                 May they, with glorious
                 Untamable might,
                 Make us victorious,
                 Now, in the fight !
CHORUS.   Look aloft ! he seeks the Farness,
                 Yet to us not small he seems.
                 As for battle, as in harness,
                 He like steel and silver gleams.
EUPHORION. Walls and towers no more immuring,
                 Each in vigour stands confessed !
                 Fortress firm and most enduring
                 Is the soldier's iron breast.

                 Would ye dwell in freemen's houses ?
                 Arm, and forth to combat wild !
                 See, as Amazons, your spouses,
                 And a hero every child !
CHORUS.   Hallowed Poesy,
                 Heavenward mounting, see !
                 Shining, the fairest star,
                 Farther, and still more far !
                 Yet, from the distance blown,
                 Hear we the lightest tone,
                 And raptured are.
EUPHORION. No, 't is no child which thou beholdest—
                 A youth in arms, with haughty brow !
                 And with the Strongest, Freest, Boldest,
                 His soul is pledged, in manly vow.

I go!
For, lo!
The path to glory opens now.[7]

HELENA AND FAUST. Thou thy being scarcely learnest,
Scarcely feel'st the Day's glad beam,
When from giddy steeps thou yearnest
For the place of pain supreme!
Are then we
Naught to thee?
Is the gracious bond a dream?

EUPHORION. And hear ye thunders on the ocean?
From land the thunder-echoes call?
In dust and foam, with fierce commotion,
The armies shock, the heroes fall!
The command
Is, sword in hand,
To: 'tis certain, once for all.

HELENA, FAUST, AND CHORUS. What a horror! We shall
rue it!
Ah, is Death command to thee?

EUPHORION. Shall I from the distance view it?
No! the fate be shared by me!

THE ABOVE. Danger his arrogance brings:
Fatally bold!

EUPHORION. Yes!—and a pair of wings
See me unfold!
Thither! I must!—and thus!
Grant me the flight!

[*He casts himself into the air: the garments bear him
a moment, his head is illuminated, and a streak of
light follows.*

CHORUS. Icarus! Icarus!
Sorrowful sight!

[*A beautiful Youth falls at the feet of the parents.
We imagine that in the dead body we perceive a
well-known form; yet the corporeal part vanishes
at once, and the aureole rises like a comet towards
heaven. The garment, mantle, and lyre remain
upon the ground.*

HELENA AND FAUST. Joy is followed, when scarce enjoyed,
 By bitterest moan.

EUPHORION (*from the depths*). Leave me here, in the gloomy Void,
 Mother, not thus alone !   [*Pause.*

CHORUS [*Dirge*].[78] Not alone ! where'er thou bidest ;
 For we know thee what thou art.
 Ah ! if from the Day thou hidest,
 Still to thee will cling each heart.
 Scarce we venture to lament thee,
 Singing, envious of thy fate ;
 For in storm and sun were lent thee
 Song and courage, fair and great.

 Ah ! for earthly fortune fashioned,
 Strength was thine, and proud descent :
 Early erring, o'er-impassioned,
 Youth, alas ! from thee was rent.
 For the world thine eye was rarest,
 All the heart to thee was known :
 Thine were loves of women fairest,
 And a song thy very own.

 Yet thou rannest uncontrolledly
 In the net the fancies draw,
 Thus thyself divorcing boldly
 As from custom, so from law ;
 Till the highest thought expended
 Set at last thy courage free :
 Thou wouldst win achievement splendid,
 But it was not given to thee.

 Unto whom, then ? Question dreary,
 Destiny will never heed ;
 When in evil days and weary,
 Silently the people bleed.
 But new songs shall still elate them :
 Bow no longer and deplore !

For the soil shall generate them,
As it hath done heretofore.

[*Complete pause.   The music ceases.*

HELENA (*to* FAUST). Also in me, alas! an old word proves
its truth,
That Bliss and Beauty ne'er enduringly unite.
Torn is the link of Life, no less than that of Love;
So, both lamenting, painfully I say: Farewell!
And cast myself again—once only—in thine arms.
Receive, Persephone, receive the boy and me.

[*She embraces* FAUST: *her corporeal part disappears,
her garment and veil remain in his arms.*

PHORKYAS (*to* FAUST). Hold fast what now alone remains
to thee!
The garment let not go!   Already twitch
The Demons at its skirts, and they would fain
To the Nether Regions drag it!   Hold it fast!
It is no more the Goddess thou hast lost,
But godlike is it.   For thy use employ
The grand and priceless gift, and soar aloft!
'Twill bear thee swift from all things mean and low
To ether high, so long thou canst endure.
We'll meet again, far, very far from here.

[HELENA'S *garments dissolve into clouds,*[79] *surround*
FAUST, *lift him aloft in the air, and move away
with him.*

PHORKYAS (*takes up* EUPHORION'S *tunic, mantle, and lyre
from the earth, steps forward to the proscenium, holds
aloft these remains, and speaks*).
Good leavings have I still discovered!
The flame has vanished where it hovered,
Yet for the world no tears I spend.
Enough remains to start the Poets living,
And envy in their guilds to send;
And, if their talents are beyond my giving,
At least the costume I can lend.

[*She seats herself upon a column in the proscenium.*

PANTHALIS. Now hasten, maidens! we are from the magic
freed,
The old Thessalian trollop's mind-compelling spell,—

x

Freed from the jingling drone of much-bewildering sound,
The ear confusing, and still more the inner sense.
Down, then, to Hades! since beforehand went the Queen,
With solemn step descending. Now, upon the track,
Let straightway follow her the step of faithful maids!
Her shall we find beside the unfathomed, gloomy King.

CHORUS. Queens, of course, are satisfied everywhere:
　　　　Even in Hades take they highest rank,
　　　　Proudly associate with their peers,
　　　　With Persephone closely allied:
　　　　We, however, in the background
　　　　Of the asphodel-besprinkled meadows,
　　　　With the endless rows of poplars
　　　　And the fruitless willows ever mated,—
　　　　What amusement, then, have we?
　　　　Bat-like to squeak and twitter
　　　　In whispers uncheery and ghostly!

LEADER OF THE CHORUS. Who hath not won a name, and
　　　　seeks not noble works,
Belongs but to the elements: away then, ye!
My own intense desire is with my Queen to be;
Service and faith secure the individual life.　　　　　[*Exit.*

　　　ALL. Given again to the daylight are we,
　　　　Persons no more, 'tis true,—
　　　　We feel it and know it,—
　　　　But to Hades return we never!
　　　　Nature, the Ever-living,
　　　　Makes to us spirits
　　　　Validest claim, and we to her also.

A PART OF THE CHORUS. We, in trembling whispers,
　　　　swaying rustle of a thousand branches
Sweetly rocked, will lightly lure the rills of life, the root-
　　　　born, upwards
To the twigs; and, or with foliage or exuberant gush of
　　　　blossoms,
Will we freely deck their flying hair for prosperous airy
　　　　growth.
Then, when falls the fruit, will straightway gather glad-
　　　　dened herds and people,

Swiftly coming, briskly pressing, for the picking and the
    tasting :
All, as if before the early Gods, will then around us bend.
    A Second Part. We, beside these rocks, upon the far-off
    shining, glassy mirror,
Coaxingly will bend and fluctuate, moving with the gentle
    waters ;
We to every sound will hearken, song of bird or reedy
    piping ;
Though the dreadful voice of Pan, a ready answer shall we
    give :
Comes a murmur, we re-murmur,—thunder, we our thunders
    waken
In reverberating crashes, doubly, trebly, tenfold flung !
    A Third Part. Sisters, we, of nimbler fancy, hasten with
    the brooklets onward ;
For allure us yonder distant, richly-mantled mountain
    ranges.
Ever downwards, ever deeper, in meandering curves we
    water
First the meadow, then the pasture ; then the garden round
    the house,
Marked by slender peaks of cypress, shooting clearly into
    ether
O'er the landscape and the waters and the fading line of
    shore.
    A Fourth Part. Fare, ye others, at your pleasure , we
    will girdle and o'errustle
The completely-planted hillside, where the sprouting vines
    are green.
There at every hour the passion of the vintager is witnessed,
And the loving diligence, that hath so doubtful a result.
Now with hoe and now with shovel, then with hilling, prun-
    ing, tying,
Unto all the Gods he prayeth, chiefly to the Sun's bright
    god.
Small concern hath pampered Bacchus for his faithful
    servant's welfare,
But in arbours rests, and caverns, toying with the youngest
    Faun.

x 2

For his semi-drunken visions whatsoever he hath needed,

It is furnished him in wine-skins, and in amphoræ and
    vessels,

Right and left in cool recesses, cellared for eternal time.

But if now the Gods together, Helios before the others,

Have with breeze and dew and warmth and glow the berries
    filled with juice,

Where the vintager in silence laboured, all is life and
    motion,

Every trellis stirs and rustles, and they go from stake to
    stake.

Baskets creak and buckets rattle, groaning tubs are borne on
    back,

All towards the vat enormous and the treaders' lusty dance ;

So is then the sacred bounty of the pure-born, juicy berries

Rudely trodden ; foaming, spirting, they are mixed and
    grimly crushed.

Now the ear is pierced with cymbals and the clash of brazen
    bosses,

For, behold, is Dionysos from his mysteries revealed !

Forth he comes with goat-foot Satyrs, whirling goat-foot
    Satyresses,

While amid the rout Silenus' big-eared beast unruly brays.

Naught is spared ! The cloven hoofs tread down all decent
    custom ;

All the senses whirl bewildered, fearfully the ear is stunned.

Drunkards fumble for their goblets, over-full are heads and
    paunches ;

Here and there hath one misgivings, yet increases thus the
    tumult ;

For, the fresher must to garner, empty they the ancient
    skin !

> [*The curtain falls.* PHORKYAS, *in the proscenium,
> rises to a giant height, steps down from the
> cothurni, removes her mask and veil, and reveals
> herself as* MEPHISTOPHELES, *in order, so far as it
> may be necessary, to comment upon the piece by way
> of Epilogue.*]

ACT IV.

—◆—

I.

HIGH MOUNTAINS.

Strong, serrated rocky peaks.   A cloud approaches, pauses, and settles down upon a projecting ledge.   It then divides.

FAUST (*steps forth*). Down-gazing on the deepest solitudes
     below,
I tread deliberately this summit's lonely edge,
Relinquishing my cloudy car, which hither bore
Me softly through the shining day o'er land and sea.
Unscattered, slowly moved, it separates from me.
Off eastward strives the mass with rounded, rolling march :
And strives the eye, amazed, admiring, after it.
In motion it divides, in wave-like, changeful guise ;
Yet seems to shape a figure.—Yes ! mine eyes not err !—
On sun-illumined pillows beauteously reclined,
Colossal, truly, but a godlike woman-form,
I see ! The like of Juno, Leda, Helena,
Majestically lovely, floats before my sight !
Ah, now 'tis broken ! Towering broad and formlessly,
It rests along the east like distant icy hills,
And shapes the grand significance of fleeting days.
Yet still there clings a light and delicate band of mist
Around my breast and brow, caressing, cheering me.
Now light, delayingly, it soars and higher soars,
And folds together.—Cheats me an ecstatic form,
As early-youthful, long-foregone and highest bliss ?
The first glad treasures of my deepest heart break forth ;

Aurora's love, so light of pinion, is its type,
The swiftly-felt, the first, scarce-comprehended glance,
Outshining every treasure, when retained and held.
Like Spiritual Beauty mounts the gracious Form,
Dissolving not, but lifts itself through ether far,
And from my inner being bears the best away.

[*A Seven-league Boot trips forward:* [80] *another immediately follows.* MEPHISTOPHELES *steps out of
them. The Boots stride onward in haste.*

MEPHIS. I call that genuine forward-striding!
But what thou mean'st, I'd have thee own,
That in such horrors art abiding,
Amid these yawning jags of stone?
It was not here I learned to know them well;
Such was, indeed, the bottom-ground of Hell.

FAUST. In foolish legends thou art never lacking;
Again thy store thou set'st about unpacking.

MEPHIS. (*seriously*). When God the Lord—wherefore, I
also know,—
Banned us from air to darkness deep and central,
Where round and round, in fierce, intensest glow,
Eternal fires were whirled in Earth's hot entrail
We found ourselves too much illuminated,
Yet crowded and uneasily situated.
The Devils all set up a coughing, sneezing,
At every vent without cessation wheezing:
With sulphur stench and acids Hell dilated,
And such enormous gas was then created,
That very soon Earth's level, far extended,
Thick as it was, was heaved, and split, and rended!
The thing is plain, no theories o'ercome it:
What formerly was bottom, now is summit.
Hereon they base the law there's no disputing,
To give the undermost the topmost footing:
For we escaped from fiery dungeons there
To overplus of lordship of the air;—
A mystery manifest and well concealed,
And to the people only late revealed.

FAUST. To me are mountain-masses grandly dumb:
I ask not, Whence? and ask not, Why? they come.

When Nature in herself her being founded,
Complete and perfect then the globe she rounded,
Glad of the summits and the gorges deep,
Set rock to rock, and mountain steep to steep,
The hills with easy outlines downward moulded,
Till gently from their feet the vales unfolded !
They green and grow ; with joy therein she ranges,
Requiring no insane, convulsive changes.

  MEPHIS. Yes, so you talk ! You think it clear as sun ;
But he knows otherwise, who saw it done.
For I was there, while still below was surging
The red abyss, and streamed the flaming tide,—
When Moloch's hammer, welding rocks and forging,
Scattered the mountain-ruins far and wide.
O'er all the land the foreign blocks you spy there ;
Who solves the force that hurled them to their place ?
The lore of learned men is all awry there ;
There lies the rock, and we must let it lie there ;
We've thought already—to our own disgrace.
Only the common, faithful people know,
And nothing shakes them in their firm believing :
Their wisdom ripened long ago,—
A marvel 'tis, of Satan's own achieving.
On crutch of faith my traveller climbs the ridges,
Past Devil's Rocks and over Devil's Bridges.

  FAUST. Well,—'tis remarkable and new
To note how Devils Nature view.

  MEPHIS. What's all to me ? Her shape let Nature wear :
The point of honour is, the Devil was there !
We are the folk to compass grand designs :
Tumult, and Force, and Nonsense ! See the signs !—
Yet now, with sober reason to address thee,
Did nothing on our outside shell impress thee ?
From this exceeding height thou saw'st unfurled
The glory of the Kingdoms of the World.
Yet, as thou art, unsatisfied,
Didst feel no lust of power and pride ?

  FAUST. I did ! A mighty plan my fancy won :
Canst guess it ?

  MEPHIS.   That is quickly done.

I'd take some town,—a capital, perchance,—
Its core, the people's need of sustenance ;
With crooked alleys, pointed gables,
Beets, cabbage, onions, on the market-tables ;
With meat-stands, where the blue flies muster,
And round fat joints like gourmands cluster :
There shalt thou find, undoubtedly,
Stench, always, and activity.
Then ample squares, and streets whose measure
Assumes an air of lordly leisure ;
And last, without a gate to bar,
The boundless suburbs stretching far.
'Twere joy to see the coaches go,
The noisy crowding to and fro,
The endless running, hither, thither,
Of scattered ants that stream together :
And whether walking, driving, riding,
Ever their central point abiding,
Honoured by thousands, should be I.

FAUST. Therewith I would not be contented !
One likes to see the people multiply,
And in their wise with comfort fed,—
Developed even, taught, well-bred,
Yet one has only, when all's said,
The sum of rebels thus augmented.

MEPHIS. Then I should build, with conscious power and
                grace,
A pleasure-castle in a pleasant place ;
Where hill and forest, level, meadow, field,
Grandly transformed, should park and garden yield.
Before green walls of foliage velvet meadows,
With ordered paths and artful-falling shadows ;
Plunge of cascades o'er rocks with skill combined,
And fountain-jets of every form and kind,
There grandly shooting upwards from the middle,
While round the sides a thousand spirt and piddle.
Then for the fairest women, fresh and rosy,
I'd build a lodge, convenient and cosey ;
And so the bright and boundless time I should
Pass in the loveliest social solitude.

Women, I say ; and, once for all, believe
That in the plural I the sex conceive !

FAUST. Sardanapalus ! Modern,—poor !

MEPHIS Then might one guess whereunto thou hast
striven ?
Boldly-sublime it was, I'm sure.
Since nearer to the moon thy flight was driven,
Would now thy mania that realm secure ?

FAUST. Not so ! This sphere of earthly soil
Still gives us room for lofty doing.
Astounding plans e'en now are brewing :
I feel new strength for bolder toil.

MEPHIS. So, thou wilt Glory earn ? 'Tis plain to see
That heroines have been thy company.

FAUST. Power and Estate to win, inspires my thought !
The Deed is everything, the Glory naught.

MEPHIS. Yet Poets shall proclaim the matter,
Thy fame to future ages flatter,
By folly further folly scatter !

FAUST. All that is far beyond thy reach.
How canst thou know what men beseech ?
Thy cross-grained self, in malice banned,
How can it know what men demand ?

MEPHIS. According to thy will so let it be !
Confide the compass of thy whims to me !

FAUST. Mine eye was drawn to view the open Ocean :
It swelled aloft, self-heaved and over-vaulting,
And then withdrew, and shook its waves in motion,
Again the breadth of level strand assaulting.
Then I was vexed, since arrogance can spite
The spirit free, which values every right,
And through excited passion of the blood
Discomfort it, as did the haughty flood.
I thought it chance, my vision did I strain ;
The billow paused, then thundered back again,
Retiring from the goal so proudly won :
The hour returns, the sport's once more begun.

MEPHIS. (*ad spectatores*). 'Tis nothing new whatever that
one hears ;
I've known it many a hundred thousand years.

FAUST (*continuing impassionedly*). The Sea sweeps on, in
   thousand quarters flowing,
Itself unfruitful, barrenness bestowing;
It breaks and swells, and rolls, and overwhelms
The desert stretch of desolated realms.
There endless waves hold sway, in strength erected
And then withdrawn,—and nothing is effected.
If aught could drive me to despair, 'twere, truly
The aimless force of elements unruly.
Then dared my mind its dreams to over-soar:
Here would I fight,—subdue this fierce uproar!
And possible 'tis!—Howe'er the tides may fill,
They gently fawn around the steadfast hill;
A moderate height resists and drives asunder,
A moderate depth allures and leads them on.
So, swiftly, plans within my mind were drawn:
Let that high joy be mine for evermore,
To shut the lordly Ocean from the shore,
The watery waste to limit and to bar,
And push it back upon itself afar!
From step to step I settled how to fight it:
Such is my wish: dare thou to expedite it!
  [*Drums and martial music in the rear of the spectators,
   from the distance, on the right hand.*
 MEPHIS. How easy, that!—Hear'st thou the drums afar?
 FAUST. Who's wise likes not to hear of coming war.
 MEPHIS. In War or Peace, 'tis wise to use the chance,
And draw some profit from each circumstance.
One watches, marks the moment, and is bold:
Here's opportunity!—now, Faust, take hold!
 FAUST. Spare me the squandering of thy riddle-pelf!
What means it, once for all? Explain thyself!
 MEPHIS. Upon my way, to me it was discovered
That mighty troubles o'er the Emperor hovered:
Thou knowest him. The while we twain, beside him,
With wealth illusive bounteously supplied him,
Then all the world was to be had for pay;
For as a youth he held imperial sway,
And he was pleased to try it, whether
Both interests would not smoothly pair,

Since 'twere desirable and fair
To govern and enjoy, together.

FAUST. A mighty error!   He who would command
Must in commanding find his highest blessing :
Then, let his breast with force of will expand,
But what he wills, be past another's guessing !
What to his faithful he hath whispered, that
Is turned to act, and men amaze thereat :
Thus will he ever be the highest-placed
And worthiest !—Enjoyment makes debased.

MEPHIS. Such is he not !   He *did* enjoy, even he !
Meanwhile the realm was torn by anarchy,
Where great and small were warring with each other,
And brother drove and slaughtered brother,
Castle to castle, town 'gainst town arrayed,
The nobles and the guilds of trade,
The Bishop, with his chapter and congregation,—
All meeting eyes but looked retaliation.
In churches death and murder ; past the gates,
The merchants travelled under evil fates ;
And all grew bolder, since no rule was drawn
For life, but : Self-defence !—So things went on.

FAUST. They went, they limped, they fell, arose again,
Then tumbled headlong, and in heaps remain.

MEPHIS. Such a condition no man dared abuse.
Each would be something, each set forth his dues ;
The smallest even as full-measured passed :
Yet for the best it grew too bad at last.
The Capable, they then arose with energy,
And said : " Who gives us Peace, shall ruler be.
The Emperor can and will not !—Be elected
An Emperor new, anew the realm directed.
Each one secure and sheltered stand,
And in a fresh-constructed land
Justice and Peace be mated and perfected ! "

FAUST. Priest-like, that sounds.

MEPHIS.   Priests were they, to be sure.
They meant their well-fed bellies to secure ;
They, more than all, therein were implicated.[81]
The riot rose, the riot was consecrated,

And now our Emperor, whom we gave delight,
Comes hitherward, perchance for one last fight.

FAUST. I pity him ; he was so frank, forgiving.

MEPHIS. Come, we'll look on ! There's hope while one is
living !
Let us release him from this narrow valley !
He's saved a thousand times, if once he rally.
Who knows how yet the dice may fall ?
If he has fortune, vassals come withal.

> [*They cross over the middle range of mountains, and
> view the arrangement of the army in the valley.
> Drums and military music resound from below.*

MEPHIS. A good position is, I see, secured them ;
We'll join, then victory will be assured them.

FAUST. What further, I should like to know ?
Cheat ! Blind delusion ! Hollow show !

MEPHIS. No,—stratagems, for battle-winning !
Be steadfast for the grand beginning,
And think upon thy lofty aim !
If we secure the realm its rightful claimant,
Then shalt thou boldly kneel, and claim
The boundless strand in feoff, as payment.

FAUST. In many arts didst thou excel :
Come, win a battle now, as well !

MEPHIS. No, *thou* shalt win it ! Here, in brief,
Shalt thou be General-in-Chief.

FAUST. A high distinction thou wouldst lend,—
There to command, where naught I comprehend !

MEPHIS. Leave to the Staff the work and blame,
Then the Field-Marshal's sure of fame !
Of War-Uncouncils I have had enough,
And my War-Council fashion of the stuff
Of primal mountains' primal human might :
He's blest, for whom its elements unite !

FAUST. What do I see, with arms, in yonder place ?
Hast thou aroused the mountain-race ?

MEPHIS. No ! But I've brought, like Peter Squence,[82]
From all the raff the quintessence.

> [*The Three Mighty Men appear*

MEPHIS. My fellows draw already near !

Thou seest, of very different ages,
Of different garb and armour they appear:
They will not serve thee ill when battle rages.

[*Ad spectatores.*

Now every child delights to see
The harness and the helm of knightly action;
And allegoric, as the blackguards be,
They'll only all the more give satisfaction.

    BULLY (*young, lightly-armed, clad in motley*). When **one**
        shall meet me, face to face,
My fisticuffs shall on his chops be showered;
And midway in his headlong race,
Fast by his flying hair I'll catch the coward.

    HAVEQUICK (*manly, well-armed, richly clad*). Such empty
        brawls are only folly!
They spoil whate'er occasion brings.
In *taking*, be unwearied wholly,
And after, look to other things!

    HOLDFAST (*well in years, strongly-armed, without **raiment***).
Yet little gain thereafter lingers!
Soon slips great wealth between your fingers,
Borne by the tides of Life as down they run.
'Tis well to take, indeed, but better still to hold:
Be by the gray old churl controlled,
And thou shalt plundered be by none.

                    [*They descend the mountain together*

II.

ON THE HEADLAND.

Drums and military music from below. The EMPEROR'S *tent is pitched.*

EMPEROR.   GENERAL-IN-CHIEF.   LIFE-GUARDSMEN.

GENERAL-IN-CHIEF. It still appears the prudentest of courses
That here, in this appropriate vale,
We have withdrawn and strongly massed our forces :
I firmly trust we shall not fail.

EMPEROR. What comes of it will soon be brought to light,
Yet I dislike this yielding, semi-flight.

GENERAL-IN-CHIEF. Look down, my Prince, where our right flank is planted !
The field which War desires hath here been granted :
Not steep the hills, yet access not preparing,
To us advantage, to the foe insnaring ;
Their cavalry will hardly dare surround
Our strength half hid, on undulating ground.

EMPEROR. My commendation, only, need I speak ;
Now arm and courage have the test they seek.

GENERAL-IN-CHIEF. Here, on the middle meadow's level spaces
Thou seest the phalanx, eager in their places.
In air the lances gleam and sparkle, kissed
By sunshine, through the filmy morning mist.
How darkling sways the grand and powerful square !
The thousands burn for great achievements there.
Therein canst thou perceive the strength of masses ;
And thine, be sure, the foemen's strength surpasses.

EMPEROR. Now first do I enjoy the stirring sight :
An army, thus, appears of double might.

GENERAL-IN-CHIEF. But of our left I've no report to make

Brave heroes garrison the rocky brake ;
The stony cliffs, by gleams of weapons specked,
The entrance to the close defile protect.
Here, as I guess, the foemen's force will shatter,
Forced unawares upon the bloody matter.

EMPEROR. And there they march, false kin, one like the
        other !
Even as they styled me Uncle, Cousin, Brother,
Assuming more, and ever more defying,
The sceptre's power, the throne's respect, denying ;
Then, in their feuds, the realm they devastated,
And now as Rebels march, against me mated !
Awhile with halting minds the masses go,
Then ride the stream, wherever it may flow.

    GENERAL-IN-CHIEF. A faithful man, sent out some news
            to win,
Comes down the rocks : may he have lucky been !

    FIRST SPY. Luckily have we succeeded ;
            Helped by bold and cunning art,
            Here and there have pressed, and heeded,
            But 'tis ill news we impart.
            Many, purest homage pledging,
            Like the faithful, fealty swore,—
            For inertness now alleging
            People's danger, strife in store.

    EMPEROR. They learn from selfishness self-preservation,
Not duty, honour, grateful inclination.
You do not think that, when your reckoning's shown,
The neighbour's burning house shall fire your own !

    GENERAL-IN-CHIEF. The Second comes, descending slowly
            hither ;
A weary man, whose strength appears to wither.

    SECOND SPY. First with comfort we detected
            What their plan confused was worth ;
            Then, at once and unexpected,
            Came another Emperor forth.
            As he bids, in ordered manner
            March the gathering hosts away ;
            His unfolded lying banner
            All have followed.—Sheep are they !

EMPEROR. Now, by a Rival Emperor shall I gain:
That *I* am Emperor, thus to me is plain.
But as a soldier I the mail put on ;
Now for a higher aim the sword be drawn !
At all my shows, however grand to see,
Did nothing lack : but Danger lacked, *to me.*
Though you but tilting at the ring suggested,
My heart beat high to be in tourney tested ;
And had you not from war my mind dissuaded,
For glorious deeds my name were now paraded.
But independence then did I acquire,
When I stood mirrored in the realm of fire :
In the dread element I dared to stand ;—
'Twas but a show, and yet the show was grand.
Of fame and victory I have dreamed alone ;
But for the base neglect I now atone !

> [*The* HERALDS *are despatched to challenge the Rival
> Emperor to single combat.*

FAUST *enters, in armour, with half-closed visor. The* THREE
MIGHTY MEN, *armed and clothed, as already described.*

FAUST. We come, and hope our coming is not chidden ;
Prudence may help, though by the need unbidden.
The mountain race, thou know'st, think and explore,—
Of Nature and the rocks they read the lore.
The Spirits, forced from the level land to sever,
Are of the rocky hills more fain than ever.
Silent, they work through labyrinthine passes,
In rich, metallic fumes of noble gases,
On solving, testing, blending, most intent :
Their only passion, something to invent.
With gentle touch of spiritual power
They build transparent fabrics, hour by hour ;
For they, in crystals and their silence, furled,
Behold events that rule the Upper world.

EMPEROR. I understand it, and can well agree ;
But say, thou gallant man, what's that to me ?

FAUST. The Sabine old, the Noreian necromancer,[a]
Thy true and worthy servant, sends thee answer :
What fearful fate it was, that overhung him !

The faggots crackled, fire already stung him;
The billets dry were closely round him fixed,
With pitch and rolls of brimstone intermixed;
Not Man, nor God, nor Devil, him could save,—
The Emperor plucked him from his fiery grave.
It was in Rome.   Still is he bound unto thee;
Upon thy path his anxious thoughts pursue thee;
Himself since that dread hour forgotten, he
Questions the stars, the depths, alone for thee.
Us he commissioned, by the swiftest courses
Thee to assist.   Great are the mountain's forces;
There Nature works all-potently and free,
Though stupid priests therein but magic see.

EMPEROR. On days of joy, when we the guests are
    greeting,
Who for their gay delight are gaily meeting,
Each gives us pleasure, as they push and pull,
And crowd, man after man, the chambers full,
Yet chiefly welcome is the brave man, thus,
When as a bold ally he brings to us
Now, in the fateful morning hour, his talents,
While Destiny uplifts her trembling balance.
Yet, while the fates of this high hour unfold,
Thy strong hand from the willing sword withhold,—
Honour the moment, when the hosts are striding,
For or against me, to the field deciding!
Self is the Man! Who crown and throne would claim
Must personally be worthy of the same.
And may the Phantom, which against us stands,
The self-styled Emperor, Lord of all our lands,
The army's Duke, our Princes' feudal head,
With mine own hand be hurled among the dead!

FAUST. Howe'er the need that thy great work be finished,
Risked were thy head, the chances were diminished.
Is not the helm adorned with plume and crest?
The head it shields, that steels our courage best.
Without a head, what should the members bridle?
Let it but sleep, they sink supine and idle.
If it be injured, all the hurt confess in't,
And all revive, when it is convalescent.

Then soon the arm its right shall reassert,
And lift the shield to save the skull from hurt:
The sword perceives at once its honoured trust,
Parries with vigour, and repeats the thrust:
The gallant foot its share of luck will gain,
And plants itself upon the necks of slain.

EMPEROR. Such is my wrath; I'd meet him thus, un-
        daunted,
And see his proud head as my footstool planted!

HERALDS (*returning*). Little honour was accorded;
        We have met with scorn undoubted:
        Our defiance, nobly worded,
        As an empty farce they flouted:
        "Lo, your Lord is but a vision,—
        Echo of a vanished prime:
        When we name him, says Tradition:
        'He was—*once upon a time!*'"

FAUST. It's happened as the best would fain have planned,
Who, firm and faithful, still beside thee stand.
There comes the foe, thy army waits and wishes;
Order attack! the moment is auspicious.

EMPEROR. Yet I decline to exercise command.

                        [*To the* GENERAL-IN-CHIEF.
Thy duty, Prince, be trusted to thy hand!

GENERAL-IN-CHIEF. Then let the right wing now advance
        apace!
The enemy's left, who just begin ascending,
Shall, ere the movement close, give up their place,
Before the youthful force our field defending.

FAUST. Permit me, then, that this gay hero may
Be stationed in thy ranks, without delay,—
That with thy men most fully he consort,
And thus incorporate, ply his vigorous sport!

                [*He points to the* MIGHTY MAN *on the right.*

BULLY (*coming forward*). Who shows his face to me, before
        he turn
Shall find his cheekbones and his chops are shattered:
Who shows his back, one sudden blow shall earn,
Then head and pig-tail dangling hang, and battered!
And if thy men, like me, will lunge

With mace and sword, beside each other,
Man over man the foe shall plunge
And in their own deep blood shall smother !   [*Exit.*

GENERAL-IN-CHIEF. Let then our centre phalanx follow
    slow,—
Engage with caution, yet with might, the foe !
There to the right, already overtaken,
Our furious force their plan has rudely shaken !

FAUST (*pointing to the middle one*). Let also this one now
    obey thy word !

HAVEQUICK (*comes forward*). Unto the host's heroic duty
Shall now be joined the thirst for booty ;
And be the goal, where all are sent,
The Rival Emperor's sumptuous tent !
He shall not long upon his seat be lorded :
To lead the phalanx be to me accorded !

SPEEDBOOTY (*sutleress, fawning upon him*). Though never
    tied to him by priest,
He is my sweetheart dear, at least.
Our autumn 'tis, of ripest gold !
Woman is fierce when she takes hold,
And when she robs, is merciless :
All is allowed, so forth to victory press !   [*Exeunt both.*

GENERAL-IN-CHIEF. Upon our left, as was to be foreseen,
Their right is strongly hurled.   Yon rocks between,
Ours will resist their furious beginning,
And hinder them the narrow pass from winning.

FAUST (*beckons to the* MIGHTY MAN *on the left*). I beg you,
    Sire, let this one also aid ;
'Tis well when even the strong are stronger made.

HOLDFAST (*coming forwards*). Now let the left wing have
    no fear !
The ground is surely held, where I appear :
I am the Ancient you were told of :
No lightning splits what I keep hold of !   [*Exit.*

MEPHIS. (*descending from above*). And now behold, how,
    more remote,
From every jagged rocky throat
Comes forth an arméd host, increasing,
Down every narrow pathway squeezing,

With helm and harness, sword and spear,
A living rampart in our rear,
And wait the sign to charge the foemen?

                              [*Aside, to the knowing ones*

You must not ask whence comes the omen.
I have not been a careless scout,
But cleared the halls of armour round about.
They stood a-foot, they sat on horses,
Like Lords of Earth and real forces :
Once Emperors, Kings, and Knights were they,
Now empty shells,—the snails have crawled away.
Full many ghosts, arrayed so, have for us
Revamped the Middle Ages thus.
Whatever Devils now the shells select,
This once 'twill still create effect.   [*Aloud.*
Hark ! in advance they stir their anger,
Each jostling each with brassy clangour !
The banner-rags of standards flutter flowing,
That restless waited for the breeze's blowing.
Here standeth ready, now, an ancient race ;
In the new conflict it would fain have place.

           [*Tremendous peal of trumpets from above: a perceptible
               wavering in the hostile army.*

FAUST. The near horizon dims and darkles ;
     Yet here and there with meaning sparkles
     A ruddy and presaging glow ;
     The blades are red where strife is sorest,
     The atmosphere, the rocks, the forest,
     The very heavens the combat show.
MEPHIS. The right flank holds its ground with vigour '
     There, towering over all, defiant,
     Jack Bully works, the nimble giant,
     And drives them with his wonted rigour.
EMPEROR. I first beheld one arm uplifted,
     But now a dozen tossed and shifted :
     Unnatural such things appear.
FAUST. Hast thou not heard of vapours banded
     O'er the Sicilian coasts expanded ?
     There, hovering in daylight clear,
     When mid-air gleams in rarer phases,

And mirrored in especial hazes,
A vision wonderful awakes :
There back and forth are cities bending,
With gardens rising and descending,
As form on form the ether breaks.

EMPEROR. Yet how suspicious ! I behold
The tall spears tipped with gleams of gold :
Upon our phalanx' shining lances
A nimble host of flamelets dances :
Too spectral it appears to me.

FAUST. Pardon me, Lord, those are the traces
Of spirits of the vanished races,—
The fires of Pollux and of Castor,
Whom seamen call on in disaster :
They here collect their final strength for thee.

EMPEROR. But say, to whom are we indebted,
That Nature hath our plans abetted,
With shows of rarest potency ?

MEPHIS. To whom, indeed, but that old Roman
Whose care for thee at last is proved ?
By the strong menace of thy foemen
His deepest nature has been moved.
His gratitude would see thee now delivered,
Though his own being for thy sake be shivered.

EMPEROR. They cheered my march, with every pomp in
vested ;
I felt my power I meant to see it tested ;
So, carelessly, I found it well, as ruler,
To send the white beard where the air was cooler.
I robbed the Clergy of a pleasant savour,
And, truly, have not thus acquired their favour.
Shall I, at last, since many years are over,
The payment for that merry deed recover ?

FAUST. Free-hearted help heaps interest :
Look up, and cease to watch the foemen !
Methinks that *he* will send an omen :
Attend ! the sign is now expressed.

EMPEROR. An Eagle hovers in the heavenly vault :
A Griffin follows, menacing assault.

FAUST. Give heed ! It seems most favourable

The Griffin is a beast of fable :
How dare he claim a rival regal,
And meet in fight a genuine Eagle ?

EMPEROR. And now, in circles wide extended,
They wheel involved,—then, like a flash,
Upon each other swiftly dash,
That necks be cleft and bodies rended !

FAUST. Mark now the evil Griffin quail !
Rumpled and torn, the foe he feareth,
And with his drooping lion's-tail,
Plunged in the tree-tops, disappeareth.

EMPEROR. Even as presaged, so may it be ?
I take the sign admiringly.

MEPHIS. (*towards the right*).
  From the force of blows repeated
  Have our enemies retreated ;
  And in fight, uncertain, shifting,
  Towards their right they now are drifting,
  Thus confusing, by their courses,
  All the left flank of their forces.
  See ! our phalanx, firmly driven,
  Moves to right, and, like the levin,
  Strikes them in the weak position,—
  Now, like waves in wild collision,
  Equal powers, with rage opposing,
  In the double fight are closing.
  Gloriously the weapons rattle ;
  We, at last, have won the battle !

EMPEROR (*on the left, to* FAUST).
  Look ! it yonder seems suspicious ;
  For our post the luck's capricious.
  Not a stone I see them throw there ;
  Mounted are the rocks below there,
  And the upper ones deserted.
  Now !—to one huge mass converted
  Nearer moves the foe, unshaken,
  And perchance the pass hath taken.
  Such the unholy plan's conclusion !
  All your arts are but delusion.   [*Pause.*

MEPHIS. There come my ravens, croaking presage ;

What nature, then, may be their message?
I fear we stand in evil plight.

EMPEROR. What mean these fatal birds enchanted?
Their inky sails are hither slanted,
Hot from the rocky field of fight.

MEPHIS. (*to the Ravens*).
Sit at mine ears, your flight retarded!
He is not lost whom you have guarded;
Your counsel's logical and right.

FAUST (*to the* EMPEROR).
Thou hast, of course, been told of pigeons,
Taught to return from distant regions
To nests upon their native coast.
Here, differently, the plan's succeeded;
The pigeon-post for Peace is needed,
But War requires the raven-post.

MEPHIS. The birds announce us sore mischances.
See, yonder, how the foe advances
Against our heroes' rocky wall,
The nearest heights even now attaining!
Should they succeed the pass in gaining,
Our fortunes, then, were critical.

EMPEROR. Defeat and cheat at last are on me!
Into your meshes you have drawn me:
I shudder, since they bind me fast.

MEPHIS. Courage! Not yet the die is cast.
Patience and knack, for knot-untying!
The close will be the fiercest stand.
Sure messengers for me are flying:
Command that I may give command!

GENERAL-IN-CHIEF (*who has meanwhile arrived*).
To follow these hast thou consented;
Thence all the time was I tormented:
No fortune comes of jugglery.
The battle's lost, I cannot mend it;
'Twas they began, and they may end it:
My baton I return to thee.

EMPEROR. Retain it for the better season
Which Fortune still to us may send!
I dread the customers with reason,—

The ravens and their ugly friend.   [*To* Mephis,
As for the baton, thou must leave it ,
Thou'rt not, methinks, the proper man.
Command the fight, canst thou retrieve it !
Let happen all that happen can !
                [*Exit into the tent with the* General-in-Chief

Mephis. The blunt stick still be his protection !
        'Twould naught avail in *our* direction ;
        There was a sort of Cross thereon.
Faust. What's to be done ?
Mephis.   The thing is done !—[94]
Now, my black cousins, speed upon your duties
To the mountain-lake !   The Undines, watery beauties,
Entreat, the appearance of their floods to spare !
By female arts, beyond our sharpest seeing,
They can divide the Appearance from the Being,
And all will swear the Being's there !   [*Pause.*

Faust. Our ravens must, with flattery beladen,
Have sweetly coaxed each winsome water-maiden;
The trickling streams at once descend.
The bald and rocky shoulders of the mountains
Give birth to full and swiftly-flowing fountains ;
Their victory is at an end.

Mephis. To such reception they're not used :
The boldest climbers grow confused.

Faust. Now brook roars down to brook with mighty
                bubble ;
Then from the mouths of glens they issue double,
And fling themselves, in arches, o'er the pale ;
Then suddenly spread along the rocky level,
And to and fro foam onward in their revel,
As down a stairway hurled into the vale.
What boots their gallant, hero-like resistance ?
The billow bursts, and bears them down the distance ;
Before such wild uproar even I must quail.

Mephis. Nothing I see of all this moist illusion :
To human eyes, alone, it brings confusion,
And in the wondrous chance I take delight.
They fly in headlong, hurried masses ;
That they are drowning, think the asses :

Though on the solid land, they see an ocean,
And run absurdly with a swimming motion.
It is a most bewildering plight.   [*The Ravens return.*
To the high Master will I praise you duly ;
But would you test yourselves as masters fully,
Then hasten to that smithy eerie,
Where the dwarf-people, never weary,
Hammer the sparks from ore and stone.
Demand, while there you prate and flatter,
A fire to shine, and shoot, and scatter,
As in the highest sense 'tis known.
'Tis true that distant lightning, quivering far-lights,
And falling, quick as wink, of highest star-lights,
May happen any summer night ;
But lightning, loose among the tangled bushes,
And stars that hiss and fizzle in the rushes,
Are shows that seldom meet the sight.
Take no great pains, you understand ;
But first entreat, and then command !
          [*Exeunt the Ravens. All takes place as prescribed.*
Upon the foe falls Night's thick curtain,
And step and march become uncertain !
In every quarter wandering blazes,
And sudden glare, that blinds and dazes !
All that seems fine ; yet we should hear.
Their wild, commingled cries of fear.

FAUST. The hollow armour from the vaulted chambers
In the free air its ancient strength remembers :
It rattles there, and clatters all around,—
A wonderful, a cheating sound.

MEPHIS. Quite right ! The forms there's no restraining :
Already knightly whacks are raining,
As in the splendid times of old.
The brassarts there, as well as cuisses,
Are Guelfs and Ghibellines ; and this is
Renewal of the feud they hold.
Firm in transmitted hate they anchor,
And show implacably their rancour :
Now far and wide the noise hath rolled.
At last, the Devils find a hearty

Advantage in the hate of Party,
Till dread and ruin end the tale :
Repulsive sounds of rage and panic,
With others, piercing and Satanic,
Resound along the frightened vale !

> [*Warlike tumult in the Orchestra, passing into lively
> martial measures.*

III.

THE RIVAL EMPEROR'S TENT.

THRONE: RICH SURROUNDINGS.

HAVEQUICK. SPEEDBOOTY.

SPEEDBOOTY. So, we are here the first, I see !
HAVEQUICK. No raven flies so swift as we.
SPEEDBOOTY. O, how the treasure-piles extend !
Where shall I once begin ? where end ?
HAVEQUICK. But all the space is full ! And now
I know not what to take, I vow !
SPEEDBOOTY. This carpet is the thing I need !
My couch is often hard indeed.
HAVEQUICK. Here hangs a morning-star, so strong,
The like of which I've wanted long.
SPEEDBOOTY. This crimson mantle, bound with gold,
Is like the one my dreams foretold.
HAVEQUICK (*taking the weapon*). With this, a man is
quickly sped ;
One strikes him dead, and goes ahead.
Thou art already laden so,
And nothing right thy sack can show.
This rubbish, rather, here forsake,
And one of yonder caskets take !
The army's modest pay they hold,
Their bellies full of purest gold.

SPEEDBOOTY. O what a murderous weight is there !
I cannot lift it, cannot bear.

HAVEQUICK. Quick, bend and squat to take the pack !
I'll heave it on thy sturdy back.

SPEEDBOOTY. O me !   Alack ! the burden slips :
The weight has crushed my back and hips.

[The chest falls and bursts open.

HAVEQUICK. There lies the red gold in a heap !
Quick, rake and take what thou canst keep !

SPEEDBOOTY (*crouching down*) Quick, let the booty fill my
lap !
'Twill still be quite enough, mayhap.

HAVEQUICK. So ! there's enough !   Now haste, and go !

[She rises.

The apron has a hole, ah woe !
Wherever thou dost walk or stand,
Thou sowest treasure on the land.

GUARDSMEN (*of our* EMPEROR). What seek ye here with
wanton eyes ?
Ye rummage the Imperial prize !

HAVEQUICK. We hazarded our limbs for pay,
And now we take our share of prey.
In hostile tents 'tis always so,
And we are soldiers too, you know.

GUARDSMEN. Among our troops he comes to grief
Who's but a soldier and a thief :
Who serves our Emperor fair and free,
Let him an honest soldier be !

HAVEQUICK. O yes ! such honesty we know :
'Tis *Contribution*,—call it so !
In the same mould you all are made :
" Give ! " is the password of your trade.

(*To* SPEEDBOOTY). With what thou hast, the coast we'll
clear :
As guests we are not welcome here.

[Exeunt.

FIRST GUARDSMAN. Why didst thou not at once bestow
On the scamp's face a smashing blow ?

SECOND. I know not,—had not strength to strike ;
They seemed to me so phantom-like.

THIRD. Something there was disturbed my sight,—
A flash : I could not see aright.

FOURTH. I, also, can declare it not :
The whole day long it was so hot,
So sultry, close, and terrible ;
One man stood firm, another fell ;
We groped and fought, with valour rash,
The foemen fell at every slash ;
Before one's eyes there was a mist,
And something roared, and hummed, and hissed ;
So to the end, and here are we,
And how it happened, cannot see.

The EMPEROR *enters, accompanied by* FOUR PRINCES.
The GUARDSMEN *retire.*

EMPEROR. Now fare he, as he may ! For us is won the
battle,
And o'er the plain the foe have fled like frightened cattle.
The trait'rous treasure, here, the empty throne, we've
found,
That, hung with tapestry, contracts the space around.
Enthroned in honour we, true guardsmen us protecting,
The people's envoys are imperially expecting.
The messengers of joy arrive from every side,
And, loyal now to us, the realm is pacified.
Though in our fight, perchance, some jugglery was woven,
Yet, at the last, our own unaided strength we've proven.
True, accidents sometimes for combatants are good ;
A stone may fall from heaven, on foes a shower of blood ;
From rocky caves may ring tremendous strains of wonder,
That lift our hearts with faith, and drive the foe asunder.
The Conquered yielded, scourged by Scorn's immortal rod ;
The Victor, as he boasts, exalts the favouring God ;
And all responsive shout, unordered, unentreated :
" We praise Thee, God our Lord !" from million throats
repeated.
Yet as the highest praise, so rarely else expressed,
I turn my pious glance on mine own grateful breast.
A young and lively Prince may give his days to pleasure ;
Him teach the years, at last, the moments use to measure.

Therefore, without delay, I call ye, for support,
Beside me, worthy Four, in realm and house and court.

[*To the* FIRST.

Thine was, O Prince! the host's arrangement, wise inspec-
    tion,
Then, in the nick of time, heroic, bold direction :
Act now in peace, as Time thine offices may show !
Arch-Marshal shalt thou be : the sword I here bestow.

ARCH-MARSHAL. Thy faithful host, till now employed for
    civil order,
Thee and thy throne secured, shall strengthen next thy
    border :
Then let us be allowed, when festal throngs are poured
Through thine ancestral halls, to dress for thee the board.
Before thee brightly borne, and brightly held beside thee,
Thy Majesty's support, the sword shall guard and guide
    thee !

EMPEROR (*to the* SECOND). He who as gallant man can
    also gracious be,
Thou,—be Arch-Chamberlain !—not light the place, for
    thee.
Thou art the highest now of all the house retainers
Whose strife makes service bad,—the threateners and com-
    plainers :
Let thy example be an honoured sign to these,
How they the Prince and Court, and all, should seek to
    please !

ARCH-CHAMBERLAIN. To speed thy high design, thy grace
    is fair precursor :
The Better to assist, and injure not the Worser,—
Be frank, yet cunning not, and calm without deceit !
If thou but read my heart, I'm honoured as is meet.
But let my fancy now to festal service hasten !
Thou goest to the board, I bear the golden basin,
And hold thy rings for thee, that on such blissful days
Thy hands may be refreshed, as I beneath thy gaze.

EMPEROR. Too serious am I still, to plan such celebration ;
Yet be it so ! We need a glad inauguration. [*To the* THIRD.
I choose thee Arch-High-Steward ! Therefore henceforth be
Chase, poultry-yard, and manor subject unto thee !

Give me at all times choice of dishes I delight in,
As with the month they come, and cooked with appetite in !
   ARCH-HIGH-STEWARD. A rigid fast shall be the penalty I
     wish,
Until before thee stands a goodly-savoured dish.
The kitchen-folk shall join, and gladly heed my reasons
To bring the distant near and expedite the seasons.
Yet rare and early things shall not delight thee long :
Thy taste desires, instead, the simple and the strong.
   EMPEROR (*to the* FOURTH). Since here, perforce, we plan
     but feasts, and each is sharer,
Be thou for me transformed, young hero, to Cup-bearer !
Arch Cup-Bearer, take heed, that all those vaults of mine
Richly replenished be with noblest taps of wine !
Be temperate thyself, howe'er temptation presses,
Nor let occasion's lure mislead thee to excesses !
   ARCH-CUP-BEARER. My Prince, the young themselves, if
     trust in them be shown,
Are, ere one looks around, already men full-grown.
I at the lordly feast shall also take my station,
And give thy sideboard's pomp the noblest decoration
Of gorgeous vessels, golden, silver, grand to see ;
Yet first the fairest cup will I select for thee,—
A clear Venetian glass, good cheer within it waiting,
Helping the taste of wine, yet ne'er intoxicating.
One oft confides too much on such a treasured store :
Thy moderation, though, High Lord, protects thee more.
   EMPEROR. What, in this earnest hour, for you have I
     intended,
From valid mouth confidingly you've comprehended.
The Emperor's word is great, his gift is therefore sure,
But needs, for proper force, his written signature :
The high sign-manual fails. Here, for commission needful,
I see the right man come, of the right moment heedful.

    The ARCHBISHOP-ARCH-CHANCELLOR *enters.*

   EMPEROR. If in the keystone of the arch the vault confide,
'Tis then securely built, for endless time and tide.
Thou seest Four Princes here ! To them we've just ex-
   pounded,

How next our House and Court shall be more stably
    founded.
Now, all the realm contains, within its bounds enclosed,
Shall be, with weight and power, upon Ye Five imposed!
Your landed wealth shall be before all others splendid;
Therefore at once have I your properties extended
From their inheritance, who raised 'gainst us the hand.
You I award, ye Faithful, many a lovely land,
Together with the right, as you may have occasion,
To spread them by exchange, or purchase, or invasion:
Then be it clearly fixed, that you unhindered use
Whate'er prerogatives have been the landlord's dues.
When ye, as Judges, have the final sentence spoken,
By no appeal from your high Court shall it be broken:
Then levies, tax and rent, pass-money, tolls and fees
Are yours,—of mines and salt and coin the royalties.
That thus my gratitude may validly be stated,
You next to Majesty hereby I've elevated.

    ARCHBISHOP. In deepest thanks to thee we humbly all
      unite:
Thou mak'st us strong and sure, and strengthenest thy
    might.

    EMPEROR. Yet higher dignities I give for your fulfilling.
Still for my realm I live, and still to live am willing;
Yet old ancestral lines compel the prudent mind
To look from present deeds to that which looms behind.
I, also, in my time, must meet the sure Redresser;
Your duty be it, then, to choose me a successor.
Crowned, at the altar raise his consecrated form,
That so may end in peace what here began in storm!

    ARCH-CHANCELLOR. With pride profound, yet humbly, as
      our guise evinces,
Behold, before thee bowed, the first of earthly princes!
So long the faithful blood our living veins shall fill,
We are the body which obeys thy lightest will.

    EMPEROR. Now, to conclude, let all that we have here
      asserted,
Be, for the future time, to document converted!
'Tis true that ye, as lords, have your possession free,
With this condition, though, that it unparcelled be;

And what ye have from us, howe'er ye swell the treasure,
Shall to the eldest son descend in equal measure.

ARCH-CHANCELLOR. On parchment I, at once, shall gladly
tabulate,
To bless the realm and us, the statute of such weight:
The copy and the seals the Chancery shall procure us,
Thy sacred hand shall then validity assure us.

EMPEROR. Dismissal now I grant, that you, assembled
may.
Deliberate upon the great, important day.

[*The Secular Princes retire.*

ARCHBISHOP (*remains and speaks pathetically*). The Chan-
cellor withdrew, the Bishop stands before thee :
A warning spirit bids that straightway he implore thee !
His heart paternal quakes with anxious fear for thee.

EMPEROR. In this glad hour what may thy dread misgiving be ?

ARCHBISHOP. Alas, in such an hour, how much my pain
must greaten,
To find thy hallowed head in covenant with Satan !
True, to the throne, it seems, hast thou secured thy right ;
But, woe ! in God the Lord's, the Holy Pontiff's spite.
Swift shall he punish when he learns the truth—the latter :
Thy sinful realm at once with holy ban he'll shatter !
He still remembers how, amid thy highest state,
When newly crowned, thou didst the wizard liberate.
Thy diadem but made thy heart for Christians harden,
For on that head accurst fell its first beam of pardon.
Now beat thy breast, and from thy guilty stores, this day,
Unto the Sanctuary a moderate mite repay !
The spacious sweep of hills, where stood thy tent erected,—
Where Evil Spirits then, united, thee protected,—
Where late the Liar-Prince thy hearing did secure,—
Devote thou, meekly taught, to pious use and pure,
With hill and forest dense, far as they stretch extended,
And slopes that greenly swell for pastures never ended,
Then crystal lakes of fish, unnumbered brooks that flow
In foamy windings down, and braid the vale below ;
The broad vale then, itself, with mead, and lawn, and hollow !
Thus penitence is shown, and pardon soon shall follow

EMPEROR. For this, my heavy sin, my terror is profound :
By thine own measure shalt thou draw the borders round.

ARCHBISHOP. First be the spot profane, where sin was
    perpetrated,
To God's high service soon and wholly dedicated !
With speed the walls arise to meet the mind's desire ;
The rising morning sun already lights the choir ;
The growing structure spreads, the transept stands exalted ;
Joy of Believers, then, the nave is lifted, vaulted ;
And while they press with zeal within the portals grand,
The first clear call of bells is swept across the land,
Pealed from the lofty towers that heavenwards have striven :
The penitent draws near, new life to him is given.
The consecration-day—O, may it soon be sent !—
Thy presence then shall be the highest ornament.

EMPEROR. So great a work shall be my pious proclama-
    tion
To praise the Lord our God, and work mine expiation.
Enough ! I feel, e'en now, how high my thoughts aspire.

ARCHBISHOP. As Chancellor, next, the formal treaty I
    require.

EMPEROR. A formal document,—the Church needs full
    requital :
Bring it to me, and I with joy will sign her title !

ARCHBISHOP (*has taken leave, but turns back again at the
    door*). At once unto the work devote, that it may
    stand,
Tithes, levies, tax,—the total income of the land,
For ever. Much it needs, to be supported fairly,
And careful maintenance will also cost us rarely :
And, that it soon be built, on such a lonesome wold,
Thou'lt from thy booty spare to us some little gold.
Moreover, we shall want—here, most, we claim assistance —
Lumber, and lime, and slate, and such like, from a distance.
The people these shall haul, thus from the pulpit taught ;
The Church shall bless the man, whose team for her has
    wrought.   [*Exit.*

EMPEROR. The sin is very sore, wherewith my soul is
    weighted :
Much damage unto me the Sorcerers have created.

ARCHBISHOP (*returning once again, with profoundest genuflec-
tions*). Pardon, O Prince! to him, that vile notorious
man,
The Empire's coast was given; but him shall smite the ban,
Unless thy penitence the Church's wrath relaxes
There, too, with tithes and gifts, and revenues and taxes.

EMPEROR (*ill-humouredly*). The land doth not exist: far in
the sea it lies.

ARCHBISHOP. Who patient is, and right, his day shall yet
arise.

Your word for us remains, and makes secure our trover!

[*Exit.*

EMPEROR (*solus*). I might as well, at last, make all the
Empire over!

ACT V.

I.

OPEN COUNTRY.

WANDERER. Yes ! 'tis they, the dusky lindens ;
There they stand in sturdy age :
And again shall I behold them,
After such a pilgrimage ?
'Tis the ancient place, the drifted
Downs, the hut that sheltered me,
When the billow, storm-uplifted,
Hurled me shoreward from the sea !
Here with blessing would I greet them,
They, my hosts, the helpful pair,—
Old, indeed, if now I meet them,
Since they then had hoary hair.
Pious folk, from whom I parted !
Be my greeting here renewed,
If ye still, as open-hearted,
Taste the bliss of doing good !

BAUCIS (*a little woman, very old*). Gently, stranger ! lest
    thou cumber
Rest, whereof my spouse hath need !
He but gains from longest slumber
Strength for briefest waking deed.

WANDERER. Tell me, mother, art thou even
She, to whom my thanks I bear,—
I, the youth, whose life was given
By your kind, united care ?

z 2

Art thou Baucis, who the coldly
Fading mouth refreshment gave?

[The Husband appears.

Thou, Philemon, who so boldly
Drew my treasure from the wave?
From your fire, so quickly burning,
From your silver-sounding bell,
Changed my doom, to fortune turning,
When the dread adventure fell.
Forth upon the sand-hills stealing,
Let me view the boundless sea!
Let me pray, devoutly kneeling,
Till my burdened heart be free!

[He walks forward upon the downs.

PHILEMON (*to* BAUCIS). Haste, and let the meal be dighted
'Neath the garden's blooming trees!
Let him go, and be affrighted!
He'll believe not what he sees.

[Follows, and stands beside the WANDERER.

Where the savage waves maltreated
You, on shores of breaking foam,
See, a garden lies completed,
Like an Eden-dream of home!
Old was I, no longer eager,
Helpful, as the younger are:
And when I had lost my vigour,
Also was the wave afar.
Wise lords set their serfs in motion,
Dikes upraised and ditches led,
Minishing the rights of Ocean,
Lords to be in Ocean's stead.
See the green of many a meadow,
Field and garden, wood and town!
Come, our table waits in shadow!
For the sun is going down.
Sails afar are gliding yonder;
Nightly to the port they fare:
To their nest the sea-birds wander
For a harbour waits them there.
Distant now, thou hardly seëst

Where the Sea's blue arc is spanned,
Right and left, the broadest, freest
Stretch of thickly-peopled land.

II.

IN THE LITTLE GARDEN.

The Three at the Table.

Baucis (*to the Stranger*). Art thou dumb?   Of all we've
brought here,
   In thy mouth shall nothing fall?
Philemon. He would know the marvel wrought here:
   Fain thou speakest: tell him all!
Baucis. 'Twas a marvel, if there's any!
   And the thought disturbs me still:
   In a business so uncanny
   Surely helped the Powers of Ill.
Philemon. Can the Emperor's soul be perilled,
   Who on him the strand bestowed?
   Gave the mandate not the herald,
   Trumpeting, as on he rode?
   Near our downs, all unexpected,
   Was the work's beginning seen,
   Tents and huts!—but soon erected,
   Rose a palace o'er the green.
Baucis. Knaves in vain by day were storming,
   Plying pick and spade alike;
   Where the fires at night were swarming,
   Stood, the following day, a dike.
   Nightly rose the sounds of sorrow,
   Human victims there must bleed:
   Lines of torches, on the morrow,
   Were canals that seaward lead.
   He would seize our field of labour,

Hut and garden, godlessly :
Since he lords it as our neighbour,
We to him must subject be.

PHILEMON. Yet he bids, in compensation,
Fair estate of newer land.

BAUCIS. Trust not watery foundation !
Keep upon the hill thy stand !

PHILEMON. Let us, to the chapel straying,
Ere the sunset-glow has died,
Chime the vespers, kneel, and, praying,
Still in our old God confide !

———————

III.

PALACE.

SPACIOUS PLEASURE-GARDEN : BROAD, STRAIGHTLY-CUT
CANAL.

FAUST (*in extreme old age, walking about, meditative*).

LYNCEUS, THE WARDER (*through the speaking-trumpet*).
The sun goes down, the ships are veering
To reach the port, with song and cheer :
A heavy galley, now appearing
On the canal, will soon be here.
The gaudy pennons merrily flutter,
The masts and rigging upward climb :
Blessings on thee the seamen utter,
And fortune greets thee at thy prime.

[*The little bell rings on the downs.*

FAUST (*starting*). Accursèd chime !   As in derision
It wounds me, like a spiteful shot :
My realm is boundless to my vision,
Yet at my back this vexing blot !
The bell proclaims, with envious bluster,

My grand estate lacks full design :
The brown old hut, the linden-cluster,
The crumbling chapel, are not mine.
If there I wished for recreation,
Another's shade would give no cheer :
A thorn it is, a sharp vexation,—
Would I were far away from here !

WARDER (*from above*). With evening wind and favouring
    tide,
    See the gay galley hither glide !
    How richly, on its rapid track,
    Tower chest and casket, bale and sack !

     [*A splendid Galley, richly and brilliantly laden with
      the productions of Foreign Countries.*

MEPHISTOPHELES. THE THREE MIGHTY MEN.

CHORUS. Here we have landed :
        Furl the sail !
        Hail to the Master,
        Patron, hail !

     [*They disembark : the goods are brought ashore.*

MEPHIS. We've proved our worth in many ways
    Delighted, if the Patron praise !
    We sailed away with vessels twain,
    With twenty come to port again.[55]
    Of great successes to relate,
    We only need to show our freight.
    Free is the mind on Ocean free :
    Who there can ponder sluggishly ?
    You only need a rapid grip :
    You catch a fish, you seize a ship ;
    And when you once are lord of three,
    The fourth is grappled easily ;
    The fifth is then in evil plight ;
    You have the Power, and thus the Right.
    You count the *What*, and not the *How* :
    If I hav ever navigated,
    War, Trade and Piracy, I vow,
    Are three in one, and can't be separated !

THE THREE MIGHTY MEN. No thank and hail?
        No hail and thank?
        As if our freight
        To him were rank !
        He makes a face
        Of great disgust ;
        The royal wealth
        Displease him must.

MEPHIS. Expect no further
        Any pay ;
        Your own good share
        Ye took away.

THE MIGHTY MEN. We only took it
        For pastime fair ;
        We all demand
        An equal share.

MEPHIS. First, arrange them
        In hall on hall,—
        The precious treasures,
        Together all !
        If such a splendour
        Meets his ken,
        And he regards it
        More closely then,
        A niggard he
        Won't be, at least :
        He'll give our squadron
        Feast on feast.
        To-morrow the gay birds hither wend,
        And I can best to them attend.

                        [*The cargo is removed.*

MEPHIS. (*to* FAUST). With gloomy gaze, with serious
    brow,
Of this great fortune hearest thou.
Crowned is thy wisest industry,
And reconciled are shore and sea ;
And from the shore, to swifter wakes,
The willing sea the vessels takes.
Speak, then, that here, from thy proud seat,
Thine arm may clasp the world complete.

Here, on this spot, the work was planned;
Here did the first rough cabin stand;
A little ditch was traced, a groove,
Where now the feathered oar-blades move.
Thy high intent, thy servants' toil,
From land and sea have won the spoil.
From here—

FAUST.   Still that accursed *Here !*
To me a burden most severe.
To thee, so clever, I declare it,—
It gives my very heart a sting;
It is impossible to bear it !
Yet shamed am I, to say the thing.
The old ones, there, should make concession !
A shady seat would I create :
The lindens, not my own possession,
Disturb my joy in mine estate.
There would I, for a view unbaffled,
From bough to bough erect a scaffold,
Till for my gaze a look be won
O'er everything that I have done,—
To see before me, unconfined,
The masterpiece of human mind,
Wisely asserting to my sense
The people's gain of residence.
No sorer plague can us attack,
Than rich to be, and something lack !"
The chiming bell, the lindens' breath,
Oppress like air in vaults of death :
My force of will, my potence grand,
Is shattered here upon the sand.
How shall I ban it from my feeling !
I rave whene'er the bell is pealing.

MEPHIS. 'Tis natural that so great a spite
Thy life should thus imbitter quite.
Who doubts it ?   Every noble ear,
Disgusted, must the jangle hear ;
And that accursed bim-bam-booming,
Through the clear sky of evening glooming,
Is mixed with each event that passes,

From baby's bath to burial-masses,
As if, between its *bam* and *bim*,
Life were a dream, in memory dim.
FAUST. Their obstinate, opposing strain
Darkens the brightest solid gain,
Till one, in plague and worry thrust
Grows tired, at last, of being just.
MEPHIS. Why be annoyed, when thou canst well despise
them?
Wouldst thou not long since colonize them?
FAUST. Then go, and clear them out with speed!
Thou knowest the fair estate, indeed,
I chose for the old people's need.
MEPHIS. We'll set them down on other land;
Ere you can look, again they'll stand:
When they've the violence outgrown,
Their pleasant dwelling shall atone. *[He whistles shrilly.*

THE THREE *enter.*

MEPHIS. Come, as the Master bids, and let
The fleet a feast to-morrow get!
THE THREE. Reception bad the old Master gave:
A jolly feast is what we crave.
MEPHIS. (*ad spectatores*). It happens as it happed of old:
Still Naboth's vineyard we behold!

————————

IV.

DEAD OF NIGHT.

LYNCEUS, THE WARDER (*singing on the watch-tower of the Palace*).

For seeing intended,
Employed for my sight.
The tower's my dwelling,
The world my delight.

I gaze on the Distant,
I look on the Near,—
The moon and the planets,
The forest and deer.
So see I in all things
The grace without end,
And even as they please me,
Myself I commend.
Thou fortunate Vision,
Of all thou wast 'ware,
Whatever it might be,   [*Pause.*
Yet still it was fair !
Not alone that I delight me,
Have I here been stationed so :—
What a horror comes, to fright me,
From the darksome world below !
Sparks of fire I see outgushing
Through the night of linden-trees ;
Stronger yet the glow is flushing,
Fanned to fury by the breeze.
Ah ! the cabin burns, unheeded,
Damp and mossy though it stand :
Quick assistance here is needed,
And no rescue is at hand !
Ah, the good old father, mother,
Else so careful of the fire,
Doomed amid the smoke to smother !—
The catastrophe how dire !
Now the blackening pile stands lonely
In the flames that redly swell :
If the good old folk be only
Rescued from the burning hell !
Dazzling tongues the crater launches
Through the leaves and through the branches ;
Withered boughs, at last ignited,
Break, in burning, from the tree :
Why must I be thus far-sighted ?
Witness such calamity ?
Now the little chapel crashes
'Neath a branch's falling blow ;

Soon the climbing, spiry flashes
Set the tree-tops in a glow.
Down to where the trunks are planted
Burn they like a crimson dawn. [*Long pause. Chant.*
What erewhile the eye enchanted
With the centuries is gone.

FAUST (*on the balcony towards the downs*). Above, what
    whining lamentation ?
The word, the tone, too late I heed.
My warder wails : I feel vexation
At heart, for this impatient deed.
Yet be the lindens extirpated,
Till half-charred trunks the spot deface,
A look-in-the-land is soon created,
Whence I can view the boundless space.
Thence shall I see the newer dwelling
Which for the ancient pair I raise,
Who, my benign forbearance feeling,
Shall there enjoy their latter days.

MEPHIS. AND THE THREE (*below*). We hither come upon
    the run !
Forgive ! not happily 'twas done.[87]
We knocked and beat, but none replied,
And entrance ever was denied ;
Of jolts and blows we gave good store,
And broken lay the rotten door ;
We called aloud, with direst threat,
But still no hearing could we get.
And, as it haps, with such a deed,
They would not hear, they would not heed ;
But we began, without delay,
To drive the stubborn folks away.
The pair had then an easy lot :
They fell, and died upon the spot.
A stranger, who was there concealed,
And fought, was left upon the field ;
But in the combat, fierce and fast,
From coals, that round about were cast,
The straw took fire. Now merrily
One funeral pile consumes the three.

FAUST. Deaf unto my commands were ye !
    Exchange I meant, not robbery.
    The inconsiderate, savage blow
    I curse !   Bear ye the guilt, and go !
CHORUS. The proverb old still runs its course :
    Bend willingly to greater force !
    If you are bold, and face the strife,
    Stake house and home, and then—your life !

                                           [*Exeunt.*

FAUST (*on the balcony*). The stars conceal their glance and
    glow,
    The fire sinks down, and flickers low ;
    A damp wind fans it with its wings,
    And smoke and vapour hither brings.
    Quick bidden, and too quick obeyed !—
    What hovers hither like a shade ?

V.

MIDNIGHT.

Four Gray Women enter.

FIRST. My name, it is Want.
SECOND.   And mine, it is Guilt.
THIRD. And mine, it is Care.
FOURTH.   Necessity, mine.[88]
THREE TOGETHER. The portal is bolted, we cannot get in :
The owner is rich, we've no business within.
WANT. I shrink to a shadow.
GUILT.   I shrink unto naught.
NECESSITY. The pampered from me turn the face and the
    thought.
CARE. Ye sisters, ye neither can enter, nor dare ;
But the keyhole is free to the entrance of Care.

                                         [CARE *disappears*

WANT. Ye, grisly old Sisters, be banished from here !

GUILT. Beside thee, and bound to thee, I shall appear !

NECESSITY. At your heels goes Necessity, blight in her
      breath.

THE THREE. The clouds are in motion, and cover each
      star !

Behind there, behind ! from afar, from afar,

He cometh, our Brother ! he comes, he is————

————Death !

FAUST (*in the Palace*). Four saw I come, but those that
      went were three ;

The sense of what they said was hid from me,

But something like "*Necessity*" I heard ;

Thereafter, "*Death*," a gloomy, threatening word !

It sounded hollow, spectrally subdued :

Not yet have I my liberty made good :

If I could banish Magic's fell creations,

And totally unlearn the incantations,—

Stood I, O Nature ! Man alone in thee,

Then were it worth one's while a man to be !

Ere in the Obscure I sought it, such was I,—

Ere I had cursed the world so wickedly.

Now fills the air so many a haunting shape,

That no one knows how best he may escape.

What though One Day with rational brightness beams,

The Night entangles us in webs of dreams.

From our young fields of life we come, elate :

There croaks a bird : what croaks he ? Evil fate !

By Superstition constantly insnared,

It grows to us, and warns, and is declared.

Intimidated thus, we stand alone.—

The portal jars, yet entrance is there none.   [*Agitated.*

Is any one here ?

CARE.   Yes ! must be my reply.

FAUST. And thou, who art thou, then ?

CARE.   Well,—here am I.

FAUST. Avaunt !

CARE.   I am where I should be.

FAUST (*first angry, then composed, addressing himself*). Take
      care, and speak no word of sorcery !

CARE. Though no ear should choose to hear me,
  Yet the shrinking heart must fear me:
  Though transformed to mortal eyes,
  Grimmest power I exercise.
  On the land, or ocean yonder,
  I, a dread companion, wander,
  Always found, yet never sought,
  Praised or cursed, as I have wrought!
Hast thou not Care already known?

 FAUST. I only through the world have flown:
Each appetite I seized as by the hair;
What not sufficed me, forth I let it fare,
And what escaped me, I let go.
I've only craved, accomplished my delight,
Then wished a second time, and thus with might
Stormed through my life: at first 'twas grand, completely,
But now it moves most wisely and discreetly.
The sphere of Earth is known enough to me;
The view beyond is barred immutably:
A fool, who there his blinking eyes directeth,
And o'er his clouds of peers a place expecteth!
Firm let him stand, and look around him well!
This World means something to the Capable.
Why needs he through Eternity to wend?
He here acquires what he can apprehend.
Thus let him wander down his earthly day;
When spirits haunt, go quietly his way;
In marching onwards, bliss and torment find,
Though, every moment, with unsated mind!

 CARE. Whom I once possess, shall never
  Find the world worth his endeavour:
  Endless gloom around him folding,
  Rise nor set of sun beholding,
  Perfect in external senses,
  Inwardly his darkness dense is;
  And he knows not how to measure
  True possession of his treasure.
  Luck and Ill become caprices;
  Still he starves in all increases;
  Be it happiness or sorrow,

He postpones it till the morrow;
To the Future only cleaveth:
Nothing, therefore, he achieveth.

FAUST. Desist! So shalt thou not get hold of me!
I have no mind to hear such drivel.
Depart! Thy gloomy litany
Might even befool the wisest man to evil.

CARE. Shall he go, or come?—how guide him?
Prompt decision is denied him;
Midway on the trodden highway
Halting, he attempts a by-way;
Ever more astray, bemisted,
Everything beholding twisted,
Burdening himself and others,
Taking breath, he chokes and smothers,
Though not choked, in Life not sharing,
Not resigned, and not despairing!
Such incessant rolling, spinning,—
Painful quitting, hard beginning,—
Now constraint, now liberation,—
Semi-sleep, poor recreation,
Firmly in his place insnare him
And, at last, for Hell prepare him!

FAUST. Ill-omened spectres! By your treatment strays
A thousand times the human race to error:
Ye even transform the dull, indifferent days
To vile confusion of entangling terror.
'Tis hard, I know, from Dæmons to escape;
The spirit's bond breaks not, howe'er one tries it;
And yet, O Care, thy power, thy creeping shape,
Think not that I shall recognise it!

CARE. So feel it now: my curse thou'lt find,
When forth from thee I've swiftly passed!
Throughout their whole existence men are blind·
So, Faust, be thou like them at last!

[*She breathes in his face.*

FAUST (*blinded*). The Night seems deeper now to press
around me,
But in my inmost spirit all is light;
I rest not till the finished work hath crowned me

God's Word alone confers on me the might.
Up from your couches, vassals, man by man!
Make grandly visible my daring plan!
Seize now your tools, with spade and shovel press!
The work traced out must be a swift success.
Quick diligence, severest ordering
The most superb reward shall bring;
And, that the mighty work completed stands,
One mind suffices for a thousand hands.

VI.

GREAT OUTER COURT OF THE PALACE.

Torches.

MEPHIS. (*in advance, as Overseer*). Come here, come here!
    Come on, come on!
Ye Lemures, loose-hung creatures!
Of sinew, ligament, and bone
Your knitted semi-natures!
    LEMURES (*in Chorus*). Without delay are we at hand,
And half 'tis our impression
That this concerns a spacious land,
Whereof we'll have possession.
The pointed stakes, we bring them all,
The measuring-chain, for distance;
But we've forgotten why the call
Was made for our assistance.
    MEPHIS. Here is no need of your artistic zeal:
Proceed as you may think it best!
Your tallest lay full length, from head to heel,
And lift the turf around him, all the rest!
As for our fathers made, prepare
To excavate a lengthened square!
From palace to the narrow house transferred,
Such is, at last, the issue most absurd.

LEMURES [89] (*digging with mocking gestures*). In youth when
            I did love, did love,
      Methought it was very sweet ;
      When 'twas jolly and merry every way,
      And I blithely moved my feet.

      But now old Age, with his stealing steps,
      Hath clawed me with his crutch :
      I stumbled over the door of a grave ;
      Why leave they open such ?
FAUST (*comes forth from the Palace, groping his way along
      the door-posts*). How I rejoice, to hear the clattering
      spade !
   It is the crowd, for me in service moiling,
   Till Earth be reconciled to toiling,
   Till the proud waves be stayed,
   And the sea girded with a rigid zone.
MEPHIS. (*aside*). And yet, thou'rt labouring for us alone,
   With all thy dikes and bulwarks daring ;
   Since thou for Neptune art preparing—
   The Ocean-Devil—carousal great.
   In every way shall ye be stranded ;
   The elements with us are banded,
   And ruin is the certain fate.
FAUST. Overseer !
MEPHIS.   Here !
FAUST.   However possible,
   Collect a crowd of men with vigour,
   Spur by indulgence, praise, or rigour,—
   Reward, allure, conscript, compel !
   Each day report me, and correctly note
   How grows in length the undertaken moat.
MEPHIS. (*half aloud*). When they to me the information
      gave,
   They spake not of a moat, but of—*a grave*. [90]
FAUST. Below the hills a marshy plain
   Infects what I so long have been retrieving ;
   This stagnant pool likewise to drain
   Were now my latest and my best achieving
   To many millions let me furnish soil,

Though not secure, yet free to active toil ;
Green, fertile fields, where men and herds go forth
At once, with comfort, on the newest Earth,
And swiftly settled on the hill's firm base,
Created by the bold, industrious race.
A land like Paradise here, round about :
Up to the brink the tide may roar without,
And though it gnaw, to burst with force the limit,
By common impulse all unite to hem it.
Yes ! to this thought I hold with firm persistence ;
The last result of wisdom stamps it true :
He only earns his freedom and existence,
Who daily conquers them anew.
Thus here, by dangers girt, shall glide away
Of childhood, manhood, age, the vigorous day :
And such a throng I fain would see,—
Stand on free soil among a people free !
Then dared I hail the Moment fleeing :
" *Ah, still delay—thou art so fair !* "
The traces cannot, of mine earthly being,
In æons perish,—they are there !—
In proud fore-feeling of such lofty bliss,
I now enjoy the highest Moment,—this !

> [FAUST *sinks back : the* LEMURES *take him and lay
> him upon the ground.*

MEPHIS. No joy could sate him, and suffice no bliss !
    To catch but shifting shapes was his endeavour :
    The latest, poorest, emptiest Moment—this,—
    He wished to hold it fast for ever.
    Me he resisted in such vigorous wise,
    But Time is lord, on earth the old man lies.
    The clock stands still—

CHORUS.   Stands still ! silent as midnight, now !
    The index falls.

MEPHIS.   It falls ; and it is finished, here !

CHORUS. 'Tis past !

MEPHIS.   —Past ! a stupid word.
    If past, then why ?
    Past and pure Naught, complete monotony !
    What good for us, this endlessly creating ?—

What is created then annihilating ?
" And now it's past ! "   Why read a page so twisted ?
'Tis just the same as if it ne'er existed,
Yet goes in circles round as if it had, however :
I'd rather choose, instead, the Void for ever.

SEPULTURE.

LEMUR.   *Solo.* Who then hath built the house so ill,
     With shovel and with spade ?
LEMURES.   *Chorus.* For thee, dull guest, in hempen vest,
     It all too well was made.
LEMUR.   *Solo.* Who then so ill hath decked the hall ?
     No chairs, nor table any !
LEMURES.   *Chorus.* 'Twas borrowed to return at call :
     The creditors are so many.
MEPHIS. The Body lies, and if the Spirit flee,
     I'll show it speedily my blood-signed title.—
     But, ah ! they've found such methods of requital,
     His souls the Devil must oft abstracted see !
     One now offends, the ancient way ;
     Upon the new we're not yet recommended :
     Once, I alone secured my prey,
     But now by helpers need to be befriended.
     In all things we must feel the spite !
     Transmitted custom, ancient right,—
     Nothing, indeed, can longer one confide in.
     Once with the last breath left the soul her house ;
     I kept good watch, and like the nimblest mouse,
     Whack ! was she caught, and fast my claws her hide ها !
     Now she delays, and is not fain to quit
     The dismal place, the corpse's hideous mansion ;
     The elements, in hostile, fierce expansion,
     Drive her, at last, disgracefully from it.
     And though I fret and worry till I'm weary,
     When ? How ? and *Where ?* remains the fatal query :
     Old Death is now no longer swift and strong ;
     Even the *Whether* has been doubtful long.
     Oft I beheld with lust the rigid members :

'Twas only sham ; Life kindled from its embers.

       [*Fantastic, whirling gestures of conjuratio*

Come on !   Strike up the double quick, anew,

With straight or crooked horns, ye gentlemen infernal !

Of the old Devil-grit and kernel,

And bring at once the Jaws of Hell with you !

Hell hath a multitude of jaws, in short,[91]

To use as suiteth place and dignity ;

But we, however, in this final sport,

Will henceforth less considerate be.

       [*The fearful Jaws of Hell open, on the left.*

The side-tusks yawn : then from the throat abysmal

The raging, fiery torrents flow,

And in the vapours of the background dismal

I see the city flame in endless glow.

Up to the teeth the breakers lash the red arena ;

The Damned, in hope of help, are swimming through ;

But, caught and mangled by the fell hyena,

Their path of fiery torment they renew.

In every nook new horrors flash and brighten,

In narrow space so much of dread supreme !

Well have you done, the sinners thus to frighten ;

But still they'll think it lie, and cheat, and dream !

       [*To the stout Devils, with short, straight horns.*

Now, paunchy scamps, with cheeks so redly burning !

Ye glow, so fat with hellish sulphur fed ;

With necks thick-set and stumpy, never turning,—

Watch here below, if phosphor-light be shed :

It is the Soul, the wingéd Psyche is it ;

Pluck off the wings, 'tis but a hideous worm :

First with my stamp and seal the thing I'll visit,

Then fling it to the whirling, fiery storm !

The lower parts be well inspected,

Ye Bloats ! perform your duty well :

If there the Soul her seat selected

We cannot yet exactly tell.

Oft in the navel doth she stay :

Look out for that, she thence may slip away !

       [*To the lean Devils, with long, crooked horns*

Ye lean buffoons, file-leaders strange and giant,

Grasp in the air, yourselves no respite give !
Strong in the arms, with talons sharp and pliant,
That ye may seize the fluttering fugitive !
In her old home discomforted she lies,
And Genius, surely, seeks at once to rise.

[*Glory from above, on the right.*

THE HEAVENLY HOST. Envoys, unhindered
　　　　　　　Heavenly kindred,
　　　　　　　Follow us here !
　　　　　　　Sinners forgiving,
　　　　　　　Dust to make living ?
　　　　　　　Lovingest features
　　　　　　　Unto all creatures
　　　　　　　Show in your swaying,
　　　　　　　Delaying career !

MEPHIS. Discords I hear, a harsh, disgusting strumming,
　Flung from above with the unwelcome Day ;
　'Tis that emasculate and bungled humming
　Which Pious Cant delights in, every way.
　You know how we, atrociously contented,
　Destruction for the human race have planned :
　But the most infamous that we've invented
　Is just the thing their prayers demand.
　The fops, they come as hypocrites, to fool us !
　Thus many have they snatched, before our eyes :
　With our own weapons they would overrule us ;
　They're also Devils—in disguise.
　To lose this case would be your lasting shame ;
　On to the grave, and fortify your claim !

CHORUS OF ANGELS (*scattering roses*). Roses, ye glowing ones,
　　　　　　　Balsam-bestowing ones !
　　　　　　　Fluttering, quivering,
　　　　　　　Sweetness delivering,
　　　　　　　Branching unblightedly,
　　　　　　　Budding delightedly,
　　　　　　　Bloom and be seen !
　　　　　　　Springtime declare him,
　　　　　　　In purple and green !
　　　　　　　Paradise bear him,
　　　　　　　The Sleeper serene !

MEPHIS. (*to the Satans*)   Why do ye jerk and squat? Is
    this Hell's rule?
Stand to your ground, and let them sprinkle!
Back to his place each gawky fool!
They think, perhaps, with such a flowery crinkle,
As if 'twere snow, the Devils' heat to cool:
Your breath shall make it melt, and shrink, and wrinkle.
Now blow, ye Blowers!—'Tis enough, enough!
Before your breath fades all the floating stuff.
Not so much violence,—shut jaws and noses!
Forsooth, ye blow too strongly at the roses.
The proper measure can you never learn?
They sting not only, but they wither, burn!
They hover on with flames of deadly lustre:
Resist them ye, and close together cluster!—
Your force gives out; all courage fails you so?
The Devils scent the strange, alluring glow.

ANGELS.   Blossoms of gratitude,
            Flames of beatitude,
            Love they are bearing now,
            Rapture preparing now,
            As the heart may!
            Truth in its nearness,
            Ether in clearness,
            Give the Eternal Hosts
            Everywhere Day!

MEPHIS. O curse and shame upon such dolts be sped!
    Each Satan stands upon his head!
    In somersaults the stout ones whirl and swerve,
    And into Hell plunge bottom-uppermost.
    Now may your bath be hot as you deserve!
    But I remain, unflinching, at my post.

                  [*Beating off the hovering roses.*

Off, will-o'-the-wisps!   Bright as ye seem to be,
When caught, the vilest clinging filth are ye.
Why flutter thus?   Off with you, quick!—
Like pitch and sulphur on my neck they stick.

CHORUS OF ANGELS. What not appertaineth
          To you, cease to share it!
          What inwardly paineth,

Refuse ye to bear it !
If it press in with might,
Use we our stronger right :
Love but the Loving
Leads to the Light !

MEPHIS. My head, heart, liver, by the flames are rent !
An over-devilish element !—
Sharper than Hell's red conflagration !
Thence so enormous is your lamentation,
Unfortunate enamoured ! who, so spurned,
Your heads towards the sweethearts' side have turned.
Mine, too ! What twists my head in like position ?
With them am I not sworn to competition ?
The sight of them once made my hatred worse.
Hath then an alien force transpierced my nature ?
I like to see them, youths of loveliest stature ;
What now restrains me, that I dare not curse ?—
And if I take their cozening bait so,
Who else, henceforth, the veriest fool will be ?
The stunning fellows, whom I hate so,
How very charming they appear to me !—
Tell me, sweet children, ere I miss you,
Are ye not of the race of Lucifer ?
You are so fair, forsooth, I'd like to kiss you ;
It seems to me as if ye welcome were.
I feel as comfortable and as trustful,
As though a thousand times ere this we'd met !
So surreptitiously catlike-lustful :
With every glance ye're fairer, fairer yet.
O, nearer come,—O, grant me one sweet look !

ANGELS. We come ! Why shrink ? Canst not our presence
brook ?
Now we approach : so, if thou canst, remain !

[*The* ANGELS, *coming forward, occupy the whole space.*
MEPHIS. (*who is crowded into the proscenium*).
Us, Spirits damned, you brand with censure,
Yet you are wizards by indenture ;
For man and woman, luring, you enchain.—
What chance the curst adventure brings me ?
Is this Love's chosen element ?

The fire o'er all my body stings me ;
My neck I scarcely feel, so hotly sprent.—
Ye hover back and forth ; sink down and settle !
Move your sweet limbs with more of worldly mettle !
The serious air befits you well, awhile,
But I should like, just once, to see you smile ;
That were, for me, an everlasting rapture.
I mean, as lovers look, the heart to capture ;
About the mouth a simper there must be.
Thee, tall one, as enticing I'll admit thee ;
The priestly mien does not at all befit thee,
So look at me the least bit wantonly !
You might be nakeder, and modest made so :
Your shirts' long drapery is over-moral.—
They turn !—and, from the rear surveyed so,
With their attraction there's no need to quarrel !

> CHORUS OF ANGELS. Love still revealing,
> Flames, become clearer !
> All, cursed with error,
> Truth be their healing !
> Glad self-retrieval
> Free them from Evil,
> In the all-folding Breast,
> Blessed, to rest !

MEPHIS. (*collecting himself*). How is't with me ?—Like
Job, the boils have cleft me
From head to foot, so that myself I shun ;
Yet triumph also, when my self-inspection's done,—
When self and tribe I have confided in.
The noble Devil-parts, at least, are left me !
This love-attack's a rash upon the skin.
Burned out already are the scurvy fires,
And one and all I damn you, as the case requires !

> CHORUS OF ANGELS. Hallowed glories !
> Round whom they brood,
> Wakes unto being
> Of bliss with the Good.
> Join ye, the Glorified,
> Rise to your goal !

> Airs are all purified,—
> Breathe now the Soul!
> [*They rise, bearing away the immortal part of* FAUST.

MEPHIS. (*looking around him*). But how?—at once I find
 them failing!
This race of minors takes me by surprise!
They with their booty heavenwards are sailing;
Thence on this grave they cast their greedy eyes!
My rare, great treasure they have peculated:
The lofty soul, to me hypothecated,
They've rapt away from me in cunning wise.
But unto whom shall I appeal for justice?
Who would secure to me my well-earned right?
Tricked so in one's old days, a great disgust is;
And I deserve it, this infernal spite.
I've managed in a most disgraceful fashion;
A great investment has been thrown away:
By lowest lust seduced, and senseless passion,
The old, case-hardened Devil went astray.
And if, from all this childish-silly stuff
His shrewd experience could not wrest him,
So is, forsooth, the folly quite enough,
Which, in conclusion, hath possessed him.

VII.

MOUNTAIN-GORGES, FOREST, ROCK, DESERT.

HOLY ANCHORITES,

Divided in ascending planes, posted among the ravines.

CHORUS AND ECHO. Forests are waving grand,
    Rocks, they are huge at hand,
    Clutching, the roots expand,
    Thickly the tree-trunks stand;
    Foaming comes wave on wave;
    Shelter hath deepest cave;

    Lions are prowling dumb,
    Friendly where'er we come,
    Honouring the sacred place,
    Refuge of Love and Grace !

PATER ECSTATICUS [92] (*hovering up and down*).
    Endless ecstatic fire,
    Glow of the pure desire,
    Pain of the pining breast,
    Rapture of God possessed !
    Arrows, transpierce ye me,
    Lances, coerce ye me,
    Bludgeons, so batter me,
    Lightnings, so shatter me,
    That all of mortality's
    Vain unrealities
    Die, and the Star above
    Beam but Eternal Love !

PATER PROFUNDUS [93] (*Lower Region*).
As at my feet abysses cloven
Rest on abysses deep below ;
As thousand severed streams are woven
To foamy floods that plunging go ;
As, up by self-impulsion driven,
The tree its weight sustains in air,
To Love, almighty Love, 'tis given
All things to form, and all to bear.
Around me sounds a savage roaring,
As rocks and forests heaved and swayed,
Yet plunges, bounteous in its pouring,
The wealth of waters down the glade,
Appointed, then, the vales to brighten ;
The bolt, that flaming struck and burst,
The atmosphere to cleanse and lighten,
Which pestilence in its bosom nursed,—
Love's heralds both, the powers proclaiming,
Which, aye creative, us infold.
May they, within my bosom flaming,
Inspire the mind, confused and cold,
Which frets itself, through blunted senses,
As by the sharpest fetter-smart !

O God, soothe Thou my thoughts bewildered,
 Enlighten Thou my needy heart !
PATER SERAPHICUS [94] (*Middle Regions*). What a cloud of
 morning hovers
  O'er the pine-trees' tossing hair !
  Can I guess what life it covers ?
  They are spirits, young and fair.
CHORUS OF BLESSED BOYS.[95] Tell us, Father, where we
 wander ;
  Tell us, Kind One, who are we ?
  Happy are we ; for so tender
  Unto all, it is, To Be.
PATER SERAPHICUS. Boys, brought forth in midnights
 haunted,
  Half-unsealed the sense and brain,
  For the parents lost when granted,
  For the angels sweetest gain !
  That a loving heart is nigh you
  You can feel : then come to me !
  But of earthly ways that try you,
  Blest ones ! not a trace have ye.
  Enter in mine eyes : enjoy them,
  Organs for the earthly sphere !
  As your own ye may employ them :
  Look upon the landscape here !
      [*He takes them into himself.*
 Those are trees, there rocks defend us ;
  Here, a stream that leaps below,
  And with plunges, wild, tremendous,
  Shorteneth its journey so.
BLESSED BOYS (*from within him*). To a vision grand we
 waken,
  But the scenes too gloomy show ;
  We with fear and dread are shaken :
  Kindest Father, let us go !
PATER SERAPHICUS. Upward rise to higher borders !
  Ever grow, insensibly,
  As, by pure, eternal orders,
  God's high Presence strengthens ye !
  Such the Spirits' sustentation,

With the freest ether blending ;
Love's eternal Revelation,
To Beatitude ascending.

CHORUS OF BLESSED BOYS (*circling around the highest
summit*). Hands now enring ye,
Joyously wheeling !
Soar ye and sing ye,
With holiest feeling !
The Teacher before ye,
Trust, and be bold !
Whom ye adore, ye
Him shall behold.

ANGELS (*soaring in the higher atmosphere, bearing the
immortal part of* FAUST). The noble Spirit now is free,
And saved from evil scheming :
Whoe'er aspires unweariedly
Is not beyond redeeming.
And if he feels the grace of Love
That from On High is given,
The Blessed Hosts, that wait above,
Shall welcome him to Heaven !

THE YOUNGER ANGELS. They, the roses, freely spended
By the penitent, the glorious,
Helped to make the fight victorious,
And the lofty work is ended.
We this precious Soul have won us ;
Evil ones we forced to shun us ;
Devils fled us, when we hit them :
'Stead of pangs of Hell, that bit them,
Love-pangs felt they, sharper, vaster :
Even he, old Satan-Master,
Pierced with keenest pain, retreated.
Now rejoice !   The work's completed !

THE MORE PERFECT ANGELS. Earth's residue to bear
Hath sorely pressed us ;
It were not pure and fair,
Though 'twere asbestus.
When every element
The mind's high forces
Have seized, subdued, and blent

No Angel divorces
Twin-natures single grown,
That inly mate them :
Eternal Love, alone,
Can separate them.

THE YOUNGER ANGELS. Mist-like on heights above,
We now are seeing
Nearer and nearer move
Spiritual Being.
The clouds are growing clear ;
And moving throngs appear
Of Blessed Boys,
Free from the earthly gloom,
In circling poise,
Who taste the cheer
Of the new spring-time bloom
Of the upper sphere.
Let them inaugurate
Him to the perfect state,
Now, as their peer !

THE BLESSED BOYS. Gladly receive we now
Him, as a chrysalis :
Therefore achieve we now
Pledge of our bliss.
The earth-flakes dissipate
That cling around him !
See, he is fair and great !
Divine Life hath crowned him.

DOCTOR MARIANUS [96] (*in the highest, purest cell*).
Free is the view at last,
The spirit lifted :
There women, floating past,
Are upward drifted :
The Glorious One therein,
With star-crown tender,—
The pure, the Heavenly Queen,
I know her splendour.   [*Enraptured.*
Highest Mistress of the World !
Let me in the azure
Tent of Heaven, in light unfurled

Here thy Mystery measure!
Justify sweet thoughts that move
Breast of man to meet thee,
And with holy bliss of love
Bear him up to greet thee !
With unconquered courage we
Do thy bidding highest ;
But at once shall gentle be,
When thou pacifiest.
Virgin, pure in brightest sheen,
Mother sweet, supernal,—
Unto us Elected Queen,
Peer of Gods Eternal '
    Light clouds are circling
    Around her splendour,—
    Penitent women
    Of natures tender,
    Her knees embracing,
    Ether respiring,
    Mercy requiring !
Thou, in immaculate ray,
Mercy not leavest,
And the lightly led astray,
Who trust thee, receivest !
In their weakness fallen at length,
Hard it is to save them :
Who can crush, by native strength,
Vices that enslave them ?
Whose the foot that may not slip
On the surface slanting ?
Whom befool not eye and lip,
Breath and voice enchanting !

      [*The* MATER GLORIOSA *soars into the space.*

CHORUS OF WOMEN PENITENTS. **To heights thou'rt**
        speeding
      Of endless Eden :
      Receive our pleading,
      Transcendent Maiden,
      With Mercy laden !

Magna Peccatrix.[97] (*St. Luke*, vii. 36.)

By the love before him kneeling,—
Him, Thy Son, a godlike vision;
By the tears like balsam stealing,
Spite of Pharisees' derision;
By the box, whose ointment precious
Shed its spice and odours cheery;
By the locks, whose softest meshes
Dried the holy feet and weary!—

Mulier Samaritana. (*St. John*, iv.)

By that well, the ancient station
Whither Abram's flocks were driven;
By the jar, whose restoration
To the Saviour's lips was given;
By the fountain, pure and vernal,
Thence its present bounty spending,—
Overflowing, bright, eternal,
Watering the worlds unending!

Maria Ægyptiaca. (*Acta Sanctorum.*)

By the place, where the Immortal
Body of the Lord hath lain;
By the arm, which, from the portal,
Warning, thrust me back again;
By the forty years' repentance
In the lonely desert-land;
By the blissful farewell sentence
Which I wrote upon the sand!—

The Three. Thou Thy presence not deniest

Unto sinful women ever,—
Liftest them to win the highest
Gain of penitent endeavour,—
So, from this good soul withdraw not—
Who but once forgot, transgressing,
Who her loving error saw not—
Pardon adequate, and blessing!

Una Pœnitentium[98] (*formerly named Margaret, pressing closer*).

Incline, O Maiden,
With Mercy laden,
In light unfading,

Thy gracious countenance upon my bliss !
My loved, my lover,
His trials over
In yonder world, returns to me in this !

BLESSED BOYS (*approaching in hovering circles*). With
  mighty limbs he towers
Already above us ;
He, for this love of ours,
Will richlier love us.
Early were we removed,
Ere Life could reach us ;
Yet he hath learned and proved,
And he will teach us.

THE PENITENT (*formerly named Margaret*). The spirit-
  choir around him seeing,
New to himself, he scarce divines
His heritage of new-born Being,
When like the Holy Host he shines.
Behold, how he each band hath cloven,
The earthly life had round him thrown,
And through his garb, of ether woven,
The early force of youth is shown !
Vouchsafe to me that I instruct him !
Still dazzles him the Day's new glare.

MATER GLORIOSA. Rise, thou, to higher spheres ! Conduct
  him,
Who, feeling thee, shall follow there ! [99]

DOCTOR MARIÁNUS (*prostrate, adoring*). Penitents, look
  up, elate,
    Where she beams salvation ;
    Gratefully to blessed fate
    Grow, in re-creation !
    Be our souls, as they have been,
    Dedicate to Thee !
    Virgin Holy, Mother, Queen,
    Goddess, gracious be !

CHORUS MYSTICUS. All things transitory
    But as symbols are sent :
    Earth's insufficiency
    Here grows to Event :

B B

The Indescribable,
Here it is done :
The Woman-Soul leadeth us
Upward and on !

NOTES.

Denn bei den alten lieben Todten
Braucht man Erklärung, will man Noten ;
Die Neuen glaubt man blank zu verstehn,
Doch ohne Dolmetsch wird's auch nicht gehn.

GOETHE.

NOTES TO FIRST PART.

1. *The posts are set, the booth of boards completed.*

THE "booth of boards" purposely refers to the rude, transportable puppet theatres in which Goethe first saw Faust represented. There is already a foreshadowing of some of the qualities of Faust and Mephistopheles in the Poet and Manager.

2. *This, aged Sirs, belongs to you.*

It is the Poets whom the Merry-Andrew thus addresses. His assertion of the perpetual youth of Genius is not ironical, but (as appears from the Manager's remarks) is intended as a compliment.

3. CHANT OF THE ARCHANGELS.

The three Archangels advance in the order of their dignity, as it is given in the "Celestial Hierarchy" of Dionysius Areopagita; who was also Dante's authority on this point (*Paradiso, Canto* XXVIII.). Raphael, the inferior, commences, and Michael, the chief, closes the chant.

4. *Pardon, this troop I cannot follow after.*

Mephistopheles here refers to the Chant of the Archangels. His mocking spirit is at once manifested in these lines, and in his ironical repetition of "the earliest day."

5. *While Man's desires and aspirations stir,*
He cannot choose but err.

The original of this is the single, well-known line : *Es irrt der Mensch, so lang er strebt.*   It has seemed to me impossible to give the full meaning of these words—that error is a natural accompaniment of the struggles and aspirations of Man—in a single line.

6. *A good man, through obscurest aspiration,*
Has still an instinct of the one true way.

In these lines the direction of the plot is indicated. They suggest, in advance, its moral *dénouement*, at the close of the Second

B B 2

Part. Goethe, on one occasion, compared the "Prologue in Heaven" to the overture of Mozart's *Don Giovanni*, in which a certain musical phrase occurs which is not repeated until the *finale;* and his comparison had reference to the idea expressed in these lines.

7. *But ye, God's sons in love and duty.*

Here the Lord, turning away from Mephistopheles, suddenly addresses the Archangels and the Heavenly Hosts.

8. *From Nostradamus' very hand.*

The astrologer Nostradamus (whose real name was Michel de Nôtre-Dame) was born at St. Remy, in Provence, in the year 1503. At first celebrated as a physician, he finally devoted himself to astrology, and published, in 1555, a collection of prophecies in rhymed quatrains, entitled *Les Prophecies de Michel Nostradamus,* which created an immediate sensation, and found many believers; especially as the death of Henry II. of France seemed to verify one of his mystical predictions. He was appointed physician to Charles IX. and continued the publication of his prophecies, asserting, however, that the study of the planetary aspects was not alone sufficient, but that the gift of second-sight, which God grants only to a few chosen persons, is also necessary. He died in the year 1566; and even as late as the year 1781 his prophecies were included in the Roman *Index Expurgatorius,* for the reason that they declare the downfall of the Papacy.

9. *The Sign of the Macrocosm.*

The term "Macrocosm" was used by Pico di Mirandola, Paracelsus, and other mystical writers, to denote the universe. They imagined a mysterious correspondence between the Macrocosm (the world in large) and the Microcosm (the world in little), or Man; and most of the astrological theories were based on the influence of the former upon the latter. From some of Goethe's notes, still in existence, we learn that during the time when the conception of Faust first occupied his mind (1770-73), he read Welling's *Opus Mago-Cabbalisticum,* Paracelsus, Valentinus, the *Aurea Catena Homeri,* and even the Latin poet Manilius.

Mr. Blackie, in his Notes, quotes a description of the Macrocosm from a Latin work of Robert Fludd, published at Oppenheim in 1619; but the theory had already been given in the *Heptaplus* of Pico di Mirandola (about 1490). The universe, according to him, consists of three worlds, the earthly, the heavenly, and the super-heavenly. The first includes our planet and its enveloping space, as far as the orbit of the moon; the second, the sun and stars; the third, the Governing Divine influences. The same phenomena belong to each, but have different grades of manifestation. Thus the physical element of fire exists in the earthly sphere, the warmth of the sun in the heavenly, and a seraphic, spiritual fire in the empyrean; the first burns, the second quickens, the third loves. "In addition to these three worlds (the Macrocosm)," says Pico, "there is a fourth (the Microcosm), containing all embraced within them. This is Man, in whom are included a body formed of the elements, a heavenly spirit, reason, an angelic soul, and a resemblance to God."

10. *O Death!—I know it—'tis my Famulus!*

The Latin word *famulus* (servant) was applied, in the Middle Ages, to the shield-bearers of the knights, and also to persons owing the obligation of service to the feudal lords. The Famulus of Faust, however, is at the same time a student, an amanuensis, an assistant in his laboratory, and a *servitor*, in the academic sense. The term is still applied, in the German Universities, to those poor students who fill various minor offices for the sake of eking out their means by the small salaries attached to them.

11. WAGNER.

The name—and perhaps also the primal suggestion of the character—of Faust's Famulus is taken from the old legend, in which Christopher Wagner, after Faust's tragic end, succeeds to his knowledge and enters on a similar, if not so brilliant a career.

It is an interesting coincidence that one of Goethe's early associates, during his residence in Strasburg and Frankfort, was Heinrich Leopold Wagner (who died in 1779), and who was also an author. Goethe not only read to him the early scenes of *Faust*, but imparted to him, in confidence, the fate of Margaret, as he meant to develope it; and Wagner was faithless enough to make use of the material for a tragedy of his own—*The Infanticide*—which was published in 1776. Schiller's poem, with the same title (apparently suggested by Wagner's play), and Bürger's ballad of "The Pastor of Taubenheim's Daughter," in which the subject is very similar, were both written in the year 1781.

12. *Where ye for men twist shredded thought like paper.*

This line, which reads, literally, "In which ye twist (or curl) paper-shreds for mankind," has been curiously misunderstood by most translators. The article *der* before *Menschheit* was supposed by Hayward to be in the *genitive* instead of the *dative* case, and he gives the phrase thus: "in which ye *crisp the shreds of humanity!*" Blackie even says "the shavings of mankind," and most of the other English versions repeat the mistake, in one or another form. In the French of Blaze and Stapfer, however, the reading is correct. Goethe employs the word *Schnitzel* (shreds or clippings) as a contemptuous figure of speech for the manner in which thought is presented to mankind in the discourses described by Faust. Therefore by using the expression "shredded thought" in English, the exact sense of the original is preserved.

13. Or, at the best, a Punch-and-Judy play.

The German phrase, *Haupt-und Staats-action*, was applied, about the end of the seventeenth century, to the popular puppet-plays which represented famous passages of history. It seems to have been, originally, a form of announcement invented by some proprietor of a wandering puppet-theatre, and may therefore be equivalently translated, as a "First-Class Political Performance !" The phrase was afterwards applied to plays acted upon the stage, and Goethe even makes use of it to designate Shakespeare's historical dramas. In the puppet-plays the heroic figures (Alexander, Pompey, Charlemagne, etc.) were in the habit of uttering the most grandiloquent, oracular sentences ; they were as didactic in speech as they were reckless and melodramatic in action.

The word *pragmatical*, which I have adopted as it stands in the original, has a somewhat different signification in German. It indicates—here, at least—a pedantic assumption and ostentation, in addition to the sense of meddlesome interference which it possesses in English.

14. Chorus of Angels.

In this first chorus I have been forced, by the prime necessity of preserving the meaning, to leave the second line unrhymed. The word *schleichenden*, in the fourth line, which I have endeavoured to express by "clinging" (Hayward has "creeping," Blackie "through his veins creeping," and Dr. Hedge "trailing"), is nearly equivalent to the English phrase "dogging one's steps." The first of the three Angelic Choruses rejoices over Christ's release from Mortality, the second exalts him as the "Loving One," and the third celebrates his restoration to the Divine creative activity.

15. Is he, in glow of birth,
Rapture creative near ?

These two lines, in the original, are a marvel of compressed expression. The closest literal translation is : "Is He, in the bliss of developing into (higher) being, near to the joy of creating," —that is, the bliss of being born into the higher life to which He has ascended is scarcely less than the joy of the Divine creative activity. The Disciples, left behind and still sharing the woes of Earth, bewail the beatitude which parts Him from them.

16. 'Tis true, she showed me, on Saint Andrew's Night.

St. Andrew's Night is the 29th of November. It is celebrated in some parts of Germany, by forms of divination very similar to those which are practised in Scotland on Hallow E'en (October 31st). The maidens, as in Keats's *Eve of Saint Agnes*, believe that by calling upon St. Andrew, undressed, before getting into bed, the future sweetheart will appear to them in a dream. Another plan is to pour melted lead through the wards of a key wherein there is

the form of a cross, into a basin of water fetched between eleven
o'clock and midnight : the cooling lead will then take the form of
tools which indicate the trade of the destined lover.

17. *She showed me mine, in crystal clear.*

A magic crystal, sometimes in the form of a sphere, but
frequently, no doubt, as a lens, was employed for the purpose of
divination. The methods, in fact, were varied to suit the superstition which employed them. In Pictor's "Varieties of Ceremonial
Magic" (given in Scheible's *Kloster*), twenty-seven forms of
divination are described at length, but Crystallomancy is not
among them. The ancients employed between forty and fifty
different methods.

18. *Sir Doctor, it is good of you.*

It is very rarely that the first and third lines of a quatrain are
unrhymed in German. I have no doubt that Goethe intended to
represent, by a less musical verse, the more prosaic nature and
speech of the common people. The words he employs in the two
addresses of the Old Peasant are the simplest and plainest ; the *tone*
of the verse is entirely that of prose.

19. *Then also you, though but a youth.*

Düntzer conjectures that Goethe derived the idea of this helpful
activity of Faust, upon which rests the episode with the peasants,
from the history of Nostradamus. In the year 1525, when the
latter was twenty-two years old, Provence was devastated by a
pestilence. The young physician went boldly from house to house,
through the villages, and saved the lives of many of the sick,
himself escaping all infection.

20. *There was a Lion red, a wooer daring.*

The jargon of the mediæval alchemists, from Raymond Lully to
Paracelsus, is used in this description. The system taught that all
substances, especially metals, had either masculine or feminine
qualities, as well as inherent affinities and antipathies. Campanella's doctrine, that all the elements of matter were endowed
with sense and feeling, was very generally adopted by his successors
in the art. Goethe drew his description of the preparation of the
panacea partly from Paracelsus, and partly from Welling's *Opus
Mago-Cabbalisticum.*

The "Lion red" is cinnabar, called a "wooer daring" on account
of the action of quicksilver in rushing to an intimate union (an
amalgam) with all other metals. The Lily is a preparation of
antimony, which bore the name of *Lilium Paracelsi.* Red, moreover, is the masculine, and white the feminine colour. The alembic
containing these substances was first placed in a "tepid bath"—a
vessel of warm water—and gradually heated ; then "tormented by
flame unsparing" ("open flame," in the original), the two were
driven from one "bridal chamber" to another,—that is, their

wedded fumes were forced, by the heat, from the alembic into a glass retort. If then, the "young Queen," the sublimated compound of the two substances, appeared with a brilliant colour—ruby or royal purple being most highly esteemed—in the retort, "this was the medicine." The product reminds us of calomel, which is usually formed by the sublimated union of mercury and chlorine.

21. *Swift from the North the spirit-fangs so sharp.*

The belief in evil spirits inhabiting the nether regions of the atmosphere is very ancient. Paul calls Satan "the prince of the power of the air" (*Ephesians*, ii. 2), and thus gives Christian currency to a much older superstition. In the poem *Zodiacus Vitæ*, of Marcellus Palingenius (written about the year 1527), the different atmospheric demons are minutely described. Their names are Typhurgus (Mist-bringer), Aplestus (the Insatiable), Philokreus (Lover of Flesh), and Miastor (the Befouler). Wagner's classification indicates the effects of the four winds upon the weather and the human frame. In Germany, the east wind is dry and keen, and the west wind brings rain.

"The air is not so full of flies in summer, as it is at all times of invisible devils: this Paracelsus stiffly maintains."—Burton, *Anat.*, Part I.

2. *Seest thou the black dog coursing there, through corn and stubble?*

The appearance of Mephistopheles in the form of a dog is a part of the old legend. Manlius, in the report of his conversation with Melancthon, quotes the latter as having said: "He (Faust) had a dog with him, which was the devil."

23. *'Tis written: "In the Beginning was the Word."*

This passage is not, as Blackie supposes, a fortunate inspiration of Goethe. It is directly suggested by the legend. In Widmann's "Veritable History of Dr. Faust" (Hamburg, 1599), I find, in the fifteenth chapter, that Mephistopheles thus answers Faust's proposition to discuss with him certain questions of theology: "In so far as it concerns the Bible, which thou again art of a mind to read, there shall be no more permitted to thee than, namely: the first, second, and fifth books of Moses; all the others, except Job, shalt thou let be; and likewise in the New Testament thou mayest read the three Disciples that write of the deeds of Christ, that is to say, the tax-gatherer, the painter and the doctor (meaning Mattheum, Marcum and Lucam); *but John shalt thou avoid*, and I forbid also the chatterer Paul, and such others as wrote Epistles."

24. *The Key of Solomon is good.*

Solomon's fame as a magician is mentioned by Josephus, and also by Origen, who was acquainted with a work on the manner of citing spirits to appear, ascribed to the Hebrew king. There seems to be no doubt that Solomon was a chief authority with the Jewish exorcists, from whom his name and some of his supposed formulæ of invocation were transmitted, until we find them in the Cabbala of the Middle Ages. The *Clavicula Salomonis* is mentioned by Welling, Paracelsus, and other writers, and some copies have been preserved. It is claimed that the genuine original contained only instructions by which good spirits might be invoked to assist in good works, but the variations give also the method of summoning evil spirits. In *Faust's Dreifacher Höllenzwang* (copied in Scheible's *Kloster*), the *Clavicula Salomonis* is given as it was communicated to Pope Sylvester by Constantine, and translated in the Vatican, under Pope Julius II. It is called "The Necromantic Key of Solomon, or the Key to the Magic Wisdom of Solomon, and to compel the Spirits to every Manner of Service," and commences: "At first, pray (or sing) the following *canticum hebraicum—Aba, zarka, maccaf, sofar, holech,* (*segolta*), *pazergadol,*" etc. Then follow a number of similar invocations, together with the "Seal of the highest wisdom of Solomon,"—a very complicated figure of hexagonal form,—which must be held in the hand. Faust, as the reader will remark, employs an entirely different method of exorcism.

25. *The Words of the Four be addressed.*

The universal belief in elementary spirits, during the Middle Ages, was a natural inheritance from the ancient faith. So much of their former half-divinity clung to them that they were assigned an intermediate place between men and genuine spirits. They were supposed to have positive and unchangeable forms, of a finer, more ethereal flesh and blood, and to be soulless, although the children born of their intercourse with human beings received human souls. They were classified, according to the element in which they lived, as Salamanders (in Fire), Undines (in Water), Sylphs (in Air), and Gnomes (in Earth). Of these, the two latter classes were supposed to be most familiar and friendly.

Faust, it will be noticed, uses "the Words of the Four," but without effect. He then repeats the adjuration, in another and stronger form. Here, however, the word *Kobold* (Gnome) is omitted, and *Incubus*, the dwarfish, triksy, household spirit, is substituted. In German fairy-lore, there is a relationship between the two, but they are not identical. There seems to be no reason for the change ; and, as Goethe attached no great importance to the passage, the rhyme, alone, may have suggested it.

26. *Now, to undisguise thee,*
Hear me exorcise thee!

The original is : "Thou shalt hear me more strongly exorcise !" Suspecting that an infernal spirit dwells in the beast, Faust makes "the sign" of the cross, and the effect is immediately manifest. Düntzer says, " He presents to him the name of Jesus,"—which is certainly a misconception. Blackie quotes a passage from Cornelius

Agrippa, declaring that evil spirits are affrigh ed by the sign of the cross.

Goethe, also, may have remembered the verse in the Epistle of James (ii. 19): "Thou believest that there is one God; thou doest well: the devils also believe, and tremble."

27. *The One, unoriginate.*

Here Christ is described, but not named. The four lines are literally:

> The Unoriginated,
> Unuttered,
> Diffused through all the Heavens,
> Guiltily transpierced

28. MEPHISTOPHELES.

The original form of this name was *Mephostophiles.* There has been much discussion in regard to its meaning; but Düntzer's conjecture is probably correct,—that it was imperfectly formed by some one who knew little Greek, and was intended to signify *not loving the light.* The expressions which Mephistopheles uses, in explaining his nature to Faust, would seem to indicate that this was also Goethe's understanding of the name.

Although, in most of the popular Faust-stories, Mephistopheles is often referred to as "the Devil," it was well understood that he was only *a* Devil. In "Faust's Miraculous Art and Book of Marvels, or the Black Raven" (1469), the powers and potentates of the Infernal Kingdom are thus given: *King*, Lucifer; *Viceroy*, Belial; *Gubernatores*, Satan, Beelzebub, Astaroth, Pluto; *Chief Princes*, Aziel, Mephistophilis, Marbuel, Ariel, Aniguel, Anisel, and Barfael.

Goethe took only the name and a few circumstances connected with the first appearance of Mephistopheles from the legend; the character, from first to last, is his own creation. Although he sometimes slyly used it (though less frequently than Faust) as a mask through which to speak with his own voice, he evidently drew the germ of some characteristics from his early associate, Merck.

"Merck and I," said Goethe to Eckermann, in 1831, "always went together, like Faust and Mephistopheles. . . . . All his pranks and tricks sprang from the basis of a higher culture; but, as he was not a productive nature,—on the contrary, he possessed a *strongly marked negative tendency*,—he was far more ready to blame than praise, and involuntarily sought out everything which might enable him to indulge his habit."

29. *In names like Beelzebub, Destroyer, Father of Lies.*

In the original, the first of these names is given as *Fliegengott*, Fly-god. For the sake of metre, I have substituted our familiar Hebrew equivalent, Beelzebub,—or, more correctly, *Baalsebub.* "Destroyer" and Liar, or "Father of Lies," are also familiar to us as *Abaddon* and *Satan.* Faust must be supposed to accept the orders of the infernal hierarchy, as given in the cabalistic writings, whence his endeavour to identify the particular fiend whom he has invoked.

30. *I am the Spirit that Denies.*

In declaring himself, first, to be part of that power "which always wills the Bad, and always works the Good," Mephistopheles is unexpectedly frank. His expression coincides exactly with the declaration of The Lord, as to the service he is obliged to perform.

In the passage which follows, he is equally honest, and the above line clearly describes the part which he plays, from beginning to end. He is the Spirit of Negation, and his being exists through opposition to the positive Truth, and Order, and Beauty, which proceed from the never-ending creative energy of the Deity. The masks which we find him assuming in the Second Part of *Faust* are all explained by this necessity of Negation. His irreverence and irony are not only a part of his nature, but they are further increased by the impotence of his efforts—which he freely admits in the following passages—to disturb the Divine system.

Mephistopheles draws his theory of the primeval darkness from the Theogony of Hesiod. His reference to "bodies" shows that he understands the physical and spiritual identity of light and life. Since we have seen that, in Widmann's Faust-book, he prohibits to Faust the reading of the Gospel of John, we may surmise a connection between his hostility to light and these verses from the first chapter of that Gospel :—

"In him was life; and the life was the light of men.
"And the light shineth in darkness; and the darkness comprehended it not."

31. *The wizard's foot, that on your threshold made is.*

In the original, *Drudenfuss*. *Drud*, from one root with *Druid*, was the old German word for "wizard." The wizard's-foot, or pentagram, was supposed to possess an especial potency against evil spirits. It is simply a five-rayed star, thus :—

Its efficacy undoubtedly sprang from the circumstance that it resolves itself into three triangles, and is thus a triple symbol of the Trinity. Paracelsus ascribes a similar, though a lesser, degree of virtue to the *hexagram*. Another peculiarity of the pentagram is, that it may be drawn complete from one point, without lifting the pencil, and therefore belongs to those *involuntary* hieroglyphics which we sometimes make, in moments of abstraction.

32. SONG OF THE SPIRITS.

This remarkable chant is known in Germany (Goethe himself being, I believe, the first to so designate it) as the *Einschläferungs-lied*, or Lullaby. It is one of the few things in the work which have proved to be a little too much for the commentators, and they have generally let it alone. By dropping all philosophical theories, however, and applying to it only the conditions of Poetic Art, we shall find it easily comprehensible. Faust is hardly aware (although Mephistopheles *is*) that a part of his almost despairing impatience springs from the lack of all enjoyment of physical life ; and the first business of these attendant spirits is to unfold before his enchanted eyes a series of dim, dissolving views—sweet, formless, fantastic, and thus all the more dangerously alluring—of sensuous delight. The pictures are blurred, as in a semi-dream : they present nothing positive, upon which Faust's mind could fix, or by which it might be startled : but they leave an impression behind, which gradually works itself into form. The echo of the wild, weird, interlinked melody remains in his soul, and he is not supposed to be conscious of its operation, even when, in the following scene, he exclaims to Mephistopheles :—

> " Let us the sensual deeps explore,
>   To quench the fervours of glowing passion ! "

The rhythmical translation of this song—which, without the original rhythm and rhyme, would lose nearly all its value—is a head and heart breaking task. I can only say that, after returning to it again and again, during a period of six years, I can offer nothing better.

33. *I come, a squire of high degree.*

The word *Junker*, which Mephistopheles uses, corresponds exactly with "squire," as a term of chivalry. In the text of the puppet-play, when he makes his appearance the second time, he is described as *wohlgekleidet*—respectably dressed. His costume on the puppet-stage was a red tunic, under a long mantle of black silk, and a cock's-feather in his hat. Goethe purposely retains this costume, because it is sufficiently appropriate to his conception of the character, which he expressly declares is too negative to be *daimonic.*

34. *This life of earth, whatever my attire,*
Would pain me in its wonted fashion.

The first fragment of the *Paralipomena* possibly belongs here, although there is also a place for it towards the close of the scene. In the following lines, omitted alike in the editions of 1790 and 1808, Mephistopheles continues to advise a change of costume :—

MEPHISTOPHELES.
When with externals thou art well endowed,
All will around thee flock, and flatter ;
A chap who's not a little vain or proud,
Had better hang, and end the matter.

I have not been able to find any evidence concerning the date of these rejected passages of *Faust.*

35. Chorus of Spirits.

Faust's curse, which includes even the sentiment of childish faith that overcame him on the Easter morning, places him, unconsciously, in the power of Mephistopheles. The Chorus of Spirits indicates, in a few powerful lines, his rupture with the order of life. The first words of Mephistopheles which follow, would lead the reader to suppose that the spirits were infernal, and thus a singular discrepancy between their character and their expressions is implied. In Leutbecher's work, however, I find a hint of what I believe to be the true intention of this Chorus. He says: "The pure spirits who direct the harmonies of existence lament over his (Faust's) step, and encourage him to commence another and fairer career. But Mephistopheles calls these voices precociously shrewd, and proposes the conditions of his compact, promising delights which, in advance, appear worthless to Faust." The lament is certainly not ironical.

36. *When thus I hail the Moment flying:* "*Ah, still delay—thou art so fair!*"

Here Faust becomes earnest and definite. The one moment of supreme contentment is for him a symbol of endless capacity for happiness. The wager with Mephistopheles rests upon this couplet, which the reader must bear in his memory until he meets with it again, at the close of the Second Part.

There is no condition of this nature in the Faust-legends. The compact there is, that Faust shall have whatever he desires for the term of twenty-four years, when he passes, body and soul, into the power of Mephistopheles. The only slight resemblance to this passage, in any of the various versions, may be found in the Augsburg play, where Mephistopheles says: "Faust, have I not said to thee, thou canst thyself break the hour-glass of thy time? Thou hast done it in this moment."

37. *Then at the Doctors'-banquet I, to-day.*

Mephistopheles refers to the inauguration feast, given on taking a degree.

38. Encheiresin naturæ, *this Chemistry names.*

With the introduction of the Student (whom we shall meet again, in the Second Part, as *Baccalaureus*), Mephistopheles not only assumes the mantle of Faust, but Goethe also assumes the mask of Mephistopheles. The episode, which is wholly his own invention, was written during his intercourse with Merck, and while his experience of academic teaching was still fresh and far from edifying.

The "Spanish boots," of which Mephistopheles speaks, were

instruments of torture used in the Middle Ages. They were cases of wood, into which wedges were driven until the calves of the victim's legs were compressed into the smallest possible space.

The phrase *encheiresin naturæ* signifies, properly, "a treatment of Nature." Here, however, Goethe seems rather to indicate the mysterious, elusive force by which Nature operates.

39. *The little world, and then the great, we'll see.*

The programme of both parts of *Faust* is given in this line. No reference to the cabalistic Microcosm and Macrocosm is intended: "the little world" is here Faust's individual experience of human desires and passions. "The great world" is life on a broader stage of action; the narrow interests of the individual are merged in those of the race; and Government, War, activity on a grand scale and for universal, permanent ends, succeed, in order that Faust's knowledge of the life of man shall be rounded into completeness. The Second Part of the work is devoted to this latter experience.

40. *I feel so small before others, and thence Should always find embarrassments.*

The following passage is the second of the *Paralipomena,* and was undoubtedly designed as an answer to the above lines. It seems to have been written at a later period, and we may conjecture that Goethe omitted the lines because they are not in accord with the manner of Mephistopheles throughout the scene :—

MEPHISTOPHELES.

Learn then from me to meet Society !
I come, both cheerful and collected,
And every heart is well-affected :
I laugh, and each one laughs with me.
Rely, like me, upon your own pretences ;
There's something to be dared, you must reflect :
For even women easily forgive offences
If one respectfully forgets respect.
Not in divining-rods nor mandrake tragic,
But in good humour lies the best of magic :
If I'm in unison with all,
I do not see how trouble could befall.
Then to the work, and show no hesitation !
I only dread the preparation.

41. AUERBACH'S CELLAR IN LEIPZIG.

The locality of this scene possesses a double interest, through its connection with the early Faust-legend and with the academic years of the young Goethe. If the stranger who visits Leipzig will seek the large, ancient house, No. 1, *Grimmaische Strasse,* near the Market-Place, the sign "AUERBACHS KELLER," nearly on a level with the sidewalk, will guide him down into the two vaulted chambers which have echoed to the wit and song and revelry of four centuries of jolly companions. He may still take Faust's and Goethe's place, at the head of the table in the farther room, order his wine from the seventieth or eightieth successor of the original landlord, and, while awaiting the preparation of some old-fashioned dish, study the two curious paintings, which have filled semicircular spaces under the arches perhaps since the year 1525.

Legends of Faust are as plentiful in Germany as those of kobolds or subterranean emperors; but these pictures, I believe are the only local records left to our day.

42. *Soar up, Soar up, Dame Nightingale.*

The couplet which Frosch sings belongs to several of the early songs of the people. The "Message of Love," written in 1639, commences :—

> " Soar up, Dame Nightingale, speed high,
>   And to my sweetheart's window fly !"

Another song, of the same period, has these lines :—

> " Dame Nightingale, Dame Nightingale,
>   Many thousand times my sweetheart hail ! '

The term "Dame Nightingale" was first used by the Minnesingers as early as the eleventh century, and has been perpetuated in the popular songs and ballads. The second fragment which Frosch sings, to annoy Siebel (who has been jilted and resents these strains of love), appears to be Goethe's.

43. *No doubt 'twas late when you from Rippach started !*
Now draw the stoppers and drink your fill !

Rippach is the last post-station before reaching Leipzig, on the road from Weissenfels. The remark of Frosch is a part of the "chaff" with which the older *Burschen* were accustomed to entertain the *Foxes*, or Freshmen. "Hans von Rippach" is a slang name, denoting a coarse, awkward, boorish fellow,—in fact, an equivalent for the Scotch *Sawney*, as it is used in some localities. By hinting that Faust and Mephistopheles have been supping with Hans von Rippach, Frosch takes a delicate way of saying that they are ignorant country clowns, in comparison with the refined Parisians of Leipzig.

Goethe took the specimen of jugglery from the legend, where, however, it is not performed by Mephistopheles but by Faust.

44. *Witches' Kitchen.*

Neither this scene nor the Walpurgis-Night (Scene XXI.) has any connection with the Faust-legend. The chief motive of the Witches' Kitchen is, of course, the passional rejuvenation of Faust, as introductory to the episode of Margaret; but Goethe, with a wilful spirit, not unfrequently manifested in his life and writings, seems to have also designed burlesquing the machinery of witchcraft and its use in literature.

There has been a great deal of not very important discussion as to the meaning of the word *Meerkatze*. It has been translated

"Monkey," "Baboon," "Cat-Ape," "Cat," and "Little Ring-tailed Monkey." I follow Mephistopheles, himself, in using the word "Ape," (*Wie glücklich würde sich der Affe schätzen !*) which will answer as well as any other for those who insist on symbolism. Goethe probably took his *Meerkatzen* from the legend of Reinek*r* Fuchs, wherein they are introduced.

45. *Full thirty years from my existence.*

There is here an apparent contradiction between the age of Faust and that which is implied in the first scene. The deduction of thirty years, we must suppose, should leave him as a youth of twenty, to begin his new experience of life ; yet we can hardly imagine the man who has been teaching for only ten years, and has barely attained his Doctor's degree, to be more than thirty-five. Düntzer thinks this is an oversight of Goethe, arising from the long interval between the composition of the two scenes.

45.* *Wert thou the thief.*

The art of divination by means of a sieve (*koskinomancy*) was known to the ancients : it is mentioned in the third idyl of Theocritus. In the life of Campanella—the Dominican monk, with whose work, *De Sensu Rerum,* Goethe appears to have been acquainted—the following story occurs : "Some boys had lost a mantle, and in order to find out whither it had taken its flight, they hung up a sieve by the middle on a peg, and then uttered the words 'In the name of St. Peter and in the name of St. Paul, has not so and so stolen the mantle ?' They went over a number of names in the same manner, but the sieve remained immovable, till they pronounced the name of Flavius, and then it began to wheel round about. Campanella, who saw it, was much astonished, and prayed with the boys that God would not suffer them to be blinded by the devil ; and, on making the trial again, as soon as the name of Flavius was pronounced, it began to wheel round about in a circle."—*Adelung,* Blackie's translation.

46. *This is the Witch's once-one's-one !*

The common schoolboy term for the multiplication-table in Germany is *Einmaleins,* from its commencement, *Einmal eins ist eins*—once one is one ! The jargon which the witch declaims from the book is nothing but a nonsensical parody of the cabalistic formula of the Middle Ages, wherein mystical properties are attributed to numbers.

In the *Paralipomena,* there is a verse which is generally attributed to the omitted Disputation, yet which seems more appropriate in this place. Mephistopheles says (apparently to Faust) :—

> Now, once for all, mark this, I pray—
> A maxim weighty for thine actions !
> No mystery the numbers here convey,
> Yet there's a great one in the fraction*n.*

47. Margaret.

We now take leave of the original Faust-legend, which will not again be encountered until the appearance of Helena, in the Second Part. The episode of Margaret is Goethe's own creation, from beginning to end, and here, even more than in the first monologue of Faust, he "delved in his own breast" for the passion which he represents. Margaret is drawn partly from her namesake, whom Goethe, as a boy of sixteen, imagined he loved; and partly from his betrothed, Lili (Anna Elizabeth Schönemann, the daughter of a banker in Frankfurt), for whom he felt probably the strongest love of his life, at the time these scenes of his *Faust* were written.

48. *In Padua, buried, he is lying,*
Beside the good Saint Antony.

If this is anything more than a random statement of Mephistopheles, the irony is neither keen nor especially important. The Saint is not the Antony of the Desert and the temptations and the Irish ballad, but Antonio of Padua, a relative of Godfrey of Bouillon. He was born in Lisbon in 1195, preached with such fervour that even the fishes rose to the surface of the sea to listen to him, and died in Padua in 1231. The splendid basilica in which his ashes rest was not completed until two centuries later. His chapel, with its *alti rilievi* by Lombardi, Sansovino, and others, still attracts the student of art.

Interments within the walls of cathedrals and churches in Italy were not prohibited until the year 1809.

49. *For thou art right, especially since I must.*

Faust, in this line, admits his dependence on the aid of Mephistopheles, and the necessity of giving false testimony in order to procure an interview with Margaret. No change in the character of his passion is implied.

There is a passage in the *Paralipomena* which seems naturally to belong here, although some of the German commentators have given it a different place. Mephistopheles says, apparently after Faust's departure, when he has impatiently spoken the above line :— —

> 'Tis hard indeed, the younker's ways commanding;
> Yet, as his tutor, I've no fear
> I shall not rule the madcap, notwithstanding,
> And nothing else concerns me here.
> His own desires I let him follow slowly,
> That mine, as well, may be accomplished wholly.
> Much do I talk, yet always leave him free;
> If what he does should quite too stupid be,
> My wisdom, then, must make a revelation,
> And I must drag him forth, as by the hair;
> Yet, while one strives the folly to repair,
> One gives for other folly fresh occasion.

50.   *She plucks a star-flower.*

The original, *sternblume*, may mean either a china-aster, a star-of-Bethlehem, a variety of primrose or of jonquil. Various modes of amorous divination by means of flowers were known to the ancients (one of them is mentioned by Theocritus), and the Minnesinger, Walther von der Vogelweide, describes a very similar method of ascertaining whether a lover's affection is returned. The single daisy (*Gänseblümchen* in German) is sometimes used for the same purpose, but it is a garden-flower, of course, which Margaret plucks.

51.   *It's as if nobody had nothing to fetch and carry.*

The effect of a double negative in German is precisely the same as in English, and it belongs equally to the vulgar dialect. Goethe introduces it intentionally here as well as in Scene XVI., where Margaret says, speaking of Mephistopheles: "One sees that in nothing no interest he hath." I have not felt at liberty to correct these purposed inelegances, as most translators have done. They are trifling touches, it is true, but they belong to the author's design.

52.   *" Were I a little bird !" so runs her song.*

This is an old song of the people in Germany. Herder published it in his *Volkslieder*, in 1779 ; but it was no doubt already familiar to Goethe in his childhood.

53.   *And we'll scatter chaff before her door.*

The word *häckerling* signifies either chaff or chopped straw. The old German custom, which is still observed in some parts of the country, allowed the bridal wreath only to chaste maidens. If one of sullied reputation ventured to assume it, the wreath was torn from her head, and sometimes replaced with one of straw, while on the eve of the marriage chaff or chopped straw was scattered before her door. A widow who marries again is allowed to wear a wreath, but not the myrtle of the maiden bride.

Church-penance for unchastity was also formerly common in England. In Germany the guilty person was obliged to kneel before the altar, clad in a "sinner's shift," while the clergyman severely rated her conduct, and read her petition for pardon.

54.   DONJON.

The word *Zwinger*, which Goethe uses, corresponds to our "stronghold" or "donjon keep," but is also sometimes applied to the open angular space between the wall of a town and one of the fortified gates. Goethe seems to use the word in the latter sense. The shrine of a saint was frequently placed in the re-entering angle, between which and the city-wall there would be a partly enclosed space. Mephistopheles represents Margaret as watching the clouds "over the old city-wall," from her window, whence her home must have been in the street nearest to it, and the shrine of the *Mater Dolorosa*, being close at hand, would become her accustomed place of prayer. I have followed all other translators in using the word *donjon*, simply because we have no English word to describe the locality.

55. *Saw splendid lion-dollars in't.*

The remark of Faust refers, apparently, to some buried treasure which Mephistopheles has promised to raise for him. "Lion-dollars" are of Dutch coinage, and so called both from the city of the Louvain (in German, *Löwen*—lion), in Brabant, where they were first struck, and from the figure of a lion on the obverse. They are also sometimes named "Brabanters." A few specimens are still occasionally seen in Germany : their value is about eighty-five cents. Hayward is mistaken in saying that the lion-dollar is a Bohemian coin.

56. *Rat-catching piper, thou!*

Browning's poem of "The Pied Piper of Hamelin" is so well-known that I need not give the old German legend to which Valentine's exclamation refers. Goethe's song, *Der Rattenfänger*, expresses still more clearly the meaning which he attaches to the phrase. The man who charms innocent maidens by his seductive arts, even as the piper by the notes of his magical pipe charmed the rats of Hamelin, is a rat-catcher.

57. *Dies iræ, dies illa.*

Goethe has elsewhere acknowledged the powerful impression which this old Latin chant made upon himself. Some have attributed its authorship to Gregory the Great, and others to Bernhard of Clairvaux; but the scholars seem now to be generally agreed that it is not of later origin than the thirteenth century, and that Thomas of Celano was probably its author. It was accepted by the Roman Church, as one of the *sequentia* of the requiem, before the year 1385. The original text is engraved upon a marble tablet in the church of St. Francesco in Mantua. The present form of the chant is supposed to have been given by Felix Hämmerlin (in the early part of the fifteenth century), who omitted the former opening stanzas, and added some others at the close. In this form it has appeared in the Catholic missals, since the Council of Trent. The chant has been translated upwards of seventy times into German, and fifteen times into English.

58. *Neighbour! your cordial!*

The original word, *Fläschchen*, means simply a phial ; but it is evidently the neighbour's pocket-flagon of smelling-salts for which Margaret asks. In most of the English versions we find "smelling-bottle," but Mr. W. Taylor of Norwich, in his "Historic Survey of German Poetry" (London 1830), says "Your Dram-bottle !"

c c 2

59. Walpurgis-Night.

The title and character of the Witches' Sabbath on the summit of the Brocken, on the night between April 30 and May 1, spring equally from the old and the new religion. Walpurgis (or Walpurga, which is the most usual form of the name) was the sister of Saints Willibald and Wunnibald, and emigrated with them from England to Germany, as followers of St. Boniface, in the eighth century. She died as abbess of a convent at Heidenheim, in Franconia, and after the extirpation of the old Teutonic faith became one of the most popular saints, not only in Germany, but also in Holland and England. The first of May, which was given to her in the calendar, was the ancient festival day of the Druids, when they made sacrifices upon their sacred mountains, and kindled their May-fires. Inasmuch as their gods became devils to their Christian descendants, the superstition of a conclave of wizards, witches, and fiends on the Brocken—or Blocksberg—naturally arose, and the name of the pious Walpurgis thus became irrevocably attached to the diabolical anniversary. The superstition probably grew from the circumstance that the Druidic rites were celebrated by night, and secretly, as their followers became few.

60.　*How raves the tempest through the air !*

The word which I have translated "tempest," is *Windsbraut* (wind's-bride) in the original. It is the word employed by Luther, in his translation of the Bible, for the italicized words in the following verse from Acts (xxvii. 14) : "But not long after there arose *against it a tempestuous wind,* called Euroclydon." A sudden and violent storm is still called *Windsbraut* by the common people, in some parts of Germany.

61.　*Sir Urian sits over all.*

Sir Urian is a name which was formerly used to designate an unknown person, or one whose name, even if known, it was not thought proper to mention. In this sense it was sometimes applied to the Devil. In the *Parzival* of Wolfram von Eschenbach, the unprincipled Prince of Punturtois, is called Urian.

62.　*Alone, old Baubo's coming now.*

Baubo, in the Grecian myths, was the old nurse of Demeter, or Ceres ; who, when the latter was plunged in grief for the loss of Persephone, endeavoured to divert her by indecent stories and actions, and thus, finally, provoked her to laughter. Goethe, therefore, makes her symbolize the gross, shameless sensuality, which, according to all popular traditions, characterized the congregations of the witches, wizards, and devils.

63.　*Make room !　Squire Voland comes !*

" In the poets of the twelfth and thirteenth centuries we frequently meet with the word *Vâlant* as a designation of the Devil.

In Berthold's Diary we find the Evil One once named as *Squire Volland*—in the play of Frau Jutta as the *Evil Volland*. The word means either 'seducer' or 'the Wicked One.'"—*Düntzer*.

64. MEPHISTOPHELES (*who all at once appears very old*).

The remaining fragments (*Paralipomena*) which belong to the Walpurgis-Night may properly be given here :—

MEPHISTOPHELES.

Though but a bagpipe, give us music ! Haste !
We have, like many noble fellows,
Much appetite and little taste.

MEPHISTOPHELES.

The piper famous
Of Hamelin, also mine old friend,
The dear rat-catcher who can tame us,
How goes —

THE RAT-CATCHER OF HAMELIN.

I'm very well indeed, I thank you ;
I am a hale and well-fed man,
Of twelve Philanthropines the patron,
And therewithal [*a charlatan*].

65. *Adam's first wife is he.*

Burton, in his "Anatomy of Melancholy," says : "The Talmudists say that Adam had a wife called Lilis before he married Eve, and of her he begat nothing but devils."

The name, from the Hebrew root, *Lil*, darkness, signifies *the Nocturnal*. The word occurs in Isaiah (xxxiv. 14) ; in the Vulgate it is translated *Lamia*, in Luther's Bible *Kobold*, and in our English version *screech-owl*. According to the Rabbinical writings, Lilith was created at the same time with Adam, in such a manner that he and she were joined together by the back, as it is written, "male and female created He them, and called their name Adam." In this condition they did not agree at all, but quarrelled and tore each other continually. Then the Lord repented that he had made them so, and separated them into two independent bodies ; but even thus they would not live in peace, and when Lilith devoted herself to witchcraft and courted the society of Devils, Adam left her altogether. A new wife, Eve, was afterwards created, to compensate him for his domestic misfortune.

Lilith is described as having beautiful hair, in the meshes of which lurk a multitude of evil spirits. She has such power over infants—for eight days after birth for boys, and twenty days for girls—that she is able to cause their death. It was therefore the custom to hang an amulet, inscribed with the names of the angels Senoi, Sansenoi, and Sanmangeloph, around the child's neck at birth ; and from the Latin exorcism *Lilla abi !* sung by the mother, some have derived our word *Lullaby*, although it has also a more obvious derivation. Lilith was equally a seductress of young men, using her golden hair as a lure to captivate them; but the youth who loved her always died, and after his death a single hair from her head was found twisted around his heart. Mr. Dante Gabriel Rossetti has embodied this tradition in a fine sonnet.

66. Proktophantasmist.

In Goethe's original manuscript and in the first edition of _Faust_ this name is given as "Broktophantasmist," as in Shelley's English and Stapfer's French version. The mistake was therefore Goethe's and not theirs, as later translators have charged. The word (from πρωκτός. the buttocks) points so directly to Friedrich Nicolai, the Berlin author and publisher, that there is no difficulty in interpreting Goethe's satire.

67. _We are so wise, and yet is Tegel haunted._

Nicolai's arrogant manner is parodied in this passage. Since _he_ does not believe in the spirits, it is incredible that they will not vanish. His annoyance at their appearance in Tegel—a small castle, a few miles north-west of Berlin, originally built as a hunting-lodge by the Elector of Brandenburg, and more recently known as the home and burial-place of Wilhelm and Alexander von Humboldt— is explained by the circumstance that in 1797 apparitions were declared to have visited the castle. So much excitement was created by the report, that an official visit to Tegel was made by the authorities, and attempts were instituted, but without success, to discover the cause of the ghostly sights and sounds.

68. _A red mouse from her mouth._

Goethe here refers to an old superstition concerning one of the many forms of diabolical possession.

69. _The Prater shows no livelier stir._

The Prater (from the Latin _pratum_, a meadow) is the famous public park of Vienna, which the Emperor Joseph II. dedicated "To the Human Race." It is an island enclosed by arms of the Danube, covered with a fine forest which is intersected in all directions by magnificent drives and walks. On holidays, Sunday afternoons, and pleasant summer evenings half the population of Vienna may be found in the Prater, which is one of the liveliest and cheerfullest places of recreation in Europe.

70. Servibilis.

This term corresponds to the "supernumerary" of our theatres.

71. Oberon and Titania's Golden Wedding.

This _Intermezzo_ had no place in the original plan of _Faust_, and Schiller is chiefly responsible for its insertion.

72. *Sons of Mieding, rest to-day.*

Mieding was a theatre-decorator at Weimar, and a great favourite of Goethe and the Ducal Court. After his death, in 1782, Goethe celebrated him in the poem, "Mieding's Death."

73. ARIEL.

Ariel is called from the "Tempest" to join his fellow-elves. Here he evidently represents Poetry,—the pure element, above and untouched by the fashions of the day.

74. A LITTLE COUPLE.

Hartung thinks the Counts Stolberg are the couple; but this is improbable, since they are afterwards introduced as the Weather-cock. Düntzer asserts that the verse represents the union of bad music and commonplace poetry.

75. INQUISITIVE TRAVELLER.

This is Nicolai, in another mask. The meaning of his reference to Oberon is not very clear, unless the latter represents the classic school. When he speaks the second time in this *Intermezzo* the Inquisitive Traveller describes himself much more distinctly.

76. ORTHODOX.

Here speaks the class of bigots who persecuted Lessing, assailed Klopstock and Goethe, and declared Schiller's splendid poem, "The Gods of Greece," to be "a combination of the most out-rageous idolatry and the dreariest atheism." This phrase is from Count Friedrich Stolberg, who became one of the mouth-pieces of the sect. His attack is thus answered in the *Xenien :*—

"When thou the Gods of Greece blasphemed, then cast thee Apollo
Down from Parnassus ; and now goest thou to Heaven instead."

77. NORTHERN ARTIST.

Some suppose this to be the Danish artist Carstens, who died in Rome, in 1798 ; others select Fernow, a writer on art, who spent some years in Rome with Carstens ; others again insist that it is Goethe himself. Inasmuch as the point made in the verse has become very obscure, and was probably not originally brilliant, the reader may take his choice of these conjectures.

78. WEATHERCOCK.

Undoubtedly the Counts Stolberg.

79. XENIES.

The word signifies gifts, presented to a visitor. After their publication in the *Musenalmanach*, the storm which arose against them became so furious that they were denounced in some quarters as having been directly inspired by the Devil. Hence the allusion to "Papa Satan."

80. Hennings.

The Danish Chamberlain Friedrich von Hennings, in his literary journal, the "Genius of the Age," attacked Goethe and Schiller.

The first verse parodies his abuse of Goethe and Schiller; the second hints that he would be more at home among Blocksberg witches than as a leader of the Muses; and the third satirizes his practice of giving a place on the German Parnassus to such authors as flattered him by an obsequious respect for his critical views.

81. Crane.

"Lavater was a thoroughly good man, but he was subjected to powerful illusions, and the severe and total truth was not his con cern : he deceived himself and others. . . . . His gait was like that of a crane, for which reason he appears as the Crane on the Blocksberg."—*Goethe to Eckermann,* 1829.

82. Worldling.

Weltkind, literally "world-child," a term which Goethe applies to himself in his epigrammatic poem.

83. Idealist.

It is generally admitted that this is Fichte, who, to borrow the words of a German commentator, "comprehended the Not-Me itself as a product of the self-determined Me, and not as something existing externally to the Me." When Goethe heard that a company of riotous students had collected before Fichte's house and smashed his windows in with stones, he remarked that Fichte might now convince himself, in the most disagreeable way, that it was possible "for a Not-Me to exist, externally to the Me."

84. *And all is dissipated.*

The transition from this *Intermezzo* to the succeeding scene of *Faust* is too violent, and we cannot help wishing that the course of the drama had not been thus interrupted. Goethe, however, not only projected, but partly wrote an additional scene, devoted exclusively to the pure diabolism of the mediæval traditions. While we must admit that a correct instinct led him to withhold it, we still must feel that an intermediate scene is necessary. The gap which we recognize was felt by the author, whose work was produced at long intervals of time, and in fragments the character of which was determined by his moods of mind. But he always preferred an abrupt chasm to an unsatisfactory bridge.

The projected scene is generally styled "The Broken Scene" by the German commentators, although Hartung takes the liberty of calling it "The Court of Satan." I translate it (with the exception of one short passage) precisely as it is given in the *Paralipomena,* with its rapid short-hand outlines, its incomplete dialogues and omitted lines, and leave all comment to the reader :—

THE HARTZ MOUNTAINS.

A Higher Region.

After the Intermezzo: Solitude, Desert, blasts of trumpets. Lightning, thunder from above. Columns of fire, stifling smoke. Rock projecting there-from: 'tis Satan. Much people around: delay: means of pressing through: injury: cries. Chant: they stand in the inner circle: the heat almost insupportable. Who stands next in the circle. Satan's address: presentations: investitures. Sinking of the apparition. Volcano. Disorderly dissolution, breaking and storming away.

SUMMIT OF THE BROCKEN.

SATAN *on his Throne.* A Crowd of People around. FAUST *and* MEPHISTOPHELES *in the nearest circle.*

SATAN (*speaking from the throne*).
The goats to the left hand,
The bucks to the right !
The goats, they have scented
The bucks with delight :
And though in their nostrils
The sense were increased,
The goats would endure it,
Nor shrink in the least.
  CHORUS. Fall down on your faces,
Your Master adore !
He teaches the people,
With pleasure, his lore.
To his oracles hearken :
He'll show you the clews
To the endless existence
That Nature renews !
  SATAN (*turning to the right*).
Two things are before you,
Both splendid and grand ;
The glittering gold

The one is purveyor,
The other devours ;
Then blest, who possesses
Together their powers !
  A VOICE. What says then the
    Master ?
Remote from his station,
I catch not so clearly
The precious oration.
I cannot detect them,
The beautiful clews,
Nor see the existence
That Nature renews !
  SATAN (*turning to the left*).
Two things are before you
Of brilliancy clear :
The glittering gold

Then learn, all ye women,
Through gold to enjoy

  CHORUS. Fall down on your faces,
Adoringly stirred !
O blest, who is nearest
And heareth the word !
  A VOICE. I stand at a distance
And listen so steady,

Yet many a word has
Escaped me already.
Who'll clearly repeat them ?
Who'll show me the clews
To the endless existence
That Nature renews ?
  MEPHIS. (*to a young witch*).
Why weep'st thou, lovely little dear
'Tis not the place to shed a tear.
Hast thou been in the crowd too
    rudely pushed and penned ?
  MAIDEN. Ah, no ! The Master
    speaks so singular

And all are so delighted, it appears ;
Perhaps the great ones, only, comprehend ?
  MEPHIS. But, sweetheart, come
    now, dry thy tears !
So that the Devil's meaning reach
    thine ears,

  SATAN. Ye young ones before us
    To stand ye are bidden ;
    I see that on broomsticks
    Ye hither have ridden:

SEPARATE AUDIENCES.

  X. Let me attain to that-
The power whereto thou knowest me
    aspirant,
Then gratefully, though born a Democrat,
I'll kiss thy hoofs no less, O Tyrant !
  MASTER OF CEREMONIES. The
    hoofs ! but once may that befall :
Thou must make up thy mind to go
    still further.
  X. What, then, requires the ritual ?

  SATAN. Vassal, thou tested art !
Now o'er a million souls thy freehold
    reaches :
He who can praise like thee the
    Devil's——
Shall never lack in sycophantic
    speeches.

ANOTHER PART OF THE BROCKEN.

LOWER REGION.

Vision of Judgment. Crowd. They climb a tree. Remarks of the people. On burning soil. The Idol naked. The hands bound on the back.

CHANT.
Where hot and fresh flows human blood,
For magic spells the reek is good.
The brotherhood, both black and gray,
Wins power for works that shun the day.
What hints of blood, we most require ;
What spills it, answers our desire.
Round fire and blood a measure tread !
For now in fire shall blood be shed.

The wench she points, we know the sign ;
The toper drinks, 'tis blood, not wine.
The look, the drink, end what's begun ;
The dagger's bare, the deed is done.
Flows ne'er alone a fount of blood,
But other streamlets join the flood :
From place to place they gush and glide,
And gather more to swell the tide.

The head falls off: the blood leaps and extinguishes the fire. Night. Tumult. Chattering of Devil's changelings. Thereby Faust learns.

Some of the German commentators suppose that the "black and gray brotherhood" of this concluding chant of the Franciscan and Dominican monastic orders, and therefore that the fragment refers directly to the Inquisition. Düntzer asserts that the heading "Another Part of the Brocken" indicates that this is a separate outline for the whole scene, intended as a substitute for the foregoing fragments, not as a continuation of them.

85. THE RAVENSTONE.

The "Ravenstone" is the old German word for a place of execution. Byron probably remembered the expression, from Shelley's oral translation, when he wrote, in a rejected chorus of the "Deformed Transformed" :—

> "The raven sits
> On the raven-stone."

86. *My mother, the harlot.*

The song which Margaret sings is a variation of one in the Low German dialect, in a story called the *Machandel-Boom* (The Juniper-Tree ; the English translator, mistaking *Machandel* for *Mandel*, renders it "almond-tree"), included by the brothers Grimm in their well-known collection of popular fairy lore.

NOTES TO THE SECOND PART.

1. ARIEL.

This first scene has the character of a Prologue to the Second Part of *Faust*, the action of which commences with the following scene. An indefinite period of time separates the two parts of the drama. Neither in his own life nor in his poetical creations did Goethe ever give space to remorse for an irrevocable deed. When Faust disappears with Mephistopheles, all his later torture of soul has been already suggested to the reader, and nothing of it can properly be introduced here, where the whole plan and scope of the work is changed.

2. *Four pauses makes the Night upon her courses.*

Goethe here refers to the four *vigiliæ*, or night-watches, of the Romans, each of three hours; so that the whole, from six in the evening until six in the morning, include both sunset and sunrise.

3. CHORUS.

The four verses of the Chorus correspond to the four *vigiliæ*. The first describes the evening twilight; the second, the dead of night; the third, the coming of the dawn; and the fourth, the awaking to the day. The direction in regard to the chanting of the verses by the alternate or collective voices of the elves was added, in view of the possible representation of the drama upon the stage.

4. *Look up!—The mountain summits, grand, supernal.*

The scene described is Swiss, and from the neighbourhood of the Lake of the Four Forest Cantons. Goethe's projected journey to Italy in 1797 terminated with a tour in that region, in company with the artist Meyer.

5. *The spheres of Hour and House are in his ken.*

The astrologers divided the celestial hemisphere into twelve parts, which were called Houses. In casting a horoscope, it was necessary to have, first, the hour of birth and the latitude and longitude of the birthplace. The location of the sun, moon, planets, and the signs of the zodiac in the different houses, was then ascertained. As each house represented a special human interest or passion, and each planet a special controlling force, the various combinations which thus arose furnished the material out of which the horoscope was constructed.

The speech of the Astrologer, prompted by Mephistopheles, refers to the seven metals, to which the mediæval alchemists attached the names of the seven planets. The sun is gold, the moon silver; Mercury is quicksilver, Venus copper, Mars iron Jupiter tin, and Saturn lead.

6.   *There lies the fiddler, there the gold!*

Clemens Brentano, in his "Boy's Wonder-horn," states that it is a common superstition in Germany, that, when one accidentally stumbles, he is passing over the spot where a fiddler is buried.

The expressions of Mephistopheles refer to the power of divination supposed to be possessed by certain persons.

7.   *He seeks saltpetre where the clay-walls stand.*

Old walls, especially in damp cellars and subterranean passages, become covered with an incrustation of saltpetre, the collection of which was formerly a government monopoly.

8.   *A cask of tartar holds the wine.*

It is a general belief in Germany that when a cask of wine has been kept for centuries, it gradually deposits a crust of tartar, which may acquire such a consistency as to hold the liquid when the staves have rotted away. The wine thus becomes its own cask, and preserves itself in a thick, oily state. It is then supposed to possess wonderful medicinal powers.

9.   Carnival Masquerade.

In the "Carnival Masquerade" we reach the first entangling episode of the Second Part of *Faust.* That the entire scene is an allegory is evident; and we can scarcely be mistaken in assuming its chief motive to be the representation of the human race in its social and political organisation.

The scene of the Masquerade is not in Italy, as some suppose, but at the German Court, after the Emperor's return from his coronation by the Pope, at Rome. Maximilian I. was the first German Emperor who omitted this ceremony.

10.   Olive-Branch, with Fruit.

If the allegory is consistently developed, we must suppose that the Olive-Branch, the Wreath of Ears, and the Fancy-Wreath are types of female character, or of the different forms of attraction whereby women draw towards them the complementary male characters.

11.   *What our name is, Theophrastus.*

The reference is not to Theophrastus Paracelsus, but to Theophrastus of Lesbos, born B.C. 390, the disciple of Plato and the successor of Aristotle. Among his extant works is a "Natural History of Plants," a translation of which, by Sprengel, was published at Altona, in 1822; and his name was probably thereby suggested to Goethe.

The "Fancy Nosegay" seems to be designed as a type of the wilful, artful, bewildering power of woman, which does not attract all of the opposite sex, but the more surely fascinates a portion of it.

12.   Wood-Cutters.   Pulcinelli.   Parasites.

The ruder and less attractive—nay, frequently repellent—elements of Society are represented in these three classes

13. DRUNKEN MAN.

Goethe's object, here, is to represent sensual indulgence, of which intemperance is but one form.

14. THE GRACES.

Here the masks represent social qualities and forces, not varieties of individual character. In the Graces we see giving, receiving, and thanking or acknowledging, not in the narrower sense of an act, but as symbolical of the intercourse of men—the communication of one nature to another, the impressions bestowed and received, the reciprocal appreciation of character.

According to Hesiod, the Graces were Aglaia, Euphrosyne, and Thalia. In place of the latter Goethe substituted Hegemone (one of the two Graces revered by the Athenians), perhaps for the reason that the name of Thalia is better known as that of a Muse.

15. THE PARCÆ.

Here, Goethe has purposely changed the parts of Atropos and Clotho. The former carefully spins a soft and even thread, warning the maskers that it must not be stretched too far, even in enjoyment. Clotho, the youngest of the Fates, announces that the shears have been given to her, because Atropos prolonged useless lives and clipped the threads of the young and hopeful, and she, therefore, thrusts the shears into the sheath, in order to make no similar mistakes. I confess I am unable to explain the exact significance of this action. Some find in it a hint that the ancient gloomy, inexorable idea of Fate is banished from modern society; others that the needful moderation and self-control will make the threatening shears unnecessary.

16. *They are* THE FURIES.

Here we have the activity of evil forces in society. Goethe changes the Erinnys of the Greeks, who were represented as fierce, baleful figures, with snakes and torches in their hands, into fair, young, wheedling creatures, seemingly harmless as doves. His design cannot be for a moment doubted. The unresting Alecto of modern society is the insinuation that breeds mistrust, the slander that wears an innocent face, the power that in a thousand ways thrusts itself between approaching hearts and drives them apart. Megæra typifies the alienation which arises from selfish whims, from indifference or satiety; and Tisiphone alone, the avenging Fury, remains true to her ancient name and office.

17. *And here Asmodi as my follower lead.*

Asmodi (or *Ashmedai*), the Destroyer, was an evil demon of the Hebrews. He is mentioned in the Talmud, and Jewish tradition reports that he once drove Solomon from his kingdom. Since, in the Book of Tobias, he kills in succession the seven husbands of Sara, he has been credited with a special enmity to married happiness. In this quality he appears as the follower of Megæra. As "Asmodeus" we find him in Wieland's *Oberon*, and the *Diable Boiteux* of Lesage, through which he is almost as widely known as Mephistopheles.

18. *You see a mountain pressing through the throng.*

The Herald's expression, "For that which comes is not to you allied," seems to indicate a change in the character of the allegory; and I am disposed to agree with those who attach a political meaning to the coming masks, rather than with those who would include the latter in the representation of society. The former interpretation is certainly the more simple and complete. The elephant is Civil Government, or The State, as another form of organised human life. He is guided by Prudence, while on either hand walk Fear and Hope, in fetters. Fear, who shrinks from every undertaking, and Hope, who would undertake all things without considering results, are, as Prudence declares, "two of the greatest of human foes." They thus represent the political elements of blind conservatism and reckless passion for change. In an ordered and intelligent State both these forces are chained, Prudence guides the colossal organism, and the Goddess of all victorious active forces sits aloft on her throne. Each change in the course of the allegory, the reader will observe, commences with the bright and attractive aspects of life and then advances to the opposite.

19. ZOÏLO-THERSITES.

Goethe takes Thersites from the *Iliad*, and unites him to the Thracian barrator, Zoïlus, who, in the third century before Christ, became so renowned by his venomous abuse of Plato, Isocrates, and especially Homer, that his name was applied by the Greeks to all vulgar, malicious scolds. The two characters, combined, represent the class of political slanderers, defamers of all good works, pessimists in the most offensive sense. The characteristics of this class are exhibited in still stronger and more repulsive forms, when Zoïlo-Thersites is changed into the Adder and Bat by the magic wand of the Herald.

The "Murmurs of the Crowd" are here introduced, as in Scene II., to supply the place of a Chorus, and assist in describing the action.

20. *Black lightning of the eyes, the dark locks glowing.*

The costume of the Boy Charioteer, as described by the Herald, is that of the Apollo Musagetes.

21. *I am Profusion, I am Poesy!*

The episode of Plutus and the Boy Charioteer is a double allegory. The first and most direct interpretation is that which belongs to the characters as a portion of the masquerade. The boy is not only Poetry, but the poetic element as it is manifested in all Art; and we may therefore say that he represents the highest intellectual possessions, as Plutus represents material possessions. Further on, we shall see the manner in which the gifts of both are received by the multitude.

22.   *Thy brow when laurels decorate*
        Have I not them with hand and fancy braided?

The Chancellor von Müller, in his work, "Goethe as a Man of Action," was the first and only one to discover the key to these expressions. The noble and intimate relation which for fifty years existed between the Grand Duke Karl August and Goethe—the Ruler and the Poet—is here most delicately and feelingly drawn. The manner in which the Grand Duke assisted Goethe in his flight into Italy; the care with which he watched lest the duties of his office should interfere with his poetic and scientific activity; the beautiful renown given by the latter in return for this freedom,—are all indicated in a few lines. When the Herald first describes Plutus, it is neither Faust nor Wealth whom we see, but Karl August as Goethe saw him:—

> " Blest those, who may his favour own !
>   No more has he to earn or capture;
>   His glance detects where aught's amiss,
>   And to bestow his perfect rapture
>   Is more than ownership and bliss."

The correspondence between Goethe and the Grand Duke so thoroughly justifies this interpretation, that I do not see how it can be avoided.

23.   *Then Avaritia was my name.*

Mephistopheles, true to his character of Negation, wears the mask of Avarice, which is the opposite of active and ostentatiously exhibited wealth. His address to the women is suggested by the difference of gender between the ancient Latin word, *avaritia*, which is feminine, and the German, *der Geiz*, which is masculine. The Women are perhaps introduced here, instead of the former mixed crowd, because avarice is more repulsive to their nature and habits than to those of the men.

24.   Gnomes.

Düntzer asserts that the Fauns represent unrestricted indulgence in all forms of sensual appetite; the Satyrs the arrogant will of a Ruler who looks down upon and despises the people; the Gnomes the unbounded greed of power and wealth; and the Giants the stupid and stubborn nature of those counsellors who surround the throne and endeavour to crush every movement arising from the development of the people. Neither this nor any other of the more particular elucidations of the scene seems to me infallible. According to Hartung, the Fauns are peasants (*Bauern*), and the Satyrs demagogues.

The Gnomes are the only ones who have something more than an allegorical part to play. They are evidently introduced as the guardians of buried treasure, in connection with the financial scheme of Mephistopheles.

25.　*They house within their special Hades.*

Goethe now returns to the original Faust-legend in giving Faust the task of invoking the shades of Paris and Helena. In the legend, however, Mephistopheles voluntarily produces Helena as a *succuba*, to be the spouse of Faust: here he remains true to his Gothic character and his negation of Beauty. The heathen race, he confesses, has its own special Hades, with which he has no concern. His disinclination to assist Faust is so very evident that we may almost ascribe to him an instinct of the elevating and purifying influence which Helena, as the symbol of the Beautiful, will afterwards exercise. Being, nevertheless, bound by the terms of the compact, he consents to point out the method of invocation, leaving the performance to Faust.

26.　*They are* THE MOTHERS!

Here is the second enigma, a complete and satisfactory solution of which is not to be expected.

Plutarch's mention of the Mothers is to be found in his Life of Marcellus: "In Sicily there is a town called Engyium, not indeed great, but very ancient and ennobled by the presence of the Goddesses, called the Mothers. The temple, they say, was built by the Cretans; and they show some spears and brazen helmets, inscribed with the names of Meriones, and (with the same spelling as in Latin) of Ulysses, who consecrated them to the Goddesses."

The reader must bear in mind that Paris and Helena are together typical of the highest and purest physical embodiment of the idea of Beauty—the Human Form—and that Helena, alone, afterwards becomes the symbol, both of Beauty and of the Classic element in Art and Literature. The Mothers, therefore, (admitting the significance of the *name*, which suggested their use to Goethe) must of necessity symbolize the original action of those elemental forces in Man, out of which grew the æsthetic development of the race, in whatever form. We may find the primitive source of all science in material necessity; our other knowledge is based upon the operation of natural laws: but the Idea of the Beautiful has a more mysterious origin, springs from a diviner necessity, and finds only hints, not perfect results, in the operations of Nature.

27.　*Here, take this key!*

The symbols of the Key and the Tripod have given rise to much speculation. Their meaning, of course, is entirely dependent upon that which may be attributed to the Mothers, since the key is to guide Faust to the latter, and then enable him to gain possession of the tripod, the incense-smoke of which will shape itself into the ideals of Human Beauty. Schnetger and Kreyssig agree that the tripod is a symbol of the profoundest wisdom, and the former attaches to it the idea of "intuition."

28. *A gentle kick permit, then, from my foot!*

The motive of this scene seems to be to renew the contrast between the shallow, artificial society of the great world, and pure devotion to ideal aims. At the same time it enables Mephistopheles to resume his old character, and Goethe (through him) to satirise the homœopathic theory of medicine, in the cure of the Brunette.

In the *Paralipomena* there are two fragments which seem to belong here :—

MEPHISTOPHELES.

Court-doctors must do every service:
We with the stars begin, and then
Come down at last to corns and bunions.

The dapper race of courtiers here
Was only born for our vexation:
If some poor devil once is right, 'tis clear
The King thereof will never hear narration.

29. ARCHITECT.

The scene upon the stage is a Doric temple ; the massive character of the pillars is here hinted, and the triglyphs are afterwards mentioned. By introducing the Architect, Goethe means not only to satirise the exclusive devotion of the German mind to Gothic art, but also to show how the Classic and Romantic repel each other when first brought into contact.

30. *The form, that long erewhile my fancy captured.*

This is one of the few references to the First Part, which we find in the Second. Faust remembers the form which he saw in the magic mirror, in the Witches' Kitchen (First Part, Scene VI.), and which, we may now be sure, was neither Margaret nor Helena.

Kreyssig alone, of all the German commentators, seems to have comprehended the spirit of this scene. He says: "The Artist has seen his Ideal. His joy, his yearning, rises to a burning desire, to a resolution so powerful that nothing can intimidate it. Again the old, passionate blood seethes, although now warmed by a nobler fire. The impetuous, rash attempt to win at one blow as a permanent possession that which has only been revealed in a fleeting glimpse, fails, like his former attempt, through that radical law, which only gives the most precious gifts in return for labour and patience. The apparition vanishes, and in the abrupt reaction we see him, who would fain be superhuman, lying senseless on the earth. The first assault of his ambitious claim has been resisted, but his resolution remains irrevocable. He cannot, now, remain longer at the Emperor's Court. The man of ideal vision and creation must equally fail to find his place there, as formerly among the dissolute groups of the Blocksberg. The period of his intellectually-artistic development and maturity commences, and the poet inaugurates it by a series of sometimes varied and fantastic allegories, in order to complete it afterwards in the Third Act, the scenes of which are excellent and truly dramatic, in spite of all their symbolism and allegory."

D D

31.   Crotchets for ever must be hatched.

There is a pun in the German which cannot be given. *Grillen* means both *crickets* and *crotchets* or splenetic humours, the first reference being to the insects which Mephistopheles has shaken out of the old fur.

Taking these two words in connection with the foregoing satire of Mephistopheles, we may conjecture that the "Chorus of Insects" is intended to represent all the whims, crotchets, and theories of mechanical scholarship,—the verminiferous life which is bred in the mould of pedantry.

32.   BACCALAUREUS.

The new Famulus, who is a spiritual descendant of the Wagner of the First Part, is introduced to give Mephistopheles the opportunity of continuing his irony.

33.   But don't go, absolute, home from here.

There is a philosophical antithesis implied in the words "resolute" and "absolute," in this couplet. Mephistopheles uses the former word in its double sense of "determined" and "dissolved," while the latter, according to Kreyssig, is a sarcastic allusion to the Hegelian philosophy. It would seem from what follows, however, that Goethe had Fichte in his mind, rather than Hegel.

34.   When one has passed his thirtieth year,
One then is just the same as dead.

The reference to Fichte is here not to be mistaken. The following passage occurs in his works : " When they have passed their thirtieth year, one well might wish, for their own reputation and the advantage of the world, that they would die ; since, from that age on, their lives will only be an increasing damage to themselves and their associations."

35.   HOMUNCULUS.

This whimsical, artificial mannikin is, in reality, the chief personage in Act II. Since he is no less an enigma to the critics than the mysterious "Mothers," and suggests even a greater variety of meanings in the course of his adventures, it will not be so easy to give, in advance, a full and satisfactory explanation of his character. The name and mode of origin of Homunculus are taken from Paracelsus, and some hint of the character, possibly, from Sterne. Paracelsus gives minute and exact directions how the Homunculus may be created ; and the attempt has no doubt been actually made thousands of times. Sterne, in the second chapter of Tristram Shandy, treats the subject with more than his usual wit and grace, averring that the Homunculus is as much a man and a brother as the Lord Chancellor of England. The attraction which such a conception (intellectually speaking) presented to Goethe's mind may be readily guessed.

36. *Fair scenery!*

In this passage Homunculus describes the dream of the sleeping Faust, which is visible to him alone.

37. *I may detect the dot upon the " I."*

This expression (which Goethe sometimes uses in his correspondence to denote finish, completion) is explained by the endeavour of Homunculus, afterwards, to break the glass in which his artificial being is confined, and commence a free and natural existence.

38. CLASSICAL WALPURGIS-NIGHT.

This allegory occupies the same place in the Second Act as the Carnival Masquerade in the first, and, like it, is a digression from the direct course of the drama. Unlike it, however, its substance is poetic rather than didactic.

When we have once accepted his double intention of conducting Faust to a higher plane of life through the awakening and development of his sense of Beauty, and, at the same time, of bringing together the Classic and Romantic elements in Literature and Art, in order to reconcile them in a region lofty enough to abolish all fashions of Race and Time, we have no difficulty in fancying how the plan of a Classical Walpurgis-Night must have presented itself to Goethe's mind, as a *pendant* to the Walpurgis-Night of the First Part, which is Gothic, Mediæval, Romantic.

39. *Here, on Grecian land.*

Faust recovers from his trance as soon as he touches the classic soil : his artistic instinct tells him at once that he is on the track of Helena.

40. *I find myself so strange, so disconcerted.*

Mephistopheles, on the other hand, is entirely out of his proper element. His disgust with the nudity of the antique forms is an admirable bit of humour, through which we can detect Goethe's own well-known defence of the chastity of ancient art. The delicate satire of the line, *Doch das Antike find' ich zu lebendig,* is lost in translation. We may almost surmise that when Mephistopheles speaks of overplastering the figures according to the fashion, Goethe referred to the indecent rehabilitation of the statues in the Vatican.

Mephistopheles finally addresses himself to the Griffins and Sphinxes, as the most grotesque and unbeautiful of the forms around him.

41. *The source, wherefrom its derivation springs.*

Düntzer explains that this passage is in ridicule of certain philologists, who, in Goethe's day, grouped words together at random according to their initial letters, and then attempted to trace them to a common root. The answer of Mephistopheles is a play upon the words *Greif* (Griffin) and *greifen* (to grip)—sufficiently like the English words to be intelligible in translation. The Griffin accepts this explanation, and confirms it by slightly changing the Latin proverb *Fortes Fortuna juvat,* which he applies to his own advantage.

42. The Arimaspeans.

According to Herodotus, the Arimaspeans were a one-eyed race who inhabited a distant part of the Scythian steppes, and were engaged in continual conflict with the gold-guarding Griffins. The colossal Ants, which were somewhat larger than foxes and dwelt in Central Asia, threw out gold-dust in making their subterranean burrows.

I confess I can offer no satisfactory explanation of the appearance of these creatures, beyond that of their repulsive forms.

43. *Express thyself, and 'twill a riddle be.*

It is evident that the Sphinxes immediately recognized Mephistopheles, and their questions are only "chaffing." When they say that their spirit-tones become material, to him, they hint that he sees nothing more than their semi-bestial form. In the answer of Mephistopheles to the demand for his name, Goethe uses the English words "Old Iniquity." This term was given, in the Moralities, to a personification of Vice, or Sin, who accompanied the Devil when he appeared, teased him and beat him with a whip.

44. Sirens.

The Sirens are first mentioned by Homer as two in number, but two more were afterwards added by the Athenians. They were located in various places—Crete, Sicily, or Capri—and there were contradictory accounts of their origin and character. It was generally believed, however, that they were fated only to live until some one should pass their island without being captivated by their song, whence the corresponding myths of the Argonauts and Ulysses.

After the confused and uncertain forms with which the Classical Walpurgis-Night opens, Goethe seems to have selected the Sirens as a point of departure for the opposite paths of Faust and Mephistopheles. They were generally represented as beautiful maidens to the waist, the lower half having a bird-form, with hideous falcon claws. The grotesque and beautiful are more intimately blended in the woman and lion of the Sphinx : in the Sirens Beauty and Ugliness are simply and sharply joined to each other. After leaving them, Faust begins to rise towards his Ideal, while Mephistopheles descends towards his.

45. *In the Repulsive, grand and solid features.*

This line throws a clear light all along the path we have chosen. Faust recognizes the far-off predictions of the Beautiful in the forms of Indian and Egyptian art, the forerunners of that of Greece. He is even reconciled to what is repulsive in them, by their association with the early memories of Grecian History and Literature. He is filled with fresh spirit, for he now feels that he has a clue which shall guide him to Helena. To Mephistopheles, who remembers Faust's disgust for the grotesque phantoms of the Blocksberg, his satisfaction is of course incomprehensible.

The Sphinxes direct Faust to Chiron, the Centaur, who is not only purely Greek, but also the last struggle of the artistic Ideal of Beauty with animal forms ; while, after recalling the Stymphalic birds and the heads of the Lernæan Hydra for the benefit of Mephistopheles, they shrewdly send him after the Lamiæ, who have aroused his desire at the first view.

46. PENEUS.

The Pharsalian Fields lie upon the Enipeus, a branch of the Peneus, and many of the commentators charge Goethe with having made a mistake ; but it is very evident that he meant to include in the scene the whole region from Pharsalus to the base of Olympus and the shores of the Ægean Sea.

In the river-god, Peneus, with his attendant Nymphs and Tributary Streams, we reach a higher plane of development. Here the forms, though representing Nature, are entirely human, and an atmosphere of Poetry, as well as of Art, encircles them. The verse changes, also, suggesting a clearer moonlight and fresher air.

47. CHIRON.

The Centaur Chiron was the son of Saturn and Philyra, the daughter of Oceanus. Homer calls him the wisest and most just of the Centaurs. He was said to have taught the human race oaths, joyous sacrificial services, and music. In his grotto on Pelion he educated the grandest Grecian heroes, among them Peleus, Ajax, Achilles, Æsculapius, Theseus, and Jason.

Schuetger has a very ingenious explanation of the symbolical significance of Chiron in this scene. He interprets the expression of the Sphinx to Faust :

> Our very last was slain by Hercules,

as indicating the overthrow of the monstrous forms of early Art ; and Hercules therefore marks the commencement of the Human period.

48. *No second such hath Gœa granted.*

There is a seeming contradiction in this passage. When Faust suggests the name of Hercules, which Chiron has omitted from the list of his Argonautic pupils and friends, the Centaur's burst of enthusiasm for the hero whose poisoned arrow accidentally caused his own death is, to say the least, unexpected ; while Faust's following speech,

> " The fairest Man hast thou depicted,
> Now of the fairest Woman speak ! "

couples Hercules with Helena as the Ideals of male and female beauty. But it was *Paris* and Helena whom he called from the Shades. We must assume that when he speaks of the latter pair to Mephistopheles, in Scene V. Act I., as "the model forms of Man and Woman," he is merely repeating the conventional ideas of the Emperor and the Court circle.

49. MANTO.

Goethe has wilfully taken Manto from blind Tiresias, "prophet old," whose daughter she was, and given her Æsculapius as a father, perhaps to account for her familiarity with Chiron, and enable the latter, through her, to send Faust further on his ardent pilgrimage. She was, in reality, devoted to the service of Apollo. After her ather's death, she wandered to Italy, where her son, Oknus, founded and named for her the city of Mantua.

50. SEISMOS.

Goethe makes a personification of the Earthquake (Σεισμός), in order the better to satirize the Plutonists.

51. GRIFFINS.

For their significance, we must remember the extent to which Goethe was irritated by the general acceptance of the Plutonic theory. The Griffins and Ants, we may guess, represent those who at once give in their adherence to every new scientific *régime*, and fancy that its principles are so many great intellectual treasures, which they hasten to collect and possess. The Pygmies and Dactyls (Thumblings and Fingerlings) are the crowds of students and smatterers who are unable to free themselves from the chains of the new theorist ; who find themselves, without knowing how it happened, under his authority, intellectual serfs, forced to service and obedience, without any reference to their own wills. The Pygmy-Elders and the Generalissimo are, of course, the rulers : it would hardly be too much to say that the former represent the members of the French Academy, and that the latter is Elie de Beaumont or Leopold von Buch. Homer's account of the battle between the Pygmies and the Cranes suggested the introduction of the Herons as Neptunists. The Generalissimo orders the slaughter of these water-haunting birds, that the Pygmies may feather their helmets with the crested plumes.

52. THE CRANES OF IBYCUS.

The "fat-paunched, bow-legged knaves" of Plutonists are triumphant, and wear the plumes they have plundered from the slaughtered Neptunists. But the Cranes, in their airy voyage, have seen the murder, and like the "Cranes of Ibycus," in Schiller's ballad, they are the agents appointed by Fate to revenge the deed.

Ibycus, the poet, on his way from Rhegium to attend the Isthmian games, was attacked by robbers in the pine-grove dedicated to Neptune, near Corinth. Far from all help, cut down, and dying, with his last breath he called to a flock of cranes, flying in a long file over the grove, and invoked them to bear abroad the news of the murder. His body was found, carried to Corinth, and recognized ; and the grief of the populace, assembled at the games was loud for the loss of their favourite singer, Ibycus. Suddenly, during a pause in the performance, while the great amphitheatre was silent, a file of cranes passed overhead, and a mocking voice was heard, saying, "There are the Cranes of Ibycus!" The suspicions of the people were instantly aroused, the speaker and his accomplice were picked out from the audience, and the amphitheatre became a tribunal of judgment. The murderers confessed the deed, and the Cranes revenged Ibycus. Such is the story which Schiller has embodied in one of his most admirable ballads.

When Goethe wrote, in 1827, "Certainly some young man of genius will arise, who shall have the courage to oppose this crazy unanimity," he anticipated the overthrow of the Plutonic theory. In his selection of Schiller's "Cranes of Ibycus," to summon his Neptunic kindred to the revenge which is only announced, not immediately performed, there is a touching suggestion of his own loneliness. The "endless hate" which is sworn is not the true substance of hate (which Goethe declared to be a passion only possible to youth) : it is merely an impatient exclamation, veiling a pang of longing for the great friend who had passed away, and of disappointment that no one came to his side to help him turn his intrenched defence into an open assault.

53. Lamiæ.

The original Lamia, the daughter of Belus and Libya, was beloved by Jupiter, and then transformed, through Juno's jealousy, into a hideous, child-devouring monster. Lilith, the nocturnal, female vampire of the Hebrews, mentioned in Isaiah, is rendered *Lamia* in the Vulgate. In the plural, they appear to have corresponded, very nearly, to the witches of the Middle Ages, who, indeed, were then frequently called *Lamiæ.* Keats's poem of "Lamia," in which the bride, recognized by the keen-eyed sage, returns to her original serpent form, represents another of the superstitions attached to the race.

Mephistopheles (probably remembering the Thessalian witches promised by Homunculus) is attracted by forms having so much family likeness to those with which he is familiar.

54. *Empusa, with the ass's foot.*

Empusa (the "one-footed," as the name denotes) had one human foot and one ass's hoof, and is therefore fairly entitled to call Mephistopheles "cousin." Goethe probably took her, as well as some other characters of the Classical Walpurgis-Night, from Böttiger, with whose works he was well acquainted. Empusa is mentioned in "The Frogs" of Aristophanes, and also in the life of Apollonius Tyana, by Philostratus. She had not the same habit of transformation as the other Lamiæ, but surpassed them all in her hideous appearance and her cannibalic habits.

Mephistopheles, however, is too ugly and repulsive for even these. They simply amuse themselves with him, and then send him further. The transformations which they undergo when he attempts to grasp them are characteristic of the Lamiæ, but, at the same time, they suggest some additional meaning. What it is I cannot guess, and I find nothing in any of the commentaries which throws the least light on the passage. Düntzer's explanation is entirely inadequate.

55. OREAD (*from the natural rock*).

Here the Oread is the spirit of a primeval mountain, created according to the Neptunic theory.

56. ANAXAGORAS (*to* THALES).

The representatives of the two geological theories are now introduced. Goethe's choice of Anaxagoras and Thales is too evidently dictated by what is known of the systems of those philosophers to need any further explanation. The former wrote of eclipses, earthquakes, and meteoric stones ; the latter derived all life and physical phenomena from water ; yet both based their theories on "Nature," and equally sought to solve her mysteries.

57. *Then were it true, Thessalian Pythonesses.*

This is a reference to an old Grecian myth, mentioned in the *Gorgias* of Plato and the *Clouds* of Aristophanes. Horace, also (*Carm.* V.), has the lines :—

> "*Quæ sidera excantata voce Thessala*
> *Lunamque cælo deripit.*"

We are to suppose that only a meteoric stone has fallen, but that Anaxagoras, in his excited fancy, imagines that the orb of the moon is rushing down upon the earth. Thales perceives nothing but that "the Hours are crazy" ; the moon is shining quietly in her place. But a meteoric mass has really fallen, giving a pointed head to the round Hill of Seismos, and crushing Pygmies and Cranes in one common destruction. Perhaps Goethe meant to hint, satirically, that the theory of creation "from above" (as Homunculus says) is quite as rational as that of creation by upheaval. If so, he has curiously anticipated one of the most recent scientific ideas,— that of the growth and physical change of planets, by accretion from the meteoric belts.

58. *The Phorkyads!*

The Phorkyads, or, more correctly, *Phorkids*, were the three daughters of Phorkys (Darkness) and Keto (The Abyss). Their names were Deino, Pephredo, and Enyo : Hesiod, in his Theogony, gives only the two last. They were also called the *Graiæ.* They were said to have, in common, but one eye and one tooth, which they used alternately, and to dwell at the uppermost end of the earth, where neither sun nor moon beheld them. They represent the climax of all which the Greek imagination has created of horrible and repulsive. Mephistopheles, consequently, is ravished with delight : he has found the Ideal Ugliness.

59. *Steering away to Samothrace.*

We must suppose that the scene opens on the Thessalian coast, near the mouth of the Peneus, and therefore almost in sight of the mountain-isle of Samothrace. The purpose of the Nereids and Tritons, in their journey thither, will be presently revealed. Meanwhile Thales conducts Homunculus to Nereus, the Graybeard of the Sea, whom Hesiod describes as just and friendly, and well-disposed towards the human race.

60. *The Graces of the Sea, the Dorides.*

The Dorides were the daughters of Nereus and the sea-nymph Doris, but are called Nereids in the Grecian mythology. Goethe's object in calling them *Dorides,* and presenting them as the daughters of Nereus, while the Nereids are introduced without any hint of their relationship, has puzzled the commentators ; and since any attempt at explanation must be merely conjecture, without evidence, I leave the question as it stands. There seems, also, to be no ground whatever for the declaration of Nereus that Galatea was worshipped at Paphos in the place of Cypris (Aphrodite). Thus far, none of the Olympian Gods or Goddesses have been introduced ; and the fresco of Galatea by Raphael, which Goethe knew, together with the description of a very similar picture, mentioned by Philostratus, undoubtedly suggested to him the propriety of giving her the place which really belongs to Aphrodite, as the representative of Helena (Beauty).

It is possible that the reason why Nereus refuses to help Homunculus to being, and refers him to Proteus, is, that Goethe intends the former to be an embodiment of accomplished, completed exist-ence, while the latter represents Transformation, and therefore—since Homunculus must begin with the lowest form of organic life—he must be first consulted.

61. *Three have we brought hither.*

The Cabiri were originally three. In Memphis they had a temple and were worshipped as the sons of Phthas (Hephæstos). They appear to have been colonized on Samothrace by the Phœnicians, and their mysteries were celebrated there with orgies borrowed from the phallic worship of the Egyptians. Three female deities were subsequently added to their number ; but Creuzer insists that there were seven, corresponding to the seven planets, with a possible eighth, representing the sun. The names of the first three were Axierus, Axiokersus, and Axiokersa, and the fourth, Kadmilus, being added as a uniting principle, they became together, according to Creuzer, a symbol of the spheral harmony. This may explain Goethe's allusion to the fourth.

The Hebrew word, *Kabbirim,* is translated by Gesenius, " The Mighty." Fürst says that *Kabbirim* was the name of the seven sons of Tzadik, in Phœnician mythology. The Arabic word *kebeer* (great), still in use, is evidently the same.

62. *Had earthen pots for models.*

Creuzer asserted that the Cabiri were originally worshipped under the form of thick-bellied earthen jars, or pots. Schelling's interpretation of the names had been opposed, not only by Creuzer, but by Paulus, De Sacy, Welcker, and others,—whence the mention of "stubborn noddles."

63. *One starts there first within a narrow pale.*

Homer describes the transformations of Proteus in the Fourth Book of the Odyssey, where Menelaus forces him to appear in his proper form. Thales makes use of the curiosity of Proteus to accomplish the same result.

64. TELCHINES OF RHODES.

The Telchines of Rhodes, who were called Sons of the Sea, were the first workers in metals. They made the knife of Kronos and the trident of Poseidon, and cast the first images of the Gods in bronze. Their appearance, here, indicates the dawn of the age of higher Grecian art. Pliny and Theophrastus are Goethe's authorities for the sunny weather and pure atmosphere of Rhodes. The very movement of the verse suggests brightness; we feel that the sun and air are not those of Rhodes alone, but of all Classical art and literature.

The Telchines exalt Luna as the sister of Phœbus, who was the tutelar deity of Rhodes : the conclusion of their chorus seems to indicate the union of Religion and Art, and suggests Coleridge's "fair humanities of old religion." Proteus exalts organic being, life in the waters, over the dead works of the Telchines, and hints at the overthrow of the Rhodian Colossus by an earthquake.

65. PSYLLI AND MARSI.

Goethe took from Pliny the Psylli and Marsi, who were snake-charmers in Southern Italy and on the Libyan shore. He arbitrarily makes them guardians of the chariot of Cypris, in which they still conduct Galatea by night, "unseen to the new generations," fearing neither the Roman eagle, the winged lion of Venice, the crescent of the Saracen, nor the cross of the Crusader. Why they are here introduced is not so easy to explain. Düntzer insists that, being magicians, they represent the magic power of Beauty ! Schnetger says they are nearer to Galatea than the Telchines of Rhodes, because they destroy snakes, which are ugly, and which, according to the Bible, are hostile to woman !

66. *Galatea approaches on her chariot of shell.*

Galatea, the lovely Nereid, here takes the place of Helena, as Homunculus takes the place of Faust. She is the Ideal Beauty, the sea-born successor of Aphrodite.

67. HELENA.

The Third Act is known in Germany as *The Helena*, not only because it was separately published in 1827 under the title of

" Helena : a Classico-Romantic Phantasmagoria," but also because
it is a complete allegorical poem in itself, inserted in the Second
Part of *Faust* by very loose threads of attachment.

68. Chorus.

The opening of the act appears to be imitated from " The
Eumenides " of Æschylus. Until the appearance of Faust, the form
of the verse is purely classic, the iambic hexameter, and afterwards the trochaic octameter, alternating with the irregular yet
wonderfully metrical strophes of the Chorus. Some features in the
description of the burning of Troy, in this Chorus, are taken from
the Æneid, but the form and character are Goethe's own.

69. Phorkyas.

The reader will not have forgotten the transformation of Mephistopheles into a Phorkyad, in the Classical Walpurgis-Night, and
will thus understand how he, as the Spirit of Negation, here appears
in a female mask, as Ugliness, to torment and threaten Beauty.
Carlyle says : " There is a sarcastic malice in the 'wise old
Stewardess' which cannot be mistaken."

70. *Queen, the offering art thou.*

Goethe here follows one of the many Greek legends in relation to
Helena. Although Homer relates that Menelaus threw away his
sword, overcome by her beauty, when he again met her, yet there
are frequent references in the poets (Euripides, among others) to a
story of her having been sacrificed. Goethe makes a skilful use of
it, to account for Helena's migration from Classic to Romantic soil.
Phorkyas maliciously amuses herself with the terror of the Chorus :
the summoning of the dwarfs to prepare for the sacrifice is but a
grim joke; she is bound, as Mephistopheles, to obey Faust's
command. Her threat of death to the Chorus is suggested by the
punishment which Telemachus, in the Odyssey (Book XXII.),
inflicts on the faithless maids.

71. *Forth from the East we hither pressed.*

The second address of Lynceus describes the migration of the
races from the East, under which the whole Classical world was
buried, until it slowly arose from the inundation to assist in shaping a new phase of human culture. The chief import of the verses
seems to be, that all which War and Colonization achieved—
territory, power, wealth, permanence—becomes null and vain
beside this new vision. It can only be restored, and to a better
value, through the abiding presence of the Beautiful, the worship
of which is the crowning element of civilization.

72. *Each sound appeared as yielding to the next.*

Goethe has taken a Persian legend (related in his own *West-
Œstlicher Divan*) of two lovers, Behram-gour and Dilaram, who invented rhyme in their amorous dialogues, and has applied it here

with consummate skill, as a means of bringing Faust and Helena nearer. The gifts are not all on one side: the Romantic welcomes and worships the Classic, but in return it adds the music of rhyme to the proportion of metre. Thus the new element continues to absorb the old, through the loving mutual approach of the two. The allegory becomes so incarnate in the chief characters that it impresses us like an actual human passion, and is so described by the Chorus. The very soul and being of the antique world—the proportion, the reality of form, and the sublime repose of Classic Art—are wedded, in a union perfect as that of love, to the sentiment, the passion, and the freedom of Romantic Art: and the latter, equally yielding, forgets Time, Place, and Race, and feels only that it now possesses the supreme Ideal of Beauty.

73. *All worlds in inter-action meet.*

The original :

> Denn wo Natur im reinen Kreise waltet,
> Ergreifen all Welten sich,—

is one of those pregnant expressions which make the translator despair,—for, the more thoroughly he is penetrated with the meaning, the less does it seem possible to express that meaning in any words. The literal translation is, " For where Nature sways in a pure circle (or orbit), all worlds (human and divine) reciprocally take hold on one another."

74. *Call'st thou a marvel this,*
Creta's begotten !

The son of Faust and Helena, as he is first described by Phorkyas, is Poetry, not an individual. In his naked beauty, his pranks and his sportive, wilful ways, he suggests not only the greater freedom of the Romantic element, but also the classic myths of Cupid and the child Hermes (Mercury).

The Chorus describes the birth and childish tricks of Hermes, as they are related in Homer's hymn and Lucian's dialogues of the Gods. There is, perhaps, a "poetic-didactical word" for the reader, in their relation, as well as for Phorkyas. Hermes may possibly typify the Poetic Genius, which boldly steals the attributes of all the Gods, and even longs to grasp the thunderbolts of Zeus, the Father.

75. EUPHORION.

In the original legend, Faust has by Helena a son, to whom he gives the name of Justus Faustus, and who disappears with her when his compact with Mephistopheles comes to an end. In one of the ancient Grecian myths, Helena bears a son to Achilles (recalled from Hades) on the island of Leuke. This son, born with wings, was called Euphorion (the swift or lightly wafted), and was slain by the lightning of Jupiter. Goethe unites the two stories, and adds his own symbolism to the airy, wilful spirit, resulting from them.

76. *Midst of Pelops' land,*
Kindred in soul, I stand!

We may accept the lawlessness of Euphorion as, to a certain extent, reflecting Byron's wild, unregulated youth. Some of the German commentators, however, force the parallel quite too far, endeavouring to discover definite incidents of the poet's history in his dances with the Chorus, and his pursuit of the maiden who turns into flame. The individual character of Euphorion is very gradually introduced, and is first declared in the above lines.

77. *The path to Glory opens now.*

The Chorus entreats Euphorion to bide in the peaceful Arcadian land of Poetry ; and his answer is entirely in accord with the spirit of the Philhellenes, during the Greek Revolution. The heroic struggle of the Suliotes, in which even women and children shared, is indicated in the preceding verses, and then follows the closing chant, in which the wail of the coming dirge is fore-felt through the peal of trumpets and the clash of cymbals. I am not able to state whether Goethe had read Byron's last poem, written at Missolonghi, on his thirty-six birthday, when he wrote the concluding portion of the *Helena*. It is strangely suggested here, in spite of the allegory, and the difference of metre.

78. CHORUS. [*Dirge.*]

Here all allegory is thrown aside : the four stanzas are a lament, not for Euphorion, but for Byron. They express Goethe's feeling for the poet, while the profound impression created throughout Europe by the news of his death was still fresh.

79. *Helena's garments dissolve into clouds.*

Since Faust is only temporarily typical of the Artist, the symbolism embodied in the disappearance of Helena, and his elevation upon the clouds into which her garments are transformed, is not difficult to guess. The Ideal Beauty is revealed to few ; but even its robe and veil form a higher ether over all the life of Man. In the direct course of the drama, æsthetic culture is the means by which Faust rises from all forms of vulgar ambition to that nobler activity which crowns his life.

80. *A Seven-league Boot trips forward.*

Goethe means to indicate by this image, and the first words of Mephistopheles, that Faust has been borne far away from his previous life, so that the former is obliged to make use of the seven-league boots of the fairy tale, in order to overtake him.

81. *They, more than all, therein were implicated.*

We must suppose that Mephistopheles, bound to obedience, unwillingly serves in the fulfilment of plans which he cannot comprehend. Although he implicates Faust in the coming military movements, ostensibly for the purpose of acquiring possession of the ocean-strand through the help which the latter shall furnish to the Emperor, he is ever watchful to bring the affair to another issue. In the passage commencing, "A mighty error!" Faust gives us Goethe's impression of Napoleon. Mephistopheles naturally casts upon the priesthood the heaviest responsibility for the anarchy of the realm, and here, again, we have another view which Goethe frequently expressed.

82. *No! But I've brought, like Peter Squence.*

Shakespeare's Peter Quince becomes, in some English farce into which the comic parts of the "Midsummer Night's Dream" were worked, pedant and schoolmaster ; and in Gryphius's translation of this farce was introduced to Germany as "Herr Peter Squenze." — *Düntzer.*

83. *The Sabine old, the Norcian necromancer.*

"From whatever cause the mountains of Norcia, between the Sabine land and the Duchy of Spoleto, acquired the name in old times, they are called to this day the Mountains of the Sibyls. Old writers of Romance made use of this locality in order to conduct their heroes through the most wonderful adventures, and thus increased the belief in those magical figures, the first outlines of which were drawn by the Legend. An Italian story, Guerino Meschino, and an old French work, relate strange occurrences, by which curious travellers have been surprised in that region ; and Messer Cecco di Ascoli, who was burned in Florence in the year 1327, on account of his necromantic writings, is still remembered, through the interest felt in his history by the chroniclers, painters, and poets."

84. *The thing is done !—*

The apparent advantage of the enemy, in carrying the position occupied by the left wing of the Emperor's army, makes Faust's aid (through Mephistopheles) indispensable to victory. The latter, therefore, employs all his magic devices, in turn. Goethe seems to have ransacked the superstitions of History, and combined their most picturesque features. We are reminded of the storm and flood described by Plutarch, of St. Jago fighting for Spain, of the apparitions and *roises* which are reported to have accompanied many famous battles ; but the most effective *ogent*, after all, is *transmitted* party hate.

85. *With twenty come to port again.*

Mephistopheles, still forced to serve, turns his commercial into a piratical voyage, and hopes to secure Faust's complicity in Evil by tempting him to accept the precious spoils of all climes, and the vessels which he has accumulated. His argument, that War, Trade, and Piracy are "three in one," makes no impression on Faust, who, as we learn from the Three Mighty Men, turns away from the bribe in disgust.

86. *No sorer plague can us attack,*
Than rich to be, and something lack.

The reader must remember Faust's age, and his long course of successful achievement, in order to understand his present impatience and petulance. He loses all joy in his vast possessions, because the neighbouring sand-hill, whereon he wishes to build a lookout for a view over all his new, thickly-peopled realm, is the property of another who refuses to sell or exchange it. Goethe has borrowed this incident from the story of Frederick the Great and the miller of Potsdam.

87. *Forgive ! not happily 'twas done.*

Faust, impatient at being so long thwarted in his plans, so far yields to Mephistopheles that he consents to employ force. Here is yet another—and the last—chance for the Spirit of Evil to win his wager. Like Jezebel, he compasses the death of Naboth-Philemon. The result is incendiarism and murder, not forcible removal; and Faust, instead of accepting the coveted property, curses the rash, inhuman deed.

88. *Necessity, mine.*

I have followed Dr. Anster in thus translating *Noth,* which may also be rendered "trouble" and "need," for the reason that Care, in this scene, includes the former meaning, and Want the latter.

The character of the three gray sisters, Want, Guilt, and Necessity, is explained when they declare that they cannot enter the house of the Rich ; but Care, the *atra cura* of Horace, has free entrance everywhere. Goethe's conception of her being seems to be the embodied Worry, and the other three have no further apparent significance than to separate her from the other tormenting powers of life, and thus the more clearly define her nature.

89. LEMURES.

Goethe has here borrowed (probably from Percy's *Reliques,* which he knew) the original song of Lord Vaux, a part of which Shakespeare puts into the mouth of the grave-digger in "Hamlet." But he has taken only the first half of the verses, completing them with other lines of his own. Therefore I have only translated these latter.

90. *They spake not of a moat, but of—a grave.*

The original line contains a pun which cannot be given in translation :—

> Man spricht, wie man mir Nachricht gab,
> Von keinem *Graben,* doch vom—*Grab.*

91. *Hell hath a multitude of jaws, in short.*

Goethe's first plan was to send Mephistopheles into the presence of The Lord, for the purpose of announcing that he had won. This, however, would have interfered with the effect of the closing scene, and he selected, instead, the machinery of the Miracle-plays, as better adapted to his purpose. The open jaws of Hell, as they are still represented in many chapels of Catholic countries, and the two varieties of Devils, are intentionally introduced as a coarse, almost vulgar framework for a scene which is meant to include the sharpest contrast of two principles, Heaven stooping down, and Hell rising up to take hold of the soul of Man.

92. PATER ECSTATICUS.

It is generally agreed—and the tendency of Goethe's mind during his last years justifies the belief—that the three *Patres* symbolize different forms or manifestations of devotional feeling. Their appearance, as we afterwards feel, was suggested by the necessity of avoiding a sudden transition from the blasphemous sensuality of Mephistopheles to the "indescribable" exaltation of the closing mystery ; but they also have their appropriate place in this ever-rising and ever-swelling symphony, with its one theme of the accordance of Human and Divine Love.

93. PATER PROFUNDUS.

We might almost say that the Pater Ecstaticus represents Devotion as manifested through temperament or exalted sensation ; the Pater Profundus, Devotion as it shapes the intellect, which perceives symbols in all things, feels the limitations of the senses, and aspires towards Divine Truth as the highest form of knowledge ; and finally, the Pater Seraphicus Devotion as it possesses the soul in the purest glow of self-abnegation.

94. PATER SERAPHICUS.

This name was given to St. Francis of Assisi, who is mentioned by Dante (*Paradiso,* XI.), and Goethe may possibly have borne him in mind, without borrowing anything from the story of his life.

95. CHORUS OF BLESSED BOYS.

These boys, whom Goethe calls "midnight-born," are the spirits of those who died in birth, barely given to Life and then taken from it before the awakening of sense or mind. The meaning seems to be that they are still undeveloped in the spiritual world,— in other words, that, in the scale of ascending Being, they have missed our sphere, and feel only the delight of existence (*allen ist das Daseyn so gelind*), without the intelligence, from which must be born the aspiration for what is still beyond and above them.

96. DOCTOR MARIANUS.

Some see in this name a reference to Marianus Scotus, who died, as an eremite, in 1086. Others, again, suppose it to be *the celestial name of Faust*, although the soul of the latter has not yet awakened to the change.

97. MAGNA PECCATRIX.

I have retained the references attached to this and the two following stanzas, because I am not sure whether they were originally written by Goethe, or afterwards added by Riemer. Mary Magdalene and the Woman of Samaria require no comment; Mary of Egypt is described in the *Acta Sanctorum* as an infamous woman of Alexandria, who, after seventeen years of vice, made a pilgrimage to Jerusalem. On approaching the door of the Church of the Holy Sepulchre, an invisible arm thrust her away. Weeping, overcome with the sudden sense of her unworthiness, she prayed to the Virgin, and was then lifted as by hands and borne into the Temple, and a voice said to her : "Go beyond the Jordan, and thou wilt find peace." She went into the Desert, where she lived alone forty-eight years, only visited by a monk who brought her the last sacrament, and for whom, when she died, she left a message written upon the sand.

These three sinful yet penitent and glorified women are made intercessors for the soul of Margaret, which has not yet been admitted to the higher spheres.

98. UNA PŒNITENTIUM.

Margaret sees her full pardon in the face of the Mater Gloriosa, before it is spoken, and the prayer (First Part, Scene XVIII.) which was a despairing cry for help now becomes a strain of unutterable joy. The Blessed Boys approach, bearing the soul of Faust, already overtowering them as it grows into consciousness of the new being. By him, who has learned so much of Life, they shall be taught at last. Margaret, no longer an ignorant maiden, but an inspired Soul, sees the beauty and glory of the original nature of Faust, now redeemed, releasing itself from its earthly disguises and shining like the Holy Host. But we hear no voice : we only know that it awakens.

99. *Who, feeling thee, shall follow there.*

The literal translation of these two lines must be added :—

> " Come lift thyself to higher spheres !
> When he has a spirtual sense of thy presence, he will follow."

The reader who knows the original need not be told how difficult it is to render the word *ahnet.*

E E

THE CHRONOLOGY OF FAUST.

FAUST is the only great work in the literature of any language which requires a biography. The first child of Goethe's brain and the last which knew the touch of his hand, its growth runs parallel with his life, and reflects all forms of his manifold study and experience. While, therefore, its plan is simple, grand and consistent from beginning to end, the performance embraces so many varieties of style and such a multitude of not always homogeneous elements, that a chronological arrangement of the parts becomes necessary as a guide to the reader.

During the illness which lasted for nearly a year after Goethe's return from Leipzig in 1768, while he was discussing religious questions with Fräulein von Klettenberg, reading cabalistic works and making experiments in alchemy, the subject of Faust, which was already familiar to him as a child, through the puppet-plays, took powerful and permanent hold on his imagination.* He carried it about with him in Strasburg, concealing it from Herder during their intercourse in the winter of 1770–71, and postponing it to write his first great work, Götz von Berlichingen. He passed the summer of 1772 at Wetzlar, but did not begin the composition of Werther, which was the direct result of his residence there, until

---

* The premonitions of the "Storm and Stress" period, which were by that time felt throughout Germany, directed the attention of many authors towards Faust, as a subject for dramatic poetry. Lessing was the first to take hold of it, but only fragments of three or four scenes of his tragedy have been preserved. The work was completed before his journey to Italy in 1775, and despatched from Dresden to Leipzig in a box which was lost, and never afterwards came to light. Captain von Blankenburg, in 1784, gave the following testimony concerning the tragedy, the manuscript of which he had read : "He undertook his work at a time when in every quarter of Germany Fausts were announced as forthcoming ; and I know that he completed it. I have been positively informed that he only delayed its publication in order that the other Fausts might first appear."

Of these other Fausts one was published at Munich in 1775, another at Mannheim in 1776, that of the painter Müller, Goethe's friend, in 1778, a fragment by Lenz in 1777, and a fifth in Salzburg, in 1782. Between the publication of Goethe's "Fragment" in 1790 and that of the completed First Part in 1808, nine additional Fausts, by various authors, made their appearance ; and between the latter date and the publication of the Second Part, in 1832, fourteen more ! Therefore, including the work of Lessing, the material of the Faust-legend was employed by twenty-nine different authors, during the period which Goethe devoted to the elaboration of his own original design !

the following year. *"Faust,"* he says to Eckermann, originated (in manuscript?) at the same time as *Werther."* Thus the conception which he had grasped at the age of twenty had been shaping itself in his brain for four years, before any part of it was put into words. Gotter, whose acquaintance he had made in Wetzlar, sends him in the summer of 1773 a poetical letter, in which he says : "Send me, in return, thy Doctor Faust, *as soon as he has stormed out of thy head."*

It is not probable that more than the opening monologue was written in 1773. Perhaps one or two of the first scenes with Margaret were added the following year ; for when Klopstock visited Frankfurt in September, 1774, Goethe read to him "some scenes" of *Faust,* which the older poet then heartily praised, though he spoke slightingly of the same scenes after they were published. In January, 1775, Goethe read all that he had completed up to that time to his friend Jacobi, who wrote to him in 1791, alluding to the published "Fragment" : "I knew nearly the whole of *Faust* already, and precisely for that reason I was doubly and trebly impressed by it. I have the same feeling now as I had sixteen years ago." Except the "Cathedral" and "Dungeon" scenes, nearly all the parts in which Margaret is introduced, as well as "Auerbach's Cellar," and the conversation of Mephistopheles with the Student, were written in the spring of 1775. It is very evident that Merck was also allowed to see the manuscript, and that Goethe's design was freely discussed among his friends. The publisher Mylius, in Berlin, writes to Merck towards the end of 1774, that he will take the manuscript of Goethe's *Stella* for twenty thalers (!), although he fears that the author may expect "fifty thalers for his next work, and perhaps a hundred louis d'or for his *Doctor Faust !"*

Goethe says : "I brought the work with me to Weimar in 1775. I had written it on foolscap, without any erasures ; for I was very careful not to write down a line which was not good and might not be allowed to stand." In this form he read it to the Court circle, which at that time included Wieland, Knebel, and Musæus. As nearly as can be ascertained, the manuscript comprised the first half of Scene I., the latter half of Scene IV., and the following series of scenes to XVIII., with the exception of VI. and XIV. In addition to these, there were probably several scenes which were afterwards omitted before the publication of the work, and one (Scene XXIII., in prose) which was restored, many years later. It is also evident that the plan of the whole work was at least roughly outlined by this time. Its development, however, — except through that secret, unconscious growth which kept it alive under the production of so many other works, — was now arrested for a long while. The conceptions of a young poet are always in advance of his power but there is a good attendant genius who thwarts and delays the performance until the auspicious season.

In 1780, after the completion of *Iphigenia in Tauris* and while his mind was still bathed in the Grecian atmosphere, Goethe wrote portions of the *Helena*, for the Second Part of *Faust*. There seems to be no doubt that the manuscript was read to the Duke, Karl August, his mother, the Duchess Amalia, to Herder and Knebel; but the scenes must have been afterwards suppressed, for the existing *Helena* is certainly of a later origin. This is, nevertheless, the only positive evidence that anything was added to the work between 1775 and 1788.

Goethe's journey to Italy was not only the realization of an early desire, but it was also a necessary escape from the irksome duties of his position at Weimar. He broke away forcibly from affairs of state in order to recuperate himself for poetry, and his eagerness and anxiety may be guessed from the circumstance that he kept his plan secret from every one except the Duke, fearing that he would never succeed if his intention should become known. It was the old superstition of keeping silence while lifting a buried treasure. The only manuscript he took with him was that of *Faust*, which he had brought from Frankfurt, and which was now so yellow and worn and frayed, that he says it might almost have passed for an ancient *codex*. Nevertheless, he did not succeed in returning to the work until the spring of 1788, just before his final departure from Rome. He writes in March : "It is a different thing, of course, to complete the work now, instead of fifteen years ago; but I think nothing is lost, since I feel sure of having regained the thread. In so far as regards the tone of the whole, also, I am comforted : I have already finished a new scene, and if the paper were only smoked, I think no one could pick it out from the old ones." This new scene is the "Witches' Kitchen." It is doubtful whether the "Cathedral" and "Forest and Cavern" were also added in Rome, or after his return to Weimar.

Finally, in 1790, in Göschen's Leipzig edition of Goethe's works, *Faust* appeared as "A Fragment." The impression which the publication produced was not encouraging : the fragment was not generally understood, and the power exhibited in the separate scenes was only partially appreciated.* Goethe, occupied with *Wilhelm Meister* and *Hermann und Dorothea*, banished it for a time from his thoughts; and the first instigation which led him to resume the work came from Schiller, who thus wrote to him on the 29th of November, 1794 : "But I have no less desire to read those fragments of your *Faust* which are not yet printed; for I confess that what I have already read seems to me the torso of Hercules. In these scenes there is a power and fulness of genius which clearly

---

* Heyne, in Göttingen, wrote : "There are fine passages in it, but with them there are such things as only he could give to the world, who takes all other men to be blockheads." Wieland expressed his regret that it was such a patchwork of earlier and later labours. Schiller was then unsatisfied with the impression it produced, and only Körner and August Schlegel seem to have had some presentiment of Goethe's design and the grandeur of his fragmentary performance.

reveal the highest master-hand, and I wish to follow as far as possible the bold and lofty nature which breathes through them." Goethe wrote in answer: "I can at present communicate nothing of Faust; I do not dare to untie the package in which he is imprisoned. I could not copy without continuing the work, and I have no courage for that, now. If anything can restore it to me in the future, it is surely your sympathy."

It seems, however, that during the following winter Goethe took the manuscript to Jena, and discussed the plan of the work with Schiller, for in the summer of 1795, Wilhelm von Humboldt writes to the latter, thanking him for his information concerning *Faust*. "The plan," he says, "is gigantic: what a pity, therefore, that it will never be anything else than a plan!" If Frau von Kalb's memory is to be trusted, Goethe wrote about this time the Interview between Mephistopheles and the Baccalaureus (Part Second, Act II.), which has generally been referred to a much later date.

There is no evidence that the First Part of *Faust* was resumed before 1797, when the "Dedication" and the "Prologue in Heaven" were probably written, together with the *Intermezzo* (Oberon and Titania's Golden Wedding), which was afterwards inserted by accident rather than design. In 1798 the "Prelude on the Stage" and perhaps the conclusion of Scene I., together with Scenes II. and III., appear to have been written. It is probable that the concluding scene of the First Part (the "Dungeon") was either produced or rewritten at this time. Goethe writes to Schiller that he is favoured by "the lyrical mood of Spring," and in several letters announces the progress he is making in the work. During the year 1799 little, if anything, was accomplished; but in 1800 Goethe commenced the composition of the *Helena*, which is frequently mentioned in his correspondence with Schiller during that year. He writes on one occasion: "During these eight days, I have fortunately been able to hold fast the conception of the situations, of which you already know, and my Helena has actually entered on the stage. But now the beauty in the *rôle* of my heroine attracts me so much that I shall be disconsolate if I must at last (since the whole can only be represented as a spectral appearance) transform her into a grinning mask." Schiller answers, apparently referring to former conversations: "It is a very important advantage, that you consciously advance from the (artistically) pure to the impure, instead of seeking a method of soaring from the impure to the pure, as is the case with the rest of us barbarians. In *Faust*, therefore, you must everywhere assert your right of force" (*Faustrecht*, an untranslable pun).

In the autumn of 1800 Goethe laid the *Helena* aside, and devoted himself seriously to the completion of the First Part. He wrote the Walpurgis-Night and the scene of Valentine's death, and then endeavoured to fill the gap remaining between the *Intermezzo* and the "Dungeon" scene. In this he was unsuccessful, and all his remaining labour from that time until the publication of the First Part, complete, in 1808, was probably merely that of adjustment and revision. The depression which weighed upon him after Schiller's death in 1805 affected his interest in *Faust* more than in any other of his literary plans.

When the First Part finally appeared, the following portions of the Second Part appear to have been already in existence : Scene I., and possibly a part of Scene II., of Act I. ; Scene I. of Act II. ; nearly the first half of Act III. (*Helena*) ; and some fragments of Act V. There is no doubt that Goethe knew, as he wrote to Zelter nearly twenty years afterwards, "*what* was still necessary to be written, but was not yet decided in regard to the *how*." It is not necessary to recapitulate here all the interruptions, the varying literary and scientific interests, which came between the plan and its fulfilment. Goethe was fifty-nine years old when the First Part was published, and the years passed by in other labours until he was seventy-five, before the impulse to complete the Second Part returned to him.

In 1824 he gave to Eckermann a programme which he had prepared for the completion of *Wahrheit und Dichtung*. It contained a prose outline of the continuation of *Faust*, and Eckermann wrote in reply : "Whether this plan of *Faust* should be communicated or held in reserve, is a doubt which can only be solved after the fragments already in existence have been carefully examined, and it is clear whether the hope of completing the work must be given up or not." This hint seems to have aroused Goethe : the plan was withheld, and the work was commenced, certainly in the following year. The *Helena*, to which he felt most strongly attracted, received a new interest for him through the idea of representing Byron in the child Euphorion, and the Act was finished in 1826. It was published in 1827, in the fourth volume of "Goethe's Works, with the Author's Final Revisions," under the title of "Helena : a Classico-Romantic Phantasmagoria," and at once excited the greatest interest and curiosity. From Edinburgh to Moscow the European critics seem to have been both delighted and puzzled by it. Carlyle wrote an admirable paper upon it, in which he shows great shrewdness in unriddling its symbolism. The encouragement which such a reception of the single act gave to Goethe stimulated him anew to complete the work, and for four years longer it became the leading motive of his life.

In the beginning of 1828 the first three scenes of the First Act—Faust's Awakening, the Emperor's Court, and the Carnival Masquerade—were published in the twelfth volume of his works, and were received with an enthusiasm equal to that which the *Helena* called forth. Goethe, now nearly eighty years old, worked slowly and with a laggard power of invention ; but he held to his conceptions with the same tenacity as in his earliest literary youth, and suffered no favourable mood of body or mind to pass without adding some lines. The portions already completed were fastened together, with blank sheets of a different colour between, indicating the gaps yet to be filled ; and he rejoiced from month to month, as the unwritten gave place to the written colour. During 1829 and 1830 the First Act was completed, and the whole of the Second Act, including the Classical Walpurgis-Night, was written ; so that, at the beginning of 1831, there only remained the Fourth Act and the opening scenes of the Fifth. This was the most laborious part of the task, and has left upon it palpable traces of labour ; but by the end of July the work was done, and on his *eighty-second* birthday, August 28, 1831, Goethe sealed up the complete manuscript of the Second Part, to be opened and published after his death. "From this time on," he said to Eckermann, "I look upon my life as a perfect gift, and it is really indifferent what I may further do, or whether I shall do anything." Seven months afterwards he was dead.

Faust is, in the most comprehensive sense, a drama of the Life of Man. The course of its moral and intellectual plot, as first designed by the author, is now and then delayed by the material added to it during the different phases of his own development, but was never changed. This plot is chiefly unfolded to the reader through the medium of two elements, which, from first to last, are combined in it, yet may easily be separated. The difficulties in the way of its comprehension have been caused by the introduction of a third accidental, and unnecessary element, which is so interwoven with the others (especially in the Second Part), that the reader is often led away from the true path before he is aware of it.

The first of the elements, and the one which gives individual colouring and reality to the characters, Goethe drew from his own experience. All the earlier scenes, he declares, were *subjectively* written : Mephistopheles and Faust were the opposite poles of his own nature. His own ambition, disappointment, love, unrest, are all reflected throughout the First Part ; and the poise of his riper nature, his æsthetic passion and his religious feeling, in the opening of the First Act, the *Helena*, and the Fifth Act of the Second Part. The second element, drawn from his objective study of men and his observation of the world, is blended with the former, but especially manifests itself in the aphoristic character of much of the Second Part, and in the symbolism which he so constantly employs for the sake of more compressed expression.

What I have called the accidental element is illustrated by the *Intermezzo*, which was wilfully inserted ; by the literary satire in the Witches' Kitchen and the Walpurgis-Night ; and in the Second Part by the paper-money scene in the First Act, the controversy of the Neptunists and Plutonists in the Second and the Fourth, and the introduction of Byron in the Third. All these features must be eliminated from the moral and intellectual course of the action, with which they have not the slightest connection. Indeed, the whole of the Classical Walpurgis-Night, admirable and wonderful as it is, in parts, forms a very roundabout mode of transition from the Emperor s Court to the allegory of Helena. Only by holding fast to the leading idea can we safely follow its labyrinthine windings.

What Goethe himself said of *Faust* in his eightieth year, in speaking of Stapfer's French translation, may be quoted in conclusion, as an estimate equally modest and just : "The commendation which the work has received, far and near, may perhaps be owing to this quality—that it permanently preserves the period of development of a human soul, which is tormented by all that afflicts mankind, shaken also by all that disturbs it, repelled by all that it finds repellent, and made happy by all that it desires. The author is at present far removed from such conditions : the world, likewise, has to some extent other struggles to undergo ; nevertheless, the state of men, in joy and sorrow, remains very much the same ; and the latest-born will still find cause to acquaint himself with what has been enjoyed and suffered before him, in order to adapt himself to that which awaits him."

THE END.

PRINTED BY MORRISON AND GIBB LIMITED, EDINBURGH